A History and Sociology of the
Willowbrook State School

David Goode, Darryl B. Hill, Jean Reiss,
and William Bronston

Library of Congress Cataloging-in-Publication Data
Goode, David, 1948–
    A history and sociology of the Willowbrook State School / David Goode, Darryl B. Hill, Jean Reiss, and William Bronston
        pages   cm
    Includes bibliographical references and index.
    ISBN 978-1-937604-05-9 (alk. paper)
    1. Willowbrook State School—History. 2. People with mental disabilities—Institutional care—New York (State)—History. 3. Developmentally disabled—Institutional care—New York (State)—History. I. Title.
    HV3006.N7G66 2013
    371.9209747'26—dc23
                                    2013004333

Printed in the United States of America

Table of Contents

"The subject of history is the life of peoples and humanity. To catch and pin down in words— that is to describe directly the life, not only of humanity but of a single people—appears to be impossible."

—Leo Tolstoy, *War and Peace,* 1904

"You could feel it, like something coming toward you, like the wind blowing, it was like dangerous."

—Ex-resident remarking to his mother why he did not want to go to Willowbrook (Fusillo, 1994)

"It is only in taking them onto the wards to see the din and stench, the misery, heaves and twists and cries that they suddenly and indelibly understand that it is not the handicap which has taken its toll, but Willowbrook. Willowbrook is the culprit."

—William Bronston, Testimony to the New York State Joint Legislative Committee for the Mentally and Physically Handicapped, February 17, 1972

Halloween Parade at Willowbrook State School

Preface

A long and circuitous road led me to writing this preface. As with any long journey, many emotions—positive and negative—were experienced, and significant defeats and victories were encountered. In retrospect I now see that I began to write this book that day in 1974 I stepped on to a ward for children born deaf and blind, at Pacific State Hospital in Pomona, California. Since then, I have had an abiding preoccupation with institutions and what they do to people who live and work in them or who have relatives who do. I admit to being the culprit who collected three other authors as co-conspirators in this project, but the reader can learn more about our respective involvements in the production of this book in the following paragraphs. In the context of this preface, I want to acknowledge people to whom I, and the other authors, are indebted.

I thank the College of Staten Island for providing me with a Presidential Research Award related to the writing of this book and for approving a sabbatical leave to work on it. The manuscript underwent several substantial revisions. Martha Bates, formerly of Michigan State University Press, read an initial manuscript and sent it out to two anonymous reviewers whose comments were helpful in the first revision. Steven Taylor at Syracuse University read that manuscript and many of his suggestions were incorporated in a second major revision to the book. While working with Lisa Marie O'Hearn of the American Association for Intellectual and Developmental Disabilities, a third substantial revision occurred. Additional revisions were undertaken, this time with the feedback of several professionals and parents: Duncan Whiteside, Mariette Bates, Jim Conroy, Henry 'Hal' Kennedy, Colleen Wieck, and many of my graduate students in Disability Studies at the City University of New York. Hal Kennedy also engaged in many hours of discussion with me about Willowbrook and Halloran Hospital about which he has a keen interest. James Kaser, Archivist of the College of Staten Island's (CSI) Willowbrook Collection, and his staff, have been extremely helpful in providing access to Willowbrook materials and photographs, and Professor Kaser contributed original scholarship to the study of the Willowbrook site. Maureen Fusillo, a graduate student studying with me and Dr. Jed Luchow at CSI, conducted most of the interviews that we use herein. Because the book is the product of four authors, an especially challenging task was given to the copy editor, Julie Palmer-Hoffman. Her contributions both stylistically and substantively require special acknowledgement. Lisa Marie O'Hearn maintained the ship on course without demanding an exact destination, and under her gentle guidance the final form of this book took shape. Last, it is important to acknowledge the many unnamed people with whom I have spoken over the years about Willowbrook, and who provided me with important insights about what happened there. Their voices, even if unacknowledged by name, inhabit these pages.

—*David Goode*

Foreword

When I was asked to write this foreword, my first reaction was that I was, of course, glad to do so, both for authors David Goode, Darryl Hill, Jean Reiss, and William Bronston and for the American Association of Intellectual and Developmental Disabilities. My second reaction was to wonder whether we really need another book about an institution and its closure. Now that I have read *A History and Sociology of the Willowbrook State School,* I know the answer to be an emphatic yes, we do.

The authors, two of whom were "on the ground" during the darkest days leading up to the closure of Willowbrook, combine the history and sociology of institutionalization and the general treatment of those we now call "people with intellectual disabilities," with firsthand accounts of what happened at Willowbrook—how people lived, labored, suffered, and, eventually, triumphed with Willowbrook's closure.

I interact a lot in my work with early career professionals and university students. Their values, enthusiasm, and skills give me hope for the future, particularly the future for people with intellectual disabilities and their families. What is missing from most of these emerging professionals and students is a flavor of "the bad old days," when institutions literally stank and maltreatment was rampant and a regular part of the everyday life of people confined to state institutions, whatever these institutions may have been called at the time. They mostly lack the outrage that my generation felt, and continues to feel, about those horrid conditions. Their framework is schools where children with intellectual disability are included, small groups homes and individualized settings where adults with intellectual disability live a more self-determined life, and a culture where the shame families once felt is largely gone.

However, I continue to hear of the renaming of state institutions. To quote a well-known politician, "you can't put lipstick on a pig." Institutions, even if they do not smell, even if they are not overcrowded, even when they try to get people "into the community" (as if the community were merely a physical space), even when people confined there have their own clothes, possessions, and decent food, are still violating the rights (let alone the dreams and aspirations) of the people living in them. I had hoped, at this point in my career, 35 years after hearing a presentation at a meeting of the AAIDD (then the American Association on Mental Deficiency [AAMD]) about how institutions were to be phased out, that we would no longer need to have these exhaustive discussions about the necessity of closing these institutions. But, alas, we do. This is one of the basic points of this book, that Willowbrook is really not just a historical place. Today the same social and economic forces that made Willowbrook continue to exist. With more than 30,000 people in large state facilities alone, not to mention private facilities and nursing homes, we have a long way to go. And that is just in the United States. Go north, south, east, or west from the United States, and you can still see institutions flourishing, some like the U.S. institutions of old. Some of the places are prettier, but they are still confining people and they are still unnecessary. Some are decrepit beyond anything we saw in the United States and are dispiriting and horrid at best. And if we include places that are smaller but that still control people's lives unnecessarily, even though they are physically nicer, what the authors refer to as "relatively total institutions," then many, many people with disabilities today continue to live in the shadow of Willowbrook and places like Willowbrook.

The authors did a creative job of combining information about the societal history and sociology that led up to both the opening of Willowbrook and its eventual closure. The irony that the physical site that was Willowbrook now houses, in part, an institution of higher learning should not be lost on the reader. There are other fine books about the history of intellectual disability, including two on Willowbrook itself: a scholarly account, *The Willowbrook Wars*, and a report, *Willowbrook*, by Geraldo Rivera based on his investigation of the institution. There are also countless exposés and news stories and a handful of films about other institutions, their closures, and the aftermath of those closures. What the authors here have done is provided a scholarly analysis of the conditions in the United States leading up to the creation of Willowbrook and traced the conditions that led to its closure and the impact of the closure on the people who had been there, as residents, staff, and families. By going to many local sources, the reader can understand the social conditions that led up to Willowbrook's creation. Reading further in the text, one gets a feel for what a total institution must have been like, for the staff, for residents, and for families. All that is missing is the smell.

The authors' intent is to show us how life worked at Willowbrook, which is far more complex than what the exposés and newspaper articles reveal. The accounts they present are from different perspectives within the institution and display the "multiple realities" that existed. Understanding the details of the oppression that occurred, as well as the ways in which children, adults, and workers resisted forces and conditions of dehumanization, is the heart of this book and an important contribution to the literature on institutions. I hope that the younger people entering our field will learn, by reading these stories, how to avoid reproducing in their own work what happened at Willowbrook.

I intend to use this book as a text in a course I occasionally teach. It will imbue in students and those who have not worked in or with institutions some of the passion that those of us who have done the work of getting people out of institutions have acquired firsthand. It is this passion that will carry us forward in our fight for equality for people with disabilities, whatever the future may hold.

—Steven M. Eidelman

For the children, women and men
whose lives were stolen by
the Willowbrooks of the world.
May these pages help us
remember and understand.

Introduction

On a typical school day, professors and students arrive at the College of Staten Island to a sight unusual for a New York City college: instead of tall skyscrapers and large nondescript office buildings, they see what looks like any large upstate college, spread like a little village, its redbrick buildings rising from lawns sparkling in the sun. Or, if it is rainy, as it often is on Staten Island, wet fog drifts aimlessly among the tree-lined walkways and fountains. In early mornings, deer and wild turkey venture onto the campus, the deer seeking a wide-open space to roam, a break from the adjacent woods that occupy much of the middle of Staten Island. Late at night, illuminated by streetlights reminiscent of those in Central Park, the entire 200 acres is almost empty save for security. It is truly remarkable that such a peaceful and pretty place exists within the bounds of the biggest city in the United States. Most colleges in New York City are urban, ugly, characterless places, fighting for fresh air and precious territory. In contrast, the College of Staten Island seems to have too much space and too much calm, especially considering its history.

More incredible is that such a peaceful place, where now one can hear the clicking of computers and laughing of students, haunts the history of American civil and disability rights as the Willowbrook State School (WSS). Many do not know that there was, on the very campus they are studying and socializing, a large state-operated institution for people with "intellectual disabilities" (what was up until recently called "mental retardation") that

1

operated from 1948 to 1987. Today Willowbrook has been for the most part forgotten and even students at the College of Staten Island, where two of the authors teach and that today occupies Willowbrook's old campus, may not recognize its name or have any understanding or appreciation of what happened there or its role in history. In the same places where people suffered and died by society's arrangement, today professors teach and students learn while unaware of what happened there. And, despite the fact that Willowbrook State School played quite a central role both negatively and positively in the history of disabilities in New York and the country, surprisingly relatively little has been written about it.

Just as in individual memory, a nation's collective memory can be short and selective. It can also often be viewed through lenses tinted with an unwillingness to acknowledge fault and a corresponding willingness to recognize it in others. More generally, memory tends to avoid, minimize, or aggrandize recollections that are painful or upsetting, and Willowbrook State School embodies such truths. "Never Forget!" is a phrase used by "self-advocates," people with intellectual disabilities who speak out on their own behalf, in association with their campaign to close institutions for others like themselves. Willowbrook is not something that should be forgotten. Ensuring that it not be was a primary motivation for writing this book.

For those who do remember, the Willowbrook State School is the setting of a tragic story: a place where thousands of children and adults, of varying states of health and ability, lived in squalor, abuse, and neglect. Although this is undoubtedly the most salient truth about Willowbrook, the life that occurred there belies any simple distillation or glossing. It is also true that some residents of this enormous school were resilient to the evils of the institution, were not brought down by the rampant disease or the lack of supervision and care. Remarkably, some even thrived, finding caring attendants, nurses, and doctors who would enable them to leave the school for weeks, months, sometimes even longer, to return to their families and community, becoming contributing citizens. Most residents, however, struggled with abuse or neglect, sickness, and the challenges of physical or intellectual disability. Some, despite these adversities, moved to other institutions, scarred and beaten down by their lives at Willowbrook. Yet others were put into community residences with certain assurances about their quality of life which may not have been fulfilled. Willowbrook is a tragic story, and we know that many residents did not have such "good fortune" to escape and that they died at Willowbrook, abandoned and neglected. Child and adult residents with and without disability, often otherwise physically healthy, were exposed to the filth, disease, and neglect of the school, and many suffered and died because of these conditions. Knowing these facts make working and studying at the College of Staten Island a disconcerting experience. Perhaps this is why there are just a few reminders of Willowbrook on campus—a small memorial plaque on the side of one of the buildings, a plaque mounted on a stone in a tree grove. The name "Willowbrook" identifies only the park and neighborhood beside the campus, so one might not connect the infamous school with the College. Indeed, it is often shocking for students, some of whom are not from Staten Island and do not know the local history, to discover that their classrooms were probably large rooms filled with hospital beds, that housed very sick disabled children and adults, a place that then senator Robert F. Kennedy referred to as a "snake pit" and where Geraldo Rivera shared with television viewers the unforgettable smell and sight of naked children sitting in their own excrement, bound and roped, huddled near radiators for warmth.

The story of Willowbrook State School is complicated. As much as it is a tragedy, it is also, at least partly, a story of redemption. It was an institution so horrible in its operations that it was closed by a legal decree; it was also the site of a transformation—not just a transformation from an infamous state school to a college where thousands of New Yorkers, including past Willowbrook residents, now get an education but, perhaps even more important, a revolution in thinking about how to best care for people with disabilities, the very place of a rupture between the past and the future. This book tells the story of what led to this rupture in American history. It documents what life was like at Willowbrook, the social realities of the institution, and what lessons might be learned from such an understanding.

Willowbrook has been the subject of a few documentaries, many newspaper articles, papers on medical ethics, and two books. Accounts are mostly descriptive in nature, providing anecdotes about what happened at Willowbrook but in most cases offering little explanation as to why and how things worked as they did. Rothman and Rothman's *Willowbrook Wars* (1984/2009), for example, is the only other academic book of which Willowbrook is the subject (Geraldo Rivera's *Willowbrook* is an account of his experience during the exposé), and while it provides sociological explanation for some of what occured there, it focuses mostly on the public's discovery of the conditions and the crucial civil rights litigation that followed. Documentaries focus on the experience of families, or on the residents, sometimes with the doctors talking, but usually do not contain the viewpoint of the workers. Moreover, such sources describe only the problems at Willowbrook and rarely offer evidence-based explanations for why it happened, what exactly "it" was or why it took that particular form. Accounts have tended to be one-sided, reporting only the horrors of Willowbrook but rarely about the resistance, courageous or even good acts that were done by both staff and residents. This book will attempt to fill in some of these gaps, examine Willowbrook via the stories of those who worked and lived there, and explicate their narratives via relevant findings of social science. We hope to both describe and explain life at Willowbrook State School.

This is a book about not forgetting. If we forget, then we have a short memory about disturbing facts. During the mid-20th century, at Willowbrook and many other schools and institutions in New York and across the United States, people with and without intellectual disabilities were forced to live in conditions that are today unimaginable. Without getting into the specifics in this introduction, one foreign visitor put it this way after he toured Willowbrook in the 1960s: "We do not let our cattle live this way in Denmark." In the United States, a country of democratic values that holds itself up as a beacon of humanitarianism, the fact that such a place was part of our history should not be something easy to forget. But then the central question becomes: how are we to remember Willowbrook? And for what purposes? The answers to these questions are complex, and not always obvious.

Shame and Pride

One can appreciate the historical significance of Willowbrook State School in the treatment of people with disability, which is simultaneously negative and positive. The negative significance of Willowbrook is that it actually was an example and became a symbol of extreme governmental neglect in the care and protection of people with (and, in fact, without) disability. Innocent children and adults were forced to live in such unthinkably inhumane conditions that, upon reflection, it causes any reasonable person to ask him- or herself how this could have been possible in such an enlightened society as that of post–World War II America. What forces allowed it or caused it to be such that, to paraphrase Staten Island politician Dante Ferrari, in the richest country in the world, in the richest state in that country, we could have such an abomination as Willowbrook?

Willowbrook's positive significance is that the exposure of these conditions by the *Staten Island Advance*'s Jane Kurtin in 1971 and by Geraldo Rivera's reportage in 1972 enabled its subsequent closing—what became the symbol of deinstitutionalization in America. This was achieved through the efforts of a coalition of parents, professionals at Willowbrook, not-for-profit agencies, and legal groups. Closing Willowbrook included the creation of the Willowbrook Consent Decree, a legal agreement about the closing and how it was to be done, which became a model for other such legal agreements around the country. In retrospect, there is no doubt that these were critical events in the normalization of life for people with developmental disabilities.

The closing of Willowbrook State School and the legal precedents it set profoundly influenced the deinstitutionalization movement all over the United States, and the Willowbrook Consent Decree laid the groundwork for the huge expansion of community services that constitute the service system see today. Willowbrook in this regard can be a symbol to governments all over the world, many of which still continue to operate terrible institutions for the disabled, that places like it need not exist and that alternative, more humane ways to help people with disabilities can be adopted. From the perspective of the history of disability, Willowbrook is famously both a scarlet letter and a beacon—a symbol of shame and pride. For this it deserves our particular attention and understanding.

Willowbrook: A Case Study of a Total Institution

Willowbrook has come to occupy a central place in the history of disability in the United States and even internationally. It is symbolic of public indifference to people with disabilities that has characterized their treatment throughout history and of the power of citizens to confront and defeat socially organized evil. For this reason, it is important that people understand what actually occurred at WSS and not to imagine it to be other than it was, for example, to treat it as an unusual occurrence or the result of some "bad apples." This is the only way we can actually learn its lessons. Second, although there are many books about institutions, among them books and audiovisual works related to Willowbrook, none of these combine history, sociology, and interview data to reconstruct life there in a comprehensive way or to account for Willowbrook's antecedents, why it took the form it did and produced the kinds of conditions that existed.

Despite the rich literature related to disability history and institutions, lacking are in-depth single case studies of single institutions that attempt to portray and explain daily life via history and sociology (we discuss many of these below). Some colleagues suggested that a book about institutions in the United States generally would be more useful than one about "only" Willowbrook. Although we do not disagree with the utility of such a general analysis and have included testimony about conditions at other state institutions, we believe that a detailed explication of WSS, from various perspectives, and approached via what is intellectually known about institutions and disability more generally is an important contribution to the literature. In-depth single case studies are curious animals; they sometimes reveal or illustrate general truths in a way other methods cannot.

Underlying much of the writing is the belief that social relations, both macrosociological and microsociological, need to be understood in order to account for the realities of WSS. This form of thinking emphasizes how social situations, their expectations and demands, shape the behavior of individuals subject to them. It looks to collective work, as opposed to individual action, as the *ens realissimum* of daily life. Though not apologetic or dismissive of human agency, the view taken in this book reflects the basic conviction that human behavior needs to be accounted for sociologically.

Willowbrook State School is not just a thing of the past, and understanding it is not relevant only to people with disability. The social forces that created and sustained Willowbrook still exist today in the United States and other industrialized countries. People today, anyone who is not independently wealthy, are at great peril in terms of being incarcerated in institutions that take away personal freedom and choice and even accelerate their deaths. Today these institutions are not only large developmental centers or state hospitals, which have 40,000 people still living within their confines. Today segregation, dehumanization, and regimentation of people with and without disabilities is also to be found in the nursing home (McBryde-Johnson, 2003), specialized facilities, prisons, and even in many group homes. Moreover, as has been emphasized by the disability rights movement, disability is an open minority—anyone can become a member at any time. That means we, you, and anyone else can become virtually in an instant subject to these social forces.

Another reason WSS is not just of historical interest is because deinstitutionalization was only a partially successful movement, with the vast majority of states still operating large, segregating places and with New York State having abandoned its plans to close such facilities by the year 2000. In fact, New York has built additional institutions in recent years (Castellani, 2005). Nursing homes, large group homes, and high-security settings all represent places that operate like, and mostly fit the definition of, a total institution. The social forces that allowed Willowbrook to exist are part of capitalistic society's general tendency to marginalize, and to make profit from, groups who are already or who are made to become, powerless and dependent (see discussion of Wolfensberger in Chapters 3 and 5). Many people make the mistake of thinking that understanding Willowbrook has to do with something in the past that pertains primarily to the population of people with developmental disabilities. But if we take Wolfensberger's argument seriously, those social forces operate on all of us, and we are ultimately subject to them, when we become, through aging or a variety of circumstances, unable to control our own lives. With the aging of the baby boomer generation, with the inescapable problem of caring for a very large dependent population, understanding the dynamics that go into the creation and operation of places like Willowbrook takes on an immediate and practical social relevance.

There is a long and significant social scientific literature concerning the organization of "total institutions" and the behavior of people within them. This term was coined by the American sociologist Erving Goffman (1961) to describe a variety of usually large institutions that are cut off from the main society and in which a small number of powerful people are in charge of a large number of powerless ones (Goffman's work is discussed in depth in Chapter 3 and referred to throughout the text). Many sociological studies (especially Zimbardo, 1973, discussed in Chapter 3) have shown that this form of social organization produces pathological and negative forms of behavior and interaction, independently of the particular individuals who are there. The very extreme conditions that often characterize such places provide unique circumstances under which everyday life must be conducted. We have learned much about human behavior under such circumstances that is not at all always obvious, whether at Willowbrook State School, Auschwitz, or Andersonville. We mean this with respect not only to those who suffered consignment to such places but also to those who operated them. One of the things we have come to understand is this: Whether acknowledged or not, under appropriate circumstances most of us are capable of becoming perpetrators and/or victims. Given the high likelihood of the continuing existence of total institutions, an understanding of their social dynamics takes on, again, an immediate social relevance.

There are those who would say that by remembering and understanding Willowbrook State School we will avoid recreating the mistakes of the past. This is a hopeful belief, and Willowbrook is partly a story about hope. Yet, understanding and appreciating the past do not guarantee that we act on that knowledge. "What experience and history teach us is this—that people and governments have never learned from history, or acted upon principles deduced from it" (Hegel, 1832/1956, p. 6). This is something we have to prevent from happening when it comes to Willowbrook. Its name can and should be a clarion call to remember how the common citizen can produce power to defeat evil that is organized in socially sanctioned ways. It should be a symbol for the human potential to confront and be victorious over power when used in such a fashion. This is the most important lesson of Willowbrook and reminds us of what can and should be done when we see such circumstances.

The Authors and Our Sources

David Goode

Although the above would certainly provide sufficient rationale to write a book about Willowbrook, there are also personal motives for each of this book's authors. David Goode is the faculty member at the College of Staten Island most personally knowledgeable about Willowbrook, having taught about total institutions for 40 years, having studied Willowbrook for over 20, and also having written a well-known book in disability studies about children born deaf and blind who lived in a state hospital in California (Goode, 1994). Because he possesses audiovisual and teaching materials about Willowbrook, he is sometimes asked by colleagues to lend them a video so they can discuss WSS in class. Although Goode feels that these requests promote Willowbrook-related scholarship on campus, they also make him nervous. He wonders what exactly his colleagues are going to teach about and what, if anything, they know about the sociology and social psychology of institutions or about institutions' history. What kinds of impressions will they leave with their students about what he considers to be important sociological and disability-related questions? He gets worried and sometimes even volunteers to come to their class to provide the lecture. He realized after awhile that he was suspect of what they might say. Not that someone from English or women's studies or continuing education might not have very interesting things to contribute (they do) but rather that by not understanding certain basic things about places like Willowbrook they might say things that are seriously misleading (they do that, too).

One reason Goode gets judgmental in this way is because of his experiences working in total institutions, including a place very similar to Willowbrook, Pacific State Hospital in Los Angeles, but also an L.A.-area Veteran's Administration hospital. In the 1970s, Goode spent several years doing research at Pacific State and also the Sepulveda Veteran's Administration Hospital. In both places, he engaged in observational and interview research, thus spending many hours on the wards, subjecting himself to the rounds of everyday life and, at Pacific State, even acting in the role of direct care staff for children who were deaf and blind and "profoundly retarded" (Goode, 1994). He observed many of the same kinds of things that were reported about Willowbrook: overcrowding, abuse, violation of rights, filthy conditions, regimentation, overmedication, experimentation, medical and educational neglect, and so on. In reflecting about the time spent in these places, he has come to realize that he was subject to a variety of social forces and relationships allowing him to accept what he was seeing, and to a certain extent doing, as reasonable and sensible. With hindsight, he can now understand how terrible the things he saw and did were. For this reason, when Goode teaches or writes about Willowbrook, it is both a reflexive and emotional experience, because what he is saying about people who worked at Willowbrook is also true about him.

This could be seen as a problem with scientific objectivity. Or one can turn this logic around and also see it as a kind of unique credential to speaking about institutions such as Willowbrook. Indeed, over the many years we have conducted events that assembled former Willowbrook residents and workers, we have noticed that people who worked or lived in these places can have a kind of intuitive understanding with each other when they get together; at least, this is what Goode has witnessed. They were there. They lived it, and given how extraordinary such places were—Goode and other workers referred to Pacific State Hospital as another planet—shared lived experience provides them with this unique experiential platform from which to understand such places and each other. You do not have to have been at Willowbrook in order to understand it or meaningfully teach about it, but without directly having experienced such places, the quality and degree of one's insight will be severely influenced, perhaps limited. It is no different than trying to teach about any catastrophic historical event of which one was not part.

In Goode's case, it was not only that he worked at a place like Willowbrook but that he specifically studied Pacific State as an ethnographer, trying to document and analyze everyday life on its wards. The same was true at the Veterans Administration hospital in Sepulveda. He was not just working there; he was observing it and analyzing what he saw sociologically. Goode produced huge volumes of field notes, articles, and two books about what he found. He visited other institutions, some ten or so, because he was interested in seeing how they looked and what they did there.

Goode's knowledge was not confined to firsthand participant observation. He was familiar with the sociological literature about total institutions, and this academic interest in the history and operation of such places has remained with him for the past 40 years. He has collected many articles, books, and artifacts related to such places, many of which we draw on in this book. One could say Goode became fascinated by and knowledgeable of such places both as lived realities and as objects of academic study. Moreover, this interest and his position at the College of Staten Isalnd has allowed him to meet many people over the years who lived or worked at Willowbrook or who had relatives there. He has acquired in this fashion much personal knowledge about our topic.

Darryl Hill

Darryl Hill also teaches at the College of Staten Island. He was introduced to Willowbrook State School in 2003 when he met David Goode, whose office was across the hall. Goode's stories of Willowbrook inspired Hill to begin to study the state school from his own perspective, as a social psychologist interested in the history of sex and gender. Hill supervised an undergraduate honors thesis study by Helen Starogiannis. Starogiannis and Hill (2008) interviewed eight past employees of Willowbrook as a pilot study for an oral history project. Using word of mouth, the Internet, public directories, and published documents, eight former employees of Willowbrook were contacted and asked to volunteer to reflect on their memories working at the school. The narrators for Starogiannis's oral history project were both men and women. They had worked in nursing, education, administration, occupational therapy, and medicine. They were interviewed on the telephone for about an hour on their memories of what life was like for the people at the school. The interviews were then transcribed and examined for relevant information. This initial study has been followed by a further study into the resident records held at the New York State Archives, as well as archives on Willowbrook held at the College of Staten Island and the *Staten Island Advance* and *New York Times*. Information from these sources are included in this book. Hill's participation in this research, his own research about gender and sexuality at Willowbrook, which has given him access to files of residents who were there, has allowed him to accumulate much knowledge about WSS and to develop a feel for what went on there.

Jean Reiss

A key source to show what things were like from an employee's perspective is an unpublished manuscript written by Jean Reiss called *They Learned to Do Without*. Reiss worked at Willowbrook as a laboratory assistant in a research unit. Her job was to collect blood samples from the children in studies designed to find physiological origins of mental disability. She arrived in Staten Island from Britain in 1958, accompanied by her husband, who worked at WSS as a doctor. She left Willowbrook in 1970. Her manuscript is an observational narrative written six years after she left. Reiss's purpose in writing was not to defend or condemn Willowbrook but rather to exorcise memories that haunted her.

The stories Reiss describes are candid, and sometimes naive and shocking accounts of life on the ward where she worked. Her descriptions of the daily life on her ward and the human individuality of the children who lived there provide a glimpse of Willowbrook that is both unique and revealing. The names have been changed and chronology of some incidents altered, but the children existed and the events occurred. For this book, we have selected relevant passages from Reiss's manuscript to help tell this story, but the readers who would like to read her complete narrative should consult the Willowbrook Collection at the Archives of the College of Staten Island.

William Bronston

William Bronston is one of the two authors of this book who worked at Willowbrook. His name is associated with bringing conditions at Willowbrook to the public eye. For many years, he has been known in the advocacy community as the major force behind organizing resistance at Willowbrook and eventually helping to orchestrate various aspects of the movement that ended up closing Willowbrook down.

Bronston's personal history made him a primary candidate for this role. Born into a family with radical politics, his granduncle being Leon Trotsky, he was predisposed to organizing and changing society radically, predilections he took with him into medicine. In Los Angeles, he had also received state-of-the-art training in the area of developmental disabilities and mental retardation with Richard Koch, one of the most progressive and forward-thinking physicians in the1960s. He spent some time at the Menninger Institute in Kansas, where Bob Perske was chaplain. In New York City, he became involved in radical politics, volunteering at a medical center in Harlem run by the Black Panthers. He readily admits that when he arrived at Willowbrook in 1970, he took the job because he was having difficulty finding one. (As the reader will see, this was a common credential among physicians at Willowbrook, although probably the only one Bronston shared with the others there.)

The administration at Willowbrook was extremely happy to have him—at first. They were quick to realize that they had made a serious error in hiring him, an error that was to come back to haunt them and eventually become a cornerstone in the confluence of events that finally closed Willowbrook.

Bronston is writing his own account of Willowbrook, *Public Hostage, Public Ransom,* that will be published in the future. The writing and speeches included in this book will not be those that appear in his. His presence in this book is critical as it was thought that, in a book that reports about the realities of Willowbrook from a variety of perspectives, including Bronston's perceptions of things as a physician working at Willowbrook was unique and critical in enriching our understanding of the place.

We incorporate remarks made by workers and residents at Willowbrook during interviews conducted by Maureen Fusillo while a graduate student at the College of Staten Island. Working under the guidance of Goode and Professor Jed Luchow while pursuing her master's degree in education, Fusillo conducted a series of interviews (Fusillo, 1994), the transcripts of which can be found in the Willowbrook Collection in the Archives of the Library of the College of Staten Island. We use data from these interviews freely in the second part of the book. Unless otherwise specified, interviews of former workers and residents come from her work.

In the next section, we describe how this book reflects varying experiences and conditions at Willowbrook. We note that there were many Willowbrooks, depending on where one was in its social hierarchy, what conditions existed in the place(s) one lived, worked, or visited, and the individual's perspective and sensitivities. This same truth characterizes the authors of the book, two of whom were at Willowbrook and one who worked at another sister institution, Pacific State Hospital. Each of these authors saw things from a different social vantage point: physician, nurse, and researcher or volunteer. They each experienced different kinds of environments within these institutions, and their writings reflect these differences as well as personal differences in viewpoint. It is important to acknowledge that Reiss's writings are about a relatively enriched environment at Willowbrook, a ward for children who were involved in medical research. Many of her observations reflect the material advantages her ward had over those housing large numbers of people without programs or other added resources. Bronston had a career at Willowbrook that involved responsibility over various kinds of buildings, notably some of the more overcrowded and understaffed ones, as well as a general familiarity with the various wards and programs because of his "on call" status. Thus, the reader will find contrasting descriptions of the same topics by these authors. Goode, with direct knowledge of several wards at Pacific State Hospital, adds comparative and corroborative observations. Finally, Goode and Hill have incorporated interviews of people who lived and worked at other institutions, in order to show how what was seen at Willowbrook related to what occurred elsewhere.

The Concept of the Book and Its Organization

We begin with an important insight—that there were many Willowbrooks and many ways to look at them. There were many Willowbrooks in different senses. First, what happened there varied at different time periods, in particular buildings, and depended on what "kinds" of patients were placed there, who was in charge, and who actually worked on the wards. If one happened on a ward, the way of life one might observe in any particular instance could vary dramatically. There were many different types of buildings for different kinds of residents, so visiting a baby building was not the same as visiting one that housed adult "working women" who were "high functioning" (in fact, many were not "retarded") or a ward for multiply disabled, "profoundly retarded" children. The "factors" that could affect what one saw were macrosociological, for example, the status of the budget, administrative philosophy, dominant ideas about people who are "retarded," and external funding, and microsociological, for example, just who lived on the ward, who worked there and what their particular history at the institution was, whether research was going on, and how daily life was "constructed" (i.e., negotiated among those involved). At the same time, there were certain common characteristics between almost all these buildings that made them part of a "total institution." Perhaps an exception, certainly a variant, would have been those wards where residents went out into the community daily to work, returning each night to sleep and staying on grounds for weekends. In virtually all other buildings, residents were inmates whose comings and goings were entirely controlled by staff.

There is another sense in which there were many Willowbrooks, depending on what social status a person occupied within it. One experienced Willowbrook, or Pacific State, differently as a visitor, administrator, rehabilitation professional, direct care staff, summer intern, visiting family member, or resident. The major status division within total institutions is between staff and inmate, whether one works there or is part of the group being "cared for" there. That division means you are either a person who is subject to the power of others who control virtually your entire life, or you are a person who controls others as part of your job. Which side of the divide you are on will powerfully affect how you see and understand the place. It also structures one's opportunities to express and have taken seriously one's viewpoint. As has been noted (Braddock & Parrish, 2001), the history of disability is filled with the voices of those who were in charge and powerful; conspicuously absent are those of the poor and powerless.

Yet even within these different social positions, occupied in the particular buildings at specific times of Willowbrook's history, people experienced Willowbrook in different ways. One can speak meaningfully of a "Rashomon" of Willowbrooks, in which one hears very different, even contradictory, accounts of this place and what occurred there.[1] That reporting about Willowbrook would reflect such radical individual differences in perspective should not be surprising. Any event, historical or present, is subject to highly divergent interpretations, yet when one tells this to audiences about Willowbrook, this is hard for them to accept. Thus one basic observation is that when we asks the question "What happened at Willowbrook?," we can be confronted with an incredible array of differing accounts. This can be seen as a problem in obtaining unequivocal answers or as a reflection of the various conditions people witnessed, and the differences in sensitivities expressed in their reportage.

Finally, when looking at the history of Willowbrook, there are very many disciplinary perspectives that could be sensibly and profitably brought into play. As the sociologist Harold Garfinkel would often comment, researchers' analyses are limited only by human imagination. Depending on one's discipline, different aspects of things will be emphasized or ignored, and different views of the thing studied will be produced. This is a condition of any analysis and not a criticism, but it is another path to different Willowbrooks.

Given the above, we had to make some very conscious decisions about telling Willowbrook's story. We look at Willowbrook through a combination of historical and scientific sources and firsthand accounts. Personal observations of life at Willowbrook, as well as at other institutions, are central. As much as possible, the book uses observations and accounts of people who actually were at Willowbrook, especially of direct care attendants, residents, and professionals providing care, precisely because it is just these voices that are most lacking in the history of disability and total institutions. We hope this will be at least somewhat of an antidote to the history written exclusively by academics. Thus the sine qua non of this work are the accounts from those who were on the ward who lived Willowbrook as a daily reality—and we base our analyses on their perceptions and reportage.

We use what we know about both the history of disability and the sociology of total institutions as a way to contextualize or set the sociological and historical stage for these firsthand accounts. We begin with a history of institutions for people with what is called today intellectual disability. After this, we present central insights taken from sociology's research related to total institutions. Having established a context for total institutions for people with disability, we then look at the particular history of Willowbrook State School, considering various firsthand accounts of people who lived and worked at Willowbrook or who visited relatives

1. Rahomon is a film by Akira Kurosawa that shows an event through the eyes of three persons, all of whom see it very differently, even in contradictory ways. To the consternation of American audiences, the fllm never resolves which version is the "correct" one, perhaps suggesting that there was no such thing as a "correct" one.

there. The final chapter discusses what we can learn from this case study of Willowbrook State School.

Organizing the book in this way gives balance to the particulars and generalities of Willowbrook. The history and sociology of institutions precede the narratives in order to generally frame the particular accounts. They are intellectual "sensitizing devices" to emphasize the orderly features of specific individuals' accounts and their continuities with more general observations. Although all of the accounts and observations presented are "perspectival" in the sense described earlier, they nonetheless contain elements that resonate with sociological analyses. Another way to say this is that the details of individual observations always contain general (social structure) as well as highly particular features (specific to that occasion). They are, as termed by the ethnomethodologist Garfinkel (1967), "lived orders."

The story of Willowbrook we present relies on what people actually saw when they were there. Whatever instruction we might provide the reader about how to read these stories, there is no way to ultimately decide about either their accuracy or what perspective to bring to bear on their reading.

The great Western genre writer Larry McMurtry, characterizing one of his favorite books about the Little Big Horn, Evan Connell Jr.'s *Son of Morning Star*, which was based on first- and secondhand accounts, wrote the following:

> It is part of the wonder of *Son of Morning Star* that Evan S. Connell Jr. has patiently located many of these obscurely published reminisces from both sides of the fight and placed them in his narrative in such a way as to create a kind of mosaic of first hand comment. The memoirs don't answer all the questions, or even very many of them, but it is still nice to know what the participants thought happened, even if we are left with a kind of mesquite thicket of opinion. (McMurtry, 1999, p. 90)

While Connell used primarily secondhand accounts of the Little Big Horn (there were some from American Indians who were there), McMurtry's remark about being left with a "mosaic" of firsthand comments and a "mesquite thicket of opinion" is also apropos to what we can know about Willowbrook. Willowbrook was recent enough that we have access to these personal observations. It is important to know about them, but we won't pretend that they don't lead us into a mesquite thicket of opinion about Willowbrook.

Finally, we offer a brief word about terminology. We recognize that there are groups of people with disabilities with strong convictions about the language used to describe disability. There is a convention offered by certain disability groups of "people-first language." There are those who do not want to see the term "mental retardation" used at all. Then there are members of the disability community who use the term "cripple," so as to re-appropriate a once pejorative term as a means of gaining personal or social empowerment. That is, there is no unanimity of opinion about terms in the disability community. In this work, we will generally observe the convention of people-first language, use the term "mental retardation" in places where it is appropriate to do so historically, and also use the term "intellectual disability" in parts of the text referring to the present. We will also use historically relevant terms, such as "idiots," "morons," "feebleminded," and the like when discussing the era in which they were employed.

1

A History of Institutions for People with Intellectual Disabilities

A history of disability in America presents several basic challenges. First and foremost, it needs to be situated in a larger context of disability in Western culture. History is such that there is no objective history of anything—only historians interpreting and writing history. So any historical account is by nature situated in history and provisional. This is especially evident when it is written by a small group of White, male, financially advantaged, educated, and, importantly, able-bodied authors, which has been true of disability history until relatively recently. History is written by the powerful, more often than not, and because of this has a perspective in some important way informed by privilege of wealth. These points all represent challenges to any historian of disability and institutions for people with disabilities, but there are more. The history of disability is a relatively new idea and is increasingly encompassing writings by, or at least viewpoints of, people who have disabilities. And there is an important conceptual problem: what we called *disabled* is a recent term, with a relatively short history, and is really an umbrella term made popular in mid-20th-century discourse. So this historical terrain of the history of disability is a quickly evolving geography, as historians uncover new pasts and discover new ways of thinking about history.

This topic is important because it allows the reader to see how Willowbrook fits into the overall history of how people with intellectual disabilities were treated. One way to think about disability history, found in Braddock and Parrish (2001), has been described as an "institutional history" and builds on the idea that different societies build different institutions to deal with or accommodate disability or that disability is "socially constructed." The word "institution" in sociology has a double meaning—it can mean a place (such as a hospital, bank, church, or state school for the retarded) or a way of doing things (e.g., the institution of marriage or of dating). Both these senses of institutions apply to the history of people who we today call disabled, and when we look back on even just Western societies, what we find are great variation in the places and ways of doing things related to such people.

Thus, it is crucial to acknowledge that the story of Willowbrook represents an important but small part in an overall appreciation of how people with disability have existed historically. Wolfensberger (1972), in his book on normalization, offered the observation that when casting a broad view at the historical record, we find that people who today we call "disabled" could be found in a variety of social roles, virtually all of which were "deviant," that is, seen as different from the norm in a negative way. These various social roles were associated with what were seen to be appropriate forms of social devaluation, segregation, punishment, and even death. Wolfensberger notes that these various deviant roles, while usually no longer expressed openly, still can be found in society's response to disability. They are part of the historical legacy of disability that operates in ways that are often, but not always, unconscious. The social roles that Wolfensberger discusses include being seen as not human, animal-like, a threat to society, and a medical entity. Also discussed are the roles of pitiable object, the holy innocent, and of being considered childlike. The story of Willowbrook occurs on the particular "branch" of the history of disability that deals with their treatment as medical entities, which is itself directly related to the perception of people with disabilities as social menaces. But the other roles mentioned by Wolfensberger were also found at Willowbrook. Our history discusses the various roles that people with disabilities have played in history, and their relevance in understanding certain observations of Willowbrook. As described by Wolfensberger, such roles can be found even when society proclaims positive laws and beliefs about disability. They are historical in origin but continue to influence persons pereceptions and actions at Willowbrook and today.

It is important to mention here that by acknowledging that the history of disability overwhelmingly shows that people with disabilities have been cast into these roles and treated in negative ways, Wolfensberger was not proposing that people with disability must occupy deviant roles. Societies generally have a disposition to produce groups that are seen as deviant for a variety of reasons and that there will always need to be efforts made to ensure that people with disabilities are not subject to this kind of social dynamic. Wolfensberger advocated for socially valued roles (social role valorization) for people with disabilities as a way to address this propensity of society and spent his life analyzing the dimensions of devaluation, devising solutions, and advocating for supports and services that achieved valued social outcomes. But he was also guarded about the idea that the old roles would ever go away and that people with disability would ever be in a position where they were not at risk. Wolfensberger's theory, and its relevance to Willowbrook, is discussed more in Chapters 3 and 5.

In our history of disability, we concentrate on the medicalization of disability and the creation of institutions for people seen as medically damaged. For purposes of this writing, an important aspect of the wider medical context for a study of Willowbrook State School is an institutional history of disability. This is a topic that needs its own book-length treatment, and indeed, there are several other sources that address it (Braddock & Parrish, 2001; Rothman, 1990; Trent, 1994; Wolfensberger, 1982). It is important to establish our framework for this work and to situate it within the history of this intellectual tradition. There are a few basic points that most agree on. One thing is that the idea of institutionalizing people with disability is a recent invention. Most people with disabilities have either lived with their families or fended for themselves. We know that early Christian monks and early Islamic healers founded places for poor and sick people and those judged "mad" or "innocent." As these societies transitioned to secularism and science led the Renaissance, satanic causes of disability persisted, but some, for example, Quakers in Eastern United States, had more charitable views of those with disabilities. Eventually, these sympathies aligned with European scientific and medical knowledge, where institutions were built for poor and sick peoples.

Most accept that the creation of modern institutions designed for the care of specifically disabled people emerged largely in the 18th century. This was especially true for people who were deaf and those who were blind but also included the continued operation of places that housed those who were "mad" or those who were "idiots" or "cripples." In the 18th century, both public and private facilities existed that were more places of confinement than treatment, as very little was known about the latter (at least in our current sense of the term). In the early 19th century shortly after the American Thomas Gallaudet visited the first public residential school for deaf children in Paris, he opened a similar school in Hartford, Connecticut. Similarly, other American physicians visited or read about pioneering European efforts. This process, American adaptation of developments related to disability that began in Europe, especially in England, France, and Switzerland, was what was occurring during the late 18th and early 19th centuries. American physicians basically liberally borrowed from what had been developed in Europe, not only with respect to treatment of people with disabilities, but with regard to all medical and social institutions.

Well before the revolutions of the late 18th century, there were many expressions of public support for people with mental disability, including those with mental illness and intellectual disability. A variety of mechanisms were in place to deal with the growing number of people affected by such problems. These institutions (not conceived of as medical until the 19th century), in both senses of the term, were taken from European innovators such as Jean Marc Gaspard Itard, Philippe Pinel, Johann Guggenbuhl, Jean-Étienne Dominique Esquirol, and Édouard Séguin, but it also needs to be stressed again that the social and political context of society was very different in America than in the European countries where these approaches originated. This was especially true about the youthfulness and hopefulness of America, a democratic experiment (even if by today's standards of universality of citizenship very limited) based on individual rights. Many of the reformers during and after the Revolution had a kind of optimism and zeal one might expect to find in a newly and violently established country.

An interesting, if not defining, characteristic of institutions that cared for the insane and idiots was the contradiction that existed between their expressed purpose, care and treatment of incapable persons, and the actual conditions of life and "treatments" such people were subject to. Admittedly, in the 18th century the state of medical knowledge was primitive. Physicians were human beings who also maintained quasi scientific views about disability such as phrenology or held negative religiously inspired beliefs about disability. These factors may help explain why there were torture-like treatments and harsh conditions for patients in order to cure them. Often, these were based on quasi-scientific beliefs about the causes of various conditions. Such treatments, and harsh daily routines of life, were found in European institutions and continued to be evident in Europe well into the 19th century. They consisted of the use of spinning devices that were thought to address the imbalance of brain fluids; prolonged cold and warm baths; use of water showers, mechanical restraints, gags, and "anxiety pears" to prevent screaming; crib beds, small cages, and other imprisoning devices; threats of drowning; forced ingestion of purgative substances; bloodletting; and other assaults on mind and spirit, often because these were seen as necessary to drive out the patient's evil or illness.

Trent (1994) has reviewed the history of services for mental retardation in the United States. After the Civil War, people who had cognitive limitations were often visible in rural small-town life as the *village idiot,* living with their families and sometimes jailed, but they were not feared, nor were they considered mad or criminal. Indeed, idiots were worthy of sympathy, and many Christians in early America were sympathetic and offered help.

By the mid-1800s, innovations in the care of idiots in Europe, especially at Paris's Bicêtre or Guggenbuhl's Abendberg, captivated and inspired Americans. Samuel Gridley Howe and another Massachusetts native, Hervey B. Wilbur, were two of the first physicians to open schools for idiot children. Howe was head of the Massachusetts Asylum for the Blind, and in 1847 he convinced the Massachusetts legislature to build a school for idiots, taking his first idiot students to his School

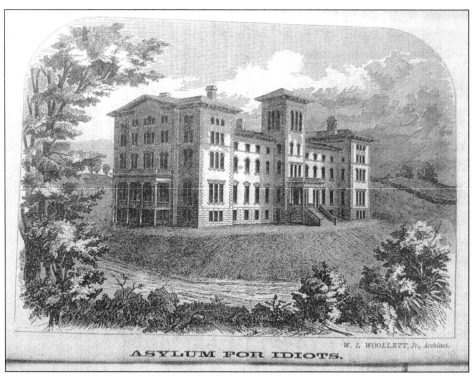

ASYLUM FOR IDIOTS.

Syracuse Asylum for Idiots

for the Blind in South Boston. Wilbur went on to become the first superintendent of the New York State Asylum for Idiots. The Syracuse Asylum was the first state-funded, residential institution for people with intellectual disability in New York and, thus, the first in the system of state-operated schools and hospitals of which Willowbrook was eventually a part.

Two Early Pioneers: Howe and Wilbur

According to Hornick's (2012) history, state schools were started in Massachusetts by Howe. Howe had also founded the Perkins School for the Blind in the 1830s. A Harvard-educated physician, Howe wanted to provide care that before this was done in almshouses. Howe founded his school based on humane and scientific principles: "The school, if conducted by persons of skill and ability, would be a model for others," that the idiot could be "trained to industry, order, and self-respect; that they can be redeemed from odious and filthy habits, and that there is not one of any age, who may not be made more of a man, and less of a brute, by patience and kindness, directed by energy and skill" (Howe, "Report on Idiocy," 1848, pp. 53–54, as cited in Hornick, 2012, pp. 11–12).

In Howe's view, idiocy was a social disease, the result of immorality or sinfulness, either one's own or one's parents (the sins of the father visited on the sons), according to a philosophy known as "degenerationism." Howe had problems reintegrating the residents back into society because of a lack of acceptance from the community; schools accepted profoundly retarded individuals who had little hope of returning to society and those with physical disabilities, such as epilepsy. According to Hornick (2012), Howe's school, like others, had to become large in order to become self-sufficient: There was no state money for them. Most adopted farms and light industry.

After Wilbur read an account of a visit to Édouard Séguin's school for idiots in Paris, he opened his own home in Barre, Massachusetts, to such students. About the same time Howe was opening a small school wing for children with idiocy, Wilbur became involved in efforts in New York State to open a school for this population. Although these efforts initially failed to convince the legislature to fund such an initiative, the group involved was eventually successful, resulting in the opening of a small school in Albany, with Wilbur as director. Wilbur then moved the school to Syracuse, establishing the Syracuse Asylum for Idiots. In its *First Annual Report* (State of New York, 1852), Wilbur documents Dr. Frederick Backus's pioneering attempts to convince the legislature to turn its attention to the care of idiots in New York State. In 1851, Wilbur and his staff (assistants Miss Frances H. Clark and Miss Adeline E. Coley) took over a building "on Troy Road, about two miles from the capitol, belonging to Stephen Van Rensselaer, who with great liberality agreed to lease it to the State for two years at a rent, not more probably than one half the actual annual value" (State of New York, 1852, p. 2). The state provided $6,000, and the school accepted 20 children, two from each district. The second year, there were 30 children.

By today's clinical standards, many of these students would have been regarded as being severely developmentally delayed or intellectually disabled; some possibly had multiple disabilities:

Of the 25 pupils we have received at our asylum, 12 could not speak a single word. Of these 12 who were speechless, 6 had no idea of language, could not comprehend a single word or command addressed to them. Of those who are not dumb, 3 say but a few words and those indistinctly; and 2 others who did not speak till nine years of age, and now but indistinctly, and with very limited number of words. . . . Seven walked imperfectly, 3 were subject to partial paralysis, 11 had been subject to convulsions, 8 were subject to excessive flow of saliva, 7 were utterly inattentive to the calls of nature, and several others required constant watching to preserve cleanliness, and 5 were described as very irritable. A greater portion were unable to dress or undress themselves, and but four of the whole number were able to feed themselves with propriety. None of them could read or write, or count, or distinguish colors by name. (State of New York, 1852, p. 13)

Wilbur's writing seems very modern in his reliance on empirical observation and science to understand his students. Acknowledging their individuality did not prevent him from seeing patterns, from creating different groups or types of idiots, and recognizing that the educational goals for these different groups would need to be different. This was very much the view that prevailed at Pacific State Hospital and Willowbrook and was probably found in every institution in the United States at that time.

Another interesting feature of Wilbur's writing about New York's first residential school for children with intellectual disabilities has to do with the role of parents. In his remarks written in 1854, having operated his school for three years and in which there were now 40 pupils (State of New York, 1854), he emphasizes parental perception and evaluation of his work. Wilbur and others involved in the establishment of the school were clear that it was intended primarily for people who were poor and could not afford exceptional means to educate or take care of their disabled relative. Parents of the students paid sometimes, depending on their circumstances, but it is safe to think that most of them would not have been from influential or wealthy families. There would have been something of a class difference between the school superintendent and the parents of those he was educating. Despite this, Wilbur afforded parents tremendous respect and central importance in his work. He wrote of them:

> But the most satisfactory evidence of the good results already in progress at the asylum, has been furnished by the expressed opinions of parents and friends of the pupils. The value of their testimony will be appreciated when it is understood that most of the children entrusted to our charge have been, by reason of their infirmities, objects of very strong affection. No place, therefore, away from home, no matter if conducted with the utmost reference to the comfort and happiness of the inmates, would be regarded as a fitting one for their children, as a mere asylum for custodial purpose. They expect an educational system suited to the capacities and necessities of their children, and they look for the evidence of a positive development, to compensate for the trials of separation. (State of New York, No. 54, 1854, pp. 18–19)

Thus, parents' involvement and expectations seemed to have played a central role in how Wilbur thought about and judged what he was doing. They are portrayed as generally very attached to their children, enduring separation, and wanting to see progress being made. That this would have been the case is from today's perspective commendable. The superintendent of a residential school would want parents like this and would listen to what they had to say. By the time we get to the massive institutions such as Willowbrook, this kind of parent involvement is almost absent (there were parent groups at places like Willowbrook but usually very small in membership relative to the total population in the institution) and, as we will read, the attitude of the administration toward families is cold and manipulative.

Eventually, the city of Syracuse offered the school either $7,500 (at that time a very large sum) or 10 acres of land. The school chose the land, and in 1854 a cornerstone was laid; a year later, a permanent home for up to 100 children was opened. The institution expanded over the years, was renamed several times, and eventually, in the 20th century, during the Willowbrook era, became known as the Syracuse State School. It is the second freestanding institution built for people with intellectual disabilities in the United States (Fernald School in Massachusetts being the first). Wilbur remained its superintendent until his death in 1883; he helped develop New York's residential system for people with intellectual disabilities, including the Randall's Island Asylum for Idiots in 1868.

Howe and Wilbur, among others, had success with Séguin's physiological method, turning "idiots" into productive citizens. These early pioneers clearly believed that idiots were able to learn and become contributing members of society, and they were documenting their successes. Braddock and Parish (2001) and Trent (1994) have argued that after their initial establishment, schools and institutions for people with intellectual disabilities grew rapidly during the 19th century and underwent a change of philosophy from being training schools to being custodial institutions. The growth and change in attitude took place for many reasons. These included the general population growth, particularly among the poorer classes, under conditions of surplus value and open immigration. Because of recurrent economic problems in the 1870s and 1880s, it became increasingly difficult to return residents to communities in which there were no jobs for them. Trent (1994) argued that the schools needed the "high-grade" students as workers in the school. They started accepting students with epilepsy and others with multiple disabilities but did not have the the funds or knowledge to support care for more serious cases. These more serious cases became "custodial" and as the schools filled with more and more of these cases, they changed in their mission to custody and segregation. Wilbur himself argued that, despite the name, the New York Asylum for Idiots was a school, yet it was obvious that the primary mission was custody and not education (Trent, 1994). As a result, residents were used as free labor to offset the costs of institutions (see Bartlett, 1964; Knight, 1891). This practice was common in institutions for the insane and for idiots throughout Europe and then in the United States. Importantly, in the early European efforts work was also rationalized on a therapeutic basis; working was thought to promote mental and physical health. "Institutional peonage," as it later became called, was a general feature of institutions in the 19th and 20th centuries, including Willowbrook.

Superintendents lacked motivation to educate or habilitate residents so that they could be returned into the community. Institutions began to take on a custodial role not intended by their founders such as Séguin or Wilbur.[1] As more were built, and as they began to grow in size, it was Wilbur who had the prescience to write in 1870, "Let us hope that the State institutions for idiots will escape that evil of excessive growth . . . in which patients are so numerous that the accomplished physicians who have them in their charge cannot remember the name of each" (Séguin, 1870, p. 21). This is exactly what ended up happening.

Under these conditions, the states did not stop their efforts in building institutions. In fact, historians have argued that superintendents during this period were entrepreneurial, using their positions and the increased demand for places to house both mentally ill and mentally deficient people as a way to grow their institutions, solidify their own careers, and gain power (Rothman, 1990; Trent, 1994). The leaders of these institutions embraced the growing idea that idiocy was a social problem, a burden, with the hope of securing more funding for their mission (Trent, 1994) or, put another way, for their own hospitals (Rothman, 1990). As it was widely believed that idiots were also morally incapacitated, a just society would take on the burden of caring for and protecting imbeciles, especially women of child-bearing age.

The dominant model for these institutions, by the end of the 1880s, was the "colony plan," large institutions, located as much as possible in relatively remote areas with farms; often, these were almost self-sustained villages, with separate buildings to segregate residents by gender, age, and ability.[2] Their mission had now

1. As we will discuss under the topic of eugenics, a darker current of thought about people with disabilities existed throughout the 19th century, ideas that construed disability as a serious threat to society and were to serve as the basis for the eugenics movement, given this name in 1883, and used as justification for involuntary incarceration, sterilization, and even euthanasia. There can be no doubt that those involved with the development of institutions for idiots, such as Wilbur and Howe, knew of these ideas. They were commonplace, as found, for example, in phrenology as early as the 1840s, with journals stating that "human degeneracy" was responsible for most social ills, openly advocating euthenasia, and animal husbandry approaches to human reproduction (see Fowler, 1844). By the latter part of the 19th century, those who were running these institutions were already responding to this perception of people with disabilities, which soon would dominate the society.

2. An interesting example was the Guislain Hospital. Goode took two tours and also collected several publications of the Guislain Museum in Ghent Belgium. The mental institution, which housed both idiots and the insane, was initially built by the city of Ghent to house male insane patients but later expanded to include mentally retarded children and adults. The facility was built as a large enclosed enclave or cloister of buildings that was by and large self-sufficient.

transformed from education to the protection of vulnerable people (again, with an increasing undertone of also protecting society from people with genetic taints). New York responded to this call by opening several institutions for people with intellectual disabilities in the 19th century, including facilities in 1866 on Randall's Island in New York City (Trent, 1994). In addition, a branch of the Syracuse Institute was opened in 1878 in Newark for women of child-bearing age. In 1894, the state opened Rome State Custodial Asylum (later Rome State School) for "low grade and delinquent cases" (Lerner, 1972, p. 24). By 1900, there were estimated to be 25 institutions for people with intellectual disabilities (Kuhlmann, 1940), with an estimated 11,800 residents (Fernald, 1917, as cited by Braddock & Parish, 2001, p. 37). In 1909, the state built Letchworth Village Home for the Feeble Minded and Epileptics in Thiells, New York. In 1930, the Wassaic State School was opened in 1931; Willowbrook State School was scheduled to open in the late 1930s but was delayed due to World War II.

Trent (1994) described what it would be like to live and work at institutions for people with intellectual disabilities in the early 1900s in the United States. One change was that institutions fully embraced their custodial powers and began accepting everyone from juvenile delinquents to epileptics, even those accused of petty crimes—some of whom may have been slow and backward but not feeble-minded. Residents' days were regimented for discipline and routine, some work or chores, cleaning, eating, and a few leisure activities, such as baseball, skating, or music. The food was fried or boiled beef, oatmeal, bread, and coffee; younger residents were given milk, eggs on special occasions. The genders were strictly separated largely because of fear of pregnancy, perhaps reasonably so given that in many cases new admissions arrived pregnant. Moreover, young feebleminded women were considered weak and prone to victimization from men. "High-grade" inmates were given free range during their "work day": Men did the hard labor, women the domestic labor; "low-grade" inmates did construction; "high-grades" did the labor usually done by staff. Farms were popular and necessary, as a source of fresh food and an outlet for labor.

It was operated by a religious order, the Brothers of Charity. The hospital opened in 1815; Jozef Guislain, who was appointed director in 1828, designed and built in 1857 the facility Goode saw when he visited. The hospital essentially functioned as a city within a city. There were many "ateliers" where patients worked to produce things (shoes, mattresses, weavings, painting, carpentry) that were both used at the institution and sold. There was a kitchen, tailor's shop, bakery, and blacksmith shop, also manned by patients. Patients also worked in the fields. There was an institutional brass band, choir, gymnastic club, and even a uniformed military group. The institution issued its own currency, which was used to pay inmates who could then purchase items controlled by the institution. In the United States, we find similar facilities, such as Letchworth Village in New York, or later Pacific State in California, that adapted this self-sufficiency model of running institutions.

There was little schooling going on, but classrooms existed, and—inspired by Séguin—instructors taught basic living and practical life skills, domestic skills, and school or vocational training, even for those who were more developed. Care included supervision of residents, cleaning, laundry, feeding, bathing, and clothing. Epidemics were common among both residents and staff, often causing attendant shortages. There were scandals, involving castration of inmates, violence, or inadequate medical care. Physical punishment was controversial, and some schools, such as the Rome State School, banned corporal punishment in 1903.

New York City's First Willowbrook: The Nurseries or Juvenile Department on Randall's Island

> The City of New York, with its immense suburbs, cannot much longer send its idiots to the northern climate of Syracuse, depriving them of the warmth of the seashore, and of the visits of their family and friends. But more, New York City must have its institution for idiots, because it contains the mature talents and growing capacities of all the branches of human inquiry, whose concourse must be insured to perfect the method of treatment of these children, and to deduce there from the important discoveries justly expected in anthropology. (Édouard Séguin writing in 1866, as cited in Goddard, 1914, p. xxii)[3]

The orphanage on Randall's Island was a place where indigent children of all kinds, with and without disabilities, would have been placed. It was created in 1848. In 1830, New York City had purchased the island located in the East River between Manhattan and Queens. Previously used as a quarantine, farm, and a station for British soldiers, the island was purchased by the city for the purpose of creating a relatively isolated area on which to locate a burial grounds for the poor, a poorhouse, a House of Refuge for Delinquents, and later an Idiot Asylum, homeopathic hospital, Inebriate Asylum, rest home for Civil War veterans, and a complex for children called the New York Nurseries. Other islands, particularly Ward's Island and Blackwell's Island, were used in the 19th century to house various indigent, criminal, ill, poor, and disabled populations. We will see that these places of isolation were not unrelated to one another.

---

3. Séguin had moved to New York by this time. His remarks must have been echoed by Wilbur and others, as the Asylum for Idiots on Randall's Island was established in October of 1866, under the direction of a former staff member at the Asylum in Syracuse. Although we cannot say that Séguin's was the first call for an Asylum for Idiots in New York City, his remarks were certainly influential. As the reader will see, the closing of the Randall's Island facility in the 1930s was related to the need to build another institution for mentally deficient persons in the New York City area, Willowbrook.

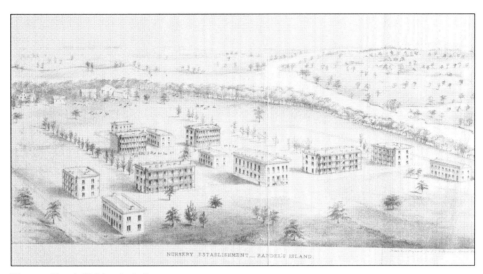

Nursery, Randall's Island 1849

We can get a glimpse into the life of The Asylum for Idiots on Randall's Island, which contained a school for idiot children and other children with disability because of a firsthand account of visits made by W. H. Davenport, who wrote for *Harper's New Monthly Magazine* in the 1860s. *Harper's* published two accounts by Davenport of his visits to institutions in New York City: one to Blackwell's Island Lunatic Asylum (see Davenport, 1866) and another to the orphanage and Asylum for Idiots on Randall's Island (see Davenport, 1867). His article about Randall's Island can be read as a narrative of a Willowbrook of its era. One very important difference was that the orphanage complex at Randall's Island was intended for all "types" of children, including those with disabilities. There were no adult residents, and its resident population was mostly kids without disability. Willowbrook, in contrast, was created specifically for children with disabilities but for various reasons had a population of nondisabled children and disabled and nondisabled adults who also lived there. Another important difference was that the orphanages were by and large not custodial institutions, although some children did live there for a long period of time. Finally, when one examines the conditions and details of everyday life, it is not possible to compare the degrading conditions found at Willowbrook to anything like what existed at Randall's Island. Still, Randall's Island, especially after the opening of the Idiot Asylum, was the place where intellectually disabled children of the poor in New York City might be sent. This part of the complex expanded greatly over the years and eventually served the function of caring for many people, adults and children, with all levels of intellectual disabilities from the New York City area. By the time it was closed in the 1930s, it was an immense facility that housed thousands of people, children and adults, with mental deficiency, and its closure was directly linked to the need to build another New York City institution, which eventually became Willowbrook State School.

Davenport's account of life at the nurseries is also a firsthand account based on what appear to have been multiple visits to the facility, although he does not specify how many times he was there. It is also written from what is a very sympathetic view toward the children he met. Davenport describes the complex of buildings on Randall's Island that were part of the nurseries or juvenile division of the New York Alms House, which opened on Randall's Island in 1848. Originally there had been nine buildings, but these had been much modified and added to. The complex was connected by wooden walkways (so was Willowbrook while it was an army hospital, and probably for the same reasons—that is, poor drainage and excessive mudiness). The facility was designed to house children above the age of three and younger than 16, children younger than three being sent to the Foundling Hospital on Blackwell's Island and then transferred to the orphanage at the appropriate age.

At the beginning of his article, Davenport comments that the men and women of the House of Refuge were used in various capacities to help run the institutions on the island, which may have been a way to pay for their stay, a form of "workfare." Generally speaking, the residential facilities appeared to have been segregated by both age (small and large boys) and gender, with the exception of the hospital complex in which no regard for either was given and children were grouped strictly according to the needs of their condition. The buildings he visited also seem to have had multiple functional areas: gymnasiums, dining areas, dormitories, and baths. Within the nursery complex were a school building and offices, as well as a quarantine building where new children were brought, cleaned up, and observed to ensure they had no infectious diseases before they were introduced into the main population. The buildings were supplied with "Croton water" brought in by pipes across the Hudson and had a complete sewerage system for waste removal (these latter features, fresh water and waste removal, were acknowledged throughout the 19th century as critical elements in asylum architecture).[4] Davenport also comments in the article about the cleanliness and even attractiveness of the interiors of these buildings, again maintained by other institutional inmates. This description of the physical plant is in stark contrast to that of Willowbrook.

We learn a little about the size of the nursery operation. There was about 80 full-time staff to serve approximately 1,000 children. Thirty were in the hospital department. In each of eight buildings where children resided there was a matron in charge. There were 10 nurses and 45 assistants. Also among the employees were keepers, a watchman, an engineer, a gardener, a cox-swain, a master tailor, and a teamster. About 1,500 admissions and discharges took place each year. (This is in marked contrast to Willowbrook, which had very few discharges but many deaths annually.)

4. The reader will see that this orientation was absent in the consideration of site selection for Willowbrook, accounting for unrelenting sewerage, building and plumbing problems.

Like the other institutions we have thus far discussed, the day was a long one. At the nurseries, school occupied a good part of the day, from 9:00 in the morning until about 3:30 in the afternoon for most. There was both a primary school and grammar school that were under the control of the New York City Board of Education and ranked sixth in its twelve wards. In addition to school, the older boys and girls were expected to work—boys on the grounds (there is an engraving of a work group of younger boys being supervised by an adult) or in shops (the tailor shop, for example) and the girls in sewing rooms. They would work before and after school for a total of 3.5 to 4 hours. In addition, there was religious and exercise instruction, and somehow, Davenport noticed, opportunities for free play. An interesting event he observed was that of a trip to Manhattan on July 4. After being entertained by the Twelfth Ward, the children returned to the island and continued with their celebration. "A military drill has long been one of the exercises of the institution, and several of the boys are adept in the rataplan and other performances of a drum-corps," Davenport noted (1867, p. 19).

Davenport describes some of the younger children being called to dinner by a bell. They quickly form a line, two by two, and enter the building where the meal is served. Davenport's illustration shows four tables, two for girls and two for boys, about 125 children in total, supervised by three matrons or attendees. The boys have no shoes but are wearing an institutional uniform of smock and pants. The girls wear a dress and shoes.[5] They are all standing while eating; there are no chairs. The meal began with a short prayer, with students standing away from the table. Once the prayer ended, each child "attacked instantly the viands before it." The meal was beef soup, with the accompanying meat and bread. Also served at dinner were fish, potatoes, gravy, roast beef, and cabbage. At breakfast the children had cocoa (no mention of the food), and at supper the drink was sweetened milk and water. There are no utensils, so children "follow their natural instincts as to means of conveying food to their mouths." The meal was eaten in silence. This kind of meal is characteristic of the regimentation found in total institutions in which everyone eats at the same time in the same place and under the same rules of behavior and similar to mealtimes Goode and others observed in the state institutions in the 1970s. In contrast, the emptiness of the routinized life of Willowbrook or Pacific State stands in contrast to the very busy lives of children at institutions back in 1866.[6]

5. It is significant that meals at Randall's Island were opportunities for boys and girls to be with one another. This indicates less of a separation between genders than was characteristic at Willowbrook, where opportunities to interact with the opposite gender were very limited. This consequence of this gender separation is discussed in Chapter 5 of this book.

6. For an account of life at Perkins School for the Blind, where deaf, deaf-blind, and mentally defective children were educated by Howe, see Freeberg's (2001) *The Education of Laura Bridgman*. Howe programmed literally every hour of the waking day, and the children's schedule included cold baths in the morning, healthy eating, exercise, instruction, work, prayer, and sleep.

It is easy to identify with many of the situations that Davenport faced as he roamed the grounds. His first encounter with the older boys playing in the field was not something that Goode ever saw at Pacific State or something that would have common at Willowbrook, although such games did sometimes take place there. It was of boys playing in a large field during a recess, more or less supervised only by some older boy "monitors." He concludes after watching them that these were by and large healthy boys who, although their play was not marked by "strict attention to the rules of etiquette," were friendly and of good nature.

On more than one occasion during his narrative, Davenport is surrounded by children whom, he writes, "smother" him. This is something that Goode experienced many times at Pacific State. He would walk on a ward where he was not known and immediately be surrounded by its residents, sometimes feeling uncomfortably crowded in. Davenport experiences this on several occasions. In one instance with the older boys, they crowd him while issuing multiple demands of "Take me out West"; "Take me with you"; "Are you going to take us to Harlem?" When people are incarcerated, powerless, and impoverished, the neediness of their situation comes "naturally" to the fore when they encounter a stranger from the outside. This was the same at Pacific State, where residents on the wards Goode visited who were complete strangers would ask him to take them to MacDonald's or to take them home.[7]

Davenport's introduction to the younger children of the nurseries is pathetic. Many were brought to Randall's Island after being abandoned by their parents. Their placement at the nurseries or at the Foundling Hospital on Blackwell's Island is coordinated via the Office of Commissioners:

> They reach the office of the Commissioners in a variety of ways. Some have been confided in cars or stages to the momentary care of benevolent gentlemen, the mothers never again appearing; others have been left on door-steps. Some have been found in open lots, ash barrels, and in alleys. A large number are sent or brought by their mothers who pay their board. It is not desirable to look in the depths of city depravity, or more could be written. (Davenport, 1867, p. 18)[8]

7. The topic of going out west or to Harlem is actually very pertinent for these older youths, many of whom faced leaving the nursery. This was not just idle chatter or a shotgun of "whatever" requests. The older boys exhibited ambivalence toward freedom. On the one hand, in one conversation Davenport reported that they were anxious to leave ("I don't believe there is a boy here who wouldn't rather be in New York"), which is interesting when one bears in mind the sad conditions of life that would have awaited them. On the other hand, there were very few elopements from the nurseries. Davenport reported 33 in the last year, which is actually quite few considering the number of children who were resident there.

8. Here the author is probably alluding to infanticide. In New York City during the 18th and 19th centuries, unwanted children were killed or left to die, and being dumped into the Hudson or East Rivers was not an uncommon method for doing so.

"GIMME PENNY, POPPY?"

Gimme a Penny

The first thing we see in Davenport's piece is an engraving of these young children crowding a window with smiling but also pleading expressions. The image is one of many drawn by the author while on his visits.

The caption beneath reads "Gimme penny, poppy?" The image conveys the children's neediness not only in material terms but also in emotional ones. The children Goode knew at Pacific State, the children at Willowbrook and other institutions, and even adults who had lived as children in institutions would call strangers by the names "poppy" or "mommy." There were practical reasons for doing so, but it also seems obvious that it was better to have a "made up" mommy or poppy than none at all. Sometimes at Pacific State and at Willowbrook, these fictional family roles evolved into something more than manipulative or compensatory devices. As we will see, certain staff, for example, could actually take on the role of being a mommy or daddy.

Davenport's article gives the impression that life on Randall's Island was hard but not unhappy. This is in stark contrast to life at Pacific State or Willowbrook. Children with disabilities come up in two ways in Davenport's piece. First is a discussion of the tailor shop where all "lame" boys were taught the craft and worked to produce goods that would be sold. Davenport remarks "there are many such in the institution." He also notes that while accommodations were provided for these children in the hospital section, many preferred to live with "their more healthful companions" (Davenport, 1867, p. 18). It is unfortunate that the author does not say more about these "lame" children and their relationship to the other children or about the hospital facility where children with more severe disabilities may have lived. But it is significant that he notes their presence in number and that, as one might surmise, the nurseries served children with disabilities of various kinds.

The other reference to children with disabilities in his article is in the account of the Idiot Asylum within the nursery complex. He describes it as follows:

> The Idiot Asylum stands at the rear of the Hospital, with its front towards the main avenue of the Island. It is built of fine brick, and its architecture, though simple, is elegant. The present edifice was constructed in 1860. My attention was turned to the school therein, and I made the inspection under the most favorable auspices—Commissioner Bowen, the then President of the Board, having the kindness to introduce me to the teacher. This young lady had repaired to the State Asylum for Idiots in Syracuse, and there familiarized herself with the method of instruction successfully pursued by Dr. Wilbur. The school was opened for the first time in October, 1866. (Davenport, 1867, p. 22)

Its purpose is explained by Davenport in an uncited quotation:

> The principal object sought is to increase the capacity of idiots for useful occupations. "To this end simple and rational means are employed to develop and improve both the physical and mental powers. The intellect is awakened by judicious discipline to a better comprehension of social relations, and the capacity to act in accordance with the demands of these relations is increased; the senses are instructed; the affections are cultivated; will strengthened, obedience and self-control secured, and vicious disagreeable habits corrected. In like manner, by progressive muscular exercises, the enfeebled body is invigorated." (Davenport, 1866, p. 22)

This connection between New York City's first Idiot Asylum and the Syracuse Asylum is not a surprising discovery. Wilbur's influence at this time was very strong, and Séguin's arrival in New York must have helped spur interest in and support for education of idiots. With Séguin's physiological approach the accepted standard, it is also not surprising to find its elements in these two institutions. The Idiot Asylum on Randall's Island appears to be a replication of Wilbur's Séguin-based approach.

In most of the classes and activities, Davenport observes that the children appear to have a desire for orderliness, to cooperate with others, and to obey those in authority. This was as true at the Idiot Asylum as in other parts of the nurseries. Davenport reports no evidence of punishments or reprimands in his articles, something that, especially if one made multiple observations, would have been unavoidable to see at Willowbrook or Pacific State. Overall, one cannot escape the impression that the conditions at the asylum were far better than those that ever existed at Willowbrook and that the children on Randall's Island, by virtue of the care and instruction given to them, were not as unfortunate as those children in later institutions who experienced extreme neglect and deficiency of education.

Through Davenport's eyes, we can visit what was the closest thing to a Willowbrook State School that existed in New York City during the 19th century. On the one hand, one cannot but find similarities in some of the observations made by him and those made later about children who lived at Willowbrook and other institutions in the 20th century. On the other hand, the high standard of living, care, and teaching that existed on Randall's Island in 1867 would never exist at Willowbrook or other places like it. In 1930, the Metropolitan Conference on Parks recommended that Randall's Island be cleared of its institutions and used only for recreational purposes. In 1933, the city acted on this recommendation and transferred ownership to the Department of Parks and Recreation. Thus began the process of the island's transformation to recreational uses, which was completed by Robert Moses, the then parks commissioner. The result of these changes was that there was no longer any large facility in the New York City area that could care for people with intellectual disability.

Although we do not know the exact number of individuals with intellectual disability who lived on the Randall's Island facility, photographs from a 1915 "Report to the State Commission to Investigate Provision for the Mentally Deficient" show that by 1914 the Randall's Island Asylum for Idiots had grown. It was a large campus of big specialized buildings, including a very large school for the feebleminded, a hospital building, a medical surgical pavilion, two buildings for custodial cases (one for males, one for females), a large male dormitory for "high-grade feebleminded," an industrial school, gymnasiums, and other buildings. The residents are shown in a variety of classes learning academics, cooking, basketry and chair making, hammock and rug weaving, folk dancing, and gymnastics. The interiors are homelike, the residents dressed in very standard but also quite clean and normal-looking dress. The children are shown in uniforms playing baseball, and there is a band, also with uniforms and instruments. Of course, the report would have tried to present the institution in the best light, so it is impossible to say what conditions were like there day in, day out. However, what can be said is that this was a very large facility that would have housed very many people with

THE AUTHOR SKETCHING.

Davenport Sketching at Randall's Island

intellectual disabilities from New York City. When it closed, residents would have had to have been transferred to other probably already overcrowded state facilities, the nearest of which was Letchworth Village in Thiells, New York. In the 1930s, for most New Yorkers, even by car, such a move would have meant four or five hours' travel each way, probably more, depending on one's starting point. By subway and train (and then taxi from the railroad station to the facility and back), it was a prohibitively long and expensive trip.

The institutional care system in New York State had for a long time been largely located upstate, and thus, the closing of the Randall's Island facilities exacerbated an already existing problem and created an unacceptable situation for city parents of children with intellectual disability. There had been created a tremendous need for another facility in the New York City area, which is the basic reason why we ended up with Willowbrook.[9]

9. Most of the residents at Randall's Island were transferred to Wassaic State School, which had been opened in 1930 (Castellani, 2005).

Randall's Island Asylum for Idiots

Johnny, Randall's Island Resident

Tailor Shop, Randall's Island

Bathing Boys, Randall's Island

Boys Working in Garden, Randall's Island

Eugenics and American Disability

In order to understand what happened at Willowbrook in the 1940s and subsequent decades the reader will need to have some familiarity with the eugenics movement. Trent's (1994) history of intellectual disabilities in the United States characterizes the late 1800s as a time when science increasingly was used to explain the plant and animal world, and because of Charles Darwin's popular theory of evolution, there was a growing interest in heredity. If genetics predicted traits, then it was possible to breed humans for selective traits, and many in the day became interested in topics such as racial purity, perfecting the human race, and, by extension, imperfections in humans. In light of this scientific revolution, a new view was emerging that feeblemindedness was not a problem of education or custody but rather of menace and degeneracy. And the picture painted of mental defectives depicted them as unable to control their sexual and moral behavior.[10]

---

10. We hope the reader will forgive this long but important footnote. It is essential to understand that ideas about curtailing human degeneracy, the need to adopt husbandry or animal-breeding ideas in order to prevent social and moral degeneracy in human beings and human society, had been openly and widely expressed in the writings of European and American phrenologists for half a century or more before eugenics was invented. The American phrenologist O. W. Fowler in *American Phrenological Journal,* in an edition from 1844, explores the issue of human degeneracy that society faced. He linked human degeneracy to all kinds of problems in society. He argued that the death of persons born with idiocy and depravity is a kindness, as life for those persons is a torture not worth living. He recommended that human beings adopt the same procedures as animal breeders in order to better the human race and prevent degeneracy. While praising the early natural deaths of children with degeneracy, he stopped short of recommending euthanasia. The point here, and it is an extremely important one when we think about the eugenics era, is that many of the ideas of the eugenics era had been popular, under another name, for half a century or more before Francis Galton dressed them up with Mendelism and Darwinism, inventing yet a new pseudoscience that he named "eugenics." The idea of people with disabilities being threats to society was given scientific clothes during this period. It is generally true that eugenics began with and continued to practice pseudoscience, that is, research that was claimed to be scientific but that failed, to many scientists of the era, to live up to credible scientific standards. Perspicuous examples of pseudoscientific inquiry done under the rubric of eugenic research included Francis Galton's composite photography, which claimed to be able to capture the essence of a family, mental defective, criminal, prostitute, thief, and so on, through the superimposing of multiple images; Rogers and Merrill's 1919 account, *Dwellers in the Vale of Siddem,* about people living in an isolated valley in Minnesota who they say were a result of a group of mental defectives immigrating there, intermarrying, and fostering children who, in the overwhelming majority, had some sort of degenerate condition (this group were isolated and did intermarry but suffered from poverty and complete lack of education rather than genetic defects); and, perhaps most offensively, Crookshank's 1924 work, *A Mongol in Our Midst,* that uses photography and radiographic images of hands to demonstrate how people with mongolism (in current parlance Down syndrome) represent atavistic throwbacks to more primitive forms of human beings. The point is, we cannot read about or judge eugenics by looking at it scientifically. It really had no credible scientific basis.

As stated by Braddock and Parrish (2001, p. 38):

> The period from 1880 to 1925 was a time when persons with intellectual disabilities were viewed as deviant social menaces, and intellectual disability was seen as an incurable disease. . . . The eugenic belief widely held during this period was that intellectual disability was inherited as a Mendelian characteristic. . . . Intellectual disability was linked in numerous studies to criminality, immoral behavior, and pauperism.

Eugenics was promoted as a "scientific perspective" but also one that was linked to specific programs of social action, including institutions for people with intellectual disability. By the 20th century, there were two parts of this social program: positive eugenics, which looked at the ways scientific understanding of human beings could enhance the production of healthy children and their upbringing; and negative eugenics, which focused on the elimination of negative "inherited traits" of human beings and the associated social problems (everything from tuberculosis to mental illness to prostitution and crime). This would be accomplished by controlling who would be capable of reproduction (through incarceration and sterilization) and/or who would be allowed to live (through euthanasia or mercy killing). Thus eugenics thinking linked people with idiocy to various social problems, but further all sorts of social problems, including idiocy, were linked to genetics. This precipitated an era where certain genes and those who carried them were seen as the basic threat to a stable and good society.

Over the course of the 18th and 19th centuries, religion was increasingly replaced by science as the way to think about and intervene in social problems. The notions of population control within sciences such as phrenology, sociology, or economics eventually became linked with the scientific works of both Gregor Mendel and Darwin. Mendel provided the biological details about "inherited characteristics"—they were in the form of what he called "unit characteristics" or today "genes"—that controlled the later development of the plant (he experimented on peas) or animal. Darwin supplied an alternative explanation, though misunderstood by eugenicists, for what were "good" or "bad" human characteristics. They were not immutable things of godly origin but a result of natural processes, and natural processes could be brought under man's control.

The early eugenicists such as Francis Galton and, most vocally, Herbert Spencer, who coined the phrase "survival of the fittest," advocated what was called "social Darwinism," which was a misinterpretation of Darwin's theory of natural selection. Social Darwinism interpreted natural selection to mean that the smart, strong, and powerful were the humans that nature picked to survive. This is an inappropriate extension of Darwin's concept of fitness, which actually referred to a relationship between changing organisms and their changing environment. Natural selection did not refer to the idea that those who are strong or smart, or had any other particular characteristic, were more "generally" fit. However, this survival of the fittest (strongest and smartest) became a theme of eugenics and was used by its proponents in scientific writing and propaganda.[11]

The history of the development of eugenics in the 20th century is somewhat shocking to most Americans. Most do not understand America's role in helping to develop eugenics not only in the United States but also in Germany prior to World War II. Even among scholars of disability, it has not been until relatively recently, with the publication of Martin Pernick's (1996) *Black Stork* and Edwin Black's (2003) *War Against the Weak,* that America's leadership in the eugenics movement has been fully appreciated.

The first book, by Pernick, was something of a shock to people interested in disability history. It was about a film, *The Black Stork,* which was made in 1917 and advocated euthanasia of children born with disability. The book is also about disability and film more generally, but the first part, dealing with the film *The Black Stork,* was somewhat of an eye-opener at the time. The film was made as part of an American physician's attempt to influence the public to accept mercy killing of children who were born disabled. Dr. Harry Haiseldon, a Chicago-based physician, used eugenics ideas and reasoning to justify killing children who were born with disability. In 1915, he was involved in a highly publicized case (in the *Chicago Tribune,* this story's headlines supervened those of World War I), Baby Bollinger, whom he "allowed to die" with permission of the baby's mother. Haiseldon was brought up on charges. He was not convicted and thus felt that his actions had been "vindicated." Haiseldon, like other eugenicists, believed that science could determine "where natural selection was heading and that eugenics could help get us there more efficiently" (Pernick, 1996, p. 79). Haiseldon differed from eugenicists of his era, such as Charles Davenport or John Kellogg in the United States or Karl Pearson in England, in the use of euthanasia rather than preventive measures to eliminate

---

11. For example, eugenics-era films, such as the American *The Black Stork* in 1917 or propaganda films of the German eugenicists in the 1920s and 1930s, would have scenes showing weak and feeble animals and insects being killed and eaten by more powerful ones. The message was that it was Nature's way of ensuring that only the strong survive and that weakness was something it wanted to prevent or get rid of, because it was contrary to Nature. This kind of argument was turned toward developing specific interventions, including sterilization, control of intermarriage, immigration control, and euthanasia. The same logic was used to argue against people who had unwanted inherited characteristics, including race (in the United States), poverty (in England), and religion (in Germany). This logic took yet other twist in Russia, with its emphasis on manipulating genes to produce a population of geniuses and athletes. Sweden had yet another take on eugenics. Each country fitted its general approach to its particular situation and culture.

undesirable characteristics. Davenport, who later played a central role in the development of eugenics in the United States, disavowed such measures as early as 1911.

However, once vindicated, Haiseldon led a campaign to convince Americans that mercy deaths of children born with disability were not only good science but good social policy. He became a celebrated figure in the eugenics movement and toured the United States advocating euthanasia of the unfit.[12] With the topic of euthanasia in the headlines, Hollywood came knocking, and Haiseldon actually starred in a silent movie that showed the evils of human degeneracy and defectives and advocated the killing of retarded and disabled persons. It was shown all over the United States, after 1917, in an attempt to convince the American public that such action was necessary and humane. The film predates similar efforts in Germany and later in Nazi Germany.

It would not be an underestimation to say that the news that Pernick's research about euthanasia of children with disabilities in the United States was somewhat shocking. Most people in the field did not appreciate how open and public the debate about mercy killing of children with disabilities was in the early part of the 20th century. Black (2003) describes how the Carnegie Institute for Experimental Evolution at Cold Springs Harbor, Long Island, coordinated a program of research, propaganda, and social engineering aimed at achieving racial purity. This was done largely under the leadership of Charles Davenport, acknowledged to be at the center of American eugenics efforts and a staunch supporter of eugenics in other countries, including Germany. Davenport retired from the Carnegie Institute in 1934 but continued his role as "elder statesman" in the 1940s. Davenport, supported by the incredible wealth of the Harriman and other foundations, ensured that research justifying eugenics was done both here and in Germany. He also specifically supported the German efforts in this area in a host of ways, including by spreading Nazi propaganda in the United States, sending American eugenics research and legislation to Germany for their adaptation, and funding research projects conducted in Germany.

Eugenics research is most interesting as a historical phenomenon. Were it not for the fact that its reports were taken seriously and used as rationale for the killing and inhumane treatment of people with disabilities and other "socially undesirable" groups, it could be called laughable, at least by current scientific standards.

It was "science" with its conclusion already in hand. Epistemologically naive and even pseudoscientific, in classic documentary fashion eugenic researchers found evidence of what they were seeking. Despite these flaws, and strong challenges from within the scientific community, eugenics research was well known and formed an intellectual backdrop against which the "problem" of disabled persons was raised.

12. Haiselden was eventually denied membership by the Chicago Medical Board both for his lecture series about eugencis and promotion of his film.

Eugenics was taught in colleges and universities all over America. Not only this, but eugenics research was used to justify the various persecutory social programs we go on to describe, which clearly affected people with intellectual disability who lived in institutions. It justified their incarceration and sterilization and provided good grounds for experimenting with residents. It was not uncommon for places like the Minnesota School for Feeble Minded and Colony for Epileptics to have a research department. When Goode entered the field in 1974, virtually all such institutions in California had research departments. Research was a part of what these places did, and Willowbrook was probably most well known in this regard (see Chapter 2).

As described in the other book about American eugenics that created a shock when it was released, Edwin Black's *War Against the Weak,* American eugenicists were a relatively small conglomeration of powerful and wealthy people who were dedicated to creating a racially pure, Nordic America. Because of their wealth and ties to academia and government, they were able to have considerable influence despite being few in number. They supported Charles Davenport's various efforts at the Eugenics Records Office, at Cold Spring Harbor, Long Island, including a national program to spread eugenics throughout the United States and actively supporting the German eugenics movement. Their efforts found their ways into law, for example, in the immigration quotas that were set up to ensure that racially, physically, and ethnically undesirable people would not enter the United States. Eugenicists were behind the compulsory sterilization laws that were enacted in 35 states and used in many institutions as a way to prevent people with suspected intellectual disability from reproducing.[13] Antimiscegenation laws, preventing marriage between persons of different races, was also an achievement of those who had eugenic beliefs and who wanted to keep the white race pure.

The ideology of eugenics, then, ultimately is the social context or milieu in which institutions that housed people with intellectual disability operated in the latter 19th and early 20th century. Eugenics was part of the fabric of American life, even if not all Americans subscribed to its beliefs. Beautiful baby contests were held at state fairs.[14] Films about eugenics or with eugenic messages were made

13. Most well known is the case of a Virginia woman, Carrie Buck, who was the center of eugenicist attempts to pass a law legalizing compulsory sterilization of mental defectives. That law was put into effect in June of 1924. It was based on a model bill that had been drafted by the eugenicist Harry Laughlin. The case of *Buck v. Bell* was appealed to the United States Supreme Court, which upheld the state's right to sterilize Buck against her will. Oliver Wendell Holmes, an advocate of eugenics thinking, presided.

14. The first American Baby Contest was held in New York City in P. T. Barnum's museum in 1851, already reflecting eugenic thinking in popular American culture. The winner, Charles Orlando Scott, as he appears in a poster from the Barnum Museum, is an overweight, white, well-dressed boy with a walking stick.

throughout the first half of the 20th century and shown in theaters all over the country (see Pernick, 1996, pp. 293–295, for an extensive list of films). The public attitude toward many groups thought to be socially undesirable or harmful to society was increasingly unforgiving. Segregation, incarceration, compulsory sterilization, and discussions about euthanasia became the dominant themes in the care of people with intellectual disability. During the beginning of the 20th century conditions in facilities for people with mental disability were deteriorating. Despite the expansion of these facilities, people with intellectual (and other) disabilities were increasingly found in America's poor farms. "In 1922, Ohio reported that 70% of its poor farm inmates had 'feeblemindedness.' . . . North Carolina estimated that 85% of inmates were 'mentally abnormal'" (Braddock & Parish, 2001, p. 39).

During this same period in the late 19th and early 20th century, public education began to establish classes for educable mentally deficient children. Sometimes called "ungraded classes," they were begun in New York City in 1900 at Public School 1 in Manhattan. In 1914, Henry Goddard (1914) wrote a book about his visits to 125 of the 131 ungraded classes that then existed in New York City. Titled *School Training of Defective Children,* the book examines the educational programs that existed for about 2,500 students, which would have represented a small portion of children who would have required such classes. Although Goddard's recommendation that the city establish additional separate classrooms staffed by teachers with special training might run against 21st-century ideas about "educational inclusion," his report shows the early efforts of special education in New York City public schools and makes recommendations about equipment, pedagogy, teacher credentialing, and administration that would have helped expand special education at that time.

As Trent (1994) argues, concurrently states across the nation were requiring children to attend school, and thus, many children who had been cared for at home came to the attention of education authorities. About this time, the study of mental defectives was becoming popular. Americans such as Goddard, G. Stanley Hall, and Lewis Terman were all working on tests to assess feebleminded people, and they started collaborating with the state schools. These scientists, Goddard specifically, linked feeblemindedness with social vices including crime, poverty, prostitution, delinquency, and drunkenness. And so the testing began, and the test results of mental subnormality helped fill institutions with newly diagnosed morons. Families were increasingly embarrassed by having a menace in their families, about having "bad blood," and if they could afford it, they sent their child away to private facilities, and if not, consign them to the poor conditions of the state institution. Testing became a major instrument in the process of institutionalization.[15]

15. The standard in history and criticism of the IQ test is Stephen Gould's (1981) *The Mismeasure of Man.*

Intelligence testing was at the same time an element of a movement of society to identify children requiring special educational help. It was part of the entry of psychology into public education, which should be, acknowledging criticisms, celebrated. Like so many other developments of the eugenics era, the testing of intelligence was born at a time when there was a deep ambivalence in the public attitude toward disability. On the one hand, we find a desire to create public institutions (state institutions, hospitals, colonies, special education classrooms) to help children with disabilities. On the other hand, we find a fear of such children and the repercussions of their being allowed to be part of society, underwriting the separateness of these solutions. These were attitudes that coexisted at the same historical time, not infrequently simultaneously in the same person, and were even held by those most involved in the care of people with intellectual disabilities, such as scientists like Goddard. The institutions that were created, in a reflection of the earlier institutions of the 19th century, also embodied this ambivalence.

At the beginning of the 20th century, institutions to house people with intellectual disabilities grew. Whether these were state schools, colonies, or hospitals, they were part of a social program that was believed to be a way to help those afflicted while at the same time protecting society from social problems resulting from inherited characteristics. The institutions were sold to the public based on rhetoric appealing to both the social good and individual welfare. They bore the stamp of eugenics thinking.

One problem from the eugenics position was how to incarcerate the increasing numbers of morons and imbeciles. Overcrowding at the existing schools made the situation seem hopeless. Moreover, once in asylums, reproduction was still possible. Thus, segregation along with sterilization was a primary way to protect society from genetic contamination. Sterilization was a controversial approach, especially in its most extreme form. Trent (1994) described how in 1895, it was discovered that the superintendent of Kansas State Asylum for Idiots and Imbecile Youth had castrated 11 feebleminded males. It was believed at the time that castration would eliminate sexual behavior, and so young idiots who were caught masturbating repeatedly were castrated with the hope that it eliminated their sexual behavior. It did not. The pro-sterilization movement had many justifications for this procedure.

Superintendents used "institutional population control" to justify sterilization via vasectomy for men or tubul ligation for women. They could both reduce pregnancies and possibly release young "high-grade" women on parole if there were no risk of sexually immoral behavior (Trent, 1994). But as the 1930s progressed, there was no work out in the community for parolees to do, families had even fewer resources, and local industries and farms were not hiring. The approaching war in the 1940s meant that many attendants enlisted or were drafted, and so high-grade residents were relied upon even more to run state institutions.

The development of institutions of care for people with intellectual disabilities in the latter 19th and early 20th century was subject to the vagaries of the economy, which consisted of regular cycles of war, recession, and depression. In the United States, major economic crises and wars occurred, which negatively affected the resources available for the care of people with disabilities. Given the combination of circumstances of economic hardship (World War I, followed by a short economic boom, followed by the Great Depression, followed by World War II) and an intellectual climate influenced by eugenic ideas, institutions for the intellectually disabled were increasingly underfunded, overcrowded, understaffed, and run through the labor of residents, many of whom, it was thought, would reside therein for the entirety of their lives.[16]

The Fernald School and Belchertown State School During Eugenics

Eugenics is the ideological background against which Willowbrook's story unfolds. Similarly, eugenics played a role in the many other institutions in this era. We will briefly look at two—the Fernald School and Belchertown State School as a way of contrasting and comparing what happened at Willowbrook.[17] Certainly, D'Antonio (2004) made this his explicit argument: Eugenics directly affected the state school system. Inspired by eugenics, "For more than fifty years, physicians and bureaucrats applied the principles of animal husbandry—attempting to weed out bad stock—to troublesome boys and girls" (D'Antonio, 2004, p. 5). For eugenicists in America, progressivism followed one of two strategies. As noted earlier, there was a positive form whereby science was applied to the development of children. This form of human betterment also promoted racial purity through intermarriage and supporting organizations, with campaigns like that of Theodore Roosevelt's attacks

16. By 1938, when it was proposed that an institution be built for the mentally deficient on Staten Island, one of the key arguments by Staten Island residents against the idea was that it was well known that conditions in such places were horrible. The impression one gets is that asylums and hospitals have been fair game for the press since they have existed. *Harper's* found them newsworthy in the 1860s (Davenport, 1866/1867), and there were newspaper articles in the 1930s describing horrible conditions for people in mental institutions. Although we have not done the systematic research, a reasonable surmise is that newspaper exposés of the increasingly crowded conditions of mental institutions probably had appeared in the press at this time.

17. Institutions in New York grew at a rapid pace: the Rome State Custodial Asylum for Unteachable Idiots opened in 1894; by 1916, it housed 1,554 inmates, 300 beyond capacity (65 were dead in the following year); and, by 1942, Rome State School had 3,950 inmates, one of the largest in the nation (Trent, 1994). We selected Fernald and Belchertown because there are books about them.

on the feminized male in favor of real "breeders" and "fighters." The other set of strategies, a negative form of eugenics, sought to contain genetically unworthy people and prevent them from reproducing by incarcerating, sterilizing, and even euthanizing them. Thus, states created schools where "the genetically inferior could be isolated forever" (D'Antonio, 2004, p. 9), and "Once locked away, they endured isolation, overcrowding, forced labor, and physical abuse including lobotomy, electroshock, and surgical sterilization" (D'Antonio, 2004, p. 5). His history of Fernald State School, which was opened in the mid-19th century, makes this clear when it examines the careers of the scientists affiliated with the school. Fernald, like all institutions in this era, bore the eventual stamp of eugenics.

D'Antonio (2004) concluded that residents were viewed by the administration and doctors as "a backdrop for their careers, the source of their authority in the outside world, and a handy reservoir of human material for research" (p. 52). Researchers at Fernald studied everything from neurological development, nutrition, the heritability of feeblemindedness, genetics, and endocrine systems. One psychiatric neuropathologist, Dr. Clemens Benda, tested the hypothesis that malformed or malfunctioning glands were responsible for feeblemindedness. Benda was known to have preserved the brains and organs of expired residents, collecting as many as 50,000 samples of brain tissue as well as thyroid and pituitary samples. He had conducted more than 3,500 lobotomies. With his large research staff of 24 scientists, Benda would secure large grants with international collaborators. This was common: Sonoma State Home in California, New Jersey State Colony for Feebleminded Men in Woodbine, and Polk State School in Pennsylvania were all involved in early studies such as those isolating polio vaccines.

D'Antonio documented how at Fernald, one ward, the Science Club, was given a special diet (an extra pint of milk a day) and other special privileges. Sponsored by Quaker Oats, the children were also fed special oatmeal. Ostensibly, the study collected all their urine and feces and examined whether phylates influenced calcium absorption from milk. In 1993, the story broke on the news that the oatmeal in Dr. Benda's study had been laced with radioactive calcium (D'Antonio, 2004). Apparently, none of the participants or parents had given informed consent because of a misleading information letter. D'Antonio described Benda as a "master mind" who "showed an unseemly callousness for a man who promoted himself as a champion of vulnerable children" (p. 251). Complicating matters is Benda's complicated history: He fled Germany before World War II and had a collection of eugenics literature, including photos of Nazis and autopsies at Dachau concentration camp.

Such a history opens up the question as to what degree Willowbrook State School was unique or a representative part of a systemic societal neglect. Hornick's (2012) new social history about the Belchertown State School for the Feeble-Minded in Massachusetts suggests a larger pattern. Belchertown, established in

1922, was part of an earlier era of schools. As mentioned earlier, Massachusetts had been home to early models, such as the Massachusetts School for Idiotic and Feebleminded, founded in 1848, which would eventually become the Walter E. Fernald State School. Belchertown opened its school 10 years after its initial opening, so its primary role was not education. It was based on the "cottage" plan, a small colony arranged on a campus setting, with dorms separated by gender, ability, or medical condition. There were dorms for residents and staff, a kitchen, a hospital, a farm, beauty parlor, a sewing facility for women, and a carpenter's shop for men. Tunnels connected most of the buildings.

Hornick explains that children arrived there either by civil commitment, voluntary application, or as ordered by the courts for observation. Only a few were not "mentally defective." The few who were viewed as educable were placed in school and taught basic reading and math skills; those who were not educable worked on basic sensory skills. It was school for half a day, then occupational training or unpaid labor. The residents also kept busy by preparing and performing a yearly minstrel show, including choruses, solos, dancing, and special acts, performed by residents in blackface; they also participated in the Fourth of July parade for the town. Contagious disease was frequent and widespread. The genders were strictly segregated, even at dances, yet there were unwanted pregnancies and sterilization was used. For most, escape or death was the only alternative to permanent residency. In the front wards, in 1970, the staff–resident ratio was 1:2; in the back wards at night, 1:60; by 1985, after a class action lawsuit, it was 3.5:1.

Foreshadowing Willowbrook, in many ways conditions were horrible. The smell at Belchertown was overpowering, and the residents, many of them nude, sat all day on benches or on the floor "in strange and grotesque positions, sometimes in pools of their own waste." Their only outside stimulation was a TV set boxed into the wall; the men stared at it for hours whether it "displayed a picture or rolling blur" (Hornick, 2012, p. 85).

Indeed, overcrowding, nudity, and preventable deaths led to a class action lawsuit, in 1972, requesting that all residents of the state school be provided with adequate treatment and humane living conditions. A decree on November 12, 1973, mandated improvements to the physical structure, increases in staffing, and implementation of community-based alternatives. These lawsuits were a part of a clear pattern paralleling Willowbrook: Among others, the residents of Partlow State School and Hospital in Tuscaloosa, Alabama, filed suit in 1970; in 1974–1975, class action lawsuits were filed by residents of Fernald State School in Waltham, Massachusetts (Hornick, 2012).

Toward midcentury, criticism of the state school system was mounting. A 1941 photo essay on Letchworth Village portrayed a less than ideal village with "naked residents, unkempt and dirty, huddled in sterile dayrooms" (Trent, 1994,

p. 226). By 1948, Albert Deutsch had written *Shame of the States* (1948), in which he argued that the state school system was "euthanasia through neglect." In the 1950s, parents of children at state schools joined in, launching a genre of writing documenting parents' confessions of "forgotten children," justifying their decisions about abandoning their children (Trent, 1994). A few postwar exposés showed the bare and dilapidated state school system; at the same time, many families were beginning to claim their lost child, and some began forming relationships. And then in 1965, one sibling of a person with mental retardation, Robert F. Kennedy, led a highly public attack on Rome and Willowbrook State Schools.

Conclusion

History shows that most societies have relegated people with disabilities to deviant statuses and that such statuses have been the basis for their exclusion, incarceration, cruel treatment, and even killing. With the growth and centralization of the population during the Industrial Revolution, a large underclass of poor people began to be recognized as a social problem that society needed to explicitly address. Under the socio-economic conditions of the Industrial Revolution, with its possibilities of surplus wealth, and then political democratic revolution, with its emphasis on individual freedom and rights, specific institutions were created to care for people who previously had either lived in villages and cities with their families, or who had been forced to become beggars or criminals, or who had failed to survive on their own. As these institutions were created, the disabled poor began to find their way into almshouses. Before the establishment of specific institutions to take care of people with disabilities, the United States followed very much the European, especially British, traditions of almshouses, workhouses, community support, and also practices of weeding out or dumping. Western societies invented institutions (in both senses of the term) to deal with a growing underclass of poor within which, with notable exceptions, could be found the overwhelming majority of people with disability. These changes can be observed in changes in European laws about the poor in the 17th and 18th centuries.

By the 18th century, freestanding institutions for people with mental illness, deafness, blindness, idiocy, and other forms of disability or illness throughout Europe were increasingly common. When considering the establishment of such places in the United States, it is clear that American physicians, many of whom had studied medicine at European universities, were fully aware of these efforts and even cited them when trying to convince legislators in the 1840s in New York State to fund similar efforts. Early examples of public support for institutions for the insane can be found in the Province of Pennsylvania in 1751 or in Kentucky in 1793. Some of the earliest of these efforts related to idiots were founded in

Massachusetts by Howe and Wilbur and then by Wilbur in New York State. Thus, these early pioneers sought to help children and protect society, and gradually city and state governments in America adopted this as their mission, helping not just disabled but a host of categories of people linked to social problems. New York State's central role in the history of institutions in the United States is appreciated only when one considers that it produced the second freestanding institution for people with intellectual disability in Syracuse, then created perhaps the most extensive system of institutions for this population, and finally created Willowbrook, the place most singly responsible for deinstitutionalization in our country. Yet when one reads about the Syracuse Asylum and what went on there, we do not get a sense that what was to come was a place like Willowbrook. There was not any of the overcrowding or neglect that came to be associated with institutions for the mentally retarded later in the century and in the 20th century. There was great concern for the individual child and that child's family.

Davenport's account of the orphanage on Randall's Island provides a glimpse into Willowbrook's precursor. Some of the things he reported about Randall's Island sound eerily familiar to those who know Willowbrook, but there were also differences. Both institutions were somewhat isolated and pastoral (at least compared to the slums and poorer areas in the city) and self-contained. Randall's Island was a busy place and offered instruction and programming to promote release into the community; children generally lived in conditions better than they would have experienced on the street.

In trying to understand some of the things that happened at Willowbrook, it is important to appreciate the role of the United States in pioneering some of the modern medical attitudes about disability. This occurred in the latter part of the 19th century, with the formation of a national organization of superintendents for such institutions in the 1870s, but continued especially in the era of eugenics, which resulted in the imprisonment, sterilization, and even euthanasia of people with intellectual disability. Appreciating this history allows one to better understand places such as Willowbrook, in which we find many practices associated with the eugenics movement, this even though Willowbrook began operating in 1948, in a technically "post-eugenics" climate. In the first quarter of the 20th century, sterilization of the mentally deficient was the law in 35 states. In the United States, from at least the second decade of the 20th century, euthanasia of children with disabilities was actively advocated for by physicians and eugenicists, who also favored miscegenation laws, restricted immigration, and public education about racial (i.e., Aryan) purity in America.

Descriptions of Belchertown and Fernald State Schools in Massachusetts present similar overall conditions to those seen at Willowbrook. Analyses of life at these schools suggested a very different quality of life than that seen on Randall's

Island. In many ways, what happened at Willowbrook had been foreshadowed by Belchertown and Fernald, indicating that Willowbrook was part of a systemic policy of neglect against people with physical and intellectual disabilities, reflecting over a century of thinking that people with disabilities posed a menace that needed to be contained. By the time Willowbrook was built, institutions betrayed the original humanitarian intent that led to their foundation.

2
A Social History of
Willowbrook State School

Settled by the Dutch, Staten Island was the last of New York's boroughs to be connected by bridge to the city, in 1964. Until then quite rural, with many parks, farms, and undeveloped land, it has always been a beautiful island. Staten Island has a long history of institutions being built on it, including quarantine hospitals, orphanages, poor farms, and homes such as Sailor's Snug Harbor. In the 19th century, island residents revolted against too many such places being located on the island or just off it and burned one of the quarantine hospitals. In the latter 1930s, after the closure of Randall's Island, the idea of building another institution in the New York City area was discussed in state government. Staten Island was not the only site considered. It is difficult to say exactly what plans were being made by the Department of Mental Hygiene before the announcement of the possibility of building an institution on Staten Island in March of 1938. Castellani (2005) describes the general situation that New York was facing in the Depression:

> The Great Depression and the 1930s have become synonymous with notions of uniform deprivations. World War II and the years just before Pearl Harbor are often portrayed as a period during which the American economy pulled out of the Depression and a boom began that would last for decades. In many ways, for people with developmental disabilities in New York, the conditions were reversed. During the Depression,

New York took full advantage of the federal Works Project Administration to substantially increase its institutional capacity.[1] Wassaic State
School opened in 1930 and was rapidly filled from transfers from Randall's Island. New and remodeled buildings at Letchworth Village State
School added 660 beds to its capacity in 1936, and the completion of
new buildings at Rome State School enlarged the capacity of that institution by 532 beds. (Department of Mental Hygiene, 1936, as cited in
Castellani, 2005, p. 25)

Castellani reported that between 1935 and 1940, the number of individuals on the
books of the state schools increased by over 25%, from 13,839 to 17,498, and the
institutional census jumped from 12,797 to 15,952; every expansion in capacity
led quickly to overcrowding. This perverse phenomenon would plague the state
for decades.

Chronic overcrowding and the opportunity to take advantage of federal aid
in the construction of public facilities framed the state's discussion of the development of state institutions for the mentally deficient. The lack of such a facility in
the city of New York would also have been part of the state's considerations, as it
would have been aware of the situation of families there. Families, aided by professionals in the field, advocated for the creation of such an institution in New York
City, and the state knew that its system of upstate facilities did not meet the needs
of families in the New York City area. As we will see in our review of newspaper
articles, it is clear that the state wanted to build a school for mentally deficient
children in New York City. What is not as apparent is whether they had in mind
a site at Willowbrook Park, Staten Island, in discussions earlier than those made
public in 1938.

Goode was able to view a few census maps from the 1870s at the Staten Island
Historical Society and can say about this period that, as indicated on the maps, it
was an area of largely rectangular plots of farmland surrounding a central brook
connecting two lakes.[2] Near these two lakes were two factories, one for iron combs,

---

1. This was equally true for many states who took advantage of these federal dollars during this era to build institutional capacity, accounting for a similarity in architecture across the
country for institutions built in this era (Wolfensberger, 1982).

2. An investigation of the earlier history of the Willowbrook area was undertaken by
James Kaser, archivist of the Willowbrook Collection at the College of Staten Island Library.
Kaser found that the area had been a wetlands traveled by canoe by the Lenapi Indians before the
settling of the island by the Dutch in the mid-17th century. The changes in water flow described
in footnote 3, most likely engineered initially by early settlers, took advantage of a large brook,
Willowbrook, that was used for manufacturing, although it is not possible to say at this time
exactly when this began.

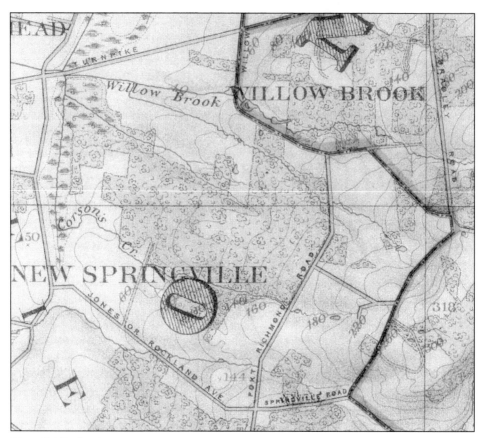

Map of Willowbrook, 1891

owned by J. Standring, and another for hardware, owned by J. Hall.[3] The 1874 map shows some residential structures, especially along Richmond Turnpike (now Victory Boulevard) as well as a farm colony to the south, which was the poor house farm. By the time the site was being looked at by the state in 1938, there was considerable residential development along Victory Boulevard, a 110-acre park, a golf course (the Willowbrook Golf Club at Butt's Head), and other residential structures scattered throughout the area. Among the arguments used by residents to defeat

---

3. The name "Willowbrook" implies a flowing body of water that could, and apparently was, used in the days before electricity to drive water wheels used in the process of manufacture. It is entirely probable that the lakes shown on the brook in the 1870s maps were manmade, This was a common strategy in the 18th and 19th centuries to ensure water flow to drive water wheels during times of drought, and a comparable two-lake system constructed on a large brook for similar purposes was built near Feltville, New Jersey, an 1840s industrial village that made paper.

the idea of building a state institution there was that it was one of the most beautiful spots on Staten Island (of course, a more sympathetic resident used this same idea to argue in favor of putting the school there so that the children could have the benefit of such beautiful surroundings).

There were articles in the *Staten Island Advance* that dealt with the proposal to establish a state institution on Staten Island. They appeared from around March through June of 1938 and reveal, not surprisingly, an overwhelmingly negative response from Staten Islanders themselves, virtually all their civic associations, and both political parties. When Willowbrook was mentioned as the possible site, Robert Moses, then commissioner of the Department of Parks and Recreation, added his voice to a chorus of objectors. If one uses the coverage of the *Advance* as an indicator of public sentiment, only one group, labor unions, openly came out in favor of the building of the institution on Staten Island. The paper, which in its editorials was also openly against the building, recognized its responsibility to publish a few dissenting letters from community members (i.e., those supporting the institution). But even these were from individuals only, not organizations, and were less much less frequent than the letters against. In an April 15, 1938, article in the *Advance,* state senator Rae Egbert, who stayed publically neutral about his own view on an institution on Staten Island, said that he received about twelve letters a day with less than a quarter of those in support of the state's initiative.

Newspaper coverage provides the only data available about what happened at this time; it tells the public story, or the story of what could be said publically, but it obviously could not tell what might have been going on behind the scenes. There is intimation about that in the press. When one reads the files of newspaper clippings about Willowbrook at the College of Staten Island's archives, one cannot help but come to certain conclusions, at least about the public face of Willowbrook. Bateman-House (n.d.) integrated these clippings with other newspaper and public writings and did a good job in pointing out certain recurrent themes, so we will use her document as the source for some of our observations.[4]

---

4. Alison Bateman-House, a Columbia University graduate student, was hired by the archivist at the College of Staten Island to write a timeline of Willowbrook by using the extensive holdings of newspaper articles, mostly from the *Staten Island Advance,* dating from 1948 onward, on loan there from the New York State Office of Mental Retardation and Developmental Disability. It should be noted that the articles are not a complete collection of articles about Willowbrook from any newspaper. She did more than was asked and integrated other public media sources with those at the archives and came up with an extensive, though not complete, compendium. Before she wrote this work, an undergraduate student and Goode had gone through the clippings as part of her undergraduate research study and had reached similar conclusions about their content.

Staten Island Advance, *Editorial Cartoon*

Staten Island state legislators first heard about the idea of a state institution on Staten Island in January of 1938.[5] The idea was announced to the public on March 3, 1938, in the *Staten Island Advance,* specifying Willowbrook and the South Shore Golf Course property in Huguenot Park as potential sites. The institution was to house 3,000 residents and was being paid for by a $40 million bond issue approved the previous year. Of this $40 million, $5.1 million was for construction of the Staten Island facility in 1938–1939. Another $7 million was appropriated for fiscal

5. After it was publically announced, State Senator Egbert revealed that legislators had been informed about this plan as early as January 1938.

year 1939–1940. The announcement set off the groundswell of overwhelmingly negative public opinion by Staten Islanders.

Many potential sites were considered, at least in the newspaper accounts: Willowbrook Park and adjacent properties, the South Shore Golf Course, a site west of Seaview Hospital, the Tysen Estate in New Springfield near Latourette Park, unspecified sites within other New York City boroughs (but dismissed as too expensive; *Staten Island Advance,* April 11, 1938), and, in the event of failing to procure a site in New York City, Columbia County, south of Albany (*Staten Island Advance,* April, 11, 1938). Not only was there indeterminacy about where the proposed institution was to be placed, there was also ambiguity about what kind of institution was to be built. The ambiguity took two forms. In the early part of the discussion, despite the fact that the original announcement talked about an institution for mental defectives, there was regular objection to a "lunatic asylum" that would house dangerous mentally ill people. Later, when it was understood that the institution would house people, primarily children, who were mentally defective, the argument changed to what guarantees Staten Islanders would have that the state would not change the purpose of the institution and later make it lunatic asylum. It is interesting that the commissioner of the Department of Mental Hygiene who was responsible for the selection of sites and types of institutions would, in the last instance, not give Staten Islanders any assurances about future decisions of the legislature (*Staten Island Advance,* April 11, 1938).[6] The idea that an institution on Staten Island would house dangerous lunatics and constitute a threat to residents was a constant argument advanced against building Willowbrook. A political cartoon published in the *Advance* shows the institution for mentally defectives as a wolf in sheep's skin, covering the real intent of an asylum for the insane.

The debate raged about an institution on Staten Island. It is interesting that arguments for and against were put before the public but the welfare of the children in such places was rarely even considered.[7] The primary arguments had to do with the impact of the facility on the island, both positive and negative.

6. In a statement to the Staten Island Lions Club on April 15, State Senator Egbert described some of the language that had been circulating in regard to the institution, "The use of the words 'asylum,' 'bughouse,' 'crazy house,' and 'nuthouse,' are passé with an institution of this kind. . . . It sounds better to say institution for mentally defective."

7. The only mention we were able to find of conditions in state institutions for the mentally deficient as a reason to not want an institution on Staten Island appeared on March 8, 1938, in the *Advance,* which reported that some Staten Island residents concluded that they did not want a state institution on Staten Island after attending a meeting in Manhattan at which three former employees of the "Rockland Institution" (i.e., Letchworth Village) "testified before a Legislative Committee in the New York County Courthouse, described immorality among the inmates, brutal treatment of the patients, and the serving of unfit food to both employees and patients." Aside from this, we do not find any remarks in the *Advance* during this period arguing that possible poor treatment of residents was a reason to not want an institution on Staten Island.

Positive arguments were almost exclusively economic. They consisted of benefits to construction workers and other laborers on Staten Island during the construction phase (these were substantial, estimated to be $58,000 per month). Possible contracts to various suppliers on Staten Island were cited. Employment of Staten Islanders at the institution once it was opened, estimated to be over $700,000 annually in salaries, was also advanced as a benefit. Housing and associated retail spending by workers would add to the economy of the island. Finally, additional revenue would come to Staten Island when relatives of those housed at the institution came to visit their family member. These many potential benefits notwithstanding, those who came out publically for the state's proposal were almost exclusively labor organizations and their representatives.[8]

The voices objecting to the state's plans were numerous and came from organizations and societies of every character—civic, fraternal, business, and financial. Political figures, especially Borough president Joseph A. Palma, Democratic county chairman William T. Fetherstone, and assemblyman Herman Methfessel, were particularly active in Richmond County's battle with the state. The state senator Rae L. Egbert maintained an active but neutral role in the debate. Many letters from individuals appear in the *Advance* during this period, and one gets the overall sense that almost all of Staten Island's 170,000 residents at the time were aware of what was going on.

Those against the institution refuted every positive argument put forth by the state and labor organizations and added a host of objections related to the negative impact of such a facility on the island. None of the economic benefits, other than those related to the initial construction of the facility, were accepted by those arguing against the proposal. They felt that those on Staten Island who were willing to profit from going along with the institution, which included labor and real estate people, were selling the community out. Those against, including Palma, argued that Staten Island would not receive the contracts related to Willowbrook (they would be issued by the state to lowest bidders); the staff of the institution would be drawn from the state workforce and not primarily from Staten Island; the presence of a facility on Staten Island would stigmatize the community, causing people to stay away rather than come; and the presence of the facility would endanger the residential development plans of the borough.[9]

8. The *Advance* reported the following quote from Egbert on April 15, 1938: "Most of the support given the state's plan to effect a $12,000,000 institution for mental defectives in this borough has been voiced by labor organizations or their representatives. . . . The majority of the few letters supporting the asylum . . . came from plumbers, carpenters, electricians, and others seeking work that would result from it."

9. For example: "The construction of the insane asylum in Richmond would put an immediate end to our progress as a borough of homes. . . . We would be stigmatized as a borough of institutions, and that stigma would keep away a majority of our potential new residents" (Palma, *Staten Island Advance,* March 9, 1938).

The *Advance* pointed to the history of Staten Island as "a Dumping Ground" and published a cartoon depicting this theme. The symbolism of the dumping ground was intended to recall various previous attempts of the city to use Staten Island as a place to dump waste and ash, which the island had successfully opposed, as well as to reference the history of Staten Island as a place on which institutions to house the diseased, infirm, and poor had been built. There was some historical truth to the claim that Staten Island already had its share of such places. Mount Lorettto, the largest child-care institution in the world, was founded there in 1883 by Father Christopher Dingle and served all of New York City. The New York City Farm Colony (later known as the Richmond County Poor Farm and then the Staten Island Farm Colony) was founded in 1829. Near the farm colony was built the Seaview Hospital, for the care of people with tuberculosis. Sailor's Snug Harbor, a community for old and incapacitated sailors, was opened in 1833 and is still in existence. The Port of New York Quarantine Hospital at Tomkinsville was part of a quarantine hospital system on Staten Island that existed at the end of the 18th century and into the 20th (Friends of Abandoned Cemeteries on Staten Island have found graves of quarantine patients dating as far back as 1799). The fear of the spread of contagious disease was so great that island residents rioted and attacked the hospital on May 6, 1857. On September 1 of the next year they burned it down , an act that those against Willowbrook pointed to as a kind of pinnacle of resistance to such places on the island. However, two additional quarantine facilities were built on islands adjacent to Staten Island, in 1870 on Swineburn Island, south of Fort Wadsworth, and in 1873 on Hoffman Island. The history of large institutions on the island was pointed to by those against building Willowbrook. Their message was "we gave already," and islanders had shown before that they would not stand for another institution.

It was not uncommon to find statements from the leaders who were against Willowbrook that they understood the need for such a place and were not arguing the state's decision to build more institutions for mentally deficient children. The problem was that it was being built on their island and in a community that did not want it. Why would the state want to spend $1,000 per acre for land at Willowbrook when it could purchase it so much more cheaply (one editorial in the *Advance* said at a tenth the cost) upstate? Why would it select Staten Island, with its small population of 170,000, with relatively few children with mental deficiency, when other boroughs had such large populations and numbers of such children? Why build it there when it was clear that "We Don't Want It!" (as the title of a March 23, 1938, *Staten Island Advance* editorial exclaimed).

Throughout the course of the year, it became clear that the state had a preference for the Willowbrook site. New York governor Herbert Lehman announced that he favored building an asylum in Richmond County but would not force it on the community. The main spokesperson for the state, Dr. William J. Tiffany,

Wolf in Sheep's Clothing

commissioner of the Department of Mental Hygiene, basically followed Lehman's lead in what looks in retrospect like a slow but steady path toward Willowbrook. Throughout March Tiffany had promised to come to Staten Island and meet with the community to discuss the state's plans. He canceled that meeting, postponing it until April 21, when it was eventually held at the Special Session Courtroom of the County Court House in St. George. State Senator Egbert facilitated the meeting, and by the time it was held, over 60 representatives from local civic groups and institutions had been invited. Only two groups had expressed their support for the idea, so the vast number of attendees were not in favor of the project. The *Advance* coverage confirms this, saying that the only people who spoke for the idea were labor representatives. In the end, 41 spokespersons were against, and eight endorsed the project (*Staten Island Advance,* March 24, 1964, as cited by Bateman-House, n.d., p. 3). Borough president Palma reassured the public that the facility would be used only for children. Tiffany used the occasion to allay fears of the public by reasserting what he and the state had said all along, that this was going to be a good thing for Staten Island and that it was completely safe for the community. He used the occasion to announce that, with Mayor LaGuardia's approval, he had selected the Willowbrook site.

One can reasonably ask why the state chose to do this in the face of assurances that it would listen to the community and knowing that islanders were dead set against the idea. Why would they choose a site that Robert Moses had publically called "stupid" and "arbitrary?" What politics or possibly even economic interests could have been at play? Was any dirty business going on?

The *Advance* intimated as much in an editorial:

> We have just finished talking with "a political realist" who believes that a State Insane Asylum would be a good thing for our community. . . . He protested indignantly that there was no allusion [sic] on the part of certain political friends, and a group of real estate entrepreneurs [located in St. George], who have been placing options on acreage in the heart of State Island with the avidity of veteran bingo players. (March 3/8, 1938)

On the same page, a letter signed by E. A. Baker asked, "Why not print the names of the realtors who are willing to cheapen our Island for the sake of a few thousand dollars now?"

This is just an allusion to what may have been going on behind the scenes with regard to political deals and money-making arrangements. It certainly is not unthinkable that part of the reason Staten Island was selected may have had something to do with people in power making money, even if the story is not as visible as the one that appears in papers. It is beyond the scope of this account, but one could well ask who profited by the selection of the Willowbrook location. Related to this, one can ask the same question about the $40 million state bond that was issued to build Willowbrook and other institutions at that time.[10] Who benefited? In fact, as

10. The question of the socioeconomics of Willowbrook was raised in an interesting way by a letter to the *Advance* written by Oscar Norring of Princess Bay: "It is my opinion that the rich residents oppose the asylum. They opposed the subway, saying that construction of such a link would bring a lot of the city's undesirables here. Why was there no kick against Ward's Island being turned into a playground for the rich, in place of keeping a State Hospital there? The city's poor people will not go there; it is too far for them to go, so golf courses and tennis courts will

the title of Paul Castellani's book, *From Snake Pits to Cash Cows*, invites us to ask, who benefited (and benefits) from the existence of Willowbrook and places like it? This topic will be taken up in later parts of the text.

World War II

Castellani (2005) described the effects of World War II on the institutional system in New York, including the transfer of Willowbrook State School to the United States Army in 1942. The Department of Mental Hygiene's annual report for 1940 stated, "Satisfactory progress was made in the construction of the new State school at Willowbrook, Staten Island, and it is expected that the first unit of this institution will be ready for occupancy in 1941" (Department of Mental Hygiene, 1940, p. 63, as cited by Castellani, 2005). The enthusiasm about the opening of Willowbrook was dashed with the onset of war. The annual report for 1942 explained that, in response to a request from the secretary of war, on September 23, 1942, this "hospital-school of modern design and equipment, erected on Staten Island for a cost over $12,000,000, to provide accommodations for 3,000 mental defectives, was transferred to the United States Army for its use as Halloran General Hospital for duration of the war emergency" (Department of Mental Hygiene, 1942, as cited in Castellani, 2005, pp. 27–29).

Because of the necessity for hospitals for members of the armed forces, the state leased the Willowbrook buildings to the army for a period of four years. Castellani writes that the transfer created enormous problems for the service system that would be felt throughout the century. In addition to the loss of 3,000 beds, the transfer of Willowbrook came at the same time as capital expenditures for institutions in New York state dropped sharply, from $5.1 million in 1941 to $15,000 in 1945. So there were no new places constructed to deal with the already crowded institutions that continued to swell. In addition, staff left during the war to work

---

be laid out for leisure class. . . . My hope is that the working people of Staten Island will not let themselves become tools of the group that is opposing the establishment of the asylum here." Norring's remarks were based on a class analysis of what was going on. New York was a hotbed for socialism in the 1920s and 1930s, so it is not surprising to see this perspective. It links the creation of the institution on Staten Island to the closing of one on Ward's Island. This may have referred to both Ward's and Randall's Island facilities, which were located next to one another. As opposed to the closing of the Ward's Island facility, which was bad for poor people, Norring believed that the opening of Willowbrook was a good thing for working people. Later, when labor played a retarding role in the closing of Willowbrook, reformers and organizers used a class-based analysis to sway them. They argued that the welfare of poor people such as those who lived at Willowbrook was not juxtaposed in opposition to the poor people who worked there and that each was victimized by a system that made profit from them.

at factories and in employment related to the armed services. The number of state institution employees dropped from 3,297 in 1942 to 2,611 in 1945. By the end of the war, there were 1,403 vacancies in an overall authorization of 4,014 employees. Twenty-five of the 63 medical officer positions were also vacant (Castellani, 2005).

Overcrowding increased during the war, as did the age of the population of younger children.[11] By 1943, 32% of institutional beds were filled with children ages 5 to 10 years. By 1945, the five state schools housed 15,361 patients, though the planned census had been 11,713. Overcrowding became extreme, with Letchworth Village, for example, reported to be 20%–30% overcrowded, with 200 children sleeping on the floor.

A situation that had been worsening for years was put under further stress as fiscal support for institutions eroded and the demands of a wartime economy took precedence. For people in mental institutions and state schools, crowding increased, as did lack of supervision. During the war, overall quality of life for both residents and workers would have significantly deteriorated, something shared by most Americans. The capacity and quality of the institutional system needed to be expanded.

Halloran General Hospital

Under such conditions of crowding, the state of New York was not overjoyed when, upon completion of the Willowbrook buildings in 1942, the United States Army requested that it lease the site to establish a military hospital there. The army, however, took advantage of the large and empty buildings to adapt them to its own use and create the Halloran General Hospital.

The more we learned about Halloran General Hospital, the clearer it became that its story deserved a book of its own. In its era, Halloran was the biggest and most sophisticated military–medical complex in the world—a virtual small city. An analysis of Halloran would be intellectually complex and methodologically challenging. What we will do here is to briefly note some of the things that happened at Halloran during the war, especially those related to disability, and describe how it was eventually taken back by the state and restored and renamed for its original purpose.

Halloran Hospital received its first patient on November 4, 1942 (*Washington Post,* June 27, 1943, as cited by Bateman-House, n.d., p. 3). Within a short while, the army transformed the buildings at Willowbrook State School into the

---

11. There had been an increased pressure to place children at younger ages into institutions for many years, partially because of professional advice to remove children with mental deficiency from the family. In 1945, state schools began to admit children under the age of 5 years.

largest, best-equipped military hospital in the country. It was described as a "medical city" in the *New York Times* (June 13, 1943). Soldiers wounded in all theaters were brought to Halloran to heal and be returned to battle or be habilitated and returned home. Newspaper clippings about Halloran that appeared in the *Herald-Tribune* and *Advance* usually show rows of ambulances driving into the facility with the wounded. The wounded arrived in New York by train (there is a photo of such a transport train with specially designed bunk beds) and by ship (which also appeared in photos in the press).

With the best of equipment and medical personnel, the army operated Halloran as a model facility. There was a vast network of social services and supports available, among them social events, sports competitions, a movie theater, and a soda fountain; a sophisticated newsletter for patients and staff called *The Halloran Beacon* was extensive and described the various activities available at the hospital and news about hospital personnel. There was a medical journal, *Professional Staff Proceedings,* that was published at Halloran and that dealt with various aspects of medical care and rehabilitation of the wounded.

When one reads the *Beacon* and looks at the newspaper articles about Halloran during and immediately after the war, when it was transferred from the army to the Veterans Administration, one gets a great sense of pride about the place, on the part of both those who worked there and those who lived there, as well as their families.[12] There are newspaper clippings of interviews with family members about their wounded loved one as well as articles about the care at the hospital itself. The tragedies and trials of some of the patients were detailed in these articles. The image of Halloran Hospital to the public was extremely positive.[13]

After the war, there was discussion about whether Halloran would be returned to New York State for its original purpose. The Department of Mental Hygiene continued to include Willowbrook in its annual reports and looked forward to its

12. One interesting document was an announcement of a February 8, 1950, wheelchair basketball competition that listed the 10 team members, coach, physician, and tour director. On the top of the announcement is printed "Ability—Not Disability—Counts." The team's name was "the Halloran Whiz Kids." Halloran contributed to the history of disability in several ways.

13. Although this is not specifically relevant to the story of the Halloran-Willowbrook connection, Goode is often asked in class, usually by students who are native Staten Islanders, whether there were German prisoners of war at Halloran. There was indeed a prisoner complex that opened in 1944 and was guarded by a Prisoner of War Guard Unit with about 45 soldiers, manning it 24 hours a day. Prisoners did forms of outside and inside labor, heavy labor such as clearing fields, planting, scrubbing floors, washing dishes, working the commissary, packing clothing, and processing tin cans. They wore uniforms of salvaged clothing marked "PW of PP" when working, but were allowed to wear their German uniforms while in the compound. They received $0.80 per day for their labor, which they were allowed to spend at the PX. They ranged in age from 17 to 50 (*The New York Sun,* April 3, 1945).

Halloran Hospital Postcard

return (Castellani, 2005, p. 45). When the lease ran out, the army turned over the hospital to the Veterans Administration (VA), on January 1, 1947, and Omar Bradley, its director, announced did not want to return the facility to New York State. A lengthy exchange between the state and army followed, including the suggestion by the then governor Thomas Dewey that the Veterans Administration consider buying the campus if it did not want to leave. This battle between the VA and New York State was eventually resolved legally in 1947 but was to continue in the press until the last paralyzed veteran left on February 15, 1951. The solution that was reached was that the VA would lease part of the campus for an additional 2-year period while it completed building a facility in Brooklyn (Department of Mental Hygiene, 1948, p. 38, as cited by Castellani, 2005, p. 45).

Although the Department of Mental Hygiene regarded Willowbrook as part of its facilities from the 1947 legal decision onward, there were actually only 58 patients from state schools at Willowbrook as of March 31, 1948 (Department of Mental Hygiene, 1948, p. 189, as cited by Castellani, 2005, p. 45). On September 4, 1948, the *Advance* reported that in addition to these children who were there in March, there were an additional 100 adults with mental deficiency living at Willowbrook,[14] with a total of 100 staff employed. What had begun was a slow

14. This is the first public indication that the assurances made by state and local politicians about Willowbrook being only for mentally deficient children were not going to be followed.

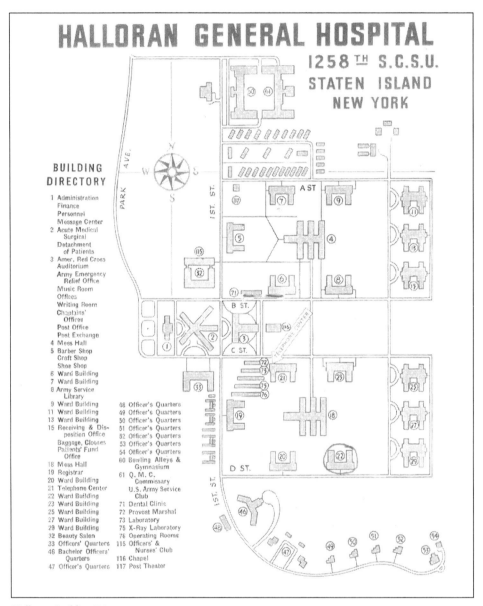

Halloran Building Directory

process of building-by-building turnover as the VA was able to secure other beds for its patients. In addition, the process was slowed on the state side by the failure of necessary equipment to arrive. A map contained within the Halloran VA Hospital brochure of 1949 shows the "State School Area" as consisting of only eight buildings. These buildings were enclosed by 5,700 feet of 8-foot-high wire fence (*Staten Island Advance*, September 16, 1947).

In an announcement inserted in the 1949 brochure, titled "Changes That Have Taken Place Since This Brochure Was Sent to the Printers" and dated March 16, 1950, the final plans for where the various VA patients would be sent is laid out. Apparently, the VA had committed to leaving the facility by June 30, 1950. The state reconsidered and granted the VA more time, which accounts for why it was not until February of 1951 that the last patient left. As the insert describes, most were transferred to other VA facilities, in Manhattan (newly built) and Brooklyn. Psychiatric patients were sent to a new VA hospital in Montrose, New York, and patients with tuberculosis were sent to Batavia and Brooklyn Hospitals.

These plans were the result of a final series of negotiations between the state and the VA, which are documented by Bateman-House (n.d., pp. 8–13). As early as September 1948, Frederick MacCurdy, commissioner of the Department of Mental Hygiene, had announced plans to place 1,400 mental defectives at Willowbrook by March 1949. Although this never came to be, and the figure was revised downward over the course of the next few months, it was clear that the Department of Mental Hygiene intended to claim back the institution sooner rather than later. The eventual census of the school was estimated at 3,800 (*Staten Island Advance,* May 9, 1951) and later 3,194 (*Staten Island Advance,* August 10, 1951, as cited by Bateman-House, n.d., p. 8).

Although MacCurdy's projection did not come to pass, the school did grow at a significant pace. In April 1950, the state notified the VA that it would not renew its lease at Willowbrook. VA administrator Carl R. Gray Jr. responded by saying that the VA needed the part of the hospital it was currently occupying and urged the state to reconsider. Pointing to the overcrowding of the state schools, MacCurdy wrote to Gray, "We, therefore, in spite of our sympathy with your problem, must maintain our position of non-renewal of the lease" (*Staten Island Advance,* April 9, 1950, as cited by Bateman-House, n.d., p. 9). Finally, Gray met with Governor Dewey to resolve the issue but without apparent outcome. Afterward Gray sent Dewey a letter reiterating his request for a lease extension until December 31, 1952. When MacCurdy replied, he asked Gray to consider the communication an official notice of lease termination. This left the VA with no choice but to halt admissions and begin emptying the hospital.

The community of Staten Island did not react well to the news of the transfer of the hospital back to the state. In fact, there was, as described by Bateman-House, quite an "uproar." The *Advance* did not feel that the new state school would benefit the community to the degree that Halloran Hospital had. Much sentiment was generated against the decision to not grant the VA a 2-year lease extension. Veterans' groups held a mass meeting on March 19, 1950, protesting Dewey's actions regarding Halloran. Dewey received a flood of protests via telegrams—approximately 400 from Halloran patients and 300 from Halloran employees. Ed Sullivan wrote in support of the veterans in his *Sunday News* column. State Senator John M. Braisted and Assemblyman Edward V. Curry introduced resolutions calling for the state to grant a 3-year lease. These died in committee. The legislators, along with Assembly-man William Reidy, met with Governor Dewey. Congressman James Murphy sent letters to the governor, the VA, and even President Truman urging that the state reconsider its position. As Bateman-House describes, the Staten Island Chamber of Commerce joined the protest writing to Dewey.

> By acquiring the entire site, the Willowbrook State School would be able to massively expand. The *Advance* reported that the institution, which had 970 patients and 325 employees in March, 1950, would increase to 3,100 patients and more than 1,000 employees once the VA vacated the premises and buildings were refurnished and retrofitted for their new uses. However, multiple stakeholders were concerned about the clos-ing of Halloran; for economic reasons, for concerns about veterans and their access to medical care, and for the anticipated uprooting of hospi-tal employees (400 of whom lived on Halloran property), patients, and their families. The public outcry forced Dewey to reconsider his deci-sion. (Bateman-House, n.d., p. 11)

After meeting with the governor, Congressman Murphy announced that the VA would not transfer patients out of Halloran pending reconsideration by the governor. Despite this assurance, transfers out of Halloran began anyway (*Staten Island Advance,* April 5, 1950). Employee transfers began at about this same time (*Staten Island Advance,* April 11, 1950). Dewey and VA officials announced that a scaled-down version of the hospital (with 740 beds) would continue to operate, with Halloran maintaining its paraplegic and tuberculosis services and general medicine and surgical section (*New York Times,* April 21, 1950, as cited by Bate-man-House, n.d., p. 12). The arrangement was slated to continue until December 31, 1952, so a compromise position between MacCurdy and Gray had apparently been reached.

As a result of this deal, Willowbrook State School gained control over the auditorium and Buildings 19, 20, 21, 22, and 23. In December of 1950, Willow-brook already had 2,072 patients and 570 employees. A clinic for patients with cere-bral palsy had been opened, additional administrators appointed, and expansion to 3,000 patients envisioned (Bateman-House, n.d., p. 12).

On January 4, 1951, Dewey and Gray made a joint announcement that the VA would vacate Willowbrook by February of 1951. This closing of Halloran before the end of the lease was motivated by the Air Force taking over the former Sampson Training Base in Geneva, New York, where the Department of Mental Hygiene had been housing 959 elderly patients, "the majority of whom would need transfer to

Willowbrook" (Bateman-House, n.d., p. 12). They needed to be there by April 1.[15] Again there was a public outcry against the plans to close Halloran. The VA patients who were still at Halloran continued to demonstrate that they wanted to keep the hospital open. A photo from January 17, 1951, shows them lined up in wheelchairs outside the headquarters of the Eastern Paralyzed Veteran Association, at 99 Park Avenue, carrying signs that read, "How Dare They?"; "We Did Our Share, Treat Us Right"; "Keep Halloran Open"; and "Don't Break Promises." The veterans who had been at Halloran, perhaps some of them for as long as 8 or 9 years, left, but not quietly. Ultimately their protests were to no avail.

The last patients left Halloran on February 13, 1951, thus paving the way for unlimited expansion by the Department of Mental Hygiene. The first group of Sampson transferees were scheduled to arrive on February 23 (*Staten Island Advance,* February 23, 1951, as cited by Bateman-House, n.d, p. 13). By May of that year, there were 2,800 patients, and by August every building on the complex was in use. Willowbrook's director Harold Berman announced that the patient census was 2,840 of a capacity of 3,194, "which would be reached in the fall. On March 12, 1952, the Department of Mental Hygiene announced that it would build an additional six buildings at Willowbrook" (Bateman-House, n.d., p. 13). The Willowbrook State School that we think of when the name is mentioned today was finally in full operation.

The Early Years at Willowbrook State School

Much of what has been written about Willowbrook concerns itself with what was going on at Willowbrook when Geraldo Rivera showed up in 1972 and he, parents, professionals, and lawyers began the process of closing the school. These efforts are well documented in *The Willowbrook Wars* (Rothman & Rothman, 1984/2009) and Rivera's book, *Willowbrook* (1972). What is not as familiar is what happened there while in operation for the 24 years before the 'explosion' was helped along by Rivera's videos. This story of Willowbrook is not an uninteresting or simple one.

Harold H. Berman, a medical doctor, was the first director of the Willowbrook State School, a position he occupied until his retirement in March of 1964. It was under his watch that the institution took shape in the early 1950s. To Berman's credit, he worked hard at fostering good relations between the community and the school. Willowbrook fit Goffman's definition of a "total institution," and

---

15. Note here the facile and open violation of assurances by the state and local politicians that Willowbrook would be for "mentally defective" children only. This violation of the promises made began as early as 1948. With the transfer of hundreds of patients from Sampson, public mistrust was again vindicated.

like all such places, the degree to which people living within it were "cut off" from the outside world was relative (see discussion of Goffman's work in Chapter 3). In such total institutions as prisons, prisoner of war camps, monasteries, or tuberculosis hospitals, an extreme degree of isolation can be imposed. Even then, the isolation is usually not absolute, and there is some contact with the outside, even if unsanctioned and illegal.[16] At Willowbrook there was always a certain degree of permeability between the inside and outside, and some residents even lived at Willowbrook while working outside, in the community. Berman both promoted involvement of community groups at the Willowbrook campus and supported trips of resident children outside the facility.

Many of these activities are described by Bateman-House (n.d., pp.141–147). In addition to establishing a Board of Visitors to monitor conditions at the school, an Auxiliary of the Willowbrook State School (also known as the Willowbrook State School Volunteer Workers) was established probably in 1951 and the Benevolent Society for Retarded Children in 1949 or 1950.[17] The Benevolent Society sponsored many events to entertain the children as well as events at which children at the institution entertained. There was a choir at Willowbrook and also a marching band (established in 1951). A fashion show was given by girls at the institution at various community sites. The Benevolent Society organized amateur entertainment nights, plays, Halloween and costume parties, and Christmas and Chanukah festivities and provided outside entertainment.

But it was not only parents of the residents who reached into Willowbrook. A wide range of community groups provided philanthropic and volunteer efforts for the school. Many of these are listed by Bateman-House (n.d., pp. 15–16).[18] She

16. For example, in concentration camps, contact with anyone outside was illegal, but there still were various kinds of exchanges that could happen, including smuggling of contraband or messages from the outside. An example of absolute isolation from the outside world is solitary confinement in a high-security prison.

17. The Benevolent Association is a group (which still exists as of this writing) formed by parents of residents at Willowbrook. Groups associated with institutions and advocating and providing activities at state schools had been around since the formation of the Council for Retarded Children in Cayuga County, Ohio, in 1932. At Letchworth, the New York State Welfare League for Retarded Children was formed in 1939. The function of such groups in most places was to improve conditions at the institutions by providing additional resources, sponsoring events and trips, and fund-raising for special projects (Boggs, as cited in Goode, 1998). Generally, they were not advocating for systemic change, just to make things better. At Willowbrook, the function of the Benevolent Association later changed as it became involved in the attempts to close Willowbrook.

18. The Vanderbilt Council of Daughters of America gave a flag to Willowbrook (1950), the American Legion gave an automatic phonograph (1950), Women of Queens County Jewish War Veterans gave Christmas presents (1952), counselors in training at the Jewish Community Center

notes that "Willowbrook opened its doors to numerous visitors" at this time (n.d., p. 16). These included groups providing care to people with intellectual disability and heads of civic and governmental agencies, including the state commissioner of mental hygiene Newton Bigelow in 1950 and 1951 and later, in 1959, Governor Nelson Rockefeller. Some of the visitors were educators and students. Willowbrook had early on established a training certificate for workers, we believe in 1952, although the first record of this is in a newspaper article describing the award of certificates to three staff in 1953. Professionals also visited the school, including, for example, members of the American Association on Mental Deficiency as part of their annual meeting in 1951. Student nurses from Central Islip State Hospital, students from a class about cerebral palsy at Columbia University (1952), psychiatric residents from Fort Hamilton VA Hospital (1952), and nursing students from Wagner College (1953) all came on the grounds as part of their education. Various open house events were also held for both local and national groups. For example, in 1953 about 80 people representing educational, social, and community organizations attended a conference as part of National Mental Health Week. The program included a tour of the campus and educational presentations by staff and, of course, a concert by the school band.

Bateman-House cites this description by Director Berman of life at Willowbrook in 1953:

> Of the 383 acres, 132 are lawns besides the woodland. This provides ample space for playground, picnic and park areas. . . . The medical surgical building affords facilities for complete care of the sick. The school building, utilized every school day . . . is conducive to academic training, occupational therapy, and soon to be inaugurated is a course for home making. Basketball games, gymnastics and daily calisthenics for groups of patients are conducted every day. . . . Academic classes are conducted for children of school age and plans are in progress to give instruction to some adults. . . . Besides choral singing, selected patients are taught to play instruments and drums. . . . Swimming, roller skating, movies, dances, picnics are other activities. Plays are staged by the patients. There are trips to the Zoo, to Island industries and to the circus and Rodeo at Madison Square Gardens. . . . Big League baseball games

---

on Staten Island made lollipop dolls (1950), Girl Scouts visited and volunteered there by rolling bandages and mending garments (date unknown), the American Legion gave two invalid walkers (1952), Girl Scouts made favors for a Purim party put on by the Staten Island section of the National Council of Jewish Women (1953), the Staten Island Rotary Club showed films and hosted a party (1956), and the band from Willowbrook played at memorial services and parades sponsored by the American Legion and Veterans of Foreign Wars (cited in Bateman-House, n.d., pp. 15–16).

at Yankee Stadium, Polo Grounds, and Ebbetts Field are attended by youngsters. . . . Professional entertainers give of their time and talent for the enjoyment of the patients. Religious training is part of the total program. (*Staten Island Advance,* May 7, 1952, as cited by Bateman-House, n.d., p. 15)

This sounds too good to be real, and it is reasonable to assume that the director was trying to paint a good picture for the press. It sounds more like a camp than an institution and an awful lot of fun.[19] One respondent to a blog about Willowbrook lived there with his parents while growing up during this period and said that patients were treated with much more respect back then, at least compared with what was going on at the time of the Rivera exposé.[20] What he says may well be true, as a comparison. But there was no time when things were "great" at Willowbrook—no honeymoon period when children were happy and safe.

There was evidence of problems from the outset. Bateman-House calls these "growing pains," but we are going to explain them, in accordance with the findings in sociology about places like Willowbrook that are discussed in chapter 3 as intrinsic to the social structure of total institutions. The problems that existed at Willowbrook were always worse than recorded in documents, whether newspaper stories or hospital records. Goode learned that firsthand at Pacific State Hospital, but it is also just a matter of common sense. More people got away with doing wrong things than got caught. At Pacific State, Goode observed a regular underground economy. Abuse occurred, but it was not reliably reported, and it is hard to say how much of it escaped undetected—much of it, one would suspect. The same would have been true of Willowbrook. The newspaper stories could have indicated only the tip of the iceberg. (We return to this topic in later chapters.)

One regular problem noted by Bateman-House's compendium was elopement (see Chapter 5). Throughout the early years, there were various cases of patients who were missing from the hospital. In the first few years, perhaps three or four cases were reported in the press. This very likely underestimates the number of

19. These kinds of idealized descriptions were common from administrators and professionals in big institutions like Willowbrook. Goode has heard many stories over the years of people who were told similar tales about the institutions to which they were being taken only to find out that what they had been told was untrue. T. J. Monroe (Ward, 1997), who did time at Southbury School in Connecticut, went there being told it was like a camp, with fishing and horseback riding. There were fenced-in horses, and children could look at them, but Southbury was a terrible, abusive place. It is also interesting to note how the idealized description by Berman resonates with earlier descriptions of institutions.

20. This blog site, willowbrookstateschool.blogspot.com, is maintained by Vanessa Leigh Debello, whose experiences related to WSS are described on pages 222–3.

residents who were found to be missing. Direct testimony of both former workers and residents indicate that individuals could be unaccounted for and not reported to the police. One resident recalled leaving to visit relatives in Brooklyn repeatedly, and getting caught and punished repeatedly, and none of this ever appearing in the newspapers. In a narrative about life on a children's ward, one staff member remembered that there were children whose overnight absence was not reported to authorities. As a worker on the deaf-blind ward at Pacific State, Goode was aware of many incidents that occurred that were never written down or reported. There was a great fear about ratting on fellow workers, and not without reason. This was also true at Willowbrook. This fear, and we will encounter it in the interviews, was an important factor in the way things were run at Willowbrook.

There were cases reported in the newspapers about either staff or residents abusing residents. One of the earliest stories about abuse at Willowbrook was of a 16-year-old resident who allegedly assaulted both residents and staff (*Staten Island Advance*, February 15, 1952, as cited by Bateman-House, n.d, p. 17). In August of that year, the first story about abuse of residents by an employee appeared in the *Advance* (*Long Island Daily Press*, August 22, 1952, as cited by Bateman-House, n.d., p. 18). This man, Ralph J. Tuccillo, was arrested for beating two residents. He eventually was indicted but got off on all but minor charges, resulting in a suspended sentence and probation for civil service law violation. In the following year, another worker was tried and acquitted after being accused by a coworker for repeatedly punching boys on a ward (*Staten Island Advance*, April 9, 1953). In May of 1955, an investigation into the alleged abuse of Catherine de Vole, a patient, cleared the institution of wrongdoing, but suspicions about her case began to raise concern about the adequacy of care at Willowbrook. Bateman-House (n.d., p. 20) writes:

> On May 23 [1953], eleven speakers, including four parents of Willowbrook residents, reaffirmed their confidence in the institution and condemned recent news stories. The meeting, held in Auditorium Building 3, attracted more than 100 Willowbrook employees and featured the report of a unanimous vote of confidence by the Benevolent Society.

Other stories indicating possible problems at Willowbrook were those involving patient deaths. There was a case of two residents who overpowered an attendant, locked him in an isolation room, and escaped down a fire escape (*Staten Island Advance*, February 2, 1955). In September of 1955, five female residents escaped after being given a key by an attendant, David Jenkins, who was convicted in January of 1956 and sentenced to 60 days in the workhouse. Two of those residents had not returned as of the date of his conviction.

Cases of residents sexually abused by other residents or by attendants are perspicuously absent from the public record during these early years. Based on several authors' experiences, this absence does not mean that such events were not occurring. The newspaper stories in these early years indicated that systemic problems at the school already existed. These were the same kinds of problems noted by Rivera and others when they exposed Willowbrook a decade and a half later. Yet the press defended Willowbrook in these early years, even, as Bateman-House puts it, "lauded" it. In a remarkable *Daily News* article (published January 26, 1955) titled "Living Dead Find Life at S.I. School," Berman is praised as having revolutionized care for the treatment of mentally retarded children. In 1957, the *Sunday News* published the following remarkable statement about Willowbrook in an article titled "At Willowbrook . . . the Children Get the Best Care Possible":

> These patients are not only mentally defective but many are most unprepossessing in appearance and habits. In wards for older imbeciles, young men of 150 pounds, for example, must be dressed, undressed, taken to the toilet, fed, washed, and put to bed. They frequently soil themselves. They are incapable of understanding simple orders. Yet the attendants serve their needs and give them affection that has to be seen to be believed. . . . Are the children neglected? Hardly ever. It does happen that because of overcrowding and shortage of help one attendant may have as many as 60 children to look after at a time. But the doctors are on an around the clock schedule and the children are examined every day in the showers for any signs of body sores, and also watched for the outbreak of childhood sicknesses. Are the children ever beaten? Rarely. An attendant who would beat a child would probably find himself set upon by other attendants. (*Daily News*, July 14, 1957)

This is an extraordinary paragraph and its writer, Dick Owen, we are sure was intending to praise the efforts of the staff and professionals at Willowbrook. At the same time, it acknowledges some noteworthy things: first, that there was very significant crowding as well as staff shortages. Anyone who has ever worked on a state hospital ward understands that one attendant cannot possibly supervise 60 residents. It is simple: As soon as anything happens, everyone else is totally unsupervised, and something, usually more than one thing, always happens. One person taking care of 60 "retarded" children means people are not receiving even the most minimal care. The article then acknowledges that children are beaten, but only "rarely." One wonders how the writer knows the frequency or where he gets his belief that other attendants would beat up anyone who hurt a child. In the interviews of attendants, the opposite is asserted—no one told the truth about such matters and attendants did not beat up other attendants for harming residents; attendants may have been beat up, however, by other attendants for ratting out abusive workers. Also note that in 1957 this reporter is already describing conditions of care and labor that in the early 1970s were the basis for closing institutions.

Goode heard two residents who arrived at Willowbrook in the early years speak about what it was like. One was a man with mild mental retardation and cerebral palsy who came during the years when there were still many military uniforms around. Gary arrived at Willowbrook when he was very young, possibly in 1949, and lived there for all his childhood and young adult years. Of these early years he remembers being on a ward with other children, some of whom were mean and would beat him up. He also remembers being afraid of some of the staff who were mean to him. Another Willowbrook resident, Gena, came to Willowbrook in 1956 at the age of 4 or 5. (Her story is told in some detail in Chapter 5.) Her account includes receiving severe beating by one staff member (resulting in that person's dismissal), taunting, and a beating from others, including other residents.[21] Gena has commented many times in public appearances that Willowbrook was never any picnic. Aside from poor conditions of life and abuse there, she remembers emotionally suffering as a young child because she could never understand why she had to be at Willowbrook and could not be with her family.

When one considers the evidence from the newspaper clippings about Willowbrook in its early years, one cannot help but come away with contradictory impressions. This is probably true because the school, like all social institutions, did embody certain contradictory elements, in this case most notably care and control, which were enacted under varying conditions in the course of its existence. At the same time that some terrible things were occurring at Willowbrook, very caring and loving things happened. The community attempted to support the institution in a variety of ways. Individual acts of kindness and care undoubtedly occurred. Educational efforts existed on the campus and extended to colleges in other boroughs. Public events and open houses were held there. Research, something we have not discussed as of yet, was also occurring at Willowbrook. At the same time, a variety of troubles plagued the institution, again, not as part of a process in which the school evolved into a healthier place, but as part and parcel of what a total institution is. This contradiction was part of the many Willowbrooks we are trying to depict.

Growth and Continued Problems

From as early as 1954, there was mention of the need to expand facilities at Willowbrook. The facility filled up quickly and required more space, more staff, and better facilities. Governor Dewey signed legislation authorizing upgrades to the laundry

---

21. We cannot find any mention of this in the newspaper files of this era. However, this does not at all mean that this event did not occur as Gena remembers it.

Willowbrook Administration Building

and other physical facilities, but this did not address the problem that Willowbrook was at this time overcrowded and could admit only "hardship cases." It was understood that "large numbers of mentally retarded persons are not receiving the care they should be" (*Staten Island Advance,* April 7, 1954).

There had been appropriations and plans in 1952 to build six additional buildings at Willowbrook, but the building program at Willowbrook did not progress for many years due to various administrative logjams and Governor William Averell Harriman's moratorium on construction.[22] Yet the census continued to grow, so that by July of 1955 there were already 4,300 residents. Completion of buildings continued to lag well behind the growth of the resident population. It was not until March of 1957 that ground was broken for six new buildings, five infirmaries, and a new kitchen and dining hall. Those buildings were not put into service until October of the following year, when Willowbrook already had 4,800 residents.

22. One upgrade to Willowbrook was the removal of a system of wooden walkways that had been built by the army during World War II. The existence of these wooden walkways is somehow part of the folklore of the local community. Goode is sometimes asked about them by students who come from longtime Staten Island families. One told him her mother remembered that there were wooden walkways all over, and apparently this was true.

In September of 1959, the *Advance* reported that Willowbrook had a staff of 1,741 employees and that three of the new buildings were in use. A dormitory could hold 160 children on four 40-bed wards, and 10 children under the age of 5 were being admitted each week. Approximately 180 new residents were admitted each month; by December of 1959, Willowbrook had a resident census of 5,200 (Bateman-House, n.d., p. 26).

What we see is an influx of patients with institutional capacity lagging behind. This was true in terms of facilities and staff. Willowbrook experienced a chronic problem in the recruitment of staff and frequently had many unfilled positions. It is not thus surprising to find an article in the *Advance* that proposed that Willowbrook perhaps had become too big for efficient operation, that it had reached the point of "saturation" (*Staten Island Advance,* December 10, 1959, as cited by Bateman-House, n.d., p. 27).

Perhaps this is why the state chose to lease five floors of Gouverneur Hospital in Manhattan in 1961. The hospital was to house 200 nonambulatory children who were then living at Willowbrook. This was to be a long-term arrangement, and Gouverneur was to become a decade later part of the drama that led to the closing of Willowbrook. Even though Gouverneur and other programs, such as foster care and family placement, reduced the patient population at Willowbrook by more than 400, the expectation was that Willowbrook would soon have more than 6,000 residents. By August 1962, the institution had 5,639 residents but a capacity of only 4,273, indicating a high level of overcrowding that was estimated by Director Berman at 32%. Overcrowding was particularly acute for children under the age of 5. Photos of the wards in the baby buildings show baby cribs almost filling the floor.

At the same time, Willowbrook continued to experience significant problems with understaffing. This extended beyond the direct care attendants to professional staff. For example, the *Advance* reported that over two thirds of the registered nursing positions were unfilled (*Staten Island Advance,* April 24, 1962, as cited by Bateman-House, n.d., p. 28). The chronic shortage of nursing staff was probably why the state established a practical nursing school at Willowbrook.

The overcrowding at Willowbrook at this time was, as Castellani (2005) argued, a chronic condition of institutional care within New York State. In August 1962, the Department of Mental Hygiene operated facilities designed for 16,980 persons with mental retardation that were occupied by 21,567 individuals. There were massive programs of construction in Huntington, on Long Island, Seneca (upstate), and the Bronx. When these facilities were opened, Willowbrook patients were scheduled to be transferred. It was a kind of a game of musical chairs because, as Director Berman put it, "If 500 or 600 of my patients were sent to another institution tomorrow . . . the space would be filled by others within a week." "It is not a

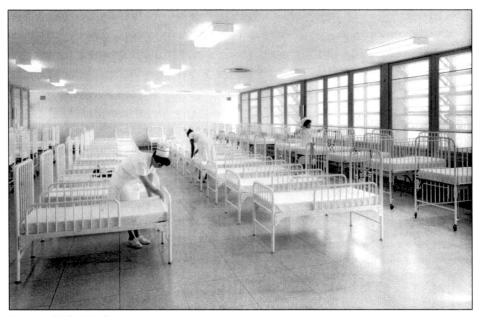

Interior of Baby Ward

question of space. . . . You can't leave these problems on the outside, even though you haven't actually got the room" (*Staten Island Advance,* August 23, 1962, as cited by Bateman-House, n.d., p. 29).

Bateman-House cites a remark made by Director Berman in 1955 about everything other than Willowbrook being "on the outside." Indeed, his remarks then and again in 1962 show how Willowbrook fit the definition of a total institution in terms of life there being closed off from the larger society. By 1964, not only was Willowbrook a total institution, it had grown into what was termed by the *Advance* "a small city," echoing an earlier characterization of the Halloran VA Hospital:

> It has its own garbage collection system, its own police, its own golf course and pool for use of patients and staff and a standby generator making it immune to power failure. Staff includes, besides the barber, carpenters, plumbers, roofers, shoemakers, and many others. (*Staten Island Advance,* March 23, 1964, cited by Bateman-House, n.d., p. 29)

Willowbrook had at this time 6,100 residents, making it the largest institution of its type in the United States and possibly in the world. It was over capacity by 2,000 residents and critically understaffed. The ages of the residents ranged from the very young to the very old. Four hundred were children below age 5, the largest grouping of such children known in the United States. There were 1,300 residents between the ages of 5 and 9 and 3,000 between 10 and 24. Of the 5,700 residents older than 5, 1,300 were classified as severely retarded, 3,200 as moderately retarded, and 900 as mildly retarded.[23]

Willowbrook Under Dr. Jack Hammond

On December 31, 1963, Berman retired. Six months later, on June 11, 1964, Dr. Jack Hammond was appointed as his successor. Hammond was to preside over the

23. An interesting and relevant question to ask is whether the reported figures are accurate and whether they can be trusted. A problem from the outset is that if they were to be trusted, then everyone who was at Willowbrook would have been retarded, and we know that this was not true. At Pacific State, staff knew and talked about residents who "shouldn't be in here." It was understood that people were institutionalized for reasons other than being retarded. At Pacific State and Willowbrook, it was easy to get in, hard to get out. Goode has a copy of a document published by the New York State Association for Mental Health, Inc., in 1961 titled *The State Institutions and How to Use Them,* which notes that the institutions were divided by population among the mentally ill, mentally retarded, epileptic, and criminally insane. It describes the requirements for admission to institutions like Willowbrook. One is voluntary, through written application of the person or by his or her parent, next of kin, or legal guardian. Thus admitted, the person could be kept in the facility for 60 days and thereafter until 15 days after written notice of intention to leave was given. The written application would need to be substantiated with thorough examination by one physician or one certified psychologist. Another method, when the individual was unwilling, was via court certification. A wide variety of individuals and organizations could initiate such an application, which would have to be substantiated by both a medical physician and a certified psychologist. What this meant in practice was that Willowbrook could be used by parents and social service organizations as a place to take children they did not want or could not control. Many interviewees involved at Willowbrook reported that it was used as a kind of dumping ground for adults and children who people did not want. Of course, we are not saying that all relatives of Willowbrook residents did this but, rather, that the institution was filled with people who had no relations outside the institution. Having a caring and involved family was an exception at Willowbrook, not the rule. For parents, all that really was required was to come to the institution, inform someone that they had a child they felt belonged there, and do the paperwork. The examination was pro forma, never yielded a negative result, and the child was in. Willowbrook became so (in)famous a place for unwanted children, children were even left in public places with signs on them saying "Take Me to Willowbrook." Given these circumstances, there is good reason to distrust the figures given to the *Advance.* Among those at Willowbrook who were not mentally retarded would have been people with autism, sensory disabilities (blindness, deafness, or the combination of the two), mental illness, physical disability (cerebral palsy being a common example), and those without disability of any type but who had gotten into some kind of trouble and Willowbrook had been selected as the place available for them. At Pacific State, where Goode had access to patient files, such trouble included chronic running away and truancy, delinquency, sexual promiscuity, drug use, possible mental illness, and violent behavior. Others had found their way into the institution voluntarily, via court certification. Once in, it was difficult to initiate the processes necessary to get out. Many residents were unable to do so. Residents and family members were often unaware that leaving Willowbrook was within patients' rights.

stormiest period of Willowbrook's history, until July of 1972, when he was transferred to Rome State School, in a symbolic victory for those who were fighting
against the deplorable conditions at Willowbrook.[24]

Over the years Goode has spoken with people active during the Willowbrook exposé, many have mentioned Jack Hammond. Some defended him, but
most spoke about him without affection. Of course, this may be because most of
those Goode contacted or heard speak were part of the movement trying to oust
Hammond and close Willowbrook. Hammond cannot be directly blamed for the
horrendous conditions at Willowbrook, which he inherited. In his first couple of
years there, he seemed to have earned the support of the community and even
the Benevolent Society, who praised his attempts to call attention to the problems
at the school. What those who wanted to close Willowbrook blamed him for are
his Machiavellian manipulation of people and situations in order to control the
institution and run it his way, often working against at least some of those trying
to change it for the better. When he was transferred to Rome State School in a
somewhat undisguised assent to parent demands, he had lost support from many
parents, workers, and professionals at Willowbrook. Parents demonstrated openly
and demanded Hammond be fired (for example, see the *Staten Island Advance*'s
coverage of the parent demonstration on January 12, 1972).

When Hammond took over, he was immediately faced with the problems that
had become permanent aspects of life at Willowbrook. These included violence
(within weeks of his coming to Willowbrook, a resident was murdered by another
resident), employee pilferage (for example, two employees were arrested for stealing 400 feet of brass pipes in December of 1964), terrible overcrowding (there were
over 6,000 residents, forcing Hammond to close the school to admissions in October), and continued labor issues.

The labor problems included objections by labor unions about the management's anti-union attitude, inability to find qualified staff (Hammond was quoted
as saying that if he had three attendants for a ward of 80 and one person for night
duty, he was lucky), and high staff turnover (50% of ward attendants dropped out
before the end of their seventh month; *Staten Island Advance,* March 10, 1965, as
cited by Bateman-House, n.d., p. 32). Hammond described the physical conditions
at Willowbrook as "deplorable." There was no pediatrician for the over 1,000 young
children who lived there. There were seven recreational directors for all 6,000 residents. Many of the facilities were in a state of disrepair. This included the outdated
water system, which apparently was responsible for the scalding deaths of two residents in May.[25]

24. Hammond died soon after, in January 1973, at the age of 55.
25. In one case, the death was caused by another resident acting in the role of a caretaker
who became scared and ran away when scalding water came out of the shower he was using to

Investigations were conducted about these deaths, and Hammond denied any attempt to cover them up and keep them out of the news. During the time Hammond was director, there were reports of deaths at Willowbrook. These reported deaths were usually newsworthy—homicide, an escaped child who died in the nearby woods, a child found drowned in the pool. One reads with horror the reports of seven or eight spectacular deaths a year. But less frequently reported on were the far more common, routine deaths caused by neglect, medical mismanagement, or conditions of institutional life (such as aspiration pneumonia, which could result when a resident was fed improperly and too quickly).

The issue of deaths at Willowbrook is complex (see our discussion in Chapter 4). Obviously, given Hammond's denial of such, people thought that there were cover-ups of deaths that were suspicious. One professional staff member reported that one of the most common forms of death listed on death certificates, aspiration pneumonia, was itself a cover-up. Ex-Willowbrook residents with whom Goode has spoken over the years have said that there were attempts to cover up all kinds of things—homicide, beatings, sexual abuse, acute neglect,[26] and stealing among them. One resident when asked about cover-ups said sarcastically, "Of course, do you think they wanted to get caught?" Given this, it would be hard to estimate the actual incidence of these acts by even just in-house reports, let alone those that reached the press.

In June of 1965, after a resident homicide in which one resident punched another in the throat, causing his death, two *Staten Island Advance* reporters, Mark Weisner and Drew Fetherston, took a tour of Building 9, where the death had occurred. Here is an excerpt of their description of the ward:

> "Patients there are the most retarded, most disturbed, strongest and most dangerous as any patient in the institution." This assessment is not from the police but from a professional, Dr. Jack Hammond. . . . Patients in 9C are at the bottom of the ladder. . . . Two of the four wards in Building 9, including C Ward, are filled with aggressive types. Hammond showed the way to Ward C on the second floor. "There are 76 patients here now," Hammond said, "The capacity is 38." The door that opens Ward C is a door opening on chaos. Milling and gesticulating men, many of them with facial or bodily disfigurements, roamed the floor of the dayroom, where the killing occurred. Others watched

---

bathe a wheelchair-bound patient. The parent, in a *Daily News* article, complained about "other retarded children doing this kind of work unsupervised" (*Daily News,* May 13, 1965, as cited by Bateman-House, n.d., p. 33). After a second scalding death a month later, the state finally replaced the outdated water system to prevent further such accidents.

26. As one example of acute neglect, a resident died of strangulation after being left in a restraint device without supervision (*Staten Island Advance,* June 15, 1965).

a Popeye cartoon on television, vacantly following the action. The patients are active, sometimes assaultive, and are kept on heavy doses of tranquilizers. Some slept leaning on each other or on the floor, or under wooden benches. (*Staten Island Advance,* July 22, 1965, cited by Bateman-House, n.d., p. 36)

This description describes an all too common picture in total institutions. It could have been made virtually in any of the state institutions in 1965. It describes a ward for violent residents. Willowbrook, as did many other institutions, assigned residents to wards by institutional logic. One of the outcomes of this logic was often to group patients with violent tendencies in order to facilitate their management. That meant assigning staff who could deal with such problems and liberally using heavy doses of tranquilizers. (At Pacific State, Goode was told that virtually 100% of the residents on the dangerous wards were on tranquilizers.) Such buildings were called by staff at Pacific "hell holes." Goode visited two such wards, one at Pacific State and one at Creedmore, in Queens, New York. In both places, the staff assigned to these buildings were known to be able to handle violence because they were themselves violent. Creating such a social setting was bound to produce only one thing, more violence, although from the institution's point of view, it was controlled because it was isolated and largely unseen.[27]

Research at Willowbrook

"One way you could get around that waiting list was to agree to have your child participate in research experiments." (Murray Schnepps, parent of a child at WSS, personal communication, College of Staten Island, September, 1993)

As already mentioned, medical research was part of what went on at Willowbrook and many institutions of its era, and its expansion was clearly part of the state's plan for that facility. In 1961, Rockefeller had announced plans for the building of the New York State Institute for Basic Research (IBR) adjacent to the Willowbrook campus. It was a unique facility, operating essentially as a state-run National Institutes of Health. It was built next to Willowbrook for an obvious reason—the

27. This kind of logic still persists in some large institutions for people with intellectual disabilities who are considered dangerous to themselves or others. Specific institutions are used for such individuals. Of course, the problem of assigning abusive staff to such places does not happen today, and there have been changes in how we manage both dangerous people with disabilities and abusive staff.

presence of a massive captive population of potential research subjects.[28] IBR's construction was delayed, and the facility would not officially open until 1967. Despite the delay, much research was going on at Willowbrook, conducted by researchers in the 1950s and 1960s, including George A. Jarvis, IBR's first director, an internationally renowned researcher brought there for the express purpose of building research at the facility, and Saul Krugman and Robert McCollum, at the time less well-known researchers, whose experiments at WSS on hepatitis have become paradigmatic of unethical research.

At Willowbrook, like Pacific State Hospital, one would have found a real variety of research projects going on at any moment. Some could be related to habilitation—for example, designing, testing, and implementing a curriculum for a particular population (such as the deaf and blind children on the ward where Goode worked at Pacific). Others could be medical, where drugs or some other form of medical treatment was being tested. Pacific was very aggressive in pursuing grants from the federal government for both kinds of research and had a large research building with labs and a library on campus. Willowbrook was even more aggressive about grants, as the intent from its inception and as a result of the State's investment in IBR. Goode noted a kind of brotherly competition, and cooperation, with Pacific State, with Willowbrook the big brother.[29]

Thus, it was not surprising to find the following remark by Harold Berman, Willowbrook's first director, speaking in 1955 about the institution's research mission:

> These projects, he said, extend into the field of nutrition disease, drugs, and electro-stimulation, with several of such projects having their beginning at Willowbrook. Among these, he said, is the use of metrazol, previously associated with treatment of brain conditions of old age, in the treatment of mentally retarded children. The project is being pursued under a grant from the Research foundation of Mental Hygiene.

28. Medical research has always been part of institutions for populations such as those with intellectual disability or mental illness and, in fact, of any public hospital, even those for people without special conditions. This is morally wrong, but it should not surprise us that it was part of Willowbrook. If there is anything exceptional about Willowbrook in this regard, it is that perhaps because of the size of the facility New York State decided to build its own large, state-of-the-art medical research center adjacent to it, thereby emphasizing this aspect of life at the institution. It is clear that the state had invested in the kind of physicians needed to develop the Institute for Basic Research into an internationally recognized center of research on disease and disability.

29. As a rough indication of the level of research, in an interview for the *Staten Island Advance* on November 1, 1976, Berman was quoted as saying that he once counted 73 separate research projects ongoing at Willowbrook (Bateman-House, n.d., p. 80).

. . . It should be clear, Berman said, that Willowbrook is "more than just a school." "I should like to have the name changed to Willowbrook State Hospital and School, thus giving a clearer definition as to its function and operation," he said. (*Staten Island Advance,* November 14, 1955, as cited in Bateman-House, n.d., p. 78)

Bateman-House describes the research ongoing at Willowbrook when Governor Rockefeller visited in 1959. It was a place at which "the latest theories concerning the etiology and treatment of mental retardation could be tested, both on human and animal research subjects" (*Staten Island Advance,* March 26, 1964, cited in Bateman-House, n.d., p. 78).[30]

The directors of Willowbrook Harold H. Berman and Jack Hammond were able to contribute to research while in their posts as administrators. Berman began his career with experiments on electro-cerebral stimulation therapy (Berman & Jacobs, 1956). Berman and Jacobs, the assistant director of Willowbrook, showed how electro-cerebral stimulation twice weekly for 5 weeks helped very young patients (2.5 to 4.5 years of age) who were violent or epileptic. In 1957, Berman teamed up with his new assistant director, M. Lazar, his supervising psychiatrist, Ossey Noé (also an associate research scientist with the New York University School of Medicine), and another physician, on a study that had terrible consequences for the children involved. They reasoned that the convulsant and respiratory stimulant Pentylenetetrazol (Metrazol) had the side effect of reducing confusion and increasing metabolism in the brain, so it might help the residents. One hundred and eleven children, from 1 to 18 years of age, were given the drug for 9 months. Unfortunately, not only did the drug do nothing for the cognitive functioning of the children, but 20 had convulsive seizures during treatment, three children exhibited disturbing behavior, and three died (although the published article, Berman, Lazar, Noé, and Schiller, 1957, asserted that the deaths were unrelated to the treatments). Later, Berman and Noé (1958) tamed things down a bit and studied the nutritional supplement Dietall; it was found to improve weight gain in underdeveloped residents for the 2 years of the study (1954–1956).

Jack Hammond was also well published and, as a clinical professor of pediatrics at the New York University School of Medicine, had an active research career. He was a coauthor on all the papers on the controversial hepatitis study (along with Krugman and Giles; see Krugman, Giles, & Hammond, 1967), although it is unclear what role he played in the study. In 1967, he teamed up with Noé and published a case study of an unusual patient: a black child with de Lange syndrome

30. This is the only mention of animal research subjects present at Willowbrook we encountered. If there were animals, their treatment is a subject of inquiry in its own right.

(i.e., Amsterdam dwarfism; Noé & Hammond, 1967). Noé (1964) had written on this topic before, but this article was a graphic account, complete with full pictures of the child's face and limb deformities. In a few years, they were joined by Max Reiss and Janet Hillman on an endocrinological study of five cases of Amsterdam dwarves plus two "bird-headed" dwarves (possibly children with progeria; Hillman, Hammond, Noé, & Reiss, 1968).

Hammond was also involved in some social research. Along with Manny Sternlicht, the chief of Adult Rehabilitation Services, and Martin Deutsch, the senior psychologist, Hammond sent surveys to 5,395 parents in December 1967 testing parental interest in children. They received only 749 responses back. Of these, 552 parents were willing to make an appointment to discuss their children, but only 77 were willing to consider moving their child back into the home. Overall, they concluded, the "sad lack of parental interest poses a very real problem," the result of which was that "institutions will continue to be overcrowded and their waiting lists for admission will grow" (Hammond, Sternlicht, & Deutsch, 1969, p. 339). Hammond was also listed as an author in an odd article that details the fall 1971 outbreak of shigellosis in the "Baby Division" cottage during the preparations for a study on shigella vaccines (Levine et al., 1974). Shigella was so endemic to Building 26, the "Baby Building," that they could not find a ward without it.

There was an influx of foreign researchers into Willowbrook in the 1960s. Max Reiss came from the Biochemical and Endocrinological Research Unit, Barrow Hospital, Barrow Gurney, near Bristol, and Bristol Mental Hospital in the United Kingdom. Reiss had some renown in British circles on the role of the thyroid in psychiatric illness. He wrote a remarkable review of a book on castration in 1960 that reported on the therapeutic aspects of castration with sex offenders, schizophrenics, "mental defectives, or epileptics showing pathological sexual behavior" (Reiss, 1960, p. 652). He concluded with the remark that sexual castration was no longer an ideal treatment because oestrone or stilboestrol would have a faster effect.

Upon arriving in America at Willowbrook, Reiss began what would be almost 10 years of research into the endocrinological correlates of "mental retardation." In 1959, Director Harold Berman teamed up with Reiss and Katherine Albert-Gasorek, researchers at the Neuro-Endocrine Research Unit, to publish a study on the relationship between sexual immaturity and mental deficiency. Squibb Pharmaceuticals donated chorionic gonadotrophic hormones, which were given to boys 9–15 years of age who were deemed to have mental deficiency and "retarded genital development" or "sexual retardation" (a condition marked by undescended testicles). They reported that the hormone treatment caused increased mental status, cooperativeness, and teachability. They also found genital maturation, overall growth, and changes in facial expression such that "The facial stigmata of the dullard have nearly disappeared" (Berman, Albert-Gasorek, & Reiss, 1959, p. 107), a point reinforced by facial pictures of young boys before and after treatment. A few years later, their research team examined and treated 102 patients for hormonal immaturity for 3 months. They ruled that gonadotropic hormones were a good treatment for "sexually retarded boys" (Reiss, Berman, Pearse, Albert-Gasorek, & Hillman, 1961, p. 112). Reiss and his team published widely on their research with boys and hormones (e.g., Hillman, Hammond, Sokola, & Reiss, 1968; Reiss et al., 1966).

Manny Sternlicht had perhaps the most varied publication history during his tenure at Willowbrook and was possibly the most prolific researcher there. His research interests seem to reflect trends in care for disabled children while he was at Willowbrook. He was also strongly connected to the academic community: While principal psychologist at Willowbrook, he was also a professor at Yeshiva University. He began at Willowbrook in 1960, but by 1971, he had become assistant director there, with a record of more than 50 published papers.

Sternlicht's first papers were with the senior psychologist Zev Wanderer. Their first article simply described 64 mongoloids (35 males and 29 females) over the age of 16 at Willowbrook, replicating a study from the West Coast (Sternlicht & Wanderer, 1962). Later, they described a volunteer psychology training program for students to work with "retardates" (Wanderer & Sternlicht, 1964). After a tour in 1960 of graduate programs in the New York area led to new connections between students and Willowbrook, they developed an internship program and accepted four master's students in the summer of 1961.

It seemed whatever Sternlicht was involved in at Willowbrook, he got a publication out of it. Some of his research focused on testing innovative therapies. He established group psychotherapy for "delinquent retarded males" (Sternlicht, 1964). He must have been involved with hiring new nurses because he published a paper on nurse recruitment (Sternlicht & Cavallo, 1965). In one study, he found that over a year of nonverbal training, such as play therapy with balloons, finger painting, and psychodramas in pantomime, was effective for a group of severely acting-out female adolescent "retardates" (Sternlicht, 1966). Sternlicht (1969) also explored alternative treatment approaches: The paper describes a group therapy intervention for the parents of children at Willowbrook who were looking for work.

His collaborations with Louis Siegel and Gabriel Pustel were also fruitful: Together they published at least nine articles on topics ranging from the effects of institutionalization, friendship patterns and orientations to time among Willowbrook residents, and the psychodynamics of humor. They found that institutionalization decreased the IQs of children after 4 years (Sternlicht & Siegel, 1968a); residents at Willowbrook were oriented to the present and had unstable friendship patterns (Sternlicht & Siegel, 1968b); and among Willowbrook residents, adults and female adolescents recalled the most unpleasant childhood memories (Pustel, Sternlicht, & Siegel, 1969).

With the addition of Michael DeRespinis, this team published a wide range of papers, but the studies seemed, as seen above, to look at either the obvious or the trivial. This team found that adolescent Willowbrook residents drew trees with color that varied with the seasons, but adults did not, perhaps because they had been institutionalized too long (Pustel, Sternlicht, & DeRespinis, 1971). They also reported that both male and female residents drew pictures of female animals more often than of male animals (Pustel, Sternlicht, & DeRespinis, 1972). And, in the category of "obvious research," they found that the longer a Willowbrook resident was institutionalized, the more frustrated the resident became finding solutions to problems as well as more helpless and defenseless (Siegel, Sternlicht, Pustel, DeRespinis, & Brandwein, 1972).

In the 1970s, Sternlicht teamed up with Martin Deutsch. Deutsch was a master's-level clinical psychologist who had worked at Willowbrook since 1964. By 1971, Sternlicht was assistant director of Willowbrook, but thanks to his collaborations, his publications kept coming. One of the first was a bizarre article exploring the value of temporary placement in an institution for a mentally retarded child. The outcome, Sternlicht and Deutsch (1971), sounds like an extended advertisement for Willowbrook, veering off into fantasy. Their rationale was that "The institutions would offer a respite from the trials and tribulations of a complex existence, a respite during which the retardate could take hold of himself before having to face the further challenges of the normal world" (p. 37). The child could live in a community of peers, and the institution would offer "an individually tailored program designed to permit him to realize his inner potentialities and to come to terms with himself" (p. 37). All this would correct the child's unhealthy personality and behavioral problems. Moreover, in this fantasy institution, the child would be surrounded by caring adults specially trained for his or her needs; the attendant, acting as a surrogate parent, would along with the teacher, occupational therapist, recreational instructor, psychologist, and social worker all work closely together on an individually designed program with clearly attainable goals. Sternlicht and Deutsch described a case where a mildly retarded 6-year-old boy spent "less than three years" during his temporary institutionalization making "enormous strides in interpersonal adjustment, remarkable improvement in classroom performance, and an almost meteoric rise in intellectual functioning which brought his IQ within the normal range of intelligence, making him a successful candidate for replacement in the community" (p. 38).

Sternlicht seems at times the consummate optimist. During this period, he and his team used basic research to assess innovative approaches to care but repeatedly were frustrated by their efforts. Hopeful that "praise" would modify residents' behaviors, they found instead that "censure" was the most effective "incentive" on motor performance in a group of Willowbrook children (Sternlicht, Bialer, &

Deutsch, 1970). An interesting paper in 1971 talks about a milieu therapy program implemented at Willowbrook. They published a program manual in 1965 called the "Willowbrook State School Remotivation Manual." The purpose of the program was to "interest the patient in the objective world, stimulate the patient . . . Make him part of a group" (as cited in Sternlicht, Siegel, & Deutsch, 1971, p. 83). Using this program, Ward attendants called "motivator-attendants" helped 24 profoundly and severely retarded youngsters over 3 months to little effect.

Sternlicht's publication record appears like a historical record of what was happening at Willowbrook. For example, he published two papers documenting "working residents." Sternlicht and Schaffer (1973) described how between 1971 and 1972, Willowbrook hired 17 former residents. Fifteen men worked as porters; two women worked as hospital attendants. All were longtime residents and had gone through the program "Training Adults for Community Living" (Sternlicht, Hammond, & Siegel, 1972). They achieved modest success: All but one (who was caught stealing) had their jobs after 9 months. Wagner and Sternlicht (1975) claimed that institutions often overlooked a valuable resource: residents. Using residents as "tutors" would help with the shortages of skilled personnel and provide growth experiences for the resident tutors. They trained 17 young women (average age of 19 years) to receive 30 hours of training in "dressing" and "eating." Unfortunately, both the experimental and control participants improved over time in eating and dressing, and the tutors did not improve in adjustment except to reduce maladaptive behavior somewhat.

Of particular interest to researchers associated with Willowbrook were infectious diseases such as German measles (rubella), mumps, shigellosis, chicken pox, and hepatitis because of both their possible link to mental retardation and their high prevalence at the institution. Dr. Saul Krugman, chairman of Pediatrics at NYU Medical Center, had been infecting children at Willowbrook with rubella and hepatitis virus since the 1950s. His first published paper on hepatitis appeared in 1957. He studied the effect of gamma globulin injections to see whether they would protect children from infection. Hepatitis had been noticed in children at Willowbrook since 1949, and research had been supported there by the army since 1951. By 1953 hepatitis was considered endemic at Willowbrook. Because of chronic conditions of multiple exposure, most children would be infected with hepatitis between 6 and 12 months after admission (Krugman et al., 1967).[31]

Krugman admitted new residents to a special 16-bed unit and fed them virus samples obtained from serum and stools of already infected residents. He infected

31. *Willowbrook* is a short, emotionally moving film by University of Southern California filmmaker Ross Cohen, that was an official selection of the Tribeca Film Festival, 2012. It documents a new physician and patient who arrive at Krugman's ward at the same time. See www.willowbrookmovie.com

hundreds of children 3 and older over the years. He then tracked the course of the symptoms and concluded that there were two types of hepatitis, one that was highly contagious with a short incubation period (type A) and one that was less contagious with a longer incubation (type B). He found that gamma globulin injections did prevent children from contracting the disease.

In 1972, as part of the escalating exposé of Willowbrook, Krugman's work came under heavy criticism from inside and outside of the medical community. Organizations on the left, such as the Progressive Labor Party, actively held rallies to protest Krugman's unethical research practices. Medical groups in New York City held meetings condemning Krugman's work. Faculty from New York colleges and universities organized protests. And ethicists and others writing in medical journals such as the *Lancet* both praised and condemned him.

Krugman defended himself by saying that he had obtained parental consent, that the pediatric hepatitis cases at Willowbrook were mild, and that the children would have caught the disease in any case because of institutional conditions and were therefore better off getting it in controlled circumstances.

Krugman had Berman attach the following letter to the parents' consent form (see Murphy, 2004):

Willowbrook State School
Office of the Director
Staten Island, New York

Date

Dear _____

We are studying the possibility of preventing epidemics of hepatitis on a new principle. Virus is introduced and gamma globulin is given later to some, so that either no attack or only a mild attack of hepatitis is expected to follow. This may give the children immunity against this disease for life. We should like to give your child this new form of prevention with the hope that it will afford protection. Permission form is enclosed for your consideration. If you wish to have your child given the benefit of this new preventative, will you so signify by signing the form.

Sincerely,

H. H. Berman, MD Director

The letter is clearly misleading, whatever might have been on the consent form. It implied that if the child did not participate, he or she would be worse off because of the institutional conditions. The letter was apparently also offered within the context of early admission, suggesting that the children of parents who allowed them to participate in the study would be given immediate entry to Willowbrook rather than being placed on the large waiting list. The letter mentions but then obfuscates the fact that some children would not receive the gamma globulin, and it does not mention the possibility of severe cases. Thus, the consent was obtained in a highly unethical manner. Krugman, in spite of developing an effective treatment for hepatitis (by 1963 it was used worldwide) and receiving recognition and many awards for his work within the medical community, is most remembered for his unethical method of conducting his research and justifying his work to parents.

This book will be unable to address the many issues related to research at Willowbrook. Goode (1994) recounted a personal experience at Pacific State illustrating how unethical methods and procedures were rationalized by very 'good' scientists and, in other respects, human beings. It concerns a child with rubella syndrome who was living on the ward Goode was observing in the 1970s. All the children were congenitally deaf and blind and diagnosed with profound or severe mental retardation. Most did not use any formal language and were unable to independently perform even the most rudimentary activities of everyday life. The children were fed seated at a table with their food in a plastic tray with compartments: one for the meat, one for the vegetable, and one for the starch. They were fed a "modified diet," which meant that the food was ground up, making it a mush. Only color told one the difference between what was what (the brown/gray the meat, the green or orange the vegetable, and the white the starch). The food was basically tasteless, texture-less, and without nutritive value. It was common for children to appear as if they were malnourished, probably because they were. One of the children Goode observed, Kim, had the curious habit of eating with her left hand on top of her head. She would leave it there for as long as a half hour. It is extremely difficult to keep your hand on your head for that long. When Goode asked someone about why, he was told the following story: Kim had been the subject of an experiment that used aversive stimulation, in her case electric shock, to eliminate undesired behavior in profoundly retarded children. In her case, that behavior was "stealing" food. What stealing meant was that while eating with her right hand, she would use her left hand to grab the food from the tray of her tablemate. Apparently this behavior was regarded as serious enough to merit Kim being subject to electric shocks in order to stop it. Goode knew a person who was involved and some of the details of the experiment. Apparently the scientist initially used a cattle prod attached to an electrode on Kim's left wrist. While at the table, when Kim reached over to steal food she was given an electric shock. The procedure was sufficient to produce the effect that Goode observed. Kim had learned not to steal food with her left hand and had removed it to a safe place, her head. This story shows how irrational and immoral science can become. Virtually none of it makes sense when looked at from the outside. Its basic premise, that Kim had an unacceptable behavior that needed to be eliminated, had to have been formulated within the culture of a total institution, cut off from the outside world, where such a crazy idea could never seem reasonable. Although it was reasonable to agencies that actually funded research like this, to us today it seems obvious that the problem Kim had was that she lived in a total institution and was not being fed enough or well. The obvious solution to her "problem" was to feed her more and better food. Instead, what was actually an arrangement of the institution was "constitutionalized" as "Kim's problem," and once formulated in this way, the solution was to shock her. There is a tendency in total institutions to blame institutional problems on the inmates, which is perhaps a reflection of the basic social structure in such places. Those in charge are representatives of good and assumed to be so, and the inmates are there because they have problems and are blameworthy (see discussion of the sociology of institutions and particularly Goffman, in Chapter 3). The use of the cattle prod was an expression of scientific indifference to the humanity of the child. The idea was to apply the research to other food stealers, but it is unknown whether this was ever done. As another expression of indifference to Kim, no one ever bothered to "de-program" her and she continued to eat in the fashion described during Goode's tenure at Pacific State. The scientist involved, who will remain nameless and passed away now many years ago, went on to receive a lifetime career award for research from the American Academy on Mental Retardation.

This kind of situation shows how researchers in the field at the time had little sensitivity to the humanity of their subjects. For a variety of reasons, they regarded them as more like animals to be experimented upon, rather than people who needed their help. We are sure that a comprehensive study of research at Willowbrook (or PSH) would uncover many examples of research that could be characterized this way.

The image of Willowbrook will always be associated with "Inhuman Human Experimentation," as one flyer by some local student and university action groups put it on their call for a demonstration during Willowbrook's exposé. The topic of research at Willowbrook could be fruitfully taken up by future scholars. Because so much research went on, just sorting out exactly what was studied during the 24 years research was permitted there would be time-consuming.

Much medical progress was made at the expense of those who were the captive research population, as is always the case under such conditions. This may be one reason why there are those who compare the experiments at Willowbrook to those conducted by the Nazis in their total institutions.

The public outcry following the exposure of the many abuses and appalling conditions at Willowbrook would, justifiably, make Willowbrook's research program one of its casualties. In 1973, a U.S. District Court ruled that "no physically intrusive, chemical or biomedical research or experimentation shall be performed at Willowbrook" (*Staten Island Advance,* September 29, 1976, cited in Bateman-House, n.d., p. 80). Research at Willowbrook was over.

Willowbrook Draws National Attention

Despite Hammond's efforts to change things, Willowbrook did not improve in the first years of his tenure. He continued to experience labor issues, incidents of abuse, physical plant problems, and monetary shortages. Like the *Advance,* Hammond seemed to find himself in the position of having to point out the flaws of Willowbrook while also defending it. The *Advance* was particularly fair-minded about its coverage, to its credit. Hammond, in contrast, seemed to be consistently defensive about criticism from the outside. This included criticism by parents who, he felt, had unreasonable and unrealistic expectations for their children; so, ironically, some of the most caring parents probably were seen by him as part of the problem.

In September 1965, Robert F. Kennedy paid a surprise visit to Willowbrook and Rome State School, and on September 9 appeared before the Joint Legislative Committee on Mental Retardation. He gave the following testimony, which was published in several newspapers:

> I have within the week visited two of the largest state institutions for the care of the mentally retarded. I was shocked and saddened by what I saw. There are young children slipping into blankness and lifelong dependence. There are crippled children without adequate medical supervision or rehabilitative therapy. There are retarded children living in the midst of severely retarded adults. There are children and young adults without education and training programs to prepare them for life in the community. And there are many—far too many—living in filth and dirt, their clothing in rags, in rooms less comfortable and cheerful than the cages in which we put animals in a zoo—without adequate supervision or a bit of affection—condemned to a life without hope. . . . There are no civil liberties for those put into the cells of Willowbrook—living amidst brutality and human excrement and intestinal disease. . . . In the year 1965 that conditions such as I saw should exist in this great state is a reproach to us all. (*New York Times,* September 10, 1965)

Kennedy showed up unannounced and thus could see conditions of life that were not manicured for visitors. Obviously not mincing words, he used the expression "snake pit" to describe Willowbrook. He appeared on television using this expression.

Hammond was quick to defend his institution and attacked Kennedy. He accused Kennedy of an unfair, sensationalist exposé and immediately conducted a tour of Willowbrook for reporters during which he stressed that the problems were due to overcrowding and that plans to reduce overcrowding were well under way. Meanwhile, Shirley Epstein, the president of the Benevolent Society and a member of the Board of Visitors, backed Kennedy. C. Ernest Smith, president of the Board of Visitors, called Kennedy's remarks, other than those about overcrowding, untrue. Some parents expressed the view that despite overcrowding, their children were treated well.

As we have seen, Willowbrook, from its inception, was a political football. After Kennedy's remarks, this public aspect of Willowbrook increased, as politicians from local, state, and federal governments became increasingly involved in assigning blame. Kennedy had earlier recommended that the state make public the contents of the Conklin Report, a report about the conditions at state schools by State Senator William Conklin. When Governor Rockefeller refused, Kennedy seems to have taken things in his own hands. When he made his remarks, one of the members of Conklin's committee corroborated Kennedy's observations, as did the *New York Times*, which had obtained a copy of the Conklin Report.

The effects of Kennedy's talk appear to have initiated events that eventually would lead to the closing of Willowbrook. After looking at the newspaper clippings and reading Castellani's (2005) book, one can see that because of Kennedy's stature, what he said, though it had been said before by others, took a first step toward putting Willowbrook in front of the public. It would take 7 years before Geraldo Rivera would expose the conditions at WSS to the public in an event that was linked directly both to public awareness and to a lawsuit that actually led to its closing. But in 1965, because of their family history, the Joseph P. Kennedy Foundation, and the activity of John Kennedy's administration in this area, people took what Robert Kennedy said seriously and Willowbrook entered the public conscience.

Kennedy's remarks also created a paranoia that he might show up unannounced again. Bateman-House describes how the Willowbrook division at Gouverneur Hospital geared up for a possible visit after an exposé was published in the *New York World Telegram*. There were 208 residents there, all under the age of 6. The headline of the *World Telegram*'s article on Gouverneur was "Snakepit for Kids: State Was Warned." The article noted that the state had begun a process of cleaning up the normal filthy conditions that were there, or so reported an anonymous worker. The Democratic mayoral candidate for the city of New York, William F. Ryan, called for an investigation and for "the wrath of God to be brought down upon those responsible" (*New York World Telegram*, September 10, 1965, as cited by

Bateman-House, n.d.). As with the main Willowbrook campus exposé by Kennedy, Hammond defended Gouverneur against this charge by the press, saying "except for its age it is about as ideal facility as you can find" (*New York Post,* September 10, 1965). He claimed that the facility had been entirely remodeled by the state to suit its current use. But the press would not relent. Over the next few days, the media published additional reports about serious conditions that existed at Gouverneur, including fire hazards and possible structural damage. On September 13, three days after Kennedy's remarks, Rockefeller was forced to announce that Gouverneur would be closed as soon as possible. (Gouverneur, however, was still open in 1972, during the Rivera exposé, and had been the subject of a suit by a parent of a child there, Willi Mae Goodman, in 1971.)

In the press, the calls to address conditions at Willowbrook multiplied. These included the New York State Association for Retarded Children, a large and influential statewide parent-run organization headed by a politically astute lawyer, Jerry Weingold. It also included the Benevolent Society, which sent a telegram demanding that conditions be improved. The Benevolent Society also sent a telegram praising Jack Hammond for his attempts to expose conditions at Willowbrook, this as part of a pattern of hot and cold relations between Hammond and the society.

For the remainder of 1965, Willowbrook remained in the news. The state had appropriated money in the supplemental budget passed in June to hire an additional 1,700 workers statewide. This appropriation, spearheaded by the Democrats, was itself a highly political matter, with Republicans accusing the Democrats of hypocrisy because of their previous attempt to remove $3.5 million from the operating budget of the Department of Mental Hygiene. According to Rockefeller, the problem was not one of money but of recruitment. The state said it would try to increase staff-to-patient ratios in all positions at Willowbrook.

Hammond continued to experience labor problems. On September 14, 1965, Council 50 of the State, County, and Municipal Employees Union held a meeting about conditions at Willowbrook. Hammond banned reporters from the meeting, but accounts of the meeting were published in the *Times* (September 15, 1965), *World Telegram,* and *Sun* (September 14, 1965). Employees complained that they were being used as scapegoats for the conditions at Willowbrook. They said that nepotism was rampant and that the lower-level employees were not well treated. They also cited doctors' lack of response to nonprofessional attendants' calls about sick residents (Bateman-House, n.d., p. 43).[32]

32. Hammond called this latter accusation a total fabrication, but given independent remarks Goode heard from former Willowbrook employees, it is possible that it was not. We will look at Bronston's account of Willowbrook in medical terms that will corroborate this accusation.

Now Willowbrook was like a game of hot potato. As each group got heat, it tried to rid itself of the blame as quickly as possible, pointing to someone else at fault. In retrospect, one can intellectually understand that all parties to Willowbrook, other than those imprisoned there, bear some part of the responsibility for it. The "nonprofessional attendants," as they sometimes referred to themselves, were particularly sensitive to being blamed for conditions there as they were not responsible for them, and in fact many were performing tasks well beyond what their job description required. There were many workers at Willowbrook who did their absolute best to help those they were in charge of, whatever conditions of labor were imposed on them. This is a theme we have heard over and over again from former Willowbrook workers. Many workers resented, and to this day continue to resent, any accusations against them.

The same hot potato game was also being played politically. Now that Willowbrook had been exposed, fingers began pointing. Alongside this, various parties positioned themselves to claim responsibility for solving Willowbrook's problems. If we are to believe what Hammond told the *Advance* five years later, that none of Staten Island's three lawmakers had ever inspected conditions at Willowbrook, then there is a certain suspicion that we must maintain about the rhetoric we see at the end of 1965 (see Bateman-House, n.d., pp. 44–45). There was a grand jury investigation of conditions at Willowbrook conducted by then District Attorney John M. Braisted that heard testimony about deaths and other abuses there. The report was submitted to New York State Supreme Court Justice James C. Crane on December 22, 1965. It was not released until September of the next year. An *Advance* article described its content as "mild," with the various conditions cited having been corrected.

Rockefeller, who was taking much criticism for the situation at Willowbrook, announced various plans to improve conditions (including providing funding for the nursing school and hiring 84 education and therapy specialists). He toured the facility personally with the Board of Visitors on November 8 and ordered construction of additional prefabricated buildings to help alleviate the overcrowding,

We know in retrospect that all of these measures had little or no effect on conditions at Willowbrook. To paraphrase from the advertisement in the *New York Herald* taken by the Benevolent Society on October 9, Willowbrook continued to suffer problems in at least the following areas: inadequate staffing in all areas; realistic salary scales to attract qualified workers; severe overcrowding; insufficient educational, recreational, and rehabilitation facilities and programs; inadequate administration by the Department of Mental Hygiene; and insufficient funds to rectify these problems.

The final realization that Willowbrook could not be fixed and should be closed did not crystallize for another 5 years. In 1966, there were many attempts on the part of the state to upgrade conditions at the institution. Prefabricated units were to be put in place, additional staff were hired, affiliations with academic medical institutions were forged, and the nursing school was enlarged. A grant of $97,871 was obtained for intensive training of 50 severely retarded residents 5 to 9 years of age.[33]

Rockefeller also signed into law a bill mandating education of state institution residents ages 5 to 21. Plans for bringing the census in Willowbrook down were made, and by March 1966 the population had decreased to 5,595, 175 fewer than when Kennedy had visited the previous September. Plans for opening additional facilities on Long Island and in the Bronx also figured into solving the overcrowding problem. Hammond had announced that the target figure was 4,000 (*Staten Island Advance*, January 28, 1966, cited in Bateman-House, n.d., p. 47). However, this depopulation did not take into account the estimated 800 children who were on a waiting list as long as 20 months to get into Willowbrook.

Exposé

In the years immediately preceding the exposé of conditions at Willowbrook by ABC Television reporter Geraldo Rivera in 1972, Hammond was faced with a continuous problem of labor recruitment and retention. In May of 1968, there were 450 vacancies (Bateman-House, n.d., p. 51), although estimates by labor organizers were as high as 500–600. Hammond was also under a hiring freeze in the middle part of the year. The executive director of Council 50 of the American Federation of State, County, and Municipal Employees, AFL-CIO accused Hammond of being anti-labor and of discriminating against Black workers. This group would be in constant conflict with Hammond, involving numerous strike threats and mutual lawsuits. At the end of November, a union organizer, Lemon Hood, was arrested for criminal trespassing when he allegedly refused to leave the grounds of Willowbrook (*Staten Island Advance,* May 29, 1969, cited in Bateman House, n.d., p. 53). Although he was found not guilty, Lemon's continued presence on campus organizing workers led to his being charged a second time; the union sued Hammond and various other members of the Department of Mental Hygiene. Eventually, charges and the lawsuit were dropped. Accusations and threats on both sides remained part of the landscape of Willowbrook until the time of the exposé.

33. As mentioned above grants, both rehabilitative and research, were driving forces at places like Willowbrook. They brought additional resources into the institution and advanced careers. They do not appear to have been primarily motivated by quality of life issues for residents. Rehabilitation grants would allow for additional staff and programming, making the lives for those within them at least theoretically improved, if only for the duration of the grant. Willowbrook was to get many such grants over the years, often, if we trust the press, with good results for the residents. If we consider other accounts, such as those contained in Chapters 3 and 4 of this book, the effects on participants of at least some of the experiments was disastrous.

When reviewing this period of Willowbrook's history, it is evident that the state was actively attempting to improve conditions at the school, even though the essential problems of staff shortage and turnover and overcrowding remained much the same. Improvements came in the form of new buildings and programs and attempts to reduce Willowbrook's population. Programs to reduce Willowbrook's census were presented as a solution to the crowding problem, even though Hammond had already said publically that people on a large waiting list would fill slots immediately. One very interesting approach was, as described earlier, to ask parents whether they were willing to take their children home. As mentioned above, the state mailed 5,395 surveys, of which 5,110 were delivered. Of these, 749 were returned. Of those returned, only 77 expressed a willingness to take their children back home. Fifty-nine of these children were mildly or moderately retarded and 17 severely retarded. The state concluded that family placement was not a feasible way to reduce Willowbrook's population (Bateman-House, n.d., pp. 53–54).[34]

In October of 1968, a new intensive therapy center for 750 children was opened. Grants continued to come into the school for special programs. But overall conditions remained much the same at the end of the 1960s and beginning of the 1970s.

34. Of course, a survey sent in the mail would not be the clinically effective way to approach a family about taking their child back home and despite rhetoric to the contrary was probably not intended to actually get families to take back their children. The lack of parental response can be interpreted in different ways, and although it did in some cases indicate indifference or lack of caring, in others it may have been a reflection of lack of community resources that could help parents or lack of knowledge of such resources, language differences, or parental illiteracy. The survey raises the issue of the parents' responsibility and blame for putting their child at Willowbrook or, for that matter, for the very need for such places. The conclusion of the researchers was an example of blaming the victim; they suggested that families were the reason a Willowbrook was needed. This is something that is foremost on the minds of many students in Goode's classes who want to know "how a parent could have taken their child to a place like that." Perhaps the best-known documentary about Willowbrook, *Unforgotten* (Meskell, 1996), in many ways is an attempt to answer that question. Katie Meskell had a sister at Willowbrook and follows several families who had children there, documenting the effects it had on the person and family. Goode shows the film in class not only because it presents life at Willowbrook through clips of Rivera's footage but also because it shows the intense suffering of families who had members living there. Of course, these were families who were involved, and clearly many were not. However, *Unforgotten* does the work of getting the students to see that many caring people took their children to Willowbrook because they were desperate and felt that they had no other option. The child was not being helped at home, the institution promised education and habilitation programs, and the family physician and clergy often recommended this as the best option for all involved. Many of the parents Goode has talked to over the years have told him that this was their position when they made the decision to place their child at Willowbrook, and it was a terrible and sad thing to have done. For others, it may have been a different kind of affair, perhaps dumping an unwanted burden. What *Unforgotten* does is to show viewers that there were families who brought their children to Willowbrook who were not uncaring, unconcerned, and uninvolved—a kind of assumption one might make without detailed knowledge.

Then, in March of 1971, possible budget cuts of $49.6 million to the Department of Mental Hygiene for the next fiscal year were announced. Along with the budget cut was a hiring freeze. Department of Mental Hygiene Commissioner Alan Miller made dire predictions about what might happen if the budget cuts were implemented. Hammond shut the nursing school and other school services at Willowbrook. Employees protested the cuts. As another aspect of the cuts, the plan to close the Willowbrook program at Gouverneur Hospital was announced. The state laid off 200 of Gouverneur's staff, and hired 60 to help with the 194 children who would be moving back to Willowbrook. Parents protested. In an almost dress rehearsal for the suit that was to follow a short while later at Willowbrook, on April 27, 1971, Willi Mae Goodman filed suit against the state to prevent the action. The case was eventually decided for the state by the appellate court in July (Bateman-House, n.d., p. 55).

All this served to highlight the problems at Willowbrook. In August, Hammond told the *Advance* that Willowbrook had lost an additional 300 workers because of the hiring freeze. In October the Board of Visitors sent a letter to Rockefeller citing shocking and appalling conditions at Willowbrook. In November, parents walked outside Willowbrook to protest the cuts. Jane Kurtin, a reporter for the *Advance,* covered the demonstration. Kurtin then wrote a series of articles that were to place the brutal conditions of Willowbrook squarely before the public. She wrote a powerful article, "Willowbrook: Inside the Cages," that was published on November 16, 1971, and documented the overcrowding and brutal conditions at the school, highlighting the stories of two residents named "Alan" and "Patty", who had been in seclusion for 1 and 2 years, respectively. Kurtin's articles included photos and interviews with Hammond in which he admitted that conditions had become inhumane, and it addressed other aspects of Willowbrook and care of persons with mental retardation.[35]

After the appearance of Kurtin's coverage pressures, internal and external, increased on Willowbrook. Politicians, local and state, called for an investigation.

---

35. When reading Kurtin's articles written at the end of 1971, one wonders why her much praised coverage did not produce the public outcry that Rivera's videos were to just a few months later in January of 1972. The same question could be asked about what were probably many local newspaper exposés of conditions at state-run institutions all over the country. In 1968 a local television channel in Philadelphia did a revealing and powerful series, "Suffer the Little Children," about conditions at Pennhurst State School, a very large institution, that were as horrifying as those done by Rivera about Willowbrook. Those videos also did not lead to the same kind of public outrage that was achieved by Rivera. Although we are not going to closely cover the Rivera exposé in this book, many people believe that the difference between what he did and what was done before was that ABC Television was syndicated. The images Rivera shot were shown all over the country on the same day, and they were released in the midst of a public conflict about Willowbrook. The impact was immediate and enormous.

Dante Ferrari, Democratic county chairman, visited Willowbrook and called for an independent investigation. Members of that task force, Andre Stein and Saul Weprin, toured Willowbrook and requested that the chair, Amman, convene a legislative hearing on Willowbrook. Amman refused on the basis that the state already knew the critical nature of the situation at Willowbrook (Bateman-House, n.d., p. 58).

At this point in the history of Willowbrook, we begin to get into a story that has been described in detail in other writings (Bateman-House, n.d.; Rivera, 1972; Rothman & Rothman, 1984/2009). For purposes of closure to this historical introduction, we will very briefly summarize what occurred.

Pressures inside and outside of Willowbrook built at the end of 1971. Within the institution were some professional staff, particularly Dr. Michael Wilkins, social worker Elizabeth Lee, and Dr. William Bronston, who were trying to work with parents and others to improve conditions on the wards. The conditions at Willowbrook had deteriorated so seriously that parents had become aware of them and were organizing and demonstrating.

Wilkins and Bronston had befriended resident Bernard Carabello, who had written a letter about conditions at Willowbrook that had been published in the *Advance* on December 6, 1971. Carabello was part of this group who was locking horns with the administration including, but not limited to, Hammond. One of the more telling incidents that occurred prior to the exposé of Willowbrook by Rivera was a questioning of Carabello by Drs. Milton Jacobs and Manny Sternlicht about his relationship with Bronston and Wilkins. Kurtin's December 22, 1971, article about this interview reported that it was done in an offensive and threatening manner (*Staten Island Advance,* November 22, 1971, as cited by Bateman-House, n.d., p. 59).[36]

Hammond, sensing that some professional staff were beginning to align with parents, issued an order forbidding them from meeting with parents, on or off duty. This was to place a check on the professional–parent coalition that was building. It was part of Hammond's strategy to manage the increasing difficulties inside and outside of Willowbrook. Lee, Bronston, and Wilkins ignored the order.

On January 5, Hammond fired Wilkins and Lee. It was a Wednesday, and that evening Wilkins called an acquaintance, ABC Television reporter Geraldo Rivera, informing him of conditions at Willowbrook, where children were being neglected

36. Goode has spoken with Bernard Carabello and to Mike Wilkins about this event. Carabello remains particularly proud that he stood up to what was going on at Willowbrook, including not being intimidated by Sternlicht and Jacobs, who had not only threatened to curtail his privileges if he did not stop making trouble but also to circulate rumors about him. Hammond tried to discredit not only Carabello but also the others involved in the "insurrection." Revelations of the leftist associations of Bronston and Wilkins and the fact that they lived together in a multifamily home were made public as an attempt to damage their reputation.

Geraldo Rivera and Crew outside Tina's Diner

and abused. Rivera and his crew agreed to meet with Wilkins the next day at Tina's Diner on Victory Boulevard. Wilkins told them that he still had a key to Building 6 and that he would take the crew there, unannounced. Thus, on January 6, Rivera's crew broke into Building 6, Ward B, and filmed what they saw. They also interviewed Lee and Wilkins in Lee's apartment before returning to the institution to film more. That evening, scenes from Willowbrook were shown on Eyewitness News broadcasts at 6:00 and 11:00 p.m. From the standpoint of the history of disability in the United States, this broadcast was an event that brought about a sea change in the treatment of people with intellectual disability.

On March 17, 1972, following a conference for parents, professionals, and civil liberty lawyers that had been held at Mount Augustine Retreat House on Staten Island the week before, a lawsuit was announced. *New York State Association for Retarded Children et al. and Parisi et al. v. Rockefeller (New York ARC v.*

Rockefeller) was filed with the federal court in the Eastern District of New York, with Judge Orin Judd presiding. This was to begin a 3-year legal battle between the litigants that was finally resolved on May 5, 1975, when the state settled with the litigants and agreed to find community placement for all residents at Willowbrook. The document prepared to govern this process, known as the Willowbrook Consent Decree, was to form a model for other closures of institutions that followed. The legislation established a "Willowbrook Class," (a large group of residents who resided at Willowbrook) that was protected under its agreements. The significance of the Consent Decree has been dealt with in a number of publications (see Ferguson, 1994; Rothman & Rothman, 1984/2009). The Willowbrook case is still open as of this writing and will not be closed until the death of the last person named as part of the Willowbrook Class.

The last section of Bateman-House's chronology deals with the years 1972 to 2002. It documents what went on at Willowbrook both before and after the signing of the Consent Decree, including all the ways that deinstitutionalization and "community placement" was effected. The newspaper articles of that era continue to describe serious problems at Willowbrook until its final closure on September 17, 1987, some 12 years after the signing of the Consent Decree. The investigation of this period in Willowbrook's history is, as the colloquial expression goes, a whole other kettle of fish. Much of the systemic change that occurred in New York State during this period can be found documented in Castellani's (2005) book. What may not be as well documented or understood is the paradoxical effect that the exposé and federal oversight had on life at Willowbrook. Several staff members interviewed said that after the Consent Decree was put into law, the state was mandated to hire a huge number of direct care and custodial staff or face significant fiscal penalties. Rather than face these penalties, they hired people without sufficient background checks who should not have been working there, and again, according to these interviewees, conditions at Willowbrook became more difficult and more dangerous than ever. The court mandates created a loss of trust in and knowledge about other workers, and this affected the overall feeling of the place, which became in some ways even worse, from a quality-of-life point of view.

Beyond these few remarks by former workers, the story of Willowbrook in the last years of its existence is something beyond the scope of this writing. As the reader will see, many of the interviewees who had been at Willowbrook for a long time claimed that the conditions deteriorated rapidly, for a variety of reasons, after the exposé. Here is what can only be described as a surreal paragraph about conditions at Willowbrook just before its final closure (Bateman-House, n.d., p. 71):

According to his autobiography, *The Soul of a Cop,* New York Police Department officer Paul Ragonese discovered an unreported chamber of horrors at SIDC [Staten Island Developmental Center, Willowbrook's new name at that time] when he visited the facility on December 6, 1985 (Ragonese & Stainback, 1991). Ragonese, a member of a NYPD emergency response team, was sent to Staten Island Community College to remove picric acid from a building. A chemist at the College informed the officers that she believed there was more picric acid in a building at Willowbrook, where she had previously worked. Ragonese stated that, upon entering building 2 and ascending to the second floor, he and his partner found pitric acid, a leaky barrel of cyanide, and other chemicals, and a room with a mattress on the floor. Beside it, was a partially eaten can of pork and beans, a spoon in it, and the bodies of a dozen pigeons. The heads had been torn or bitten off and were nowhere in sight, as if they had been eaten. Ragonese also reported seeing "more than fifty glass containers stood on shelves. Inside the containers were brains, hearts, livers and other organs. In the hallway, [h]uman body parts were strewn all over the floor. At the end of the hall, rats were eating the decaying flesh of the human body parts, many belonging to children. There were human feces, rat feces, pigeon feces and mouse feces everywhere." Ragonese claimed that his discovery was never investigated, despite of his personal notification of his superiors, the Department of Environmental Protection, the medical examiner's office, a special assistant to Mayor Koch, the Director of health and public hospitals, and the NYPD public information office. (Bateman-House, n.d., p. 71)

Ragonese's is an absolutely horrific and stunning narrative. There would be no obvious motive for him to have lied about what he saw. Conversely, there would be many reasons for his superiors, and the others he claimed to have notified, to have ignored his report and even covered it up. If it is a veridical account of what this police officer saw, his remarks reveal this about Willowbrook and institutions like it: whatever one can imagine, that imagination will never encompass the terrible, dark realities of such a place. Willowbrook was, in the words of Harold Garfinkel, "only witnessable, not imaginable." (Harold Garfinkel, personal communication, Seminar on Ethnomethodology, Department of Sociology, UCLA, 1973). And if we can return to the original reason for bringing up Ragonese's book, the neglect and inhumanity at Willowbrook apparently continued until it was finally closed in 1987.

Summary of Willowbrook's History

Willowbrook's history is a part of the more general history of New York State and Staten Island. Staten Island has traditionally served as a "dumping ground" for

New York City, taking not only ash and refuse from the city but also the diseased, infirm, and poor of New York, both children and adults. Staten Island in the 1930s was largely rural. Because the island was not linked by bridge or tunnel to other boroughs and because it had a lot of undeveloped land, the city had traditionally taken advantage of Staten Island by building various hospitals, asylums, and quarantine facilities on it. Since the 18th century, Staten Island served as a location for quarantine and other institutions for the city. It is unusually rich in the history of total institutions, from Mount Loretta, to Sailor's Snug Harbor, to Willowbrook, to name a few.

Willowbrook State School ultimately was established because of overwhelming need, after the closing of Randall's Island, to build a large facility for young New Yorkers with disabilities. The facilities already operated by the state were very crowded, and it needed to increase capacity. The institution could have been built in many other locations, but through complex political and economic processes, it ended up on Staten Island, much to the displeasure of Staten Islanders and many politicians, even ones as powerful as Robert Moses. In the end, political and economic interests overrode the overwhelming objections from the community. The governor announced that a new school for retarded children would be built on the Willowbrook site.

Upon completion in 1942, the secretary of war leased the state of the art "hospital-school" Willowbrook State School for returning veterans as Halloran General Hospital. By the late 1940s, soldiers were retreating from the halls of Halloran, and the facility began to gradually fulfill the purpose for which it was built. The early years at Willowbrook were probably never ideal, as the director blamed problems on "growing pains," but reports of abuse were evident really from the start. These were probably overshadowed by what must be regarded as the suspiciously uncritical glowing "puff pieces" in the New York papers, in which Director Berman sold the virtues of Willowbrook. There was no need to oversell the place; demand far exceeded supply. From inception, it grew, first in population, then in structure, but always under conditions of crowding and eventually more critical problems. By 1964, it had become the largest institution of its kind in the United States. Under Hammond's directorship, Willowbrook had many problems: fiscal shortages, violence, theft, alcohol and drug use, abuse, overcrowding and understaffing, labor problems, and resident deaths, among others.

At the same time, Willowbrook also became a major research institution as a large, captive, somewhat isolated population of children proved highly beneficial for researchers, and research was, in fact, part of the mission of the school. Both directors, Hammond and Berman, were well-published authors, and the establishment of research units (psychology, neuro-endocrinology) led to a cohort of well-funded published researchers. What they studied reflected much about what was going on at Willowbrook, as well as what these leading experts thought about mental and physical disabilities and their diagnosis and treatment. Eventually though, medical researchers were sanctioned for their studies on childhood infectious diseases. Although there was scientific value to the work, it was sadly at the expense of the research subjects involved and their families.

The institution as a totality evoked the image of cruel treatment and extreme confinement. It drew national attention as conditions became public, but little was actually done to improve conditions. In the mid-1960s, the investigations and inquiries began, amid heightened media scrutiny, including Robert Kennedy's series of statements after a tour of Willowbrook in 1965 and Jane Kurtin's *Staten Island Advance* articles, but the state's budget problems and politics about how to use existing funds led to even more critical staff shortages and threats to resident welfare and safety. Facing open rebellion from parents and two doctors, Bronston and Wilkins, and a social worker Elizabeth Lee, Director Hammond fired the doctors, spurring Wilkins to help Geraldo Rivera get into the school and take video of conditions there. The public outrage and legal proceedings that followed led to the creation of the Consent Decree in 1975 and to Willowbrook's eventual closing in 1987.

3

A Sociology of Total Institutions

Before reading firsthand accounts of people who lived and worked at Willowbrook, we should be familiar with the insights sociologists and social psychologists have gained about how people act in places like it. It is important to understand this body of thinking because it provides important scientific insights with which to interpret some of the details of everyday life we will encounter. As we will argue and demonstrate, without such a framework, misinterpretation of what is being said or written is a distinct possibility.

In the 19th century, social scientists were very involved in the debates surrounding the eugenics movement, and many were advocates of eugenics thinking. Some, such as Herbert Spencer, were regarded as leaders of a science of society that could lead to the solution of social problems. A perusal of the early editions of the *American Journal of Sociology* (established in 1895) will reveal many discussions in the area of biological sociology and the merits of solutions to deal with the problems of inherited characteristics. Sociology's interest in doing empirical research about institutions that housed mentally ill or mentally deficient people, however, did not emerge as a major focus of the discipline until the middle part of the 20th century, when it became part of a popular subdiscipline of the field medical sociology.

To some degree, this interest paralleled the rise of qualitative sociology—forms of sociology that used ethnographic or participant observation techniques and took root in sociology in the

1930s, particularly as part of the Chicago School of sociology. Systematic observational sociological research was well suited to describing the details of everyday events, such as a street corner gathering of men, behaviors of different cultural groups or social classes, or the workings of institutions, such as workplaces or, in the current case, mental institutions. As inhumane conditions and treatment in mental hospitals became known to the general public, sociology increasingly became interested in what went on in such places.[1] We are going to discuss several of the works included in this genre, but this is not a comprehensive survey that literature. Instead, the specific research cited embody what are key sociological insights about behavior in total institutions.

Modern observation and participant-observation research about mental institutions begin to appear in the 1930s notably with Sullivan's (1931) study of his special acute unit for schizophrenics. In 1938 and 1939, Rowland published research on patient subculture and organization in a state hospital. Freud and Burlingham's *War and Children* (1943) noted the therapeutic importance of emotional attachment between caretakers and children in children's hospitals. Devereux (1944) studied a ward for schizophrenics and reported the importance of ward organization in affecting patient behavior. Szurek (1947) in a particularly interesting observational study reported on the therapeutic impact of problems between staff and between staff and resident children, concluding that patterns of communication between staff members were critical in determining children's behavior. Bettleheim and Sylvester's (1948) study of children in institutional settings also had a similar theme, emphasizing the social milieu—that is, relationships as the primary determinant of resident behavior. Deutsch's (1948) *The Shame of the States* documented the terrible conditions in state hospitals across the country.

Many of the early studies were concerned with an analysis of the social milieu of the state hospital. Sometimes conclusions reached about the social structure were then implemented, to see if improvements could be made in clinical outcomes. One of the most compelling examples of a work in this genre was Frank Stanton and Morris Schwartz's *The Mental Hospital* (1954). Schwartz was a sociologist skilled

---

1. As was discussed earlier, there was an awareness by the end of World War II of institutional conditions. By the time Hollywood made the movie *The Snake Pit,* starring Olivia de Havilland, in 1948, there had been many articles in newspapers about the deplorable conditions in mental institutions, including those that housed children with mental deficiency. It could be said that most people knew about the problem of mental institutions, so sociology would have taken it up as an identified social problem. For example, Edith Stern, a reporter of that era who wrote an article on children with disabilities in state institutions across the country, published in the *Ladies Home Journal* of August 1948 an article titled "Take Them off the Human Scrap Heap." There were numerous descriptions of the kinds of conditions that Rivera exposed at Willowbrook some 24 years later.

in observation, and Stanton was a psychiatrist in charge of a private mid-Atlantic psychiatric facility for women. One of the author's concerns was with social processes within psychiatric hospitals that "create" or "promote" symptomatic behaviors. It is clear that they offer an alternative explanation to psychiatric theory as to why people behave as they do in such a setting. As with earlier studies, the authors focused on patterns of interaction and communication between staff and patients and within these two groups. As a general summary of a long book with many empirical chapters, they found that these patterns of interaction and communication are systematically determinative of disturbed behavior. The work focused on "the other 23 hours of the day" in which the patient was not in treatment with a "treatment psychiatrist" but under the care of a "custodial psychiatrist," psychiatric nursing staff, aides, and occupational therapists. Many interesting observations were made about interpersonal and dysfunctional communication between these three statuses and how they affected patient behavior.

Here are two examples from their book. One relates interaction on the ward to instances of "pathological excitement" (i.e., when patients act out, become out of control, aggressive, or self-abusive). This chapter of the book was based on a study done originally in 1949 and is the most complete analysis of its type within the volume. The authors describe a pattern of "covert staff disagreement" about the treatment of specific patients or acts committed by patients. Escalating conflicts over the treatment of the patient (custodial psychiatrist and staff) and therapy of patient (treatment psychiatrist) resulted in one-upmanship, especially between the psychiatrists involved. The conflict had social consequences as staff took sides. Often there were "last ditch efforts" on the part of the loser in the conflict to establish she (the patient—the study was done in a psychiatric hospital for women) was right. Emotional attitudes and resentment toward the patient on the part of staff occurred during this process. This pattern resulted in "heightened symptomatology," as patients were subjects of intense, though entirely unacknowledged to the patient, disagreements among those involved in her care. To their credit, the authors follow six cases and 15 incidents of excitability in great detail. Based on their observations and conclusion that the problem lay not with the patient but in the behavior of those around her, the authors formulated and implemented three interventions: transfer of patient, withdrawal of authority (e.g., changing either the treatment or custodial psychiatrist), and discussion between parties. When implemented, this pathological excitement stopped virtually immediately in all cases. The chapter shows how a "dissociative social field" produces dissociative reactions in patients. This same kind of logic can, and should, be applied to the residents at Willowbrook.

Another chapter was on incontinence, which is based on the authors' 1950 article on the topic. It is not the most pleasant topic, but it is an absolutely fascinating study that reinterprets incontinence not as a psychiatric symptom but as a form of social participation. The authors specifically examined the character of the incontinent act, the specific situations in which it occurred, specific situations when it did not occur, and also attitudes about incontinence among the staff. Without going into unpleasant details, it was clear in reading descriptions of the problem that these were not what one would term medically incontinent acts, that is, that the individual involved had no control over these natural acts. It was clear that they were purposeful. The authors noted this and also that 90% of incontinent acts occurred in situations of conflict, abandonment, isolation, and devaluation or those that were unconstructive. Incontinence never occurred when patients were paid attention to or got what they requested. Interviews with staff revealed pessimistic attitudes about solving incontinence and feelings of resentment, blame, anger, and disgust. Generally, aides saw the social function of the incontinent act—i.e., attention getting, avoiding a patient, or punishing a patient or staff member) as a testing device, substitute gratification, or an expression of devotion or of teasing (Stanton & Schwartz, 1954). One patient said it was a result of her loneliness. Incontinence thus had a social place and function within the institution.

These two chapters illustrate an essential insight into the people in institutions. It is the same as concluded by Goode while at Pacific State. Although he had not read Stanton and Schwartz at the time, he found that most of what he was seeing could be explained by virtue of conditions of life, rather than as a result of the cognitive deficiencies of the residents. Things that looked entirely weird and were attributed to medical causes, for example, like stereotypy, were much more due to boredom and complete neglect rather than to neurological and congenital abnormalities.[2] These two chapters point to a general dynamic in total institutions, that people incarcerated in them and with little power need to or choose to react with unofficial and unapproved ways to influence their situation or make statements about it to others. When Bronston says that Willowbrook is the culprit, it is in this way, that it created abnormal conditions that required abnormal 'solutions' by residents.

2. In *A World Without Words,* Goode (1994) spent a prolonged period "shadowing" a child with deaf-blindness who lived at Pacific State. Via observation, he realized that she spent 23 hours of the day left to her own devices, in solitary pursuits. The only thing she had reliable control over was her body, and she used it in various ways to occupy her time, including engaging in repetitive, bizarre-looking rocking, head rolling, and finger flicking. These stereotypes could be easily construed as the result of her deaf-blindness and retardation. But when Goode spent a mere 36 hours on the ward as a kind of pseudo-patient, he exhibited a propensity toward rocking and repetitive movement, possibly as a way to help relieve the tension of his situation. In many of the institutions Goode visited, residents could be seen in day areas or on lawns engaging in such behaviors. Despite the tendency to medicalize their rocking by seeing it as stereotypy due to being retarded, work such as that done by Stanton and Schwartz and Goode remind us that contextual or situational explanations may be more parsimonious than biological ones.

This same insight about institutional life, that what one sees inside is often not a reflection of organic disease but rather of social conditions, is no better explicated than in the 1971 book *Hansels and Gretels* by Dorothy and Benjamin Braginsky. The book reports the authors' observations, interviews, and experiments with children living in institutions for the mentally retarded. In ways paralleling Stanton and Schwartz's (1954) and Goffman's (1961) work the Braginskys' approach to understanding human behavior in such settings eschews the medical model and embraces a sociological one. The beginning of their book criticizes the use of a medical model to explain the behavior of children with mental retardation, of either the "organic" or "familial" type (Braginsky & Braginsky, 1971, p. 16). Through a variety of sociological research techniques, the authors question the assumption that children with mental retardation function in less human, less rational ways than children without such diagnoses. Of particular interest are their observations of children in institutions who use "impression management" (Goffman, 1961) as a way to control their lives, to work against the institutional control over them. They detail how specific strategies of adaptation by children respond to the various characteristics of their degraded social environment. Their work sees the conflict between the goals of the "retardates" and the "institutional demands" as the central social dynamic to explain children's behaviors in such settings, resonating with Goffman's (1961) view in *Asylums*. The children in the institutions they worked in emerge in the Braginskys' book as competent survivors in an uncaring capricious environment. The children's responses to this environment, far from being evidence of their mental retardation, are seen by the authors as indicating social intelligence and a great ability at impression management, a strategy for living that makes good sense when almost no other ones are available. This way of looking at children in institutions is similar to the one we take. It is embodied in the observations of children's ward life recorded by Reiss.

William Caudill's 1958 book, *The Psychiatric Hospital as a Small Society*, examined the social system of the mental hospital in terms of its statuses and roles, patterns of communication and interaction. Caudill was an anthropologist trained at the University of Chicago in the early 1950s who used multiple research methods to examine the society of mental hospitals (see also Caudill, Redlich, Glimore, & Brody, 1952). He discussed them in terms of being mobility-blocked places based on a caste system (patient and staff), with each caste having its own rules, beliefs, practices, and perceptions of life. Further, one of these castes is under the domination of the other. The author described "multiple subordination" of patients, that is, that there are different ways and different mechanisms used by staff to control patients. Caudill's book very much set the stage for Erving Goffman's 1961 work, *Asylum*, which can be regarded as emblematic of this sociological genre of research. *Asylum* is a large, rich, and complex volume, so our intention here is to pick certain key ideas and insights related to what went on at Willowbrook.

Asylum is also an odd book in some ways. Goffman wrote it after substantial fieldwork in a hospital he disguises with the name "Central," on which he reports in the chapter titled "The Underlife of a Public Institution." Most of the book, however, is not a report of his fieldwork but rather an integration of ideas coupled with illustrations taken from research and literature about what he calls "total institutions." Goffman argued that although all institutions (both ways of doing things and places) lay claim to the time and efforts of members of society, certain ones are more encompassing than others. By "total institution" Goffman means "a place of residence and work where a large number of like-situated individuals, cut off from the larger society for an appreciable period of time, together lead an enclosed, formally administered round of life" (Goffman, 1961, p. xiii).

The key elements of the definition are "cut off from the larger society" and leading a "formally administered" daily life; this certainly fits Willowbrook. However, the definition encompasses other institutions as well. He names different "types" of total institutions, including those for the harmless and incapable (arguably Willowbrook was in this category); those for people who are ill but not harmful to others (e.g., a hospital for children with chronic disease); those for people who are harmful but not intentionally so (e.g., a TB clinic or mental hospital); those for people who are intentionally harmful (e.g., prison, a POW camp); those that justify themselves on instrumental grounds (e.g., boot camp, boarding schools); and those that are retreats from the outside world (e.g., monasteries, communes). One of Goffman's important insights is that all these places, by virtue of their sharing this basic form of social organization, share certain characteristics and dynamics that structure social action for their members in similar ways.

At places such as Willowbrook for the resident (patient, trainee, religious devotee, etc.), the normal segregation of roles in daily life would be absent. Instead of living with different sets of people, under different authorities, and in different places and without an overall imposed plan, in total institutions just the opposite occurs, at least for those who reside within them. For residents there is an overall feeling of regimentation and of being cut off from the outside world. As discussed earlier, the degree to which residents are "completely" cut off from the outside varies. At Willowbrook, for example, in the early years there were many attempts to bring the community into the institution and also to allow residents to take trips to the outside. This changed over time because of staff shortages, overcrowding, and cutbacks. Generally, places like Willowbrook, which housed persons who were not criminal or generally violent, would not have the same degree of enforced segregation as, say, a prison. But eventually, because of extrinsic factors, such as those cited above, many became essentially like prisons, with very little contact occurring between patients and people from outside the institution.

Goffman emphasized the importance of social structure in determining how persons think and act in total institutions. The basic division in social structure in such places is between a large, managed, relatively powerful group and a small administration and supervisory staff whose basic job is surveillance and to promote conformity to institutional rules and procedures. There is generally a moral overlay to this division in which the large group is seen as sick, bad, inferior, blameworthy, and so forth, and the staff as representing the good, normal, and powerful. There is such great social distance between these groups, even though they are with one another day in and out, that Goffman literally writes about two "worlds," the Staff World and the Inmate World. The two groups are in a highly asymmetrical relationship both in terms of knowledge and power, with the staff having most of the power and often a tremendous amount of information about residents. This is the way the institution is supposed to function, but Goffman also points out that there is both formal and informal organization in total institutions. Informal organization exists for both staff and resident. The underlife of an institution may not at all conform to the rhetorical description, may even directly contradict it. In prisons, for example, despite the real differences in power between guards and prisoners, in the daily life of the institution prisoners and prison gangs have much power and possess consequential information about everyday life entirely unknown to those in charge. That is not the way it is supposed to work. At Willowbrook, however, residents were in a condition of relative powerlessness (although, as we shall see, they were not entirely powerless) and hence were limited in the ways they could construct an Inmate World.

Here is the basic rationale for the situation. These institutions have "inmates" who are there for some reason—for example, to be cured, educated, rehabilitated, habilitated, or enlightened. There are staff whose job it is to do this work and to make sure that order is kept. There are two distinct worlds that come into contact with one another—that of the staff and that of the residents or inmates. We will look at the Inmate World first.

Goffman talks about the inmate being subject to an institution's presenting culture and to a series of personal "abasements, degradations and humiliations" that he calls the *mortification process*. To a degree, every institution does this because the resident is going to have to fit into a new world with new rules and ways of doing things. This involves a process of disculturation from one's old life and identity and reaculturation to the institution and a new identity.[3] Sometimes this

---

3. It is supposed to work such that the adaptation to the institution and new identity creates a "better" person. The process, as any of the prison gang documentaries on television illustrate, can work in reverse. Through a process of fraternalization, the inmate is more influenced by other inmates than by the attempts to habilitate or cure him or her.

is done as part of punishment (e.g., with prisoners) and sometimes not (e.g., with mental patients), but it is always done. Admission procedures are a primary way to "mortify" the self and can involve public nudity; photographing; body searching; disinfecting; haircutting; fingerprinting; taking a case history; or being assigned numbers, issued institutional clothing, told the rules, and assigned quarters. There may be tests of deference or obedience to help ensure compliance. In general, upon admittance, everything that reminded the resident of the outside world is taken away, and none of the things that formed the basis of distinction between the inmate and other humans remains. An old identity is taken away, and a new one is "issued." Many of these processes existed at Willowbrook.

As stated above, both inmates and staff face official and unofficial versions of what is going on, what sociologists call formal and informal social organization. Formally, they are subject to the rule-governed efforts of the institution to take away an old identity and substitute a new one. Informally, residents understand how things "really work," whatever the rhetoric of attendants, professionals, and administrators. They experience what Goffman calls the "underlife" of the institution, what occurs in reality day in and out. Inmates have to contend with attendants, professionals, and other inmates, none of whom behave in accordance with codified rules and regulations or even necessarily standards of decent behavior on the outside.

Wolfensberger (1989) wrote about the relationship between the formal and informal organization in human services. He noted that these often are in direct contradiction with one another. Thus, an institution such as Willowbrook would have a formal organization based around its rhetorically declared purposes, to care for and educate mentally deficient children and adults. But the informal, unstated organization would work quite to the contrary—with few persons being educated and many being made sick to death by just being there. This kind of contradiction between the rhetorically stated functions of a human service institution and its actual functions as observed in situ, far from being uncommon, is, according to Wolfensberger, highly likely when violence of some form is part of its actual function.

In many total institutions, the process of stripping away a person's identity and substituting a new one can be harsh, brutal, and even fatal. Goffman argues that to some degree such work needs to be this way because "resocializing" an adult person must approximate the original conditions of socialization, where the parent had complete control over meeting the child's most basic needs. One might think that children and adults who were mentally deficient would not need to be subject to forms of degrading treatment to "strip away" their old identities, as it appears they were at Willowbrook, Pacific State, and other institutions of their ilk. Goffman cites various mechanisms that are used by management to strip the identity of inmates. These include personal disfigurement (beating, shock, burning, cutting, and tattooing), humiliation (forced deference, deferential speech), contamination (public nudity, urination and defecation, and physical contamination with unclean bedding, food, and facilities), and social contamination (forced age mixing, rape, and in earlier periods forced racial and ethnic mixing). These were all things that could be found to some degree at Willowbrook.

Goffman also points out that after the initial period of being in the institution, various other forms of social control are used by those in charge. Because there is no segregation of roles, those in charge know almost all there is to know about what inmates do. Without privacy, there is no preserve, no place from which the resident can defend his or her actions, as these are all public. Regimentation and tyranny are also used to control inmates. Things are done in unison with other inmates— eating, sleeping, urinating, going to the pool, sitting on the lawn—and residents are generally "herded" to these group activities. The activities are done within an overall authority structure in which staff have the right to punish inmates, both formally and informally. This is where tyranny can, and unfortunately too often did, enter the picture. Even in total institutions where inmates were far less vulnerable than those at Willowbrook, staff exercise incredible power over residents.

Goffman notes that the result of these processes of stripping away identity and other forms of social control in total institutions is that the inmate, to some degree, can begin to seek mortification and to act in ways that would appear to justify it. This resonates with the ideas of Stanton and Schwartz (1954) that people are acting in these places in accordance with how they are being treated.[4]

Residents of Willowbrook and other state institutions had a system of formal rules that specified obligations and privileges. Inmates are generally expected to know the rules, to avoid breaking them, and to understand that they will be punished if they do. They also learn that conformity to rules can be rewarded through the granting of privileges and sometimes early release. Inmates also learn the institution's lingo, how not to mess up—knowing the ropes. Knowing the ropes to some degree entails understanding the inmate code of behavior, that is, the informal rules and regulations that govern the actions of those at the bottom. This is the other part of the inmate's world in a total institution, his or her relations with the other inmates. Goffman terms this process "fraternalization," noting that inmates

---

4. The function of taking away and substituting a new social identity can be organized as a way to dehumanize persons (e.g., as in Willowbrook) or ennoble them (e.g., as in a monastery). Research about concentration camps, for example, has pointed to the function of stripping away old identity and the substitution of one that is less human looking and acting, as a basic way to facilitate the work for the soldiers who had to actually kill and torture those in the camps. It is easier to treat people inhumanely when they look and act less than human. One example that has been studied concerns the use of excrement in concentration camps as a way to make persons look and act less human, making them more available to non-human treatment.

develop mutual support and a set of counterbeliefs and practices to those of the staff. In places such as mental hospitals and prisons, these responses can be quite sophisticated and organized, for example, as with ethnic gangs in prisons.

We cannot find any evidence of political organization of residents at Willowbrook; their fraternalization did not result in gangs and groups as one sees in other total institutions. Fraternalization consisted at Willowbrook of friendships and sexual relationships. Goffman notes that sexual relationships, even in an institutional setting, can add to a sense of closeness and identification. Goffman admits in latter parts of the book that he did not focus enough on other aspects of the resident subculture. He ignored the violent, nonaffiliative aspects of resident behavior with one another. Willowbrook, as most institutions for people with mental retardation, was very violent, not only in terms of violence by staff against residents. As we shall see, violence was an institutional motif, used by everyone at all levels. Resident-against-resident violence was extremely common and was also structured sometimes into a pattern designed to maintain order on the ward. Thus as opposed to prisoners, for example, the residents at Willowbrook had no way to form a social structure of their own, like gangs in prison. They responded to the conditions set up by the administrators and staff primarily as individuals.

Once after listening to a description of the deaf-blind ward at Pacific State, Mel Pollner, one of Goode's teachers, remarked, "Every place has its own cast of heroes and villains." That would have been true at Willowbrook, too. At Willowbrook, individual residents dealt with staff and other residents who were part of a cast of heroes and villains.

Thus, from the point of view of the resident of a total institution, a bottom-up perspective, one is faced with two distinct but related processes: those being administered, both formal and informal, by the staff and by those being lived with—that is, other residents to some degree out of the control of staff. These form two spheres of institutional life for the resident, both of which could be punitive, tyrannical, and controlling or, more rarely, kind, humane, and fulfilling.

When looked at from the bottom up, life in a total institution is highly controlling. A tremendous amount of social pressure is brought on the individual in order to induce conformity and desired behavior. Again, in some kinds of total institutions, such as concentration camps, the severity of these efforts can result in brutal torture and violent death. One cannot imagine that under such conditions individuals would have much power over their actions. Yet we do know that even in such places, there were acts of resistance, even political organization. In total institutions, much of what people do is in response to how they are being controlled and forced to act. Goffman points out that different strategies emerge to deal with the conditions of total institutional life. These strategies can be typical of a person, that is, a person can adapt one particular strategy and be known for that choice. But more often, "the same inmate will employ different personal lines of adaptation at different phases in his moral career and may even alternate among different tacks at the same time" (Goffman, 1961, p. 61). Here are some of the strategies Goffman identifies: (1) situational withdrawal, where the inmate withdraws attention from everything other than his or her immediate surroundings; (2) intransient line, a sustained rejection of the institution, flagrant disobedience, requiring much effort and paradoxically deep involvement with the rejected authority; (3) colonization, where the inmate experiences mortification as a willing victim, finding institutional life preferable to outside life; and (4) conversion, where the inmate takes on the staff view of him- or herself, acts the perfect prisoner or patient. This may not be a comprehensive list, but to us it points out something very important about people's actions within even such a controlling, captive environment.

One of the insights gained from the study of total institutions is thus that people have and make choices, even under extreme conditions where freedom seems so curtailed. They can achieve a kind of "freedom," even if it is exercised under the most controlling of conditions. It is a remarkable thing to witness, as did Goode at Pacific State and as Bronston and Reiss did working at Willowbrook. We remember specific children who fit into these different, let's call them "modes," of response. It seemed back then that these were ways of coping with the conditions that fit the personality of the individual. These different ways of acting signify different ways of making meaning of their immediate experience. That people act so differently under the same conditions indicates they understand their positions differently, and this is also a very important insight about what people say about Willowbrook. Even within a group of former residents, people will speak about Willowbrook in very different ways (e.g., "it was the worst place I could imagine," "I had friends there," "it wasn't so bad," etc). As mentioned above, it may not just be a matter of memory; these contrasting expressions may reflect different modes of personal perception and adaption while residents were there, as well as different conditions of life depending on time and place. Thus reports about how they lived and experienced Willowbrook express these actual differences.

Goffman writes, too, about the Staff World. Common sense would tell most people that working at a place like Willowbrook and living there were two very different, if directly related, matters. In addition, when Goffman uses the word "staff," he means specifically attendants or those who interact face to face with inmates on a daily basis. He acknowledges that he does not really address the differences in rank between staff members, except in very general ways, as much as he looks at the interaction between staff and inmates. At a place like Willowbrook, there were many levels of authority: an administrative staff of doctors who were in charge of the institution; physicians who were assigned to various buildings to supervise and who very much had authority in these buildings; nurses, social workers,

psychologists, occupational therapists, and teachers who had professional authority (and most of whom were White); and attendants (many of whom were Black
and Hispanic) who worked on the wards directly with the residents. Though at the
bottom of the ladder of professional status at the institution, attendants had tremendous power over the individuals in their care.[5] Goffman does not write much
about the differences in working at a total institution in these various capacities or
statuses, each of which involves different expectations and demands, and, importantly, power. Nor does he comment about the relationship between the formal and
informal organization of these different groups.

Sociologists are experts at looking at interaction, so it is not surprising that
Goffman focuses his analysis of staff on those most directly in contact with the
inmates. He sets up his analysis with the term "people work." The institution provides staff with a certain rationale, goals, and rules for how they are to treat inmates.
Goffman admits that everyday life rarely approaches the ideal, and Wolfensberger
notes that covert practice may contradict the ideal. Wolfensberger describes how
organizations deal with the fact that their workers become aware that reality and
rhetoric may contradict one another (see below).

For staff, inmates become "objects" on which "work" must be done. This
work involves control and management and often some reshaping or molding of
the inmate in the institutionally stated desired direction. While doing this "people
work," those involved in direct care are simultaneously subject to several powerful social forces. They must understand and manage the demands placed on them
by their superiors, which at Willowbrook would have been the professional and
medical staff. Such expectations are usually associated with standards of efficiency,
according to Goffman. Within this work hierarchy, direct care staff face the human
demands of inmates, which vary considerably in different kinds of total institutions. At Willowbrook, direct care staff had considerable range in tasks, depending
on the kind of ward one worked on. In buildings where more severely mentally and
physically handicapped children and adults lived, staff would have been involved in
bodily care, feeding, toileting, dressing, and perhaps limited physical therapy. On
wards with less severe patients, attendants would have been involved with different
kinds of tasks, especially those related to behavioral supervision and control, and

5. This is a general feature of total institutions and was as true at Pacific State as it was
at Willowbrook (see interviews and descriptions in Chapter 4). Attendants at both places were
rarely consulted or listened to by professional staff. They were there to do the work they were
told to do and did not participate in governance of the institution or even their ward. This
dynamic of not having power contributed to the staff's difficulty on the job. Because they were
not treated with professional respect, it became more difficult for them to turn around and
treat their charges with respect. This same dynamic is still observed in many human service
agencies today.

staff would also be subject to the consequential hostility and resistance of inmates to go along with what was being demanded of them.[6]

Thus, the attendant is in a kind of "power sandwich," with efficiency and control being required by those above and humane care and freedom being sought by those below. Staff are subject to these "vertical" social forces that constitute their conditions of labor. But they also produce for one another very strong social expectations and mutual sanctions related to their work together. These are "horizontal" social forces, group expectations and a culture of attendants in the workplace, which constitute yet a third set of powerful social forces shaping staff experience and behavior. Philip Zimbardo's work, which we will look at later in the chapter, illustrates how these peer group expectations powerfully influence the behavior of staff in total institutions.

One of the things Goffman explains in this section of the book is how staff are provided with a rationale for (whatever) practices are required of them as part of their people work. Goffman gives the examples of shaving inmates' heads (on the basis of keeping the inmates healthy), extracting inmates' teeth (on the basis of keeping the inmate and others safe), or giving women hysterectomies (on the basis of avoiding countertherapeutic circumstances from arising), all of which were done at places like Willowbrook. When staff are required to do things that are morally objectionable and difficult, they are provided with an institutional rationale, support for compliance by those above, and support from other staff who are being required to do similar work. As Wolfensberger (1989) argues in an analysis of human service institutions, when actual practices required of human service workers are in contradiction with stated rhetorical goals of an institution, workers are provided with ways of rationalizing or even making unconscious what they are actually doing. In fact, Wolfensberger states that the more severe the contradiction is between rhetoric and reality, the more likely the worker is to be unconscious that he or she is doing something wrong or bad.[7] This dynamic, as it unfolded at a particular place and

6. Reiss, who worked on a ward for persons who were largely independent and took care of themselves, visited a ward where the persons were not toilet trained and were highly disabled. During Reiss's visit, she observed one of the residents defecate on the floor, while being apologized for by a member of the staff. She left the ward horrified and disgusted. This reveals how "people work" at Willowbrook could vary considerably from ward to ward.

7. One of the most graphic depictions of people work and inhumane treatment of inmates of a total institution is probably Frederick Wiseman's documentary film *Titticut Follies,* named for the annual show put on by both inmates and guards at a state prison for the mentally ill. The film is a veritable survey of phenomena identified in Goffman's analysis. It captures the controlling and often inhumane treatment of the guards but done in such a way as to be unconcerned with the fact that they were being filmed. The film showed that, among many other things, guards had become so accustomed to doing these things as a matter of daily routine that it had become natural and acceptable to them and that they were unaware that what they were doing

time, constituting a sui generis reality, needs to be understood in its own right if one wants to understand why staff acted as they did at places such as Willowbrook. Another kind of social dynamic, one of affiliation and the ability of staff to resist and see through institutional rhetoric, requires yet a different explanation.

Goffman notes that the total institution provides opportunities for a more sympathetic relationship between staff and inmate, what he calls "role release," where the usual social distance and power asymmetry is suspended between these two groups. He argues that certain ceremonies play this role in total institutional life, for example, the house organ (i.e., the newsletter, which at Willowbrook was called *Plain Talk*[8]), the annual party, the Christmas party, the institutional theatrical, and the open house,[9] all things found at Willowbrook. These events perform a certain "safety valve" function in total institutions. They did at Pacific State and Willowbrook.

---

would look to an outsider as brutal or morally wrong. In one instance, Wiseman captures a prolonged exchange where staff horribly taunt and tease one inmate until he exhibits, to use Stanton and Schwartz's (1954) term, "heightened symptomology." The sequence shows how institutional culture and group ways of seeing things had become dominant in the staff's actions and that, despite their very severe treatment of this person, they had virtually no sense that they were doing something wrong.

8. The September 1963 edition of *Plain Talk,* a copy of which is in Goode's possession, is four double-sided legal pages and includes stories about community organizations and staff members, announcements, a building-by-building news column titled "Here and There," for sale ads, thoughts for the day, a building-by-building "Chit Chat" column, and a building-by-building column titled "Gripes," wherein various complaints and reservations are expressed. In the particular edition Goode has, there is an announcement of a Twenty-Five Year Club (persons who had worked for the state for 25 years), which included mostly members of upper administration (the director, assistant director, nursing director, and other professional staff). Members of this group constituted an institutional power elite that basically ran Willowbrook without input from those below. This in-house organ was a big production. To have put it out each month required much effort and care. It signifies, partly at least, that the administrators at Willowbrook understood the value of having a means to distribute (and mold or shape) information at the institution.

9. Goffman notes that when total institutions hold open houses, they produce a reality that is intended for visitors only. Generally speaking, they have to manage their social image. "All the glory disappeared as quickly as it had appeared," commented one ex-mental patient about an open house. This is something known to every staff or resident. The institution needs to be careful about the way it presents itself to outsiders and to carefully conceal the reality of institutional conditions from visitors, so it "dresses up." At Pacific State, for example, there was an Office of Public Relations that conducted tours for physicians and other visitors. These visits were carefully orchestrated and went to specific wards, usually what were called Hospital Improvement Program (HIP) wards, which had additional funding for staff and equipment, and to a ward specifically designed for the purpose of entertaining touring guests. Finally, there was an auditorium, where a final show was given to the visitor. They were never taken to the back wards or allowed to roam unescorted. It was careful management of the institution's public image. Willowbrook had many open houses, and they all would have had this character.

Those who worked at Willowbrook and places like it were appreciative of the fact that residents had their own view of themselves that emerged out of their fraternalization. In subsequent chapters, you'll read observations, especially from Jean Reiss, showing that staff understood the kind of lives the children lived and why they acted in disturbed and disturbing ways sometimes. Staff understood naturally how children were constructing identities for themselves, in reaction to the conditions of life imposed on them. Even when they condemned what residents did, staff understood its social logic. In practice, we believe, people who worked on the wards appreciated the different identities afforded to the children and to some extent their own role in that process.

Experimental Social Psychology and Behavior in Institutions

A good question relevant to reading about life at Willowbrook is why there was so much violence there, especially if we assume there was nothing particularly remarkable about staff or residents that would have biologically or psychologically predisposed them to be either aggressive or passive. To help answer this question, there are another set of studies from the field of experimental social psychology that very much inform how we should appreciate behavior in total institutions. These include the work of Solomon Asch, Stanley Milgram, and Philip Zimbardo, all of which profoundly demonstrate the power of group expectation on human activity and perception. The topic was of particular interest in post–World War II social science, perhaps stemming directly from the recently witnessed inhumanity of that war. The question of personal responsibility and collective action, of the relationship between moral agency and political authority, understandably loomed in the minds of many people.

Asch's work, published in the 1950s (e.g., Asch, 1955) dealt with the effects of group pressure on perception and verbal behavior. In one of his most well-known experiments, a group was asked to compare the lengths of two lines projected onto a screen. Except for one actual subject in the experiment, the group was composed all of Asch's accomplices. At one point in the experiment, the accomplices all said that a line that was obviously shorter was longer than the one that was actually longer. This put the subject in a position of having to disbelieve his or her eyes in order to comply with the other group members' reported perception. Many subjects, especially when none of the accomplices reported the correct answer, went along with the group opinion. If one of the accomplices in the group was willing to support the real subject, the subject's compliance to reporting the "wrong" answer went down dramatically. Asch's work clearly demonstrated the effects of group pressure on individuals' willingness to say something they did not believe.

Following Asch was the publication of Stanley Milgram's work on obedience to authority. Milgram (1965) published the first results of a series of experiments designed to show how people would react when told to do something that was against their moral beliefs. He created another fake situation, what is called in experimental psychology a "facade," in which subjects were made to believe that they were electrically shocking someone to that person's great personal injury and even possibly death. Milgram's work became infamous in the annals of experimental social psychology. Milgram also produced a black and white video of his experiment, which was widely distributed in colleges and universities in the early 1970s, when his work was both highly acclaimed and criticized.[10]

Although part of Milgram's notoriety surrounded the ethics of his work, its results captured social science's attention. Ethical or not, he set up a situation in which people thought that they were delivering electric shocks to a person who was complaining of chest pains and then eventually remained silent and could well have had a heart attack or seizure. The "real" subject sat at a shock generator that (he thought) was delivering severe electric shocks to another subject in the experiment. The fake story told to the real subjects was that this was an experiment in the use of electric shock in learning. The subject at a shock generator was told to read word pairs to a fake subject in another room whom he could not see and could hear only through speakers. The fake subject (a confederate of the experimentor) was asked to remember the different word pairs. When he got an answer wrong, the real subject was to deliver a shock from the generator. The shocks escalated as the experiment progressed, from mild to moderate to severe, as labeled on the generator. Through the speakers, the real subject heard reactions to the shocks, even light ones, from the fake subject. As they got to the severe level of shocks, screams were heard through the speakers and then complaints about the learner having a

---

10. Milgram's experiment continues to fascinate us. There have been several recreations of Milgram's work including *The Tenth Level,* a 1975 production for CBS television starring Ossie Davis, William Shatner, and John Travolta. A 2005 film, *Atrocity,* is a re-enactment of the experiment. Chip Kidd's 2008 novel "The Learners" is about the Milgram experiment, and features Stanley Milgram as a character. "The Milgram Experiment" is a 2009 film by the Brothers Gibbs that chronicles the story of Stanley Milgram's experiments. For a more complete list of media representations of Milgram's shock experiment see the Wikipedia article on "the Milgram experiment." There is a reason for this continued fascination, the way the experiment so clearly illustrates a deeply felt social dynamic, compliance to legitimately perceived authority. This dynamic will be critical to our interpretation of what happened at Willowbrook.

heart problem, that his heart hurt him, and so forth. The real subject was instructed by the experimenter to proceed with the shocks in spite of the protests, yells, and screams of the learner. At one point, the fake subject did not respond, and the real subject, those who had gotten that far, was instructed by the experimenter to continue to deliver high-level electric shocks. No subjects detected that the experiment was a deception. They continued without real knowledge of the status of the learner, who, given the escalation of protests and screams and then total silence, could well have been dead.

There were no real shocks given, and the feedback from the fake subject, the learner, was (in one experimental condition depicted in a film of the experiment) actually tape-recorded, preprogrammed responses designed to slowly bring the real subject to a point where he (all subjects of his original experiments were men) is asked to hurt someone, or at least so he would believe, for the sake of the experiment. The real subject would have believed that he had hurt the learner repeatedly, at escalating levels of shock, until finally the learner did not or could not respond and was silent.

Under these conditions, over half of the adult male subjects shocked the learner to the point where he could have, again given what they were hearing through speakers, been seriously injured or even dead. In the film made by Milgram, he follows one subject for a long period of time, showing the escalating tension and pressure as the subject proceeds up the shock generator and the fake subject's protests escalate in severity. It is evident from watching the real subject that he feels extremely tense in the situation. At one point, when the fake subject does not respond, the real subject refuses to continue, turns to the experimenter, and asks whether he can check on the learner to see if he is all right. The experimenter says no and that the real subject needs to continue with the experiment. The distraught subject turns to the experimenter and says he will not take the responsibility. The experimenter responds and says, "I will take the responsibility. Please continue." The real subject then returns to the generator and continues to shock the fake subject at the highest level of shock, even though the fake subject is silent and does not respond.

This moment in the experiment is a sociologically significant one. It captures a person giving up his own agency in a matter he thought to be of dire consequences, in this case with much angst and anguish, because of the expectations of another person in the situation. In the end, he went ahead, with minimal prompting from the experimenter, and continued to shock a person whom he believed "might be dead in there."

Milgram studied the effects of proximity on how subjects behaved. He found, consistent with what common sense would tell us, that the closer and more directly available the authority figure giving the instructions, the higher the compliance rate of the subjects to shock the fake learner. When commands were given on a prerecorded audiotape and no actual person was issuing the instructions to continue, compliance was low. When the authority figure was present in the room, compliance with instruction was high. Conversely, when the learner, the fake subject, could not be seen but heard only from another room, the real subject was much more likely to shock the fake one than when the fake subject was in the same room and could be seen. Thus, it is easier to disobey authority and to do violence at a distance.

In general, Milgram showed the dynamics of authority in consequential situations. He demonstrated that under many kinds of situations, both face-to-face and less direct, many people will comply with the instructions of persons perceived to have legitimate authority, even when these instructions violate their own personal feelings and morality about what is right and wrong.

At this point, the reader might be thinking, *interesting, but what does this have to do with Willowbrook?* A lot, at least when it came to the attendants who were in a similar position to the real subjects of Milgram's experiments, asked to do things against their better judgment by a legitimate authority over them and often provided rhetorically justifiable reasons. An important difference between Milgram's subjects and Willowbrook's attendants, however, was the social context within which each operated. Unlike an experimental laboratory, Willowbrook had a climate of violence and of not openly questioning things that affected both staff–resident interaction and staff–staff interaction. Because violence was so prevalent in the institution, staff would have become accustomed to it as an unremarkable aspect of daily life. Also, unlike Milgram's subjects, direct care staff at Willowbrook became experts at handling violence as part of their everyday job. They had tremendous discretionary power over the residents, delegated via institutional rules and regulations and also via the informal social organization or underlife of the place. Finally, the authority and power of an experimenter in an academic laboratory during a short encounter is far less consequential than that of a superior at Willowbrook.

Probably the single clearest illustration of the power of institutional roles to determine behavior in a total institution is the work of Philip Zimbardo at Stanford University. His research became very popular at the time and even appeared in the *New York Times Magazine* in an article titled "A Pirandellian Prison" (1973). Zimbardo, a social psychologist, came up with a clever idea of building a fake or mock prison and staffing it with "normal" people. That is, he reproduced the social form of prison life but staffed the form with people who were neither prisoners nor guards. They were students at Stanford. What happened was so unexpected, and so striking, that Zimbardo's work appeared in journals, audiovisual slide shows, and film. Most social scientist do not have their work published by New York Times.[11]

Zimbardo built a fake prison in the basement of the Psychology Department building at Stanford. It had locked cells running along either side of a long, locked corridor. At one end was a dark storage closet used as solitary confinement called "the hole." Outside the locked area were the superintendent's and warden's offices, roles that were played by Zimbardo and his graduate assistant, respectively. It was run the way a real prison was. There were parole hearings, daily routine counts of prisoners, and other imposed routines of everyday life. All cells were wired for sound, and there was a video camera taking a shot of the main corridor. This provided much audiovisual data. The experimenter employed a consultant, a person active in the prison system in California, to ensure that conditions approximated those of a real prison. Zimbardo recruited paid student subjects for a 2-week experiment in which half would be arbitrarily assigned the role of prisoner and the other half to that of guard. Subjects were tested with subscales of the Minnesota Multiphasic Personality Inventory to eliminate those who scored high on subscales related to authoritarianism and sadism. He ended up with a pool of presumably relatively "average" young men.

Students who were assigned the role of prisoner were told that their civil liberties could be temporarily violated while in the mock prison and they had agreed to this condition. The students who acted in the role of guards were told that they would be working shifts, as regular guards, and while on duty would be responsible

---

11. Like Milgram's work, Zimbardo's experienced a certain public media cross-over, becoming the object of many recreations and representations. These include:

- In 1992, ''Quiet Rage: The Stanford Prison Experiment", a documentary about the experiment, was made available via the Stanford Prison Experiment website. The documentary was written by Zimbardo and directed and produced by Ken Musen available at: http://www.brcc.edu/library/videolist/videojustice.html Justice videos
- The novel ''Black Box", written by Mario Giordano (writer) and inspired by the experiment, was adapted for the screen in 2001 by German director Oliver Hirschbiegel as ''Das Experiment."
- In 2010, Inferno Distribution released the film ''The Experiment (2010 film)", which is an English-language remake of the 2001 film.
- The experiment was featured in a 2012 episode of Science (TV channel) ''Dark Matters: Twisted But True" in the documentary short "Creative Evil."
- ''Broadening", a play in the 2012 Dublin Fringe Festival was based on the Stanford experiment.
- Zimbardo's work, as Milgram's, became emblematic of a basic insight about human behavior—when persons accept a certain definition of a situation, the expectations associated with social roles within that situation are overwhelmingly powerful influences on human action.

for enforcing prison procedure and rules. The day the experiment began, students who were prisoners were arrested by the Palo Alto Police Department in the early hours of the morning. They were processed, fingerprinted, and then taken to the psychology building's mock prison. There they were issued institutional clothing (a baggy smock, flip-flops and a nylon stocking cap to simulate a head shave) and a chain fastened around one ankle. They were placed in groups in cells. The students playing the roles of guards were issued uniforms and reflective sunglasses so that the prisoners could not see their eyes. They were given rules of the prison that they were told to enforce. The prisoners were given these same rules and they had to obey. No other instruction was given to the guards or prisoners.

We will not attempt to convey to the reader in great detail what transpired over the next several days, as these can be read in the many published accounts of the experiment. Here is a summary of what is important for our current discussion.

In the early hours of the experiment, prisoners did not take the authority of guards seriously. This is indicated both in the recorded verbal behavior and by the fact that on the first night, prisoners staged a "revolt" and refused to come out of their cells. The guards on duty took no action against the prisoners, who had barricaded themselves in their cells. The experiment took a serious turn when the next shift of guards arrived the next morning. The guards on duty during the night were asked why they did not do anything about the prisoner revolt. The new shift said that the prisoners should not be allowed to get away with their action. Adopting a course of action, the previous shift guards volunteered to help the new shift deal with the revolt. This was not something they had to do, as they were technically already off duty, but they did so out of a sense of failure to have performed their responsibility. So they stayed on after their shift had ended to clean up the mess they had allowed to happen. The decision of these student "guards" was similar to that of Asch's and Milgram's subjects. In a situation where they faced peer pressure and a legitimated rationale, they acted as they did because of peer group dynamics and social expectation.

The guards sprayed CO_2 extinguishers into the cells to get prisoners away from the doors, then broke in, gathered the prisoners, assigned them new cells, and put the ringleaders of the rebellion in the hole. From this point on, the power of the guards over prisoners was exercised with little restraint, especially when one considers the actual circumstances of being in a psychological experiment on a college campus.

Guards escalated their control over the prisoners during the next two days. Abuses forced on the prisoners included conducting prisoner counts (where prisoners are lined up and asked to identify themselves by number) in a verbally and physically abusive fashion, including forcing prisoners to do push-ups while a guard sat on their backs. Guards rubbed blankets used by prisoners in plants with thorns, causing them to have to pick the thorns out by hand in order to use their blankets. Prisoners were force-fed. Some prisoners, in punishment for bad behavior, were forced to clean toilets with bare hands. On the other side, prisoners began to feel and act as though they were inferior and bad and as though deserved the punishment they were receiving, also reacting to social expectation.

Over the course of the first days, several prisoners began to have uncontrollable behavior, including anxiety and crying. Some were actually released because of the severity of their reaction to the situation, indicating that conditions at Zimbardo's prison were bad—at least some average guys were having problems coping with mock prison. This kind of "psycho-somaticizing" of stress probably also occurs in real prisons. But in real prisons, it does not earn one an early release or even a trip to the infirmary.

Within a very short while, conditions for the mock prisoners in the mock prison became in reality harsh, with abuses common. One could well ask, where were the experimenters while this was going on and why did they allow an experiment where people were clearly being subjected to severe stress continue? It is one of the remarkable parts of Zimbardo's experiment that both he and his graduate student assistant were exposed to the same kinds of powerful social forces as the student subjects. Each played social roles in the mock-up, superintendent and warden, and each began to act in accordance with the social demands of these roles, rather than as research scientists conducting an experiment. Their responses to events were tactical, from within their roles within the experiment.

The experiment continued in a somewhat out-of-control fashion until an odd incident occurred. One of the prisoners who had been let out early because of psychosomatic problems had said that he was going to come back with his fraternity brothers and break everyone out. When Zimbardo became aware of this rumor, his reaction was to attempt to transfer his prisoners to the Palo Alto jail, which was refused by the Palo Alto Police. Plan B was to break the prison down and put the prisoners in the hole. When the fraternity brothers came, they would find no prison or prisoner and leave. These were the thoughts that occupied Zimbardo, who himself had become completely immersed in his role in the mock prison, acting like a prison superintendent rather than as a social psychologist.

Zimbardo finally came to his scientific senses via a conversation with a colleague, who must have become aware of Zimbardo's lack of scientific attitude and shocked him back to his senses. Commenting on his own behavior as well as that of his subjects, Zimbardo writes:

> We were no longer dealing with an intellectual exercise in which a hypothesis was being evaluated in the dispassionate manner dictated by the canons of the scientific method. We were caught up in the passion

of the present, the suffering, the need to control people, not variables, the escalation of power and all of the unexpected things that were erupting around and within us. We had to end this experiment. So our two-week simulation was aborted after six (was it only six?) days and nights. (Zimbardo, 1973)

Like the guards, the experimenters themselves had surrendered to their roles in the mock prison. These roles and their associated expectations, rather than the logic of the experiment, had become the primary determinants of their behavior. Like the guards, they began to act in ways that were "appropriate to the prison culture." The guards' punitive and severe behaviors were a product of "their transaction with an environment that supported the behavior that would be pathological in other settings, but was 'appropriate' in this prison" (Zimbardo, 1973).

The student prisoners were subject to conditions similar to those of real prisoners and began to act like real prisoners within a short while. This phenomenon had been observed before, in other mock-ups. Zimbardo reported about staff from Elgin State Hospital in Illinois, where staff played the roles of patients for one weekend on a hospital ward. "The mock mental patients soon displayed behavior indistinguishable from that we usually associate with chronic pathological syndromes of actual mental patients: incessant pacing, uncontrollable weeping, depression, hostility, fights, stealing from each other, complaining" (Zimbardo, 1973).

Zimbardo's (2007) research extended his theory to other historical events, such as the torture of prisoners at Abu Ghraib prison. Arguing that situational and systemic pressures make good people capable of evil, Zimbardo makes the point that many working in institutions must fight the forces of obedience, conformity, deindividuation, and dehumanization or succumb to these pressures. Thus, there are no, or at least few, bad apples, only bad barrels. Put another way, constraints of the immediate situation, like those in large institutions, can override individual conviction. In the case of Abu Ghraib prison, it was not that the torturing guards were evil but that the government and military created an incarceration situation that was the product of political and societal pressures, pressures to which the guards acquiesced.

Looking at Asch's, Milgram's, and Zimbardo's work, we can learn about the social forces that shaped behavior in institutions such as Willowbrook. Most "regular people" are capable of finding themselves in situations whose demands and logic dominate their behavior and cause them to do things they think they "normally" would not. More often than not, they act in conformance with the social expectations of the situation, whatever their internal convictions and psychology. These experiments lead one away from explanations of behaviors of staff or patients at Willowbrook that are *psycho*-logical rather than *socio*-logical. What one observes at places like Willowbrook is not primarily the expression of psychological predispositions of individuals, or of kinds of persons (mentally ill, mentally retarded, criminal, etc). At Willowbrook and places like it, one sees a certain form of social organization capturing those who staff it, like Zimbardo's students. This is an extremely important thing to realize. Despite the fact that there was widespread neglect and even abuse, most staff did not act the way they did because they were sadistic or unusual in some way, predisposed to hurting or neglecting people, any more than patients acted the way they did because they were retarded.[12] Instead, both were part of a social organization in which, hidden from the outside, the all-powerful few control the powerless many, as defines the total institution. The difference between what happened in the experiments compared with Willowbrook was that at Willowbrook the power of this social form over staff and resident behaviors was far greater than what could be produced in any experiment.

Thus, the observations of total institutions by early sociologists advance the idea that behaviors within them, even symptoms, can be explained sociologically rather than psychologically. What we learn from social psychology and sociology should help frame the reader's interpretation of firsthand narratives about life at Willowbrook that appear in the following chapters.

Conclusion

These studies constitute a considerable corpus of knowledge demonstrating that behaviors of people often conform to their roles within in social situations. This can be true even when what is being required goes against their better judgment. This

---

12. Many people, lay and professional, think psychologically when they explain why people behave the way they do. Common sense, our "stock of practical knowledge," sees behavior as the outcome of a person's beliefs and psychological makeup. When Milgram asked psychiatrists to predict how many of his subjects would shock the learner in the conditions described above at the high levels of shock once the learner had stopped responding, the psychiatrists estimated that less than 1% would comply with the experimenter. In fact, more than 60% complied with the experimenter's instructions to continue. Similarly, if you ask students after seeing the film about Milgram's work how many think they would shock the learner to the end if they were the subject, almost nobody thinks they would. That is because people tend to think psychologically and fail to understand that social forces can override one's beliefs and better judgment. Many students, too, tend to think psychologically about Willowbrook. Staff were "sadistic"; patients were "crazy" or "retarded." This is why it was such a bad place. It is to correct this very incorrect interpretation that we present the works discussed in this section. Most worrisome is the results Milgram (1965) found when replicating the experiment with a group, similar to that of Asch, in which only one member was a real subject and the others accomplices. Under this condition, when the group indicated no desire to stop shocking the unresponsive "learner," virtually no actual subject protested. This latter condition much more approximates "real life."

aspect of human behavior maximizes the possibilities for various kinds of social pathology to be produced by those staffing a socially dysfunctional system. This sociological orientation becomes critical when reading the narratives about life at Willowbrook.

What is interesting, though, is that not all research about total institutions reports exclusively negative findings. Not everything that happened at such places was abusive or horrible. The "good" of total institutions is rarely written about, probably because it occurs in the main under conditions so horrible and degrading that to bring up contrary examples is often only to prove the rule and also perhaps perceived as undermining of an appreciation of the overall inhumane conditions. Relatively early on, in Braginsky, Braginsky, and Ring's 1969 book, *Methods of Madness: The Mental Hospital as a Last Resort,* the researchers noted that the mental institution afforded residents certain benefits, including relief of responsibilities usually required of people on the outside. The word "resort" in the book's title is used ironically. The authors noted that many recidivists (people who return to total institutions) may have "good reasons" for doing so, including the care they receive there, relief from the normal responsibilities of daily work, friendships and romances with other patients or with staff, and the availability of other benefits of hospital life, both official and unofficial. Although residing at Willowbrook offered residents few benefits and few opportunities for close and nurturing human relationships, it would be a mistake to think that these did not exist. Staff members extended themselves sometimes extraordinarily to help particular residents. Residents fell in love with each other. Staff fell in love with residents—relationships that were both illegal and immoral. (A medical director at Pacific State once commented about them, "They are always confused but not always abusive.)[13]

Some readers may interpret our inclusion of an understanding of the sociology of institutions as a kind of apologia for them and the actions people took within them. It is not. Understanding what went on at Willowbrook, during the Holocaust,

---

13. Although this sounds like a completely callous and perhaps even ridiculous comment, 30 years after it was said, we can understand what he meant. While at Pacific State, Goode heard about a couple of staff members who had formed relationships with residents. Although he did not know the staff involved, those who did told him that both were very nice people but a little "disturbed." One of these staff expressed the desire to marry one of the residents. This may seem incredible to a naive reader, but from the perspective of a person who spent much time in such a place, you could not ask for a more perfect environment in which to become confused about what is right and wrong. What this medical director meant was that the people involved in such relationships did not think that they were doing anything to hurt the resident or patient involved; sometimes they believed quite the reverse. It is logical that there would have been staff–resident romances, hetero- and homosexual, in every institution. We are sure readers who worked at state hospitals could supply many of their own examples.

or in other collective tragedies in history does not require forgiving those involved; nor does it require demonizing them, especially because 'they' were, in fact, just 'ordinary' people. This is one of the basic lessons from the Holocaust. An analysis of dynamics is not a framework to dispel or mitigate responsibility. The intent of including this material is to tell what we know sociologically about behavior in places like Willowbrook and to point out that in reading the narratives, one may be tempted to think that the stories are about people different in some qualitative way from oneself; *they* were "retarded," the staff "sadistic," "uncaring," and so forth. Instead, these are stories about people just like you or us, but people who found themselves in a bizarre, alien landscape not of their own making, requiring of them a complete change in seeing, thinking, and acting.

4
Day-to-Day Life at Willowbrook

As noted earlier, little has been written about everyday life at Willowbrook beyond what is described in newspaper articles, television news stories, and the documentary film Unforgotten. The most recognized book written about Willowbrook, *The Willowbrook Wars* (Rothman & Rothman, 1984/2009), focused on the legal and political movement to close the school, giving scant coverage to day-to-day life there, except to note what the popular media already observed: the stench, the maltreatment, and the failures. These are general observations and were not intended to establish an empirically based historical record of life at the institution. The book is the seminal work about Willowbrook and does an excellent job in presenting the social and political forces that came into conflict during the years following the Willowbrook exposé, but it was not intended to, and does not, inform us about the details of everyday life at the institution.

Another book, *Willowbrook: A Report on How It Is and Why It Doesn't Have to Be That Way,* was written in 1972 by Geraldo Rivera after his experience exposing conditions there. It is a moving account, its content in many ways recapitulated in later broadcasts he did on this subject, and captures the horror of the conditions there, the emotions one might have felt as an unknowledgeable outsider coming upon such things, and the reflections Rivera had at that time about building something better for people with cognitive limitations. But the account is not science, is not an analysis of the institution, and does not begin to reveal Willowbrook's inner workings and kinds of events that will be found in this volume. The film *Unforgotten* is similar. It is a moving account of the experience of the families featured in the movie. It does expose the viewer to the horrors of the place, at least to some degree. Although it contains vignettes about life related to the institution (some of which we include), it reveals much more about how families reacted to having a family member at Willowbrook than about Willowbrook itself. In fact, as we shall see, families were not permitted on the wards, and often were not told the truth about what was going on. Thus, this part of our book takes up what has been largely glossed over in previous accounts.

What was life like at Willowbrook? What was it like to live, work, or visit relatives there? If we look at the sources available, an accurate response to these questions is that there is no one answer to any of them. As we already noted, there were many Willowbrooks, and there were different experiences people had while there. Life differed greatly depending on the building, who was working there at the time, and what was going on more generally politically and economically both within and outside the institution. Thus, the reader will find in these pages contradictory accounts on what life was like, sometimes reflecting these real differences in circumstance.

Willowbrook meant many things to different people, partly because of their own proclivities and sensitivities and how these affected their perceptions and actions within the institution. Accounts of Willowbrook reflect the position the person occupied and for how long, the time and the place, as well as the individual's sensitivities. These two dimensions—'real' differences in circumstances and different viewpoints about things—created what we referred to in the Introduction as a Rashomon of Willowbrook. The following are accounts of life at Willowbrook that can offer more concrete detail, providing a historical legacy of what went on at the school. Their consistencies, and inconsistencies, are part of the phenomenon of what Willowbrook "actually" was to particular people who lived and worked there.

Some readers may feel that there is no point reviewing the day-to-day social organization of Willowbrook, because what happened, happened, and we should simply move beyond and forget. We hope to convince them otherwise. We believe it is crucial to document and understand the details of what happened. News accounts often describe but do not explain, and explanation is crucial for understanding. Understanding is necessary, if not sufficient, to prevent future Willowbrooks, because the same social forces that created places such as Willowbrook still exist today. The same motivations to profit off of those who are least able to defend themselves and who are least powerful in the society still exist today. To think that Willowbrook is a matter of the past is a naive and incorrect view of our current situation. Understanding of that past is critical to our understanding of the present. Finally, Willowbrook, or at least places like it, can be "one budget cut away." No one, given the history of disability we have discussed, should ever think that places like Willowbrook could not come back in a blink of the historical eye.

It is important to consider some limits on the analysis that follows. Most of the evidence is selected from four different points of time, and even so, they are snapshots that just begin to capture all the complexity of Willowbrook. The accounts reflect our Rashomon effect: the social position of the person at Willowbrook, his or her personality and experience, the particular places in Willowbrook they worked or lived, and the particular time they were there.

We will use five major sources for our accounts: Jean Reiss's report of life at Willowbrook written in the 1970s while she worked there as a nurse; interviews of former workers and some residents done by College of Staten Island student Maureen Fusillo; interviews and statements made by William Bronston who worked at WSS as a physician; Helen Starogiannis and Darryl Hill's interviews of former workers recalling their experiences of many years ago; and data taken from accounts of life reported many years afterward by an early resident named Gena and written up by Goode. The accounts are retrospective and affected by the passage of time, sometimes clouded and perhaps faded recollections. Conversely, one is often struck by how vivid some of the individuals' memories of Willowbrook appear to be when recalled and how real their feelings to those describing them. This can be seen in the documentary *Unforgotten* and has been observed by Goode at events that have been held over the years where Willowbrook survivors have showed up.

Our data consist of first- and secondhand accounts mostly produced as part of research, personal reflection, or public presentations and that differ in some ways from those given in legal testimony and news media. We have included excerpts from one such piece of legal testimony, but the vast majority of the interview and ethnographic data we draw on are firsthand retrospective accounts produced in research. We blend these with observations made of other institutions, such as Fernald State School in Massachusetts (D'Antonio, 2004), Willard State Hospital in New York (Penny & Stastny, 2008), and Weston State Hospital in West Virginia (Pratt, 1998), and with what we already know from Rothman and Rothman's (1984/2009) book on Willowbrook. Goode provides additional observations from his research experiences at Pacific State Hospital during the 1970s.

So far in this book, we have reviewed some of the relevant history leading up to Willowbrook and offered some basic theoretical assertions about why Willowbrook happened. Now we will see whether, and how, available accounts of day-to-day life at Willowbrook support these ideas. We have taken data from the described sources, analyzed them, and organized them thematically. What follows integrates observations from all our sources and portrays selected aspects of life at Willowbrook.

Physical Environment

The descriptions of the physical environment of Willowbrook evidence the contradictions and inconsistencies described earlier, and for the reasons cited. This is clearly seen in contrasting the relatively benign descriptions available in Reiss's writings with those that appear in Bronston's statements or those of some of the direct care staff workers. Reiss, working primarily on a ward for children involved in research protocols who experienced a higher quality of life than on the larger custodial wards, visited other parts of the hospital only later in her career and then probably only to treat residents brought to the nursing station. She did not have much direct knowledge of the large, anonymous, dehumanizing conditions on the kinds of wards Bronston knew intimately.

The external physical environment of Willowbrook belied the events that took place there. Clearly, to most who visited Willowbrook, it seemed as if it was rather idyllic.

Reiss describes the setting of the school in a way commonly found in our sources:

> The grounds are beautiful. An entrance road winds between woods and wide lawns on which are spaced gracious, old willow trees. Pheasants and squirrels haunt the woods, all adding to the first impression of a lovely park, a quiet retreat. The main road continues past large, stolid red brick buildings, uncompromising in appearance, but somehow dwarfed by their surroundings. It soon becomes obvious that this is a place for children. Gaily painted benches, a carousel, sprinklers, swings and monkey bars abound, and indeed, in the warm weather there are children everywhere.

This romantic view was communicated widely to incoming residents. George, a resident at Willowbrook, said: "They told us it was going to be a farm, when I came there was no farm."

The many buildings were located around the largest building, Building 2:

> The largest building, in the center of the ground at Willowbrook, is designed like a cross. Four long wings are joined by a large central hall. Three wings, on one floor, were devoted to laboratories, and one wing reserved for boys between the ages of 10 and 19 years.
>
> All the seven stories of Building Two had a similar catchment area on the ground for articles that flew out of the window. . . . From the outside, Building Two gives the impression of having barred windows . . . [but] the windows are not barred but are composed of small panes set

Aerial View of Willowbrook, 1980

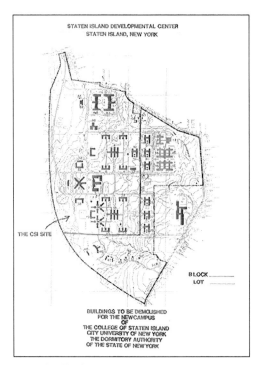

Map of Willowbrook, 1980

in horizontal sets. Each set of panes opens inward for about six inches, allowing air in but not much, one would imagine, out.

In 1969, according to the memory of a recreation worker, the wards were very basic:

> So it's like a big room and it's filled with 40 beds and then you walk out of that room and to the right of that room there's another room, and that's where the clothing room was. And it was a big thing that looked . . . like a big set of lockers but no front doors on it and some of the clothes were in there. . . . There'd be a day room, and in that day room would be maybe ten round tables, and around the round tables were . . . these big scoop chairs. . . . And usually there was a television in there.

The wing of the main building where Reiss worked was typical in some respects but unusual because there were only 20 boys who lived there in relative luxury compared with conditions in the nonresearch wards. Reiss notes:

> There were 20 white iron bedsteads in a big airy room, with brightly colored spreads and drapes. The dark green terrazzo floor shone with polish and the absence of any rugs. Beside each bed was a small battered locker in which the boys could store their personal possessions. They hardly ever had any personal possessions, so they stored whatever they could find; small pieces of pencil, scraps of paper, odd shaped stones, carefully hoarded slivers of soap or a well-chewed piece of bubble gum.

Adjacent to the ward was a large room that served as a playroom during the day: "High on the wall was a television set which was seldom off and practically never properly adjusted." Reiss continues:

> There were several card tables set around the room with bright plastic chairs beside them. Here the boys would sit and play with whatever toys the ward possessed at the time. Toys had a short life. Many were donations from richer, happier homes and had already suffered from hard use. Jigsaw puzzles were never complete, and model cars seldom had their full complement of wheels.
>
> The boys ate in a dining room off the main ward. There were usually six or seven boys to a table, and each had his special place. They were instructed in the sophisticated art of using knife and fork, no snatching, and the delights of having a paper napkin. New arrivals in the ward were frequently quite lost and bewildered at first but they learned more from imitating the other boys than from the attendant's instructions.

Each ward had its own presenting culture, how things were done there, that residents were forced to adopt. Willowbrook, like all total institutions, was not a place designed to adjust to the needs and wants of people, so much as it was a place with procedures and routines to which people were expected to conform.

Television was mentioned in most accounts of wards at Willowbrook and elsewhere. D'Antonio's (2004) history of Fernald State School is interesting because he imagines what effect television must have had on the lives of residents. They would all get to see what was happening in the outside world, how others lived, the fictions and news of American life, the warm rich homes of television families, the fun party at *American Bandstand,* as well as world events, such as the moon landing, the civil rights movement, war, and protest. What television shows were they watching and what impact did it have on their lives? Did they see the outside world as something desirable? What did they think of news reports involving Willowbrook? Was the political unrest in the outside world known to them? Or was television at Willowbrook more like the way it is portrayed in Frederick Wiseman's documentary, *Titticut Follies?* There it functioned as a kind of constant drone of sound that inmates learned to ignore or, if not, that drove them crazy. At Pacific State there were often radios, sometimes televisions, on the wards, that functioned in this latter way, offering anything but glimpses into the outside world. Ronnie, a ward aide at Willowbrook, summed up the impact of television:

> There were really no recreation activities there. We had a TV room. Most of the populations were lower-functioning, so they really did not watch much television. The TV was just there. It was something for us to do after we fed our clients and got them ready for bed. The TV was more for the staff to use.

Although these conditions of life clearly illustrate its impoverished quality compared with those of many children residing outside of institutions, they are nothing like the "subkennel" (G. Dybwad, personal communication, 1999) conditions that existed on some of the larger wards and buildings as described by Bronston.[1] First, we will look at life at a relatively privileged ward, such as Reiss's, and then look at how Willowbrook was on the larger, more custodial wards.

At Willowbrook, in Reiss's building, between the main ward and the dayroom were the shower rooms and offices and a small, disused storeroom, which became a playroom. Some buildings had wards that were large. The population in these places varied between 100 and 150 boys, according to Reiss:

---

1. This remark by Dywad was made in November, 1999 during a visit to the Howe Library at the Fernald School. Dybwad's remark is similar to that made during a visit to Willowbrook in the 1960s by another normalization pioneer Nils-Eric Bank-Mikkelson, "In Denmark we would not let our cows live like this."

They did not, at that time, have lockers by their beds or anywhere that they could store personal possessions. The few boys who had valuable articles such as a transistor radio or even a special toy would leave it in the supervisor's office. They often checked their glasses and hearing aids into the office after school, the danger of breakage in the ward was so high.

Reiss did visit buildings other than Building 2, and there she saw very different conditions:

One of the first buildings I went to was reserved for adult spastic men. Most of them had been, from birth, unable to use their arms and legs. The brain damage that they had suffered had been so severe as to leave them profoundly mentally retarded. Few could feed themselves, and fewer still were able to make understandable noises. Entering the ward that first morning was a horrifying experience. The almost palpable smell of incontinent patients and excessive steam heat was combined with grunts, groans, and honking cries. I slid through the ward, trying not to breathe and avoiding with an internal scream the twisted hands that seemed to clutch at me. I found the attendants gathered in the big washroom where they regularly started their shift. The room was completely tiled, filled with steam and the hissing of the shower hoses. All over the place were steel trolleys on which lay patients, mostly naked. Immediately in front of me was a patient whose limbs had taken on the shape of a pretzel. He was covered in feces from head to foot. A huge black man was standing, arms akimbo, looking down at him and saying, "Jesus, Henry, where's your moderation?" Catching sight of me the attendant added, half apologetically, "He just don't seem to know how to stop." Picking the boy up in his arms he carried him over to the sink and started washing him.

Elsewhere on campus, there were over 30 other buildings, most smaller, one- or two-story redbrick facilities. For example, there were the "Baby Buildings":

They are one story high, with easy access to outside playgrounds. They are modern in design, brightly decorated and have many conveniences. The wards are immense and contain, without overcrowding, some 50 beds in each ward.[2]

---

2. Other interviews describe the baby buildings as very crowded, perhaps indicating that conditions in these may have been variable.

Some of the staff lived on campus, recalled John:

> There was housing there for some employees that worked there. I know
> of a couple of attendants that actually lived on the grounds. What the
> requirements were to get the housing or anything else I don't remember
> but I do know for a fact that some of them did live out there.

There were other buildings as well: "The clothing supply store was housed in the complex of buildings near the heating plant . . . [along with] the shoe repairer, the upholsterer and electrical shop." There was also a school building about 700 yards from the main building.

Joséph described other features of the campus:

> All of the buildings were connected to each other by a series of tunnels.
> There were central kitchens. The food was sent down these tunnels on
> trays and up into the kitchens on elevators. The place had its own bak-
> ery, its own greenhouse, its own power plant, its own fuel dump, and in
> the back, its own laundry. It had a big commercial-size laundry.

Many people remember the Olympic-sized swimming pool that was a gift from veterans who stayed at Willowbrook when it was Halloran Hospital. As Reiss recalled: "Surrounded by trees it was a cool and inviting place on a hot summer's day." It was on the north side of campus, right near the area used for maintenance. Willowbrook had no air conditioning on the wards, so during the summers the heat and humidity could be brutal. Residents were brought to the pool to cool off but only during the work week. Each Friday the pool was entirely drained and refilled and became the provenance of doctors for the weekend. It was returned to the residents on Monday (note: without being drained and refilled).[3] Building 1 was the main administrative block at that time, and only staff visited it for supplies or discipline.

There was also a maintenance building that housed the gardeners and ground-skeepers.[4] According to Reiss:

> They mowed the lawns, trimmed the trees and bushes and planted a
> few flower beds. They also picked up the garbage that was strewn on the

---

3. Diane Buglioli, a former staff member at Willowbrook and currently co-director of an agency serving people with developmental disabilities on Staten Island, described this usage of the pool on several occasions at Willowbrook events held at the College of Staten Island.

4. This lovely enclave of buildings, still used to house maintenance equipment, perhaps once serving as a residence as well as a storage area, is one of the more beautiful parts of the Willowbrook campus. It belongs on any tour of the grounds and a fanciful person might be reminded, on a summer's day, of a diminutive version of the beautiful Queen's Hamlet at Versailles.

grass. Around Building 2 they not only picked up garbage, empty cans, bottles, and candy wrappers; though there were plenty of those, they also picked up shoes, clothes, towels, sheets, and even toys.

Rothman and Rothman (1984/2009) summarized some of the less idyllic aspects of the physical environment at Willowbrook: It smelled like urine and sweat; toilets and showers were often broken; water fountains were all broken; locked doors were found on every ward; there were no towels or toilet paper; and there was a lack of toys.

Arlen, a worker interviewed by Fusillo, recalled the toilets and baths:

> They had four toilets on each side of the bathroom. In the center they had a tub up as high as body level. That tub you bathe the patients in the wheelchair, those patients you couldn't put in the shower. There were no dividers between the toilets, and there was a big shower room with a washing wand so workers could simply spray residents down.

Living Conditions

Generally, the living conditions at Willowbrook were, as has been noted, offensive to any conception of humanity. Rothman and Rothman (1984/2009) described them this way: "filth ubiquitous, so that virulent intestinal deceases like shigella spread through the population. Staffing was minimal, one attendant to fifty or sixty inmates, and injuries common, with residents abusing themselves or assaulting others" (p. 15). A judge toured the facility in February 1973 and found conditions "disreputable."

These brief characterizations barely scratch the surface of the horror that was the experience of living at Willowbrook. In the 1950s, there appeared an article about Willowbrook with the headline "Living Dead at State School." It was intended to show how helpless and hopeless people were being cared for at the school. Had the headline read "Living Death at State School," it would have been more accurate, because for many Willowbrook was like a concentration camp, a living hell of neglect, endless nothingness, and deplorable conditions. It was a battle just to stay alive, and many lost the fight. This view of Willowbrook is no better captured than in the statements of Bronston, who as a physician had a fairly global impression of the institution and who meticulously documented the conditions of life. The following interview excerpts capture his characterizations of the environment at WSS:

> Willowbrook was an island in the state of New York that had been created with an internal culture with no access, no windows to look out, only steel doors, terrazzo floors and human suffering at a level that is

incalculable. [It was] a prostitution of every human being that came in there to accept and become complicit in crimes against humanity, which were the normal MO. This was framed in the rule books and in the duty statements and the records which are totally transparent, only really became properly revealed and translated, under the hand of the Federal Court when we finally filed suit against the State for constitutional abrogation. . . .

The place smells like excrement all the time. Or this incredible sickening odor of Pine Sol disinfectant, which comes in industrial cans of twenty, thirty, fifty gallons. It's mopped out on the floor by the inmates because there aren't enough staff to clean the place. . . .

The place operates just a cellophane's width above absolute chaos. Shrieking, physical outbursts, people struggling against the imposition of the tranquilizing drugs that are car-loaded into them. Any excess movement, any resistance, any human anything is immediately met with a two hundred or three hundred milligram shot of Thorazine to knock them out. . . .

In the meantime I was plunged into the two adult women's buildings and began to establish my grip on what the hell this new job was. They put me into the worst possible environment to get me to quit. Because this was truly the last place these women were ever going to be. There was no developmental anything going on. There was no school programming going on. There was just wretchedness. Wretchedness and suffering and insanity and inhumanity. Short of Dachau, or a concentration camp in Germany where they were actually burning people every day—they didn't have to burn people here. They needed to keep them alive because they needed to make money off them.

These remarks, taken from the interviews done by Kathy Cowan in 2001–2002, are in stark contrast to the life we find described on Reiss's ward. Yet even these statements only begin to uncover the horror that was life at Willowbrook. The following, taken from an interview with Bronston (2006) at the College of Staten Island, describes life at Willowbrook in even harsher terms:

[It is difficult to] get at the fabric of life in a 'city' like Willowbrook. This abysmal and underground city, this dark hellish environment of eight thousand souls, residents and workers together, you know it's as big as half the towns in the United States, you know. And it was a town that was "underground," completely out of the public sight, completely closed off, completely understaffed, completely underfunded. That essentially provided a border place for maximum human abuse. . . . I don't know whether you can imagine the gravity of the human abuse that was the norm, the violence that was the norm, and the inhumane—the dehumanization that was the norm there. I mean, it was a concentration camp! You have to understand the magnitude of what that means in terms of every minute of every day and every communication, every message, every signal that was sent in that place was aimed at crushing people or keeping them in a state of barely alive, and the consequent profitability for the system. That is as long as they were alive and the more smashed they were, the better, the more money the state would get from the feds in order to cover their daily attendance. Everything else was a holding action.

The following is from Bronston's interview in 2007:

What you're looking at is a "walpurgisnacht,"[5] a total pandemonium that exists in a continuous drum beat in that place, where everything is at the edge of "dyscontrol," at the edge of explosion, and everybody had to gird themselves, had to be ready, to repress any unique or individual expression, day in and day out, amongst people who were majorly disabled, and whose institutional sojourn aggravated their aberrant and bestial kinds of . . . inclinations because that was the norm, because there was nothing else there. So the workers, essentially, had to keep people in check. They had to somehow minimize the day-to-day carnage, which was quite extraordinary even with that effort. The place was pandemonium all the time, shrieking, stench, chairs flying, people unconscious, asleep on the floor after being drugged daily, burned both from laying against the radiators and injured by the daily detergent concentrate used to swab the floors. Many, many people were always drugged by doctors' orders, and they couldn't move, and they didn't realize, and they needed the warmth. You know, no clothing, bathrooms with no toilet paper, no flushing, everything broken, you know, most of the time . . . nudity . . . nudity and humiliation the norm, violence the norm. I mean, all the time . . . it was all blamed on "mental retardation." The notion was that the reason why things were what they were was because the people were screwed up. The people were no more screwed up than you and I, they were just in . . . an environment that was so antithetical to human behavior, civilized behavior, you know, role modeling, any kind of . . . decent

5. Celebrated differently in different countries, in Germany *walpurgisnacht* is a holiday on which witches gathered on a mountain to celebrate spring. It is similar to Halloween in the United States.

. . . progressive, educational input, which is why, you know, we closed the place down. I mean, the place was a concentration camp, it was, it was a crime against humanity in every corner and every nook and cranny. Every behavior, every relationship, the culture was completely prostituted to the enforced containment imperative of the state of New York in its design for managing this population.

Everybody had to make an adjustment just to survive: to survive disease, to survive low income, to survive the tyranny of irrational requirements, to survive the physical madness, the pandemonium of the place where at any minute . . . a plastic chair would come flying from nowhere. Shoes would come flying from nowhere. Benches would be thrown over. A person would come flying from nowhere and crash into you, or somebody would be clawing at you or bring feces and slam it into your chest—I mean . . . this was the definition of inhumanity.

A consequence of such conditions was dehumanization, descent, and death. In his interview with Starogiannis and Hill, Bronston said:

Nobody ever left the institution except when they died. They just matriculated deeper and deeper into the darkness and into the vulgarity of the conditions there as they grew older. As they left childhood and cuteness, as they left being children in the eyes of the people working there, and became adults, smelly and big and ever more broken instilled from bestial living with maladapted behaviors the violent side effects of psychotropic drugs, hope vanished and they were put deeper and deeper into the concentration camp in terms of its imposed nothingness. . . . People came in there and lost their status as human beings very quickly. I'm not saying they lost their status just as a citizen; they lost their status as a human being right away. . . . They were ground into nameless pulp, quickly, in order to not tax the institution to individualize, or to in any way communicate that there was hope for future release. The entrapped and savaged population only increased the income to the institution because, the more severely disabled an individual could be certified, the more money would come from the feds.

Willowbrook was not unique in the degree of deprivation. Before and after the famous exposé by Rivera, many state schools were reported to have similar conditions. Comparable images to those shown by Rivera were broadcast about Pennsylvania's Pennhurst State School, in 1968, on local television. The conditions at Fernald State School were described this way:

Dozens of severely disabled men—some of them stark naked—wandered aimlessly in large, cold, unfurnished rooms. Many were drugged to keep them quiet. Others babbled incoherently or rhythmically pounded on the walls and floors with their feet, hands, even their heads. Puddles of urine and smears of feces made the floors almost impassable. Attendants, at most two for a ward of thirty-six, were barely able to keep the men from harming themselves and each other. (D'Antonio, 2004, p. 49)

The following was observed in 1947 at Fernald:

In the North Building day room, puddles and piles of human waste littered the floor, and the room was filled with rhythmic moans, chirps, and shouts. [There was] a crowd of stooped and drugged men, many of whom were either half-dressed or completely naked. (D'Antonio, 2004, p. 124)

Similar examples can be found in accounts of many other institutions. The generality of such conditions nationally is challenging and important to explain about America's past. Willowbrook, for example, is an almost unthinkable abomination in almost every respect when viewed with history's eyes. Yet, as noted earlier, the Staten Island politician Dante Ferrari ironically observed that it existed in the richest city of the richest state of the richest country in the world.

The discourse on the conditions at Willowbrook contained specific details but also general conclusions, the kind of thoughts that develop over the years, with hindsight. There were several dimensions to this discourse in the interviews and documents reviewed on Willowbrook.

Jimmy, who lived at Willowbrook, conveyed the feeling of what living at Willowbrook was like:

I felt funny, in a funny way. It's like I felt something dangerous and trouble. It's like the bad neighborhood, the bad place, with bad people. Like people run away and get into fights and things like that. You could feel it, like something coming toward you, like the wind blowing, it was like dangerous.

Maria, a former resident interviewed by Fusillo, shared this impression of danger and violence:

Well . . . if the kids couldn't feed themselves, they would shove the food in their mouth.. . . They couldn't dress themselves; sometimes they would leave them undressed. And if they couldn't go to the bathroom, they would force them, or they would just forget to clean them up. They would throw them in the corner; let them stay on the floor naked and helpless. Kids took seizures. They would help them. But some kids they didn't survive. They died from the seizures. They would over-drug them. Give them too much medicine. Things like that.

Bronston observed that Willowbrook's big crisis was due mostly to inadequate funding. With a staff of 3,000 for 6,000 residents, budget cuts took away a third of Willowbrook's workforce: "So the coverage was so minimal that no programming of any consistency or scope or purpose or continuity could be implemented at the facility." The doctors and entitled staff used psychotropic medications to help maintain order.

Bronston's descriptions of the conditions at Willowbrook are vivid:

> The place was pandemonium all the time, shrieking, chairs flying, people unconscious asleep on the floor after being drugged, burned from laying against the radiators because they were drugged and they couldn't move . . . and they needed the warmth. No clothing, bathrooms, no toilet paper, no flushing, everything broken most of the time. Nudity and humiliation the norm. Violence the norm."

Irma, a former teacher, made the point that conditions at Willowbrook were not a secret:

> Everybody knew about this, it was not a secret or shocking. The state bureaucracy of mental retardation was paying millions of dollars in salaries to the people who were formulating this policy. This was the way of the State. It was condoned by everybody, lawmakers, politicians, everyone. This was what they wanted to do with the retarded. This was acceptable. When it was exposed, everybody became very righteous and said, "Oh, how could this happen? We'll never have another one of these again." They acted like this was hidden from them. When I worked at Willowbrook, nothing was hidden. There were no gates at Willowbrook. You could come and go and see what was going on any given day or night.

Irma emphasized the fiscal side of things:

> These attendants were getting paid very little. I defy anyone to go back to those days and work under those conditions and see if you could do anything differently. It was virtually impossible to [do] anything differently. The institution was run under very tight fiscal restraints and the numbers of residents was out of control. In the eyes of the state, the residents, the employees, and the institution were just not worth investing any more money into.

The one thing that communicates the conditions at Willowbrook is the smell. Everyone mentioned the smell. Helen, who worked on a research study at Willowbrook, described it best:

My first week in the building was truly an unforgettable experience. It was a scene from the classic movie *The Snake Pit*. The institution smell, feces, urine, sour milk and sour mops, was so overwhelming, as were the screams and inhuman guttural sounds issuing from the many severely disturbed patients.

Irma commented on it as well:

> The stench was awful. When you went on one of these wards for the first time you would vomit. You had to work there on a daily basis to get used to the stench, if you could. If you were a ward attendant the conditions were impossible.

Robert said: "Once you walked in there you never forgot that smell."

It's not surprising that so many people who lived and worked at Willowbrook cannot forget its smell. It haunts them to this day and Goode has heard many former staff and residents complain upon visiting the campus that the buildings still smell. On the other hand, many reported that while working there, they desensitized to the smell to a degree. One would have thought that such odors would have been signals to administration that conditions of life on the wards were unacceptable, even if they were not themselves working on or visiting the floor.

The smell would have tipped people off, and the administrators, if they had ever visited the wards. Unfortunately, the leadership at Willowbrook was not so involved in the day-to-day management, and when they did show up, things were often cleaned up. Irma, the teacher, was critical of the "hands off" administration during her time at Willowbrook:

> Dr. Hammond was rarely seen. Most of us would not have known him if we passed him on the street. He was like the "King of Willowbrook." He had a big house on the grounds and a chauffeured car. He attended the luncheons and did all of the nice things. He just let the system exist, no improvements or innovations. It was just business as usual. The people in charge of the status quo did not want to make changes. Changes make their life more difficult. Dr. Hammond and his administrators had a very nice life just letting things remain the way they were.[6]

John, a ward attendant, had no idea that conditions at Willowbrook were abnormal:

6. Administrators would not have been familiar with the details of life on the wards, but it is difficult to believe that they were unaware of the conditions in the various wards and buildings.

I never once, when I was working there, ever thought that the problem
was the administration, or the way that the place was run. I never had
any idea that there was any other way to treat mentally retarded people.

This is a shocking comment when one considers the conditions, but it is commonly heard.

Staffing

Staffing was a problem at virtually all state schools and hospitals. As at Willowbrook, staffing was a problem at Fernald State School. D'Antonio (2004) said of the
responsibility for keeping dozens of residents safe and clean for an 8-hour shift,
"the burden was so extreme that each month brought a dozen or more resignations.
It was not unusual for a new employee to simply walk away from Fernald after a
week, a day, even an hour on the job" (p. 48). As described above, overcrowding at
Fernald meant that conditions were less than perfect.

Any discussion of staff at Willowbrook needs to reflect what era of the school
one is speaking about. In the beginning, in the late 1940s and early 1950s, there was
not the same serious shortage of staff that characterized the institution in the late
1960s and early 1970s, which were partly responsible for the completely degraded
conditions there at that time. A discussion of staff members hired at Willowbrook
after the exposé and under the Consent Decree is entirely another matter. These
represent different eras in the staffing at Willowbrook

Certain traditions of staffing, reported at other state hospitals, existed at Willowbrook from its opening. There were always more women working in direct care
than men. At Willowbrook, the bulk of the work force providing the actual day-to-
day care for residents were women of color, often from the South. They, and some
men who also worked the wards, were part of a large body of direct care staff, often
with the title "psychiatric technician," who performed all the labor on the wards
with the residents but were not at all part of the decision-making process about
patient care in any way. This situation appears to have been a social fact for many
institutions of the day, which were very hierarchically organized, and it was, and is,
a notable characteristic of some agencies serving this population in the community.

In terms of power, right above the direct care staff were professional nurses,
who functioned often as representatives of administration on the wards but many
of whom also did not actually provide care or service (Bronston, 2005). They were,
as mentioned by several Psychiatric Technicians, not really trusted as they were
regarded as agents of central administration. Above these nurses in the hierarchy
were professionals, at Willowbrook mostly white men, who had, by virtue of clinical
or administrative title, power to order patients to have a procedure, attend therapy,
and so forth. There were different classes of professionals: those who worked for the
state and who were more or less permanent employees and those who worked for

private agencies, or were hired as private teachers and consultants, who had no job security and little power or authority.

Most of the staff, both ward attendants and nurses, were women, on both men's and women's wards; male attendants did not work in the female wards. According to one employee, because of the high resident-to-staff ratio, all ward attendants were able to do was change diapers and clean up messes. All the ward attendants interviewed for this book mentioned the same problem: They had received no training and were not properly screened to be childcare workers. The training ward attendants received mostly consisted of lectures on the etiology and development of mental retardation, first aid, and the rules and regulations of the institution (Bogdan, Taylor, DeGrandpre, & Haynes, 1974).

John, a direct care worker, put it succinctly: "I don't even remember having any training, or receiving any knowledge about mentally retarded people at all."[7] He continued: "The only training I got was from other attendants." Indeed, one past employee expressed concern because at one time, when Willowbrook was desperately poorly staffed, they would send buses over to Newark and hire people on the spot and investigate their references later, but there was no effort to weed out predators or those with criminal histories. Ronnie noticed that Willowbrook, as a state facility, hired people with criminal records and those coming off public assistance, without any screening or training.

As described by Bronston, physicians ruled over the particular buildings they were assigned. They had authority about what occurred on the wards but were expected to conform to the status quo of procedures as defined by the central administration of the institution—that is, as defined by the highest level of authority there, the director and assistant director who served through political appointment via the New York State Department of Mental Hygiene. Generally speaking, physicians who worked at Willowbrook and other state institutions across the country did not do so because of a deep-seated commitment to helping children with disabilities. Typically, they did not have specific training in medical or developmental services for this population. Rather, they ended up at such places because of issues, personal and or professional, that mitigated against gainful employment in more socially valued parts of medicine. This general sociology of staff at Willowbrook, with some minor changes and additions, continued for some 30 years of Willowbrook's operation, changing significantly only when budget cuts created a staffing crisis in the late 1960s and then again when the Consent Decree required an immediate, massive influx of staff in the mid-1970s, which as the reader will see had surprising outcomes.

7. There was a manual for workers at Willowbrook that was in use in the very early years. It was, according to Herbert Grossman, a past president of the American Association on Mental Retardation and witness at the Willowbrook trial, somewhat unique, indicating at least an initial intention of providing training for workers. By the time John arrived at Willowbrook, that training had disappeared.

It is important to understand that, by and large, the source of the problems at Willowbrook, including abuse, were not the direct care staff. This is sometimes assumed by those who are unfamiliar with such places and who interpret the bad acts engaged in by staff as evidence of their being bad or sadistic people. Although such people undoubtedly did work at Willowbrook, they were a relatively small minority. The idea that they caused conditions to be as they were is far from the truth. More accurately, they may have contributed to an overall atmosphere in which abuse was tolerated and in which telling about it could be dangerous, but it would be incorrect to blame these staff for the organized and institutional conditions of neglect and abuse that existed there.

The staff's position was complicated, as described by Bronston, who also provides an overview of the general power relations that existed at Willowbrook:

Most of the workers were trapped in the middle between management union control and a very nationalist, very conscious kind of organization that was not a revolutionary structure but Black power movement, which was a crucial structure in those days. So the workers were paralyzed. They had no place to go. They had nothing to work with. If they raised a stink so much as that they were out. There was a tremendous struggle to just get acclimatized in order to be who they were because these were not . . . I mean you are talking about the soul of American culture, mothers, aunts, sisters, cousins who came in to care, and they were provided with this role model, mostly from these "monstrous white foreign born doctors" who would not touch anybody. The place was utterly life threatening because of the diseases that were there: hepatitis of all sorts; intestinal parasites of all sorts; strictly from public health kind of problems; universal scabies in the place; malnutrition of every conceivable kind. And then, of course you are in a closed environment. . . .

So, the great lesson is, you have a closed environment, you have human abuse. You describe a group of people by their devalued status, you have a killing field. Nobody has an identity. Nobody has a name. Nobody has any individuality. Nobody had access from the outside to anybody on the inside. Nobody crossed that door. When a family would come to see their relative they were on the outside of that door waiting for the person to be rolled out. They would take them out, deal with incredible problem of the behavioral situation, the total involution the total autism that was created by an environment that would kill us. Anyone who could survive one or two years in that place was made of steel. And the workers were made of steel too because they were like this [makes gesture of being pulled in two directions] every minute, anything could happen. As much as from behind them, you know the nurses who were mostly white, as from in front of them, the people they were taking care of. And I tell you those people [the administration] were horrible. They were arrogant. They used their power to suppress any dissent. They defined the situation as only solvable by them, in the best possible way, because they were in charge. It couldn't be done any better. (Bronston, 2005)

Bronston further specified what conditions were like on the wards in his interview with Starogiannis and Hill:

The workers were involved heavily all the time, because there was always some crisis and major effort to manage the lives of 50 people in a closed system. The system demanded huge and meaningless paper work creating and making records constantly. There was usually only one nurse on duty.

What happens is that the workers there had to maintain order and they had to maintain a decorum which essentially meant keeping people essentially contained and under rigid control all the time. Remember the objective here is to get through the day without getting injured, to get through the day without major incidents that could get you fired . . . get through the day in a way that you could get home intact and to have successfully managed a total purgatory of wretched souls. So the workers each reacted differently with an eye to survival and sanity. There were variations depending upon who you are talking about, what ward you are on, who's on that ward given age differences, physical disabilities, degree of embedded institutional behaviors, very dangerous infectious disease levels in the population.

Insufficient staffing and the related problem of overcrowding among residents became a norm for Willowbrook and other similar institutions in the day. There always seemed to be too few employees, and those who were there were inadequately trained. There was an extremely high turnover rate in the workforce generally, even if a core of workers stayed the course and remained there for almost their entire careers (as mentioned in several worker interviews). Basically, Willowbrook was no better than Fernald State School, where one attendant was often responsible for keeping "dozens and dozens of residents safe, clean, and sheltered for eight hours straight" (D'Antonio, 2004, p. 48). Just as in the Fernald girls' dormitory, at Willowbrook one attendant supervised 80 children.

Rothman and Rothman (1984/2009) documented staffing shortages at Willowbrook as early as 1967, when an investigation from the American Association on Mental Deficiency found 59 of the 172 nursing positions filled. Then, in 1971, Governor Rockefeller slashed funding, and there was a hiring freeze. Willowbrook already had 280 staff vacancies; by mid-1971, it had lost 22% of its staff; 633 staff were lost through attrition. But staff shortages of a fairly severe level were noted by Berman as early as 1957.

The high rates of staff turnover are obvious and clear from Reiss's accounts. She recalled about conditions in the late 1960s to 1970s:

> Willowbrook had, and I believe still has, a very high turnover of employees, particularly ward attendants. Many found the work tedious and depressing; some could not cope with the necessary changes of shift, especially the unpopular 3:00 to 11:00 PM shift. Some only worked at Willowbrook until they could obtain a more congenial job.

She continued: "As the freeze continued, the remaining employees grew increasingly resentful; sickness and absenteeism rose, compounding the problem." Thus:

> The staff was plainly insufficient. A freeze on hiring had so diminished the number of available employees that, in many wards, it became a problem to get even the routine work of dressing and feeding the patients completed. Each morning became an emergency, the remaining staff growing more resentful and exhausted as the weeks went by.
>
> Very few of the wards had enough staff to carry out even the essential routine. The endless round of feeding, washing, changing and mopping had to be carried out. Cleanliness is not just a fetish in hospitals, it is essential. It is the same in an army barracks, or prison, or any place where a large number of human beings are concentrated. The physical maintenance of the patients and surroundings occupies most of the time available.

Most people who worked at Willowbrook estimated the populations somewhat similarly across the years. Many remembered there were 35–50 people in each ward, with four wards to a building. For example, in 1962, there were 8.1 patients for every attendant. Building 22 had 266 adult female residents in the severe range of mental retardation. Irma estimated ward size even larger: between 75 and 125 people on a ward. These differences may be attributed to a variety of reasons.

At the large residential dorms, Robert noted the lack of staff: "There were never more than two attendants on a ward. Okay? Each ward had thirty-five to fifty residents and there were never more than two attendants. At times there was one. It always seemed very short staffed." There would also be a nurse on each ward.

Joséph described what he said was not just overloaded staff but conditions so crowded that it made care impossible:

The beds were side by side in these wards. There were 60 beds in a ward that was not meant to have more than about 30. There were beds in the hallway, side by side. They had to climb over one bed to get to another bed. At night, I think, there were two attendants in charge of 60 residents that needed total care. Needless to say, it was nuts. It was not the fault of the workers. It was not the fault of the residents. It was just that the system was overwhelmed, with everything that was going on there.

Irma remembered: "The beds were six inches apart. They were so overcrowded on the wards. The residents would jump from one bed to another. It was packed."

A recreation worker at the school put it this way: there was such a volume of people, to get them showered, dressed, fed, and then toileted, there wasn't any way to do anything else with them.

Reiss corroborates Bronston's description of a work environment virtually filled with diseases. Lack of staff and disease rates were directly correlated. With a lack of adequate staff and overcrowding of the residents, disease became rampant. Reiss remembered that the "Baby Buildings," with 50 kids in each ward and communal washrooms, ensured a measles epidemic. Similarly, "Most of the diseases such as intestinal parasites, hepatitis, viral infections or skin eruptions became not sporadic, as they are in the community at large, but endemic. The staff fought a continually losing battle against ringworm, scabies, and diarrhea." This was also the general situation at Willard State Hospital; infection was always a concern as every communicable disease would sweep through the institution (Penny & Stastny, 2008).

Three of the past workers interviewed mentioned that they needlessly contracted hepatitis from the residents because they were not told it was a danger or that they needed to take precautions. Irma was working as a teacher in Building 78 with the kids who had been in the hepatitis research unit. She had 12 students; seven were carriers. Yet,

They did not tell us which ones were carriers. They did not identify them. After a while they got much more realistic and they started identifying which children were carriers. They would just tell you that these children were in Hepatitis Research, so be careful.

Even still, she had already contracted the disease.

Robert also caught hepatitis, and then he called in sick:

I informed them I had hepatitis and that I'd be out sick and that I had gotten it from there. They assured me that no one had hepatitis there, and there was no way I could have possibly contracted it there. That was when I first got sick. I sort of accepted that as the answer at the time.

But through my own, while I was sick and everything else, I know that just the color of the feces, the smell of the feces, the color of urine was distinct. The root beer color of urine. . . . There was no doubt in my mind that that's where I got it from. I remember calling them back up again. Eventually I never did go back to work there because while I was out sick I was fired.

Goode witnessed a similar situation at Pacific State, where workers were told to be careful with residents who were hepatitis positive but were not given specific training about how to be careful. Many workers contracted hepatitis, shigella, and other diseases that were rampant in the institution.

Arlen captured the essence of the workload of a ward attendant:

Let's say when I started, it was about 65 patients to maybe 2 aides. The nurses couldn't help you because they were so busy in the front taking care of real emergencies. Patients banging their heads with no helmets. . . . So we had maybe two aides maybe three, at 12 o'clock you maybe got a third girl and you have from 60 to 65 patients. It is not an easy job. . . . As you can bring one or two in the bathroom, you had four to eight toilets, so you filled eight toilets, you put your patients on, then you took two in the shower, so you have to thank God and hope to God they stay on those toilets. When you looked you have half on the floor, so you are running back and forth and you are trying to shower two. There had to be two in the bathroom all the time, because there were too many clients in there. And it was rough but it was nice. I really enjoyed my first ten years.

Helen told a similar story:

Each and every attendant in that building had a tremendous workload. Just the physical care of the patients was enough, but, in addition, they had to mop and clean their wards and handle the overwhelming laundry tasks. Then patients had to go the various clinics in Building 2. An attendant had to go along, thus leaving that ward short of help for at least an hour. On the ward, a severely disturbed patient had to be closely watched and/or restrained by the attendant, until calm. This, too, took an attendant away from the regular duties. Many of the patients soiled themselves badly during the day and so there were endless showers being given throughout each day. There was virtually no time for any attendant to really work with or teach a patient toilet training or the teaching of any personal grooming skills. The patients were too destructive and disturbed to be allowed any manipulative items while in the day room, there wasn't even a TV set in any of the wards. A small number of patients were calm enough to attend an hour of occupational training a day but that was all.

For Irma, the ratio of two aides for 55 girls was ridiculous:

How could they do anything other than just keep things under control? They certainly were not going to clean them or anything. There was a staffing problem. There was never anybody there. They just basically babysat to make sure that nobody ran out of the building.

Irma was a bit defensive when she explained:

Everybody says, "How could these people be so heartless and cruel? How could they let conditions like that exist?" Well, the people working at Willowbrook at that time were ordinary people. They came to work at Willowbrook as attendants and care workers. They were given very specific instructions as to what they could do and how they were to do it. These people were following strict guidelines provided by the State of New York. The guidelines were so ridiculous and the conditions were so heartless that you had no recourse. If you wanted a job, this was your job. This was what you did, if you wanted to keep your job. These were lower entry people who needed the work. Actually, they did a great job in the sense of being on a ward, alone, with a hundred people who are functioning on many different levels, from very low to high functioning, in this crammed space.

Helen explained that the conditions at Willowbrook were variable. During the time she worked at Willowbrook, in a ward that was involved in a research study, the number of attendants increased over 6 months in 1962, lowering the staff-to-resident ratio on her ward from 1:8 to 1:4.5. She observed:

The results, in even a short time, were amazing. With more attention given to them, the patients became calmer. As they became calmer they kept their clothes on. When they kept their clothes on they began to take an interest in their appearance and were motivated to learn some basic personal grooming skills. There was closer supervision in the dining rooms and so meal times became more human. The grabbing of food stopped and many patients began to learn to use spoons and sit in seats to eat. The weight of the outgoing bagged laundry decreased because the incidents of severe soiling decreased. The patients' weights

decreased, too. They were now getting outside twice a day and thus getting more exercise, as well as, eating normal portions and not grabbing
all available food.[8]

Irma and Joséph referred to these times as the "golden years," starting around 1969,
as new young professionals, including teachers, social workers, and physical therapists, came to work at Willowbrook. Joséph recalled:

> In the late 1960s and early 1970s, if you looked in the medical journals
> with regard to speech and physical therapy, all of the articles were related
> to mental retardation. All of the articles were written by people who
> worked at Willowbrook. Willowbrook was where all of the research was
> being done. There were a lot of good things to come out of Willowbrook.

It is a notable contradiction that this golden age occurred at the exact same
time that resources to Willowbrook were cut and conditions deteriorated to a
degree that parents and professionals sued the state.

Alongside and in contrast this golden age for the researchers and professionals
at Willowbrook was a worker "underlife" (as termed by Goffman, 1961) of booze,
drugs, partying, sex, and theft. Consistent with the theme of "many Willowbrooks,"
some remember this as a central feature of the institution and others do not. John
had seen the alcohol use among staff:

> There was quite a bit of drinking going on, like at the end of the days. I
> did work 4 to 12's also; I would fill in. There was some drinking going
> on amongst the attendants. . . . There was an attendants' nook with glass
> windows on two sides. They would just sit there, and some of the clients
> were intelligent enough that they would, for favors, for gifts, for candy,
> for soda, would actually keep the rest of the clients in there quiet.

Staff also enjoyed the relative social invisibility of their jobs and had what was
apparently a rich underlife at Willowbrook. As described in Chapter 3, staff were
subject to strong peer group expectations and behavior that very much set the context of their daily lives. It was common to hear stories about the staff parties. As one
worker put it: "Partying was an art form in those days. Every night of the week there
was something going on. Parties were at a person's house or the Buddy Buddy Club.
There was always something going on." The nurses and attendants who lived in a
residence on the east side of the campus always seemed to be hosting a barbecue
during the summer.

---

8. This is an example of the kinds of variation that existed within the institution, in terms
of both time and space.

Many interviewees mentioned that there were problems with theft and drugs as well. One employee characterized drugs at Willowbrook as one of the main reasons it closed:

> There were drugs. The drugs there were rampant. Again, having worked in most of the buildings, I would see that there was a lot of drug abuse. People were selling drugs and there were a lot of people that were using drugs, such as cocaine and heroin. Alcohol use was nothing. If you were just an alcoholic and went to work, that was minor stuff. In most of the buildings there were dealers. I think that the drugs are what finally closed it down.

He continued:

> At Willowbrook, it got to a point where you could buy meats, you could buy clothing, you could buy jewelry and you could buy drugs. Drug selling was a big deal. Most of the stuff that was being sold was brought in from outside. But some of the materials that were meant for the clients were disappearing too.

He had approached an office area:

> And people would just sit in there and roll their drugs, getting ready for distribution and going about their business.[9] It was rampant with drugs. I know they closed [Willowbrook] when the drugs started. They had an undercover investigation and they started arresting people and it seemed like it all happened. It all happened at once.

He believed that many of the people who sold drugs worked in Building 46, an administration building.

> The administration was aware of it. They had to be. You had to be blind not to know. You knew. You knew which buildings. They made rounds and the staff would be stumbling, you know, falling down drunk. It was tolerated, not that it was confirmed as tolerated. It was hard to do something once an employee became permanent in a state job. I have worked in other facilities and it was not like that. It had a lot to do with the way the buildings were set up. You have to have all levels of staff working together, not separately, because that allows for abuses to happen.

The interviews done by Fusillo provide us with glimpses into how direct care staff operated day to day. Not surprisingly, many attempted to make the best of what was a bad situation. Many also went beyond what was required of them, even taking children into their own homes to try and help them. Conversely, when looking

9. That is, would make marijuana cigarettes for distribution.

at these interviews, we find clear indications of mistrust because not all direct care staff conformed to high moral standards of behavior, with much evidence of stealing, abuse, drug and alcohol abuse, and other forms of crime. There is an aphorism, a few bad apples spoil the barrel, which was to a degree true at Willowbrook. In a place where the ethical thresholds were low or nonexistent, it was difficult for many to maintain a moral compass. Being morally unsure or uneasy was probably a normal condition for many.

It is thus heartening to find stories of the regular occurrence of acts of kindness and sacrifice on the part of direct care staff. Arlen thought the Geraldo exposé was hurtful to people who worked at Willowbrook:

> We got a group of children there who could not do nothing for themselves. The worse in the world, they threw in there. And . . . there was nothing to work with as far as clothes, personal things, soap, deodorant, powder, none of those things. Old employees on the wards used to take turns and buy it out of their own pocket. Since we didn't get no credit for that. We didn't look for credit, but we looked for at least decent words.

So when Geraldo brought all this attention to Willowbrook, "He made us feel as though we hurt these children, which we didn't." Arlen felt that there was a collegial spirit at Willowbrook, where everyone was pitching in to help out.

Others, like Irma, did not agree:

> Willowbrook was so big and so departmentalized that there was not a lot of collaboration between the social workers, doctors, and educators. If you were a social worker, what were you supposed to do? People were brought there to live and die. There was no future. It was the first stop and the last stop. This was where they were going to stay. What were the social workers supposed to do?

In fact, some employees spoke about the unspoken rules of working at Willowbrook. For one, you needed to "respect the chain of command." Joséph told this story:

> When I was at Willowbrook for a short time, I went on a trip to Central Park. One of the students was misbehaving. The teacher told me to get her a stick. She wanted to use it to hit one of the students. I told her that they were very clean in Central Park and they did not leave sticks lying around. When we went back to Willowbrook, I was brought up on charges of insubordination, because I refused to get a stick for a teacher so that she could hit a student. I was brought up on charges for this. I can never forget that. I said, "Wait a minute, you are telling me that I am

going to get in trouble, because I did not get a stick for somebody to hit a student with?" That was the mentality of Willowbrook. It was the chain of command. You couldn't break that.

There was a strong inclination among those who worked at Willowbrook to deal with problems without involving higher authorities in the administration. Arlen mentioned that if they could solve a problem on the ward, they would, without "taking it to the front":

> Like incidents. Kids would hurt themselves. Somebody would be hit. If we could cover it, we cover it. It was our neck as much as the next ones. Everyone wanted to lay blame when it happened. Because you were so short of help and actually why should you sit there when you see I am working like hell and a child's disturbed, so everybody's involved. So, therefore you try to clear things up as long as it didn't harm the patient too much, you try to clear it up amongst yourselves.

Some workers feared "upsetting the apple cart." They were aware they should have been doing a better job, and maybe reported abuses and problems, but then again, as one worker put it: "People get beat up. Car was slashed, and tires was messed up, you know?"

Ronnie needed the job and did not want to upset the apple cart either:

> I feel guilty. I did not do anything about it. I went to work. I did my job. If I knew stuff was going on, I would not report it. I needed a job. I was single, and I had a child. That was not really a good excuse. I never took any action. I did not abuse them. I went and did my job.

Why? Because:

> If you made a fuss, your car could catch fire. It happened many times. A friend of mine, who was mid-level, was very tough. She wanted people to do their jobs. She was in charge of the ward aides. She bought a brand new car and one night she went out and the car was in smoke. You could not prove who would do stuff like that. But, you knew.

He believed that many of the nurses and other psychiatric technicians were intimidated by other ward aides.

Such remarks would lead one to believe that an atmosphere of general mistrust characterized relationships between the direct care personnel. This conclusion, given the interviews and other remarks that we have heard over the years, is warranted—a sad fact of life at Willowbrook, Pacific State, and, one would reason, other institutions. At the same time, there were networks of people who, after years and years of working with one another, developed friendships and trust. These relationships existed within an overall climate of distrust and danger from the vast, anonymous, constantly changing workforce. These relationships were not a matter only of affection. The friendships in the workforce also had to do with survival and work at WSS—friends helped one another through rough times on the job, helped each other in job-related matters when possible, and looked out for one another's interests.

A question that arises, when one thinks about those who worked at Willowbrook most directly with those who lived there, who knew best the horrible facts of life, is: Why did they accept what they saw? Why didn't they confront what at some level they must have known was wrong? We have above some of the answers. First was ignorance about people with disabilities. Most workers did not have knowledge of disability personally and did not have anything to compare what they saw with. Next was an authority structure, of professionals, doctors, and regulations, which rationalized the system and told people working for it what to do (cf. Milgram and Zimbardo). Fellow workers did not want other workers to upset things, and there were definite expectations that a good fellow worker did his or her job and did not rock the boat (cf. Zimbardo). There was a ruthless administration that simply did not tolerate any worker, professional, medical, or otherwise, who did not go along with the program. As Bronston put it, for anyone without job tenure, all it took was one word "and your ass was out of there." For all these reasons, many people who worked in Willowbrook and places like it lacked the ability to step outside the social formation and look back at it, or they were able to do so but were desensitized to what they saw, or they were afraid of what might happen if they tried doing anything about it. Either way, they went along with what was being done.

Doctors and Nurses

Consideration of responsibility for conditions at Willowbrook is part of any account of it. One cannot help but ask questions such as: How could conditions like those found at this residential school for children be permitted to exist? In this section we consider the role of medical personnel in engaging in poor medical practices and allowing unhealthful conditions to become the norm. Bronston has commented about medicine at Willowbrook extensively, and his remarks are condemning in the extreme. They are a first-hand, observation-based account of the sorry state of medical affairs at Willowbrook. His remarks are very similar to what was observed by Goode at Pacific State. In a summative remark, Bronston states, "As physicians we were used to legitimize and rationalize that situation in the most unethical way, intentionally by the administration" (Bronston, 2007). Sadly, in even more detailed remarks, he documents the role of the medical doctor in helping to create and sustain the inhumanity found at Willowbrook. Consider the following, based on his experiences at the institution:

> My first responsibility was taking care of this mass of people who were not presented as people at all.
>
> The nurses stayed in their nursing stations. There was not enough clothing. There wasn't enough soap. There wasn't enough food. There was an overabundance of tranquilizing medication and the place was horrendous, the noise and the smell, and this was one of the better buildings. This was what was called the Baby Complex. I was initially assigned to Building No. 16 when I first came there. And so I worked in Building 16 for six months and what began to happen was—and I had a very personal relationship with Hammond, very personal relationship. I talked with him all the time. . . . I had to make sure that my judgment was valued and that my work was supported, and it was clear we had a problem.
>
> And I also had to meet with the other docs. There were about 20–25 docs assigned throughout the place and I began to realize that this was not my peer group. These guys were a different breed of cat. Many of them were immigrants.[10] Many of them were docs that couldn't get a job anywhere else. All of them had been there a long time. None of them mingled with the people on the wards, none of them.
>
> No women doctors. Men, mostly white men, mostly European white males . . . : Slavic, German, and Polish. There were half a dozen American docs. Myself, I was the youngest. I was like the kid in the field there in my early thirties. Everyone else was in their sixties or later.
>
> I began wearing a white coat to come to work and I was on the ward all the time in the midst of the folks all the time, which was unheard of. The normal procedure of interaction between the physician who was in charge of everything, wrote orders for everything and was ostensibly, you know, in loco parentis, father of the ward, the paternalistic father of the ward, essentially would come every day, in their sport coats, look in at what was happening, get the report from the nurses about what had to be done; have the workers bring the individual in question to be seen, be held, and moved around. Never touch them, never get close to them, because they were diseased, an infectious source of hepatitis, of giardia, of every conceivable kind of intestinal parasite.

---

10. There should be no implication taken here that physicians who immigrated to the United States were necessarily incompetent. Rather, that in the case of Willowbrook, many incompetent physicians were there, who happened to have immigrated to the US.

And we began to find out—well I began to find out little by little—was this place was a gigantic experimental hideout for the top virologists in the United States, who were using this population as a way of testing out and developing vaccines for hepatitis and German measles. . . . Nobody knew what was going on . . . and they were just infecting different cohorts of kids. There was all this research going on sub rosa behind the scenes, funded by the Defense Department.[11] It took me a couple of months to get my bearings in this big damn place, a lot of buildings and even though I was just assigned one building, every week I had to be on duty 24 hours. And I would be sleeping there at night of course. . . . The place was totally violent. I would be called every ten minutes to go deal with a soaring fever of 105, a laceration which I had to suture and deal with the situation, fractures that I had to deal with, somebody found dead on the floor, which usually don't get reported till the morning because if somebody was dead they'd leave them there and not report it until the morning shift came on. I was going to be a letter-perfect physician. I was not going to suture without analgesics. I was not going to suture with upholstery thread. I wanted plastic surgery fine needles. I was not going to allow the lack of soap to exist on my ward. I was not going to allow the lack of sheets in my building. I was not going to allow rotten food to be served to the people I was responsible for. . . . I was going to respond every single time a worker called me to come. I was going to be there and I was going to take care of not only the person but the workers were as sick as the people living in the place, and so they needed taking care of too, and friendships had to be built, and connections have to be built. . . . After I was there for about six to eight months I knew I needed help. . . .

I had become such an anathema to the Administration by being a perfect doctor in my Building 16. I kept on demanding all the basics in order to make sure my workers were OK and that the people, the children on the ward, had some rational identity. . . . The doctors were so upset about my relentless practice of medicine that they insisted Hammond move me. After six months I was moved from my building and it was a shock. I mean I didn't see it coming.

The doctors organized against me in there. There was a system in Willowbrook where when a doctor would come to work, the only way you would know what was happening was for the worker, the supervisor or nurse, to give you a report. So the very first thing we did when we

11. This is the kind of program in which Reiss worked.

walked in, in the morning, was sit down and get a report of how many people had fallen ill, how many people had fallen bloody, how many . . . you know, what was the status of everything?

And the only way I could manage the situation, because there was no adequate record keeping, which I began to implement wherever I went, I would tell the truth. If I went someplace and I saw what was happening, I would write in the record the truth about what was happening. I began to build a day by day record of the true situation, with no euphemisms, no covering up. You know . . . I would lay in legal language saying: this place is killing people. This is where it is coming from. This is what I saw. This is what's happening, as a doctor.

I needed to have legitimate diagnostic help because I was dealing in a completely opaque situation where the charts said nothing. The charts, that's a whole other story. So I would call for consultants in every medical specialty which would guarantee me getting a report back from the consultant, which would remind me that I had someone to watch. [It was an] unimaginable but witnessable use of record keeping in the institution] . . . The most inhumane context . . . had been completely rubber stamped as legitimate by the medical doctors, by the State of New York, by the black Cadillacs of the Commissioner, you know, by the whole Academy. The University structure supported this alternative. All of the Chairs of Special Education absolutely recognized the validity and the purposefulness of the thing and anybody who spoke out against the model was instantly, instantly marginalized from the profession or their career in the Academy or their work in the field and nobody, no real doctor, would ever want to work in a place like this because there was no future for you. There was no status in this kind of work. This had to be work that was only done, you know, by people who were . . . "angels," who could tolerate this kind of suffering and who were seen like the director . . . as a "saint," because of this association. And these people became drunk on that egotistical role, the power role that they held, and they believed in their heart of hearts that they were doing their best. They really thought they were doing it right. (Bronston, 2007)

What is portrayed here is a reflection of the professional structure of medicine. On the one hand, we have world-class virologists conducting research on a captive child population in a most unethical manner. On the other, we find a group of physicians at the margin of the profession, who were not able to work elsewhere, were doing their jobs minimally, without regard to the standards and practice of medicine, and had accepted the status quo, the power structure, and modus operandi of the place. Their behavior as described by Bronston would have to be regarded as a clear violation of their basic oath as physicians. Their practice either indicated extreme ineptitude, a deeply uncaring attitude about their clinical responsibilities, or a combination thereof. The attempt to actually practice medicine, as Bronston did in the various buildings for which he was responsible, was regarded by these doctors as institutionally deviant and requiring punishment.

Bronston's remark about how physicians perceived themselves to be angels, with the director the most angelic, is extremely telling about human behavior in formal organizations. Similar observations can be found in the writings of Wolfensberger and Dybwad, wherein the power of institutional rhetoric to name things in ways that are the opposite of what they actually are appears a basic aspect of human service organizations. As discussed in the section on the sociology of total institutions (see Chapter 3), people who are asked to do things that are morally objectionable are given a plausible, sometimes convenient, and tempting logic to justify what they are being asked to do. State hospitals such as Willowbrook or Pacific State illustrate how physicians are not inured to this process. They internalize the rhetoric; they come to believe it in their "heart of hearts." This should not be surprising about human behavior, given what we know about it in total institutions, but it is nonetheless disturbing. The social processes described in Chapter 3 operate at every level, not just that of the direct care worker. The same pressures toward conformity, meeting job expectations, protecting one's self-image, exercising power and control, and so on, exist for all groups (cf. Zimbardo).

Yet another level of medical responsibility for the creation of conditions of life at Willowbrook, and virtual lack of medical treatment there, noted by Bronston, were those academic physicians who were employed by the State of New York as consultants and who were aware of the horrible conditions and lack of treatment there. Those consultants never worked at Willowbrook. At best, they visited and were taken on tours of cleaned-up wards where care had been taken to make things look good. Consultants who actually visited and treated people at Willowbrook were also somewhat shielded from the realities of ward life, doing most of their work in the main hospital building. This "power elite" controlled entrée into the field, marginalizing and delegitimizing those who were critical. A group of high-ranking physicians and academics served to control and ensure a supportive intellectual climate surrounding services for children and adults in institutions.

Bronston's observations about the medical personnel at Willowbrook are remarkably similar to ones made by Goode while at Pacific State Hospital, where a parallel division between treatment physicians, who were almost uniformly indifferent, incompetent, and uninvolved in ward matters, and the research doctors, who were affiliated with UCLA and were receiving the highest accolades for their work, existed. Goode had associations with well-known physicians appointed at UCLA and Pacific State and at the same time was familiar with day-to-day life on several wards at the hospital. He was able to observe these different "kinds" of physicians and physicians' work. These doctors, similar to those reported by Bronston, often thought of themselves as highly dedicated, devoting their lives to a devalued population and therefore deserving of praise, and they wielded their status and power freely. These well-known physicians served as consultants for institutions all over the country (including Willowbrook), serving states in the capacity of external experts related to institutions. This group saw themselves as humane and devoted physicians, trying to improve conditions in such places.

Bronston's (2007) characterization of nurses is equally condemning:

> So you had these white, you know, old boy and old girl supervisors. You had a big nurse kind of personality who was this—I mean the chief nurses in the place were really something, this one very attractive, kind of refined pacification agent. The other was dangerous, I mean a physically dangerous dame. They would come across like something from Alice [in] Wonderland. You didn't go against those women. They had absolute power to terminate you in half a second or throw you into a pit of work that was inconceivable and intolerable, and so they made their peace because there was a secret filled society in a hundred percent of that place.

Nurses on the ward were perceived by direct care staff as agents of the central administration. They were, after the physician responsible for the ward, the next most powerful person. Their role was akin to a COO, while the physicians operated as CEOs. On the large custodal wards, either participated in the everyday care as little as possible.

The overall pattern is clear. Those who rose in the hierarchy did so because of their willingness to play along with the powers that be. Chief nurses, given their authority on the ward and direct contact with the administration, were known to all to be loyal and powerful, functioning as the eyes and ears of the administration. Physicians by and large conformed to the low or even absent levels of medical care characteristic of the place.

In spite of the extremely condemning nature of the observations presented in this section they should not be taken to mean that all physicians and nurses at Willowbrook did their jobs without caring or trying. Some doctors and nurses dispelled their professional responsibilities within an untenable medical situation. Still others tried to take advantage of the situation for their professional advancement.

Food

In the most mundane things, we can find the social structure of everyday society. It is no accident that the topic of food at Willowbrook is often absent when those who worked or lived there speak with each other. It does not generally bring up pleasant memories for those who fed it or those who ate it. An exception to this might be the description of family-style meals of fresh food on the ward that Reiss worked on.

Many memories of food at Willowbrook recalled different colors of mush (called a "modified diet" at Pacific State), ground up in order to prevent people from choking. The mush was relatively tasteless, the result of grinding already over-cooked food. It was recognizable via color. The brown mush was the meat, the white the starch, the green the vegetable. The food had essentially no nutritive value, and even if the amounts appeared to be adequate, residents suffered from chronic mal-nutrition, in spite of having eaten significant volumes of mush.

Food at Willowbrook was immediately and directly linked to life and death, especially for those who were highly physically or mentally disabled. If you could not feed yourself, someone else had to, and sometimes there was little time avail-able, as little as 3 minutes per child, as described by Rivera. This meant that simply getting enough food into the person was problematic and consistent failure to do so could lead to disease, malnutrition and even death. One ex-staff member narrated at a conference at the College of Staten Island that she would set up four or five children in a semicircle around her and feed them in sequence, finishing spooning food into one, moving to the next, and so on, and that when she was done with the last, it would be just about time to begin to feed the first again. She would put the mush for all the children into a single bowl and feed them with a shared spoon. In response to this ultimately serious matter under irrational conditions, she had figured out the most efficient rational way to get the maximum amount of food into the children in the time allotted.

Sadly, this same pressure to be efficient when feeding children and adults with severe disability sometimes led directly to death, in the form of aspiration pneumo-nia, a very common form of death at Willowbrook and a by-product of the feeding procedures that staff were forced to use.

For those with the ability to eat, doing so did not follow any kind of cultural norm, as the following description of lunch clearly indicates. Helen, interviewed by Starogiannis and Hill, felt that lunch time

> was literally a zoo. At least a third of the patients on each ward had to be spoon-fed or forcibly spoon-fed. Those patients who showed some feed-ing initiative were therefore left to fend for themselves. These patients either grabbed handfuls of food off the nearest plate (not necessarily their own) and stuffed the food in their mouths; or, if their manual dex-terity was poor, they dumped their plate of food on the floor and lapped it up like a dog.

This kind of situation has been described in many state institutions at the time (e.g., Grossman, personal communication, College of Staten Island, September, 1990).

From an administrative point of view, feeding so many people, the population equivalent to a large town, was a logistical nightmare, yet on Reiss's ward, it was reasonably successful. This is probably, again, because her ward was not part of the usual food distribution system but part of a system that was enriched because of research grants:

> The attendant in the ward served the food and supervised the meals. In many wards this meant literally spooning the food into the children's mouths, but in our ward all the boys could feed themselves, with minimal assistance. Because the ward was small we could serve the food in family style, as it was called. This meant that the vegetables and salads were in separate dishes and the children could take what they wanted. The attendant hovered anxiously, watching carefully to ensure that one child did not clean the entire dish onto his own plate if it was something he was fond of.
>
> The quantity of food was more than adequate most of the time, and the quality fairly good, though it did vary from month to month. Our personal struggle with the kitchen came over the bedtime snack. . . . Naturally, like all children, before they went to bed they wanted a snack. The kitchen was lavish with milk and would send us huge plastic containers of milk that we could keep in our own kitchen and tap when wanted. They were continually difficult about cookies, cakes or even a bit of fruit for the boys to have with the milk. It is probably that they didn't have much to give. The distant, all important, clerks in Albany did not only calculate what amount of clothes a child would need, they also calculated in ounces how much food he or she should receive. The kitchen workers had to account for all their supplies. They kept showing us their printed forms—nowhere was there a mention of "snacks." Undeterred, we pleaded, covertly threatened, and begged. We would get supplies for a few weeks and then the battle would start once again. The kitchen would fight back, slyly hinting that the cookies were eaten by the staff, infuriating the attendants, especially the evening attendants who often baked cakes at home and brought them in for the children. Like all departments in most institutions, it was a case of "us against them." Not an all-out war but a continual skirmish; a battle that went to the most dedicated nuisance maker.

In Reiss's ward, candy was used as reinforcement. Reiss recounted:

> "You be nice and you'll get a lollipop." "Hush up now and I'll give you some gum." . . . Boxes of them were donated every month by, I believe,

the Benevolent Society, though I am not certain of the source. Boxes of lollipops were kept in the Dental Department, the Nurses' offices, by psychologists, and in the school. An injection in the buttocks, or a sample of blood from a vein, rated one lollipop. It was the standard reward.

This is consistent with what another staff member observed. Irma felt that food was used as a way to control the residents:

> The children were overfed. I believe that they would do this because they felt that it would keep them calm. The amount of food that these children used to devour was unbelievable. They would steal and snatch food from the other residents, as well.

Candy, without doubt, played little or no role on other wards, for example, the large custodial ones that Bronston supervised. It is difficult to say exactly what function(s) food may have played in any specific building. To what degree was food, like cigarettes, a form of barter among residents? What happened to the food brought in by visiting parents for their children or adult relatives or by staff for the children on the wards? It may well have played such a role on other wards on the grounds, such as those involved with medical experiments or those with less disabled residents.[12]

School programs were another place where food entered into social life. A teacher at Willowbrook recalled the ice cream:

> The ice cream guy would come and all of the children would line up on certain days. After a while they would allow the residents to have ice cream whenever they wanted it. In the beginning, though, it was very regimented. Certain buildings would get ice cream on certain days. Before they relaxed the ice cream rule, you would be allowed ice cream twice a week. The kids used to love it. They would be covered from head to toe. Actually, it was pretty good. It was like Carvel soft ice cream. The ice cream was made at Willowbrook and it was good.

Two people we interviewed mentioned that meat intended for the residents was sometimes stolen by staff and sold to butchers outside the institution. One

---

12. Here is another twist on the role of food at Willowbrook: During a November 30, 2012, visit to Goode's class, Judy Moiseff, a former Willowbrook resident, revealed that she used to pay staff to get food for her from the outside. Judy has severe cerebral palsy and has extremely limited movement and speech. She had figured out that the food they were feeding her had no taste or nutrition. One wonders how many residents were aware of this and what they might have done about it. It is difficult to comment on how widespread such a practice might have been, or whether other forms of "payment" might have been used in exchange for food.

interviewee mentioned that as part of the underlife of the staff at Willowbrook, one of the things that could be bought there was meat.

Finally, food played a particular role in the social hierarchy at Willowbrook. "Pickers," as they were termed by residents in describing certain other residents, went through the garbage cans to find discarded parts of staff or visitors' meals. Pickers were regarded as low on the social ladder by other residents.[13]

Clothing

> You were a nonentity up there. You were just a mannequin up there. Everybody was the same. The clothes you are wearing now, I might be wearing tomorrow. And the clothes I am wearing, you might be wearing tomorrow. If it wasn't for the braces I had, nothing would have been mine. (Mickey Finn, as cited by Pratt, 1998, p. 18)

Clothes in an institution such as Willowbrook do not function the same way they do in everyday society. On the outside, many people, at least those who are not very poor, use clothes for more than protection or modesty. For the majority of people, clothes involve styles, choosing garments that have a certain look to them as a way to express a personal image and identity. Individuals typically own many items of clothing, far too many to justify on functional grounds. Clothing is a form of what sociologists call "conspicuous consumption." In a total institution, there is a relative lack of clothes and clothes ownership. As stated by Mickey Finn in the epigraph to this section, it was often the case that no one owned any clothes. And in total institutions, there are the often technical difficulties of keeping clothes on people who are undersupervised, undersocialized, and severely neglected. Many would take them off. Nudity was thus a massively observable fact of life. Generally, clothes at Willowbrook were primarily provided to residents for warmth and protection, and attempts were made, within resources available, to dress residents.

Despite these attempts, nudity at hospitals and schools such as Willowbrook was a normal part of daily life. This led to a great desensitization on everyone's part, so that seeing a naked man, woman, or child was, on the job, unremarkable. This irregard for nakedness was one part of the great, palpable division between the

---

13. A discussion of "pickers" by a parent of a child who lived at Willowbrook appears in the original footage for Katie Meskell's documentary, *Unforgotten*. Even lower than these were the "shit eaters," who because of lack of socialization and supervision, would eat various substances off the floors of the institution. Goode has heard several discussions of ex-Willowbrook residents who have used the term without reflection as a negative characterization of another resident. The existence of such terms ia an indication of human beings' fine sensitivity to status distinctions at whatever level of society.

inside and outside culture. It was also part of the dehumanization of the residents and was one way in which they would be made to look less human and thereby suitable candidates for less humane treatment.[14] In a most bizarre video of an unnamed institution in the Chicago area, a staff member is seen naked in a shower, washing residents. Such as scene is unfathomable to someone who has never worked in a state hospital but not so when seen by those who lived or worked in such places. Goode explained at one showing of this video that the institution did not wash staff uniforms, so these had to be cleaned at the expense of the workers. Hence, the workers would take them off when in the showers, which were, as described by residents at Willowbrook, often places where residents would have bowel movements. Being paid minimal wages, working in a place where nudity was commonplace, the most "logical" solution was to take off their own uniforms in the showers as well.[15]

Most shirts, pants, dresses, and underwear were property of the ward, not the individual. The overwhelming task of keeping clothes clean dwarfed any kind of attempt to track items individually. Photos of mounds of shoes or underwear, such as those taken by Bronston, illustrate how clothes were not items of personal property. Residents who were able to have clothes as private property—for example, at the buildings where women without intellectual disability who had jobs outside Willowbrook lived—were able to have clothes that served as signs of status, of normality. Such items were clearly status objects. At Pacific State, on the deaf and blind ward, there was an attempt to track individual items of clothing by writing on them with indelible black pen. In a relatively short while, because of the labor intensiveness required in the daily sorting of dozens of pants, underpants, shirts, and dresses, the attempt was eventually abandoned. But it was recognized that ownership of clothing and wearing clothes that fit and were gender-appropriate was an important part of life to try and produce for the children.

For those residents who were confined to 'cripple carts,'[16] they were lucky if they wore a camisole or a tunic-like hospital gown. Employees interviewed by

14. This same logic is revealed in an interview with a concentration camp officer who, when asked why Jews were forced to live in filth and even be covered with excrement, responded by saying that making them live this way made them look and act less human and therefore made it easier for his men to do their work.

15. This video, made by a doctoral student from the University of Wisconsin, was black and white and without sound, showing conditions of life that were every bit as horrible as the worst of Willowbrook. The scene of hundreds of naked men eating lunch without utensils, covered with food, is as surreal a scene of institutional life as Goode has ever seen. The Wisconsin student said that the men were hosed off afterward.

16. The term is one used by staff at Willowbrook and other institutions and usually were basically a wagon—a flat bed with walls on wheels—on which children would be placed in order to make their care easier. They could then be wheeled from area to area or cleaned up without being picked up. One staff member mentioned that carts could easily be cleaned.

Starogiannis and Hill remembered that for some time, there was a form of institutional clothing made available to residents. Irma recalled:

> They were bizarre. The clothes for the children were made from a very heavy denim material. The clothes were all made with elastic bands. No flies on the boys' pants. The clothes were very durable. I guess they had to be to withstand the industrial laundering that they were put through. Many organizations, and even people who worked there, donated clothes for the children. Everybody hated the way the kids were dressed. Unfortunately, the nice clothes would disappear. There was an awful lot of theft at Willowbrook.

For workers at Willowbrook clothes had particular job-related relevances. Laundry was partly the reason that clothing was so hard to come by. Helen described a systemic issue with the laundry:

> The washing and drying of all laundry was done in the big institutional laundry building next to the maintenance building. Each day the ward had to sort, bag and weigh the soiled laundry they were sending out to be cleaned. In addition, any items soiled with feces had to be hand rinsed by the attendant before it could be bagged and weighed. The clean laundry would be delivered to the building, but was not sorted. Thus all incoming clean laundry had to be sorted, folded and put away. The night staff was responsible for preparing the clean clothes for each patient to wear the next morning. As well as pairing the over sixty pairs of sneakers that were piled up prior to showering all patients.

Joséph noticed a similar problem with towels:

> There were 6,000 residents there. I think they were supposed to have 12,000 towels. There were supposed to be two towels per resident. One towel was in the laundry, so there was one available. That is in theory. They did a survey. They counted all of the towels in Willowbrook. Now, on inventory there were 12,000 towels. When they actually counted them, there were only 3,000 towels. When they asked the head of the laundry department, what was going on, he just said that they were missing. If you were supposed to have 12,000 of anything and you only had 3,000 of them, I think you would notice that they were missing. What happened to them, who knows?

The few clothes available, incontinent residents, and overworked staff also contributed to nudity. Anyone familiar with the *Unforgotten* video knows the Geraldo footage included these stark images of nude residents sitting on the floors. Arlen

Willowbrook Residents

believed that there just were not enough employees to keep everyone dressed. George, Helen, Irma, and John noted that residents might have been dressed in the morning, but they would tear their clothes off, and so nudity was prevalent on the wards.

It was not always like this. In buildings where kids went to school, they would dress better, usually in donated "street clothing." The photos of Willowbrook children in the local papers showed them dressed in their Sunday best. So on the one hand, the reality of life at Willowbrook denied the importance of clothing, but on the other, the image presented to the community affirmed clothing's importance in creating "normal appearances." Clothing was a key aspect of Willowbrook's image management.

In their coverage of the legal case against Willowbrook, Rothman and Rothman (1984/2009) included much of the testimony, which often focused on clothing. In their book, they mentioned inadequacies with clothing at Willowbrook 27 times: They note the lack of clothing, theft of clothing, rampant nudity, and inadequate laundry and the orders that Willowbrook residents should have "clean adequate and seasonally appropriate" clothing (p. 205).

Clothing was an institution-wide inadequacy that reached into even Reiss's "privileged" ward.[17] Reiss narrated several stories involving problems with clothes and how they were part of ward life:

> There were seldom any surplus clothes in the ward. The amount of clothing allocated was carefully calculated by clerks in Albany who, one must imagine, had no idea what a small boy and a hospital laundry could do to a piece of clothing bought from the lowest bidder.
>
> The closet that contained the new clothing, outdoor coats, and private clothes always had to be locked, and the key kept carefully by whoever was in charge of the ward. Even so, the articles were not safe. Many times the attendant would go to her cupboard to find that half her supply of new shirts, for example, had vanished. Once she lost all her pajamas, two overcoats, and some carefully reserved shoes. . . .
>
> The acquisition, allocation, and retention of clothes took hours of our working week. Complicated charts had been made out . . . listing exactly how much clothing would be required by each child. These figures, which were continually being quoted to us by the supply house and the laundry, bore no relationship to the facts of ward life.
>
> In many of the wards of the institution the whole day was spent in washing the children, and then trying to keep them clothed. In our ward it was more a matter of trying to keep them respectably clothed. Some boys had relatives or friends who would bring them jackets, shirts, or even shoes. These were greatly prized by the children and known as "outside" clothes, as compared with "state" clothes. Usually, as soon as the relative left, the clothes were whisked off the child and locked in a special closet. This was because the parents had a habit of expecting to see them again, and an experienced attendant knew that it was unlikely

---

17. We refer here only to resource issues and recognize that being a subject of research was no "privilege."

that they would be presentable by the next visit, always supposing they were still in our possession, which was also uncertain.

Some parents, and it often seemed to be the economically poorer ones, had an appreciation of this situation. They would bring a shirt, or some socks, and tell the attendant to let the kid wear them out. Next month they would turn up with another offering. One mother came every two or three months to see her son and to take him home for the weekend. She was a thin exhausted looking little lady, which was understandable enough when you learned that she had seven other children at home. She was also possessed of a desperate cunning. She would collect her son Paul neatly dressed in the best State clothes that we could find and would return him late Sunday evening dressed in his brother's castoff clothing.

We never had enough shoes. Either new shoes had not been received by the storeroom so it was "Please wait awhile, delivery is expected momentarily . . ." (Momentarily could usually be reckoned in months), or they were being repaired, which also took months. Desperate phone calls to the shoemaker brought equally desperate and irate protests from him. He had had no assistant for months, he had over three hundred shoes to sole, and while we were on the phone would we please explain what we let our kids walk on? . . . Sometimes the children's feet seemed to leap forward in size so that the pair worn last month was pinching and squeezing their feet most painfully this month.

Reiss also described the process of exchanging old tattered clothing for new clothes, widely known as "condemning":

Everyone looked forward to condemning. It was like an outing. Great laundry bags were stuffed with the torn clothing and worn-out shoes. One or two boys would help drag the bags to an attendant's car and we would all set off together for the far end of the grounds.

The rule was one new article of clothing for one torn or worn-out piece, but there was always some leeway for bargaining. The attendant would scan the shelves of new clothes very carefully while the clothing clerk counted out the rags we had brought. A great deal depended upon which clerk was on duty, but the expedition was always most successful when the senior attendant was present.

With the greatest tact and diplomacy she would enter into delicate negotiations, such as, "Could the old pajamas be replaced by shirts?" . . . And "Could our boys have some of the new raincoats she just happened to have noticed? Not the grey and brown ones—the red and blue would be better." . . . Sometimes we were allowed to wander into the next room where the donations of old clothes were kept. These clothes, cleaned and sorted into kinds and sizes, were stored in huge cardboard containers awaiting distribution to the various wards. To us this was often the highlight of our visit, and we would spend the greater part of our time combing through the collection. No one ever inspected the goods at a Flea Market as carefully and conscientiously as we raked through those clothes. We were not looking for extra clothes so much as for something different. Something to lighten the solid but unimaginative State purchases. Pants with a flare leg; belts of any kind; corduroy pants or jacket; cuff links; scarves; gloves; shirts worn and frail but colorful in pattern—anything for a change.

It was generally understood that part of the clothing shortage was due to pilferage by the staff. It angers some former employees to hear accusations that they were stealing from these disadvantaged residents because many did exactly the opposite, bringing in old clothes as well as extra food to donate to the children on their ward. Yet, clearly, interview data indicate it was happening at Willowbrook, and Goode remembers that staff pilferage also was commonplace knowledge at Pacific State. Pilferage was another example of losing one's 'outside moral compass,' a sad fact of life for many in total institutions. Staff would rationalize doing this with a variety of arguments (these things will be wasted on these children. if I don't, someone else will; my children need these more, and so forth).

It is clear that clothes, like food, was a ubiquitous, constant, and important, part of life in Willowbrook, as much in their absence as in their presence. Whether on a research or a custodial ward, much time and effort on the part of staff was spent on matters related to clothing and trying to keep residents clothed. But for the residents who owned no clothes, and who sometimes did not want to dress in them, by and large clothing played a much less significant social role, related to their relationship to their family outside the institution (having 'outside clothes.') Because anyone's clothes were anyone else's, they played no role in social differentiation or in the development of personal identity. This is not to say that clothes could not play a consequential role on the ward. For example, Goode interviewed a former resident who described being terribly beaten for "hiding my dirty underwear under my mattress." She insisted she was set up, that she never did so. For this person, clothes, in this case dirty clothes, like everything else at Willowbrook, was just one ingredient in the whole mess.

Social Hierarchies

In most introductory textbooks in sociology or anthropology, it would not be unexpected to find a statement to the effect that all human societies produce a system of social hierarchy or graded social statuses. Certainly, Goffman's (1961) book *Asylum* notes that staff and inmate hierarchies play critical roles in the social organization of total institutions. It should be no surprise that Willowbrook created similar social groupings or that terms used to describe these statuses were known to both resident and staff populations. At events related to Willowbrook, it has not been uncommon to hear former residents and staff using terms such as "low grade" or "low functioning" or "garbage picker." Other labels in common use at institutions of the time all reflected the ward attendant's typology: puker, biter, grabber, soiler, headbanger, low grade, vegetable, fighter (Bogdan et al., 1974).

Most institutions have social hierarchies. Fernald State School, for instance, created resident hierarchies based on age, physical size, toughness, and intelligence (D'Antonio, 2004). The most dominant boys were "big shots." Below them were the smart boys, who did not use force; then the boys who stuck together for protection; then the "dopes," severely retarded boys. The administration used intelligence and ability in their assessments of need. Two visitors to many such places reported that different institutions developed their own local vernacular, reflecting location and history of the particular place (Dybwad, personal communication, 1999; Grossman, personal communication, 1990).

Thus, there was a hierarchy that existed among Willowbrook residents, staff, and administration and it was produced and recognized by them in admittedly highly unusual circumstances. Again, this should not be at all surprising. Super- and subordination of others exists virtually universally in any human social grouping at any level of society. In addition, in most places, hierarchy is also accompanied by an assignation of goodness and badness—"a local cast of heroes and villains" (Pollner, personal communication, 1978). We find both hierarchy and heroes and villains in many of the interviews we examined and in the observations of Bronston, Reiss, and Goode. And, as with all matters related to Willowbrook, the way one saw and experienced these hierarchies was highly dependent on one's status within the institution.

Reiss recounted evidence of hierarchies in the social organization of the dining room and sleeping arrangements:

There was a definite pecking order in both the seating arrangements in the dining room, and the allocation of beds in the dormitory. Progress in social behavior at least could be charted from two indicators. How long it took before they were promoted from the newcomer's table to a seat with the long term residents and the distance between their bed and the attendant's office.

Naturally the night attendant liked to have the very young, handicapped or potential trouble-makers near her night station, so that she could keep a wary eye on them. One of the most effective controls the attendants had over an outraged and furious small boy was to threaten to transfer him to "where the babies sleep" or "back to the newcomer's table."

The terms *low grade* and *high grade* or *low functioning* and *high functioning* were applied both to people and to behaviors of people. These terms, used by staff and professionals, were also adapted by residents to describe each other. According to Reiss, "All bad behavior was 'low grade'; impertinence was 'sassy,' 'acting up,' or 'big shot'; aggressiveness was 'downright mean' and good behavior was 'real nice.'" At Willowbrook, it is reasonable to suspect that the vernacular reflected the large preponderance of workers of color who came from the South.

It is important to distinguish between an account such as Reiss's, which is unusually close to the everyday lives of the children she writes about and exceptionally sympathetic to their perspectives and interests, from the way residents at Willowbrook speak about social hierarchy. As stated above, most residents were aware of the nomenclature used by staff to typify residents on a social continuum. They used these terms among themselves and in conversations with staff. But—and this observation is corroborated by several witnessed conversations among former Willowbrook residents and conversations with them—residents had their own system of grading and speaking about themselves. Bernard Carabello, for example, was regarded by some residents as a sort of hero, because he was a public figure and showed courage standing up to the administration. Similarly, another resident who masterminded weekly nightly excursions into the community was looked up to by other young women in her building. An older resident known by Goode, Bertina, who died several years ago, was regarded by many of the women in her building as an older sister or even mother. These statuses were generated by persons at the bottom of society, within the resident world, and beyond them perhaps known only to direct care staff but no one else.

Violence

As described earlier, violence of various forms is an expected result in total institutions; its presence, if not form, is not a reflection of the particular personalities involved. All places like Willowbrook, including the full range of institutions mentioned by Goffman (1961) in his book, create violence as a notable feature of everyday life. At Willowbrook, given what we have heard over the years and what is available in our accounts, violence manifested itself on many levels and occurred ubiquitously. There was the initial institutional violence of setting up the place and creating conditions that were abysmal for both residents and workers. There was the violence done by the administration and their intellectual and political cronies, in cementing their control over the place and seeing to it that there was no resistance to its modus operandi, inhumanity and evilness. There was the physical and psychological harm caused by the lack of exercise by physicians of their medical duty. There was violence done by staff to residents, including rape, beatings, psychological torture, administration of chronic drugs, and murder. There was violence done by staff to other staff members, for a variety of reasons including personal vendettas, paybacks for ratting, drug dealing disputes, and mental illness. There was, finally, violence done by residents to other residents, which could include beating, rape, torture, and murder.

This institutional violence, the terrible conditions of neglect, lack of nutrition, and medical mismanagement were severe enough to result in death for many who lived at Willowbrook. It was a place "hard enough to kill anyone who wasn't made of steel" (Bronston, 2005). There are so many nameless persons who came to Willowbrook, essentially lived a "nasty, short, brutish" existence, and died. These forms of institutional violence far outweighed, by any measure, the more individual acts of violence perpetrated by "bad" staff or residents.

Gena (whose story is told in Chapter 5) arrived at Willowbrook in 1956 and was severely beaten by a staff member who took a disliking to her, as a result losing vision in one of her eyes. When her mother discovered the beating, the staff member was fired, although nothing appeared in the press about the incident. Generally, such incidents were hushed up by the administration, but because of the extremity of some cases, they could not be covered up. Sometimes one hears staff talk about the early days of Willowbrook with a kind of warmth, a feeling of *gemeinschaft*—personal connection—that existed there. Although this may well have been true among the staff, violence for residents was always a part of Willowbrook, even in its earliest days.

Many accounts mention the violence at Willowbrook. This is especially true of articles in the *Staten Island Advance*. Rothman and Rothman (1984/2009) indicated what things were like: "In the first half of 1965, a succession of violent deaths occurred which sparked a flurry of press reports and even a short-lived grand jury investigation" (p. 23). Those events? A 42-year-old resident was scalded to death in a shower; the same happened to a 10-year-old boy; then, a 12-year-old boy was accidentally strangled by his restraints; and a 26-year-old died when a fellow resident struck him in the throat. When Judge Orrin Judd visited Willowbrook in 1973, he observed a child with recent untreated head wounds, yet there was no record of the injury on the patient record or ward logs. Bronston corroborates this chronically flawed nature of medical documentation and treatment.

Another kind of violence was by staff toward residents. By "kind," we do not mean to say that all violence by staff was the same thing. At Pacific State, violence could be done by staff for a variety of reasons: retribution; as a gesture demonstrating arbitrary domination to other residents to establish authority; out of personal dislike; in response to an act of aggression; for no good reason; as a matter of self-defense; as a misguided form of teaching; or because the staff member was mentally disturbed. There is no reason to think that similar motives did not exist at Willowbrook.

Arlen noted that there had been "a lot of abuse going on there," and "We always went in and tried to stop the abuse," because "to see somebody come in and abuse them for no reason because they cried, because they soiled, or they didn't stay on the bench, little things, you wouldn't hit your own kids."

Similarly, Maria, interviewed by Starogiannis and Hill, went to Willowbrook afraid of what might happen:

> I did not want to stay there because there was too many abusers there, and too many children there getting abused, and getting hit by chains and getting abused by the attendants. And getting locked in the seclusion room.[18]

It is highly unlikely these stories were unique.

John said:

> I witnessed attendants hitting the kids. It was that intimidation, the yelling, the hitting and the intimidation, is what kept them quiet and worked most effective[ly] and was the method most used by most attendants, but not all.

Joséph similarly recalled: "Some of the attendants used to grab the residents by their ears and pull them so hard that the skin underneath the ear used to tear."

One nurse's aide told a story about a male patient that the male workers used to abuse. They used to punch the patient's stomach and grind their shoes into his genital area. This went on for 3 years, and even though it really bothered her and she wanted to yell at them, she never did, and eventually the worker lost his job.

Violence is a response to stress and anxiety, overcrowding, and generally unkind conditions. It is also a product of the social invisibility of total institutions and the climate of fear often existing in such places around reporting violence and abuse. This was evident at Willowbrook.

Some of the violence seen at Willowbrook was between residents. Irma remembered that "There was continuous fighting. Living under conditions like that you had the survival of the fittest." In fact:

18. At Willowbrook and most institutions, some form of seclusion was used for punishing patients.

There were many violent clients, who would literally kill one another. There were deaths all the time. A client would pick up a chair and pound it over a person's head, or kick a person until he couldn't breathe. It would happen all the time. The clients would bite. Fingers and ears were bitten off.

Jimmy had lived at Willowbrook and was a victim of bullying, but he had adopted a nonviolent philosophy. He admitted: "I used to get beat up," by other residents, and he fought back. Eventually he tried the following tack: "You try to communicate and talk to them, not get into a fight."

As will be seen, staff participated in this kind violence to the extent that they would have "favorites" who would serve as peacekeepers, often via violence or its intimidation. This meant that staff pre-selected among residents, as it were, who was to do violence to whom.

Reiss mentioned that fights between residents were common on occasions when the authority of good care for the residents was left to "responsible" residents, such as when working patients escorted other residents across the campus to their appointments. Out of sight of ward attendants, "trouble usually erupted the moment they were outside the building. This was the moment when resentments and arguments flared, and old scores were settled by pushing, shoving, or free-for-all fights." Perhaps imitating something they had probably seen on television, the children on Reiss's ward, led by Peter, a 14-year-old boy who organized many inventive ways to pass the time, organized a lynching.

[One of the boys] George was standing on a table, one end of a piece of string around his neck, the other end attached to the light bulb above. Peter was instructing the crowd of boys to shout, "Blood, blood!" when an appalled attendant put an end to the game.

This is an example of children "acting out" various dramas, in this case something perhaps seen on TV but oftentimes dramas reflecting institutional life. Reiss's writings contain other such accounts. In one instance, an incident that occurred during the day where a child was unfairly treated was reenacted with the ending changed, of course, to the staff member getting caught and being punished. One wonders, given this glimpse of kids' culture on the ward, in how many other places at Willowbrook, or at institutions all over the country, we could find examples of "magic theater" put on by institutionalized children. It is a remarkable observation about total institutions such as Willowbrook that children and adults can create rituals and shared culture, even under marginal, abusive conditions.

Many residents learned about force from the staff. Indeed, to some degree, through the staff's endorsement of surrogate authority figures on the ward, staff promoted the strongest or most dangerous or feared (not necessarily the same) to positions of delegated authority and implicitly if not explcitly endorsed their methods.

At the same time, it would be misleading to simplify the morality of violence within the residents' world to mere acts of mimicry. Other accounts, and the authors' experience at Willowbrook and Pacific State, show that residents of institutions, just as any social group, contained people who were unique and different from one another in many ways. There were people at Pacific State who were feared by everyone, staff and residents. Without being specifically diagnostic, one suspects these persons may have had a form of mental illness, perhaps exacerbated by personal experience, and had been incarcerated for their acts. Then the state institution served as a stage for them to act out their various dramas. Similarly, with staff, some were known as particularly violent, to everyone on the ward or in the building. In some institutions, such as Willowbrook or Creedmore State Hospital in the 1970s, violent staff were put into the same buildings and wards as violent patients, on the rationale that the latter required the former to keep order, thus creating unthinkably horrible conditions of life for those living there. At Pacific State, staff known to be violent were feared by both patients and workers. This was also true at Willowbrook, which even had relatively high-ranking administrative staff who were known as being "bad news."

Rothman and Rothman (1984/2009) summarized Bronston's testimony to the judges contemplating the Consent Decree. Bronston took pictures of the residents he treated. Pointing to one picture, he testified that it was a head injury caused by keys. After clarifying that only attendants would have keys, he presented further similar pictures. He reported the regular occurrence of violence on the wards at Willowbrook. And it is Bronston's assertions that injuries were caused by staff. This same kind of thing was substantiated by D'Antonio (2004) at Fernald State School in Massachusetts. He found that attendants threatened residents with "red cherries," the welts that rise up in response to a beating with wooden hangers. Sometimes the violence also took the form of humiliation: One attendant had ward-mates urinate in a bowl, then threw the urine in a disruptive boy's face. Resident-on-resident violence occurred, from fistfights to all-out brawls.

One way to think of violence at places like Willowbrook was that it became a kind of currency, a way of transacting business, underwritten by a social form, the total institution, that from the top down permitted, and even encouraged it to thrive through practices of informational control and willful ignorance. Violence was so much part and parcel of the place, so much built into its structure and most rudimentary aspects of daily existence, that it expressed itself in all relationships. This is one reason why, as mentioned above, acts of compassion within places like Willowbrook stood out as such notable achievements.

Furloughs, Vacations, and Release

It is difficult to estimate to what degree residents were able to get a break from the horrible conditions and boring routine life at Willowbrook. George recalled that most residents were never allowed to leave their building, except for work and furloughs or vacations. In Reiss's program, apparently such things as furloughs, vacations, and even release were relatively common. But they were not so common in the larger, nonresearch buildings. John remembered: "three of these brighter individuals, who during the time I worked there, never had any visitors at all. No one ever came to take care of them. They were just left there and forgotten." Many, many children and adults at Willowbrook did not have families or staff who cared about them. Again, it is hard to give a proportion. At the deaf-blind ward at Pacific State, Goode estimated that more than two thirds of the children on the ward did not have parents or other relatives who visited, and those that did, did so infrequently. So in presenting Reiss's account, we do not want to give the impression that this was the way it was at other parts of the institution.

On her ward, there were several ways for a resident to get a break from Willowbrook, temporarily and indefinitely. Temporary relief commonly took the form of furloughs. Either the parents, sometimes staff members, or even community members could request that a resident be released temporarily for a home visit for a day, a few days, or even longer. Reiss explained:

> Sometimes people quite unrelated to the children would request permission to take them out, either for the day or for the weekend. The majority of these people were employees of Willowbrook, ones who had grown fond of a particular child and knew how welcome the invitation would be. Some were students who had worked in the institution for a summer. Others were kindly people who had heard about the need of these children for attention and affection. These special outings were greatly prized by the boys, and the un-chosen ones, who remained in the ward, would bicker and fight all day, taking out their envy and frustration on each other.

Irma used to take female residents home with her on weekends. Others, she said, would run away from Willowbrook: "Some of the girls that I taught said they hated it and did threaten to run away. They wanted to go home. Nobody wanted to be there." Other employees recalled these home visits with staff.

Jimmy remembered that his family used to take him home for weekends, but he would also be able to go on trips for movies, shopping, and work. Eventually, he was placed on community release, living by himself in an apartment in Park Hill, Staten Island, and he found a job, paid rent and the phone bills, and bought his own food. He said: "I like the way my life is now. I'm doing good. I do work, go to school, and help my mother food shop and stuff like that. Everything else is no problem. I get along with my family." Sadly, Jimmy's experience appears to have been the exception at Willowbrook. In contrast, at Fernald, furloughs were prohibited, based on the rationale that the children often developed a "family crush" on the employee and fantasized about being adopted into a loving home (D'Antonio, 2004).

For those residents who attended school, which closed during the summer months, a home summer vacation was also a possibility; depending on their family circumstances, this vacation could last a week or up to the whole summer. Reiss explained:

> Sometimes the parents did not return the child at the end of the vacation. Either they had found the boy or girl to be appealing and manageable, or there had been some change in the family situation that made it possible for them to keep the child at home.
>
> The authorities at Willowbrook were only too happy to discharge a patient, especially to the real home. They usually arranged to put the patient on what was called "convalescent status" which allowed the parents a year in which to decide. After a year the discharge became permanent.
>
> Some of the patients were returned long before the vacation was officially over. The parents, exhausted by the difficulties of trying to fit a retarded institutionalized child into the family setting, would sadly bring him back long before the time was up.

Reiss describes how some residents would be released into foster homes,

> but only when those homes were located near a public school which had suitable facilities and would accept the child. . . . There were, inevitably, many boys and girls who had no relatives and for whom a foster home could not be found.

A few residents, like Jimmy, were very successful and, through hard work and dedication, were able to obtain a job in the community, find an apartment, and start their lives away from Willowbrook. Other's tried but without similar result. Reiss described Hector, a strong 19-year-old boy:

> The job that was found for him was as cleaner and helper in a small general store in Staten Island. Since the store was located far from Willowbrook, and the cross island journey by bus complicated and tedious, it was thought best for him to live in a boarding house nearby. He was enchanted at the prospect. He would have not only a job, and a salary, but independence. The room was neither large nor luxurious, but it symbolized his coming of age.

Everyone looked around their own homes for small things to give him, such as a bright cushion or an old radio—anything that might cheer the place up and make it more comfortable. He was instructed to work hard, listen to his employer and to make the most of this great opportunity. . . .

Hector retained his job for six months. He was never late, always clean and tidy and listened carefully to everyone. He understood about paying his rent, and he would do that the moment he got his weekly money. He then indulged his passion for clothes, well ingrained over the years, and spent the rest of his earnings on shirts, ties, shoes, etc. He seldom, if ever, remembered to put something aside for food.

Because Hector had little money for food, he would visit Willowbrook to eat; eventually, he returned to Willowbrook to live, unable to succeed permanently on the outside.

Maria also found a way out of Willowbrook. When she was a teenager, Willowbrook placed her in foster homes, and then she eventually found her own apartment and arranged to have her 3-year-old son returned to her: "I got an apartment on Jersey Street with the help of the social workers and the nurse's aide and then my son came back to me when he was three years old." She eventually married and lived with the father of her son. At last report, she was doing well:

Well at the present time I go out three days a week and I do little cleaning jobs off the books because I like to have a little extra money. Because I go out. I like to go to movies. I like to go out to the Seaport.

These are heartening stories. They are not unique to Reiss's building, as we have heard other workers over the years talk about similar efforts on other wards. But by and large, most residents at Willowbrook did not have vacations, camps, or furloughs. For the vast majority of those admitted, Willowbrook was a permanent, incarcerating place of residence.

Some few activities at Willowbrook provided for temporary exit from the grounds. There was a choir, a band, and a girls' touring fashion show each of which gave performances at Willowbrook, on Staten Island and even in other boroughs. These were activities taken seriously by those who organized them, and much time and effort was put into them. For those few residents involved, these were welcome breaks from the daily routine of institutional life.

Activities

Like Randall's Island, in the mid-19th century, Willard State Hospital seemed like a beehive: Patients were working throughout the hospital, and those who did not work had a wide range of activities to dull the boredom (Penny & Stastny, 2008).

Entertainment was considered therapeutic, so there were dances, concerts, lectures, amateur theater, and regular movies. Sports were common, with marching drills, calisthenics, basketball, baseball, and annual field days—they even had a bowling alley. Occupational therapy had just been introduced in 1914, and by the 1920s, Willard was a leader in offering arts and craft activities as primary therapy. They also offered the state's first training on "activities of daily living," such as cooking, shopping, budgeting, and grooming, especially for those getting ready for leave or release. They looked at jobs held by patients as "on-the-job-training."

Such a description is inconsistent with what happened at WSS. There boredom was the rule—a common element of the routine round of life. John reported that

> It wasn't an uncommon sight to walk on the ward and see three or four of them masturbating. Some did it all day long. There were no activities at all. There were no games. There was no training at all. There was no individual attention.

On Reiss's ward, conditions were relatively luxurious compared with other buildings, and children had many activities. She recalled:

> There was a wide range of activities for all trainable and educable chil-dren in Willowbrook at that time. . . . I am always surprised to find there is seldom any mention of the well- equipped school, the extent of the recreation department activities, the occupational department, and the outings and parties arranged by the Benevolent Society and other generous charitable groups. Yet these activities played an important role in the life of the institution from its inception. The recreation depart-ment taught the children games, organized a basketball team, arranged dances for the teenagers, movies on Saturday afternoons for all who wanted to come, taught gym, and trained the children to play many dif-ferent instruments in the band.
>
> By 1967, with improved classrooms and more teachers, the programs for educable children were searching for pupils. The patients in the two buildings which were reserved for school children, and the small group in our ward, were not only given a full day of schooling; they were pulled hither and thither by recreation staff, occupational thera-pists, organizers of special outings and the band teachers. In addition, their medical needs were well cared for. They were scheduled for dental work, eye-glasses, hearing aids, shots and physical examinations. Con-sultants came to prescribe for painful feet, spotty skins, or the more seri-ous physical malfunctions from which so many of them suffered. "These kids," said one exasperated attendant, "have more appointments than Miss Universe."

It is important to note that even within the relatively benign and activity rich conditions of life on Reiss's ward, boredom was still a recurrent feature of life. This accounts for some of the incidents she recalled where children would get adventuresome and disappear for a time, doing what kids do. Activities were scheduled for children, as a matter of routine, but freedom from adult supervision, as with all children, was a highly sought after prize. They were breaks from the boredom and routine.

On the larger wards, the custodial buildings, it was not common for people to have vacations, furloughs, or to get released. After the age of 18, no one was entitled to go to school, so this activity, insofar as it existed for the general population, was discontinued. It is accurate to say that people who lived on these custodial wards experienced a kind of endless nothingness of mundane routines: waking, dressing, eating, taking medications, sitting around, eating, waiting around, eating (getting washed and toileted if lucky), and going to sleep. The next day, the same.

The picture Reiss portrays of routine occasionally interrupted by trips or special events does not generalize to the rest of the institution. It is clear from other accounts that most residents in Willowbrook and places like it were left to their own devices for virtually the entire day. Goode observed this at Pacific State also, where children on the deaf-blind ward were unengaged with others for as much as 23 hours of the day. Thus they had no choice but to invent ways to occupy themselves with whatever here and now possibilities presented themselves. Sometimes these were so limited that the resident had control only of his or her body, which was the primary cause of stereotypic behavior on the deaf-blind ward at Pacific State. In the video of an institution near Chicago in 1968 described earlier, residents are seen nude, publicly masturbating, vomiting and eating vomit, and violently rocking back and forth, all activities that were in reaction to being totally unsupervised and unsocialized or, put more operationally, completely bored, there being nothing else that they could figure out to do.

In the large, custodially-oriented buildings at Willowbrook, such as those described by some of the attendants and by Bronston, professional programs appear to have played a minimal, or even no, role in the lives of residents. Reiss's description of medical treatment, trips, and cookies was highly unusual, according to Bronston. On these larger wards there were essentially no activities. Few opportunities existed to ever leave the ward. The total boredom of everyday existence was the most salient aspect of life there, with residents left to their own devices to occupy the endless hours of nothingness. This became their lives. Such idleness bred violence, conflict; it led to despair and involution. It created conditions where children were unable to grow, and adults regressed to an autistic-like withdrawal. The sameness of every day made it difficult, almost impossible, to appreciate the passage of time. A resident of a total institution was reported to have remarked that before he came to it, "a day meant more to me then than a year does now."

School

A point of contention in the interviews is the degree to which education and habilitation of children occurred at Willowbrook. By those who worked at Willowbrook, it is estimated that fewer than 20% of the children attended school at any one time.[19] At the age of 18, residents had "aged out" of school. The quality of the education was reported by many to be marginal. Bernard Carabello, for example, went to school for many years at Willowbrook but never learned to read and write adequately.

On Reiss's ward, some of the boys attended school. Getting the residents there was not a simple task:

> To get there . . . it was necessary to cross one of the main interior roads of the institution's grounds. In theory, the boys were supposed to be taken to school, or medical appointments, by an attendant. In practice this rarely worked out. We just did not have an extra attendant. Gradually, under the pressure of perpetual staff shortages the authorities agreed to allow the boys to be led to school by a "responsible" boy. In the morning the boys lined up by the ward door and the leader was given instructions about each child's destination. They would then clatter across the central hall and rush down the stairs to the back door. They started off in a straggly crocodile, smaller boys holding the hand of a larger boy, and trouble usually erupted the moment they were outside the building. This was the moment when resentments and arguments flared, and old scores were settled by pushing, shoving, or free for all fights. The responsible boy needed both authority and strength.

Because there were chronic staff shortages, there were not enough staff to take residents out of their building, and if the children were not in school, according to a teacher, "they didn't really do anything except lay in the ward. . . . There was really nothing organized for them to do on the wards. If they had a TV on they could lie there and watch TV." In the words of one ward attendant: "There were no activities at all. There were no games. There was no training at all for the residents." Thus, as described above, masturbation and other repetitive bodily actions were a ubiquitous and constant activity on many wards.

Irma, the teacher, worked in a temporary building, a "prefab," and it was substandard:

19. As with other estimates about percentages and proportions at Willowbrook, we rely on published and narrative sources cited in our Introduction. More adequate quantitative determination of something like the proportion of children attending school could be constructed from files of the residents. Such a task would be extremely time-consuming and costly and would have its own limitations in terms of accuracy.

There was no heat in the classrooms. The wards had heat. The temperature in the classrooms was 55–60 degrees. Sometimes we would stay in the classrooms and other times we would teach on the wards, depending on how bad it was. This building was one of the prefabs. It was a piece of garbage. They tore that building down. The building was only made for temporary purposes. It just lasted too long. Another thing about the prefab buildings was that they were painted with lead-based paint. This lead-based paint was chipping and peeling all of the time.

Irma felt Willowbrook students were relatively easy to manage:

The residents used to love to come to school. I had a really nice bunch of students. There were never any discipline problems because they did not want to go back to the wards. All you had to say was, "Well, do you want to go back to the ward?" They would shape right up.

She reflected on another reason why her Willowbrook students were so nice:

The children at Willowbrook learned routine. They were much easier to control in a classroom setting. Later, when I started teaching children who lived at home, it was much more difficult, because they had no concept of routine. The Willowbrook children sure did have the concept of routine down pat.

A recreation worker described how he saw the schooling at Willowbrook:

Building 3 was a regular Board of [Education] type of programming. So they were teaching, depending upon the cognitive level of the person, functional academic types of things like learning to tell time and color identification and they'd be working on some speech . . . basic reading, basic math, things like that.

Joséph taught at Willowbrook. He still believed in the efforts of the Education Department:

In spite of all of the abuses that were going on at Willowbrook, and there were many . . . believe it or not, the school functioned fairly well. It was amazing. The Education Department, even though it was nuts, functioned. It serviced more residents than any other department at Willowbrook. There were classrooms in almost every building.

However, critics argued that their efforts were remedial at best. Bronston (2007) described the lack of power of the educators at Willowbrook: "So the school system was a token school system. It was never reinforced. . . . It never led to anything because nobody ever left the institution except when they died." Of the teachers, he said:

> There were 20 to 30 special educators there during the period I worked there. They were trying their best to teach profoundly disabled children. The teachers were very upset because there was no communication between them and the staff who worked on the ward, and thus the things being taught at school were not reinforced on the ward. This essentially destroyed the teaching they were doing. (Bronston, 2007)

During Bronston's tenure at Willowbrook the teachers became so frustrated with the situation that, against his advice, they signed a petition asking Hammond to require the ward personnel to carry through with the teaching done at school:

> At one point the teachers filed a petition to the administration to insist that the work that they did would be carried on and that the ward workers be instructed to maintain some of the skill sets and understand what was going on so that the residents would essentially have some continuity in the way in which they were managed and supported. And Hammond fired them all. (Bronston, 2007)

They had no tenure; thus the teachers who signed the petition were summarily fired. This shows the degree to which education was valued by administration or was seen as central to Willowbrook's mission. One might say there was a veneer of education at Willowbrook. The classes existed there, but they were largely ineffective and were not attended by the vast majority of residents. There was little or no cooperation in teaching skills learned in the classroom on the wards. In this sense, despite sincere attempts by educators to make it otherwise, Willowbrook State School was mostly one in name only.

Outdoor Activities and Trips

As stated in our brief history, one of the arguments for and against putting Willowbrook State School at the chosen location was its beauty. The grounds of WSS were beautiful, as the grounds of the College of Staten Island are today. Looking out the window on a beautiful day, probably every student and faculty member has felt like those who occupied the buildings before them, trapped and wanting to be outside and enjoying the surroundings.

In some programs, the grounds became a great part of life during the spring and summers. Reiss remembered summertime as a time of great outdoor activity. College students doing summer internships would arrive and with their assigned charge "would lead the children over the grounds to a nearby park, where they learned to fish. They made barbecues and picnics, fashioned kites and played a strange form of baseball which seemed to consist mainly of running and shouting." Reiss admitted that these activities were not always available or so engaging:

> During the warm weather the patients were taken outside in long car-riages, wheelchairs, or hobbling along with the help of the attendant. Apart from this period in the sunshine they seldom left the buildings, unless they were so sick that they needed the specialized care of the hospital unit in Building 2.

Some residents might be taken to the swimming pool. Yet Reiss acknowledged that sometimes in the summers:

> The boys were in the ward for long empty hours. Once or twice a week the recreation department would take them swimming or again a group would go off on a picnic or a trip. The rest of the time the ward attendant was the sole source of entertainment for the children.

Sometimes the residents in Reiss's ward would be taken off campus to go shopping:

> Some of the boys were taken to a nearby shopping plaza, given a few dollars to spend, and treated to lunch in the diner. On the shopping expeditions the boys always behaved much too well, too shy, repressed and quiet. They watched the other children romp and scream around the aisles, while they remained close to the attendant like silent shadows.

Interviews with various people who worked at Willowbrook mentioned taking residents on trips. A teacher who worked mostly in the "Baby Building" remembered taking residents to movies at Radio City Music Hall and to museums, the zoo, and the beach. The business officer at the school recalled trips to go out for ice cream, McDonalds, or even to the opera, although she remembered refusing payment for a trip to Atlantic City because the staff simply wanted to take in the boardwalk. A recreation worker recalled many trips: to the movies in Flatbush, to Madison Square Garden, maybe once a month or every other month, but only for those residents who were perceived to be able to be out in the community.

Irma recalled that starting around 1969, there was a large influx of new young professionals. They were:

> teachers, social workers and physical therapists, who were going to be working with the retarded as professionals for the first time ever. This was an enlightenment, which actually started to take place before the exposé on Willowbrook. We came into Willowbrook and saw what was happening. We knew that this was insane. We were brand new to this

place, 21 years old, fresh out of college. You did not have that much impact on an institution that had been going on forever. We started to take the residents on trips, for instance to Washington, D.C. We were taking them for first time experiences, traveling out of state, staying in hotel rooms, swimming in the ocean. Up until now no one wanted to even be seen with the retarded. This was the beginning. No one was really concerned about being fired. We were willing to buck the system. We were young and had no responsibilities. We were not afraid to fight. I had just graduated from college and I was not threatened. There was so much injustice. Someone needed to say, "Hey, we'll go to the wall, because this is all wrong."

Joséph, a paraprofessional with the Education Department, recalled spending a lot of time on trips because they always needed male attendants to help when boys needed the restroom. He recalled:

I spent four years of my life going to the bathroom. I saw the movie "The Love Bug" eight times in two weeks. I went four times each week, going to Radio City Music Hall, with different classes. I spent my life in the bathroom of Radio City Music Hall. I knew every tile in that place. The men's room at Radio City was all ceramic tile and marble. There was nothing there to absorb the sound. I was there with the boys, waiting on line to use the stalls.

One gets a sense that chaperoning these trips could be very challenging work. Joséph told another story:

Another time, we went to the Museum of Natural History. One of the students saw the whale on the ceiling in the Hall of Fishes. It was dark. He bolts like a deer in headlights. Did you ever try to find a child inside the Museum of Natural History? This was not an easy task. The boy does not know who he is. He cannot even speak. Finally, I catch up with him down in the main lobby. If you have ever been in the Museum of Natural History you will know what I mean. Here I am fighting with this child in the main lobby. About six hundred people are staring at me. He is on the floor kicking and screaming, because he does not want to go back to the Hall of Fishes.

This was back in the late 1960s and early 1970s, when people were a lot less familiar with disabilities in everyday life. Excursions off the grounds, especially given their group nature, could not be made inconspicuously. Having taken severely disabled children from Pacific State Hospital to state fairs and amusement parks, Goode in the 1970s experienced firsthand not only the physical demands of taking care of children who were unaware of risk in an uncontrolled environment, but also the cognitive and emotional demands of handling the intense stigma that can sometimes be part of encounters in the community. With children unaware of stares or comments, as the deaf and blind were, it is left to the caretaker to 'handle' their stigma. For the caretaker, the last element of such trips was, usually, the obvious enjoyment of the experience by the children. So there was this three-part mix for the staff person: demanding work, often negative public scrutiny, and the children having fun.

Movies, Parties, and Dances

Goffman (1961) described the function of the institutional ceremonial in total institutions. *Titticut Follies,* Wiseman's 1967 cinema verité of life in a hospital for the criminally insane, is named after the annual show put on by the staff and residents there. These "breaks" from the normal routine and structure of life serve various functions for residents and staff. They may allow people to blow off steam. They can allow people to show a creative part of themselves that otherwise would not be on view (e.g., that a resident or worker was a great dancer or singer). In the cases where shows are put on jointly, they may present opportunities for staff and residents to participate in events on a relatively equal footing and temporarily relax status distinctions.

At Willowbrook, there were also trips out to the movies (as Joséph and others remembered) and sometimes to a theater in Flatbush in Brooklyn. There were also the occasional birthday parties for staff and holiday parties around Christmas and New Year's on the wards. There were also Friday-night dances sponsored by the Benevolent Society. Reiss described the dances:

> At the dances they seldom conformed to the convention of having a partner, but as soon as the music started they would prance out onto the floor twirling and whirling to the rhythm in a self absorbed individual manner, not unlike many of the participants in discotheques today [the late 1970s].

Rothman and Rothman (1984/2009) were more critical about activities sponsored by the Benevolent Society: "its functions amounted to little more than occasional social events. It sponsored a few parties, complete with circus clowns, and arranged outings to a nearby park" (p. 22). Bronston also remembered some of the parties in a more critical way: "[There] were terribly tragic kinds of celebrations with balloons and ice cream and stuff like that, completely age inappropriate, completely culturally inappropriate, and completely desperate in their production." This is similar to the experience of Goode at Pacific State. The parties were often terribly sad and shallow attempts to have fun precisely because everyone understood that the place would revert immediately back to the same deprived circumstances and unending routine as soon as the event was over.

The Band

The Willowbrook State School Band was a prized activity. The local newspaper liked to print pictures of the Willowbrook band. Reiss recalled:

> The band was a source of pride and joy to Willowbrook. A dedicated music teacher, in the earliest days of Willowbrook's establishment, had found that children of widely varying levels of ability would not only respond to music, but could learn to play an instrument. Often the children learned to play music before they learned to read and write. Many of them never succeeded in mastering the elementary academic skills, but they learned not only to play instruments but also to read a simplified music score.
>
> Of all the activities arranged for the children the most popular was the band. Everyone wanted to belong, either playing an instrument, singing, or dancing. The children not only enjoyed the music but loved the companionship and excitement of rehearsals and practice sessions. To avoid interfering with the children's school hours these practice sessions were often held in the early evening. This was yet another attraction for the children; to have special permission to leave the ward after supper for an hour or so, happy in the knowledge that they were being eyed enviously from the less fortunate ones who were left behind.

The band would put on a performance in the school auditorium at Christmas for the pleasure of the patients and visitors, and it served as a dress rehearsal for the Benevolent Society luncheon in the spring, which was always held in one of the big New York hotels. The luncheon variety show also featured dances and performances by many children, some as young as 3 or 4 years.

There were some other activities, parallel to that of the band, which allowed a very small number of children to participate and leave the institution from time to time. There was a choral group and a traveling fashion show that provided some opportunity to participate in a recreational activity and to occasionally leave the institution on trips. Many staff and residents remembered these groups. Unfortunately, we were unable to interview anyone who was directly involved with these activities.

Willowbrook State School observed Mental Health Week yesterday by holding open house for the public.

A group of students from Public School 228, Brooklyn, who have started a special project with regard to the state institution, presented a record player which was accepted by two children from the rehabilitation center at Willowbrook.

A dramatization entitled "Our Doctor Told Us" was offered by a group of employes, depicting an interview between parents of a retarded child and a social worker. The emotional problems involved in the care and treatment of such a child, were brought out. Admission procedures in a state school were discussed. The school band played selections.

Director Gives Talk

Dr. H. H. Berman, school director, welcomed guests and explained the significance of Mental Health Week. He called attention to a $350,000,000 bond issue recommended by Governor Dewey to meet the need for hospital beds and said it will in-

At open house in Willowbrook State School, visitors from Public School 228, Brooklyn, watch boys work on looms in the occupational therapy section. The Brooklyn school donated a record player.

Occupational Therapy

Occupational, Recreational, and Physical Therapy

Ironically, sometimes in the face of incredibly horrendous living conditions, human service institutions and organizations will have programs of therapy, often because they were able to get external dollars to support that particular initiative. Wolfensberger (1989) noted that such therapies can be absolutely unrelated to more critical, observable needs of the residents. This was true at Pacific State Hospital, where researchers responded to Requests for Proposals (RFPs) announcements by the federal government. If there was one for sex therapy, researchers responded to it if they thought they could get the money, and thus would they establish a program. It did not matter that the people in the institution were starving, living in filth, or had no opportunity to actually have sex. Administrators often had to convince the ward attendants to implement the programs. In one institution similar to Willowbrook, attendants were asked to implement a new program that would benefit residents, and the staff resisted, accusing the administrators of spoiling the residents with rewards given in a behavior modification program, and eventually they sabotaged the program (Bogdan et al., 1974).

Paradoxically, the 1960s were a period of great innovation in mental disability research and theory, yet little of this made it into the corridors of large state schools

Weaving Class

(Rothman & Rothman, 1984/2009). At Fernald State School in Massachusetts, there was very little school time. Rather, the philosophy was to work on building basic life skills. A state school paper, "Industrial Training for Imbecile and Moron Boys of School Age," suggested having 3–year-olds chase balls, then piling sticks and stones, stringing beads, placing pegs in pegboards, and eventually making brushes and textiles on looms. Some children even ended up working on large industrial-sized looms; cutting straw and attaching it to boards to make brooms and brushes; resoling shoes; or refurnishing and repairing furniture. In a month, the residents of Fernald would produce 350 bedsheets and towels, 150 brushes, and 25,000 sheets of stationery.

At Willowbrook, some of the older residents, those who were considered capable, kept busy with occupational therapy. Adult men wove or hooked rugs that were sold at an annual sale. Adult women learned skills in the sewing classes. For example, Maria, who lived at Willowbrook, attended cooking and sewing classes.

This was all confirmed by Jimmy, a resident at Willowbrook:

> Some of the staff were okay. No problem with them. The staff would try to teach you to learn something that you wanted to learn. Maybe, like

doing your homework in school. Teach you how to ride a bike. Learn how to use the phone, answer the phone, stuff like that. Showing you how to cook. Teach you how to learn. No problem getting along with people.

An occupational and recreation therapist who worked at Willowbrook for 3 years remembered that "in the occupational therapy they did . . . things like putting things together. Like plastic pieces and so forth, to train their concentration, to work on their concentration skills and motor skills." Irma described the Physical Therapy Department:

> The Physical Therapy Department was good, also. They used to teach some of the aides how to deal with the children, that is, teaching them to walk. It was really very interesting. Some of these aides had very little education themselves. Yet, after six months of training, they would be very good at teaching the children to walk.

Irma described the importance of these programs to the residents' routines:

> The girls would get very depressed on the weekends. Most did not get any visitors. There was nothing for them to do on the weekends. The education and recreation programs were all during the weekdays. If anything happened, if a resident got injured, it was usually on a Saturday, or Sunday night, because there was nobody there to watch them. There was some staff who really cared about the residents and some who did not. The situation was just impossible.

She continued: "There was a recreational program, also. I really never did see anyone doing anything much with the children. They were not as departmentalized as education and they had a lot more freedom to float around." A recreation worker confirmed this:

> Everything was departmentalized, so I was in the [recreation] department. And I would sign in every morning at the gym, and I would go to wherever I worked. . . . And I would provide activities. . . . When I worked in the baby unit . . . I'd pick up my class and I'd walk them down the hall to an area that had a recreational area and then I would do different activities with them and then bring them back. And then go get another group. And then bring them back. And then it would be lunch time. . . . Then I'd run a class in the afternoon. And then I'd go back to the gym . . . [to] do whatever paper work I had to do. Then I'd go home from there.

A speech pathologist remembered "activity therapy," where:

> Sometimes . . . the activity therapist or the staff would be doing an activity. So the people would be in a circle and they would talk to them, and give them a ball to toss, or give them an instrument to hit the stick to hit an instrument to make noise, you know that kind of thing.

Yet this employee admits that "some of the residents would be sitting on the floor rocking, and that's all they did all day."

This is how Jimmy remembers it:

> We walked and ride a bike and sometimes go to the gym and play basketball. . . . We had a gym. We had to work out and train. We had a gym teacher in there and he was teaching us how to play basketball. How to shoot the hoop and everything. We were doing pretty good. Stay out of trouble. Sometimes we talked and go to the movies. Maybe go out, go food shopping, go buy food. Buy clothes and things.

Such therapies appear to be very much like what had existed for many years at state hospitals and schools. At Randall's Island, for example, even in the 1860s there were many classes in all kinds of crafts and work that could serve the residents after release. At Letchworth Village, similar kinds of classes were held for residents. The critical difference between these earlier efforts and those found at Willowbrook was that the latter were largely for show, or driven by fiscal remuneration, or to relieve boredom and were not generally undertaken as preparation for the outside world.[20]

Working Patients and Institutional Peonage

As mentioned in our Introduction, since the inception of institutions for people with disabilities, residents have been used for labor and/or have been provided work-related experience as part of therapy. Working residents could be found widely in institutions in the northeast United States, including, of course, Willowbrook (Bogdan et al., 1974; Sternlicht & Schaffer, 1973; Wagner & Sternlicht, 1975). At Willowbrook there were actually some residents who worked "regular" jobs in the community. They were not the majority, but a "lucky" few, usually people who were not intellectually disabled but there for other reasons, would go out into the community to work each day and return at night to sleep (often called "working girls or working boys"). Many more residents had unpaid jobs at the institution, a practice sometimes referred to as "institutional peonage."

---

20. This is not to say that there were not those who worked at Willowbrook who did take their work in this way. The comment is intended as a systemic one. The vast majority of residents at Willowbrook were never given preparaton in life skills that would prepare them for the outside world.

This practice was not reserved for adults. There is a long history in New York and many other states of children working in the hospitals where they lived. Deutsch (1948) observed that Letchworth Village was supported heavily by child labor. A worker at Rosewood State Training School in Maryland said:

> "Virtually all of the actual work involved in the operation of the institution is done by the children." He added, "In most cases patients assigned as 'helpers' to the specialized employees are stooges for these employees—doing the actual work while the others 'supervise' and collect the pay." (as cited in Trent, 1994, p. 230)

It was thought in the early establishment of institutions for people with intellectual disability that work was part of the process of treatment or habilitation. This idea was brought over to the United States in the 19th century and formed the basis of certain institutional forms, such as the cottage or village system, where residents produced everything that was needed for daily life.

Some people consider this use of residents a form of victimization, servitude or slavery, in that individuals were given work without being paid. And this view is probably correct from a legal and civil rights perspective. It is important to bear this in mind, while at the same time appreciating what roles such unpaid work had in the lives of the residents, as they saw and experienced it.

Many residents took on work roles at WSS. This was not seen as a punishment but rather as a reward. They were known as "working patients" and were generally seen more as "elite" residents than as victims. They even competed for the work. At Willowbrook resident work was seen, at least by some staff, as a positive way to train residents in basic work skills, offer "on-the-job" training, without complications like a salary. Then there is the resident perspective. By and large, when former residents have spoken about these jobs, it has been in positive rather than negative terms. Goode heard several women who lived at Willowbrook speaking emotionally about the work they did at the Baby Buildings, helping to take care of the children there. It was important for them as woman to be able to be around children and nurture them. This served several functions in their lives, including, as one person put it, trying to make things right for them (doing for these babies what was not being done for the resident herself—that is, caring for them). Another resident indicated that this was good practice for her, because later she got married and had some disabled children herself. Work at the institution served these "good" functions for residents—providing relief from boredom, engaging them in helping activities, in some instances preparing them for future life—while at the same time being a form of economic exploitation. In Reiss's writing, and in the observations of Goode, punishing residents for wrongdoing could come in the form of denying them their work. Although no money was involved, the work role was highly meaningful, a source of pride and status, a way to occupy time, contribute, to give care when it had been denied them, and so on. It created in this sense social capital.

As was commonplace in other institutions, at Fernald higher-functioning girls became maids at the superintendent's house (D'Antonio, 2004). In Willard State Hospital, where they were heavily dependent on unpaid patient labor, patients worked in all areas of the institution, including industrial shops, the slaughterhouse, for the blacksmith or brick maker, bakeries, laundries, heating plant, and out on the farm (Penny & Stastny, 2008). This is how the colony or farm model worked, with residents involved in the production of the necessities of everyday life. At Pacific State, there were still some elements of this going on when Goode was there. Residents worked on farm, sewed curtains and mended clothes, worked in the cafeteria, and were the basic groundskeeping crew. The medical director had an assistant with Down syndrome who greeted visitors in the antechamber of his office.

The rationale behind patient work is a logical extension of the English Quaker notion of "moral treatment": Weak minds could be cured by good honest labor. But as Penny and Stastny (2008) noted, the existence of patient labor is equally a reflection of the belief that "patient work was necessary for these huge institutions to sustain themselves without an excessive burden on taxpayers" (p. 24). America never was willing to pay fully to care for the weak and feeble. In fact, once unpaid patient labor was outlawed in New York in 1973, large institutions became more expensive; the economy of scale was tilted by the burden of actually paying people (i.e., the residents) what they were worth in salaries and health benefits and providing basic human needs including dignity, self-determination, and opportunities for self-betterment—living and social skills, education, and eventually occupational training. There was not enough political will to fund these benefits with tax dollars, contributing to the closing of large institutions nationally.[21]

Reiss relayed a few stories about working residents at Willowbrook:

> The working patients in Willowbrook during the 1960s lived in special buildings, one for boys and the other for girls. They had small rooms, dressing tables, mirrors, upholstered chairs and rugs on the floor. Some of them worked within the institution; others traveled by public transport to jobs on the island and returned to Willowbrook at night.
>
> Sometimes a patient would work outside the grounds but live in Willowbrook for several years. Some clung to this pattern of living, but

21. In New York State, rates negotiated with Medicaid for reimbursement for services for patients in institutional care was extremely high, and remains so today, but is currently being renegotiated because of the reluctance of the federal government to continue to pay for services that can be as much as ten times the cost of those in smaller, community settings.

others could be gradually persuaded to live outside the institution and just return for medical or financial help.

One girl, in her thirties, worked as a daily cleaner in different private homes around the island. She was cheerful, prompt and able to use a vacuum cleaner and a washing machine. Both arts had been taught her in the training school at Willowbrook.

She could not read or write except to print her name. She knew exactly which bus to take to arrive at her different destinations on the island. She could never explain to me how she knew which bus was which, since numbers didn't seem to register with her.

I supposed that she had come to know the area in the main terminal from which her bus left, and would wait there patiently trusting it would be the right bus, but on returning home she had to be selective or she would never have gotten back to the institution.

Other patients were unable to develop such a talent, and they were generally assigned some job in Willowbrook. They worked as messengers, helped in kitchens, clothing rooms, the PX and maintenance departments.[22] They went as cleaners to staff houses on the grounds, helped on the delivery trucks, in the medical clinics, and the dental department.

Other adult residents could carry out some routine work, such as mopping or sorting laundry. One can see how these experiences may have been beneficial for these residents later in life, when opportunities for paid forms of similar labor may have presented themselves.

From the resident's perspective, work was a form of status: From several sources it appears that the more they worked, the more they felt capable. Possibly because of work experience, some of these were residents were able to eventually leave Willowbrook and find employment in the community. Gena, for example, lived at Willowbrook for all of her childhood and young adulthood. During this time, she worked on the wards where she lived, developing the custodial work skills that she continues to use to this day. George recalled, "I worked in the kitchen. And I worked as a porter. They pay me and I worked in the workshop and all that. Then I worked other places." Jimmy said that he learned "to cook or wash dishes and stuff. When I started I was doing dish washing, pots and everything. Sometimes I did

22. PX is military slang for "post exchange," a store that sells various goods of use to those on base. At Willowbrook this reference is an institutional hold-over from its earlier history as an Army Hospital.

cooking and wrapped up the food packages, pack up the bags." Maria was a porter for seven years in Buildings 20, 22, and 23: "I was a cleaner. I got paid a check, and a salary, and everything."[23]

The staff took one of two perspectives. For some, working patients were necessary for the smooth operation of Willowbrook. Staff encouraged working patients, and it created status on the wards, with working patients getting preferential treatment. Ronnie explained:

> If a client was very cute or high-functioning and could help with the work on the ward they were rarely abused. They were not hit. The attendants were nice to those patients. They would give cigarettes or extra food to them, because they were able to help you.

Irma clarified: Working patients "also took care of the ones who were lower-functioning. In that way the attendants had help." A recreation worker observed that working patients:

> used to roll the clothes to get them ready for the next day, and put them in these like cubicles so that when the people would come to get dressed in the morning they would take the stuff out of the cub . . . each cubical like a little pigeon hole type of thing.

And in return, the residents might get some cookies or soda, but she added: "there were no real chores because they didn't have anything." Arlen placed limits on working patients: "You didn't give them the complete control. You didn't let them shower them or fix their hair or anything, but they helped you dress them, put their sneakers on them."

The other perspective from staff was highly critical about working residents. Bronston (2007) observed residents doing basic maintenance, laundry, grounds care, and lodged the following criticism:

> people were recruited pretty much like slave labor to compensate for the staff shortages and inadequacies and lack of budget. There was no job protection, no worker rights, no remuneration, nothing. This was a concentration camp. People were used for a variety of functions in order to save the institution money and to engage them in constructive work. [Yet it] never meant anything more than saving the state money or just being part of the concentration camp culture.

23. Paid labor was probably through an agency that operated at Willowbrook; after the exposé and federal oversight of the facility, it could have also been part of a special grant.

It was clear that working residents

> would get certain privileges or they would get paid attention to, or whatever. And they were used for every conceivable compensatory effort there, including repression. They [were] commandeered to beat up somebody, or to physically suppress somebody that the workers needed to be controlled or contained.

There are, then, these different ways to look at working residents at Willowbrook. From the perspective of patients, there were certain positive social and personal functions, in spite of their being unpaid. From the perspective of administrators, residents represented a huge source of unpaid labor. From the psychiatric technician's point of view, work may have been seen as good for the resident as well as for the other residents whom those working helped. Of course, all these logics derived from a basic form of social organization that was not governed by the rules of ordinary society, the total institution.

Institutional Social Control

As described in Chapter 3, for Goffman (1961), the social basis of total institutional life is a division between a small powerful group in charge and the large mass of individuals whose lives the first group administers. The small group has almost total control of the relatively powerless larger group. The official version of social control is that the staff, guards, brothers, officers, or doctors are in charge and in control of the inmates, patients, novitiates, or recruits. To this official version of power and control, in Goffman's analysis, is also added an unofficial one, social control as exercised by the powerless group among its own members. In some total institutions, the power exercised by this subordinate group can be very dominant in their everyday lives. In the "underlife" of the institution, it is sometimes the residents or prisoners who control what happens, even more than the staff. In some of the narratives—Reiss's, for example—one gets a sense of this underlife, of the ways previous experience, smarts, personality, and strength may have entered into the equation of power, of control.

In this section, we will focus on how staff controlled the residents via an assortment of social and medical practices. We will examine the unofficial social strategies of control in the subsequent section, on punishment, noting that a variety of physical and mental threats and acts were used to keep residents in line and that these were routinely used throughout the institution. In the present section, we look at the more official methods.

An institution as large as Willowbrook, without adequate staff, relied on various methods of maintaining social order, some of them radical. One technique was based on assessing the needs of residents and then assigning them to a building on the basis of their age, needs, and abilities. More drastic measures were needed for many, and so doctors and staff used physical restraints and tranquillizers such as Thorazine or even stronger drugs. For direct care staff, social control also included the engagement of residents to maintain order.

Determining the Need for Control

Trent's (1994) history of institutional care for mentally retarded children in state schools argued that "care became an effective and integral part of control" (p. 5). So has been the case for many institutions that care for cognitively and physically challenged people. At Willowbrook, one key method of control was to assess the needs of residents and then place them in an appropriate setting. Despite the existence of these procedures Rothman and Rothman (1984/2009) documented the repeated failures to make any sort of meaningful assessment of need for the residents. Even in the face of increasing legal oversight, the institution was incapable of properly assessing the needs of each individual; in fact, this was a benchmark that was never cleared by Willowbrook, and this issue, assessment of need, became a central feature of the class action lawsuit against Willowbrook.

In Reiss's ward, because it was a small special research unit, boys with very different levels of ability lived together. More generally, functioning level and sex, not age or diagnosis, were the general basis of assignment to wards. This was determined through an initial intake examination, on the basis of which residents were assigned to what were thought to be appropriate wards. There is testimony, mostly from parents and staff, to indicate that these initial assessments were not thorough, often pro forma, and that results were very suspect. Nonetheless, they would determine one's initial living circumstance in the institution. Residents were grouped first by sex, then by functioning level, although most wards had a wide mix of "levels" of disability. Residents requiring total care, those who were non-ambulatory and profoundly or severely retarded were grouped together because of management reasons. In wards that were not specialized for nonambulatory care, blind, deaf, deaf-blind, severely retarded, moderately retarded, mildly retarded, emotionally disabled, and nondisabled could be found on the same ward. As noted in several of the interviews of former Willowbrook staff, this created conditions that severely limited habilitation and also fostered resident-to-resident intimidation and abuse.

Many interviewees spoke about the diversity of needs among the residents. Arlen spoke about the girls in Building 21, who were "mostly delinquent" and came from St. Joseph's Home in Brooklyn. Others noted that many at Willowbrook were not disabled at all. Irma made this point as well: "On any given ward, at the same time, there were severely retarded residents and emotionally disturbed residents. There were also normal people, who became emotionally disturbed because they were not really retarded, living in the same facilities." She felt that:

> Many people were placed at Willowbrook who did not belong there. Courts placed people from broken homes when they were very young. They became wards of the state, and would be sent to Willowbrook. These were normal kids living in an environment geared for the severely retarded.

In addition, there were residents of all ages, from babies to elderly adults. Those living at Willowbrook represented the full spectrum of humanity: male and female, young and old, able-bodied and disabled.

A speech pathologist who worked at Willowbrook also felt it was a dumping ground for unwanted children who were not necessarily disabled:

> I mean it was an institution for the mentally retarded, either way I looked at it, but a lot of people that were there were not that way. They were there because they became wards of the state and that's where they put them.

Some patients were known as "total care" residents. Reiss explained:

> Many were brain damaged, spastic patients whose whole lives had been confined to a hospital bed. The range of movement in their arms and legs was so restricted that they could not stand or walk, they could not sit up in bed without assistance and, frequently, were unable to turn themselves from side to side while lying down.

Some residents, both boys and girls, arrived at Willowbrook from criminal and family courts. Reiss recounted: "They arrived with records of arson, purse snatching, robbery and malicious mischief. They came on neglect petitions; some were lost and abandoned children who had been taken by the police to a Children's Shelter." These arrivals were tested by psychologists and given low intelligence quotient scores, but it was thought that many could benefit from an academic school environment. Yet the school was so understaffed that children received at best only a few hours of training a day. Many of the residents' IQs were so low as to classify them as uneducable and untrainable. Formal testing, however, was often a poor indicator of a child's ability, given that both language and cultural barriers existed. Thus, as Reiss described:

> The indicator which we found to be much more reliable was the primitive one; were they, or were they not, toilet trained? If toilet trained,

even if they did not speak, seldom answered to their names and were too distractible or restless for any training program, they were accepted in the ward. It was found that these children often blossomed under individual attention.[24]

The overall outcome of this inaccurate assessment process at Willowbrook was to create conditions within which staff would be dealing with people on a ward with such a variety of needs and abilities. It was impossible to use any one approach to either habilitate or control them. The mix created conditions ripe for abuse among residents and, by being impossible in these ways, made the expedient solutions available for control seem more acceptable.

Chemical Social Control: Thorazine, Mellaril, and Phenobarbitol

I remember having my full length leg braces on and having a pheno-barbital capsule forced down my throat. The way they would force it down my throat was by laying me down on my back, and then hold-ing my nose shut, forcing me to breathe through my mouth, which in turn forced me to swallow. And each time I swallowed they would simply drop the pill in my mouth. Each time they did this, I would choke, because the capsule was almost too big to go down my throat. . . . Phenobarbital, Valium and Thorazine were the most commonly given drugs. Especially Phenobarbital. It was passed out like candy. Me, I grew up on Phenobarbital and Valium. (Mickey Finn, as cited by Pratt, 1998, p. 17)

Most people know that the use of psychotropic medications, particularly tranquilizers, was widespread in state institutions for people with mental illness, but they were also heavily employed in hospitals for people with mental retardation all over the United States in the 1960s and 1970s (Grossman, personal communica-tion, 1990). This trend toward use of medication to calm and control people with disabilities continued in the community, and its inappropriate use is still a problem today. At Willowbrook and Pacific State, tranquilizers were in ready supply, and on some wards virtually everyone was put on them in order to keep things calm. Resi-dents had no choice about taking these medications. Thorazine and Phenobarbitol were extremely popular, but longer acting drugs, such as Prolixin, were also used.

---

24. At Pacific State there was also an almost complete distrust in professional assessments of children by those who worked with them on the ward. It was not uncommon for those work-ing with the children to have their own ways of assessing their capabilities and shortcomings.

Tranquilizers were routinely prescribed and often administered by nursing staff or even psychiatric technicians who had the required training. This, in practice, put the power of drug tranquilization in the hands of relatively low-level staff persons who faced dangerous, uncontrollable circumstances. Drugs became the universally accepted and sanctioned avenue for social control and punishment. Because in part of its easy availability, it was also easily mis- and over used.

Many of the accounts describe how both older and younger residents were routinely given the tranquilizer Thorazine for purposes of social control. The "State Boys" at Fernald were actually involved in the drug trials for Thorazine, proving that it created docile patients (D'Antonio, 2004). In Reiss's opinion, "The punishments allotted were never particularly severe, seldom effective and when the situation was obviously out of hand, tranquilization was the means of choice. Control had to be maintained at all times." Reiss described several residents who were given a daily dose of Thorazine to keep them sleepy, obedient, and calm.

In his interview, George mentioned that Thorazine was given to everybody. It seemed impossible, but Irma confirmed this:

> Thorazine was in common use at Willowbrook. They gave it to everybody. It was administered three times a day, in the orange juice. Everyone was on Thorazine. The higher functioning residents got wise. They knew that they were being drugged and would spit it out. After a while, even some of the lower functioning clients would fake taking it, too. It was all so crazy.

Joséph, a former ward attendant, also spoke about Thorazine use in his ward:

> The main treatment by the doctor in my building was to give out Thorazine. One of the students was receiving somewhere around 200 to 300 milligrams of Thorazine a day. That is enough to stop a charging bull. We went upstairs to complain that we just could not keep this boy in school. He was just too crazy. The doctor pulled his chart and said, "No, no, not possible, this boy is on 2–300 Thorazine, not possible." Just then, the boy ran down from Ward C with three attendants on top of him, dragging them down the stairs. The doctor looked up and said, "100 milligrams of Thorazine." That was the controlling factor at Willowbrook. Thorazine and beating the residents.

Bronston also related that drugs were the primary, routine technology used for social control on many of the wards. He noted that often residents were kept on these medications for years without being rotated off them for a period, which was medically dangerous and resulted in a host of permanent side effects, such as tics. Residents developed a tolerance for the medications, requiring higher doses to achieve desired results. Thus, the tranquilizing drugs, seen to be required by a "resource situation" that was socially created, were not used in a medically responsible manner.

Not surprisingly, the practice of medicating residents of state institutions for the purposes of controlling their behavior followed them out of the institutions into the group homes and other facilities created during the deinstitutionalization era, especially in its early days. Overmedication was a very common problem in the early days of deinstitutionalization. Medications are still used in group homes today, although laws prevent their facile administration, and at least theoretically oversight in their appropriate management exists.[25]

Punishment

A basic fact of virtually all total institutions is the use of threats and punishment to control resident behaviors. Here are three examples from other state hospitals. At Letchworth Village, in Rockland County, New York, Gene Vertefeulla, a former resident recalled:

> I used to get beat up just for crying. I got hit a couple of times with a ball bat, with a cop stick, across the feet, stuff like that. A lot of times you try to explain to people . . . and they walk away. And I say, if that was your son, would you let your son get hit! . . . One kid got his head put down the toilet, that wasn't right. Sometimes they got punished for nothing. Cause you want to walk with or talk to somebody. Sometimes you talked to somebody and you just got punished for that. Get hit with a scrub brush across your hands, or a radiator brush.
>
> Q: *There was no one to complain to?*
>
> A: You would tell the doctor and he would say, go back and get some more. At that time you would tell the doctor and they didn't believe you. They would say go back home and get some more . . . back to the cottage . . . and you had to walk back. . . . They made you clean the porch on your knees in the middle of the winter, and that was mean. . . . They hit me with a ball bat just because I asked them why they opened my private mail. (as cited by Pratt, 1998, p. 17)

At Fernald State School, residents were scared of saying anything critical because "attendants routinely preyed on their ignorance and imaginations to make

---

25. As expressed in a talk given by a parent at Goode's class at the College of Staten Island in October 2012, there is a worry that the use of drugs as a form of social control could come back to the service system if resources are severely cut, as is proposed by some politicians today.

them obedient. They continually threatened to give the boys shock treatments or lobotomies 'so you come back like a zombie'" (D'Antonio, 2004, p. 51). Yet escapes were common, and seclusion and restraints were used as control. In the 1940s at Fernald, three to four residents were housed in seclusion. By 1952, the school had a prison with approximately two dozen residents in house, six bound in leather straps or straightjackets.

One doctor, Fred Dowling, "would twist a towel around a boy's head, drag him to the bathroom, and force his face into a toilet bowl" (Pratt, 1998, p. 92). An attendant would use "pig piling" to help control behavior: The attendants would identify a resident, and all the others would jump on top of the victim, or a big shot might rough up a child. One attendant earned the moniker "slap happy" because she had the propensity to slap a resident, boxing his ears.

Hornick (2012) described punishment and control at Belchertown State School. Escapees from the school were socially devalued and embarrassed by having their heads shaved like a pie-shaped wedge or having to wear striped overalls. More broadly, Hornick found that:

> Control of residents was maintained in three distinct ways: by structuring their physical environment to restrict freedom of movement and individuality, by establishing routines and schedules that dealt with residents in groups rather than individually, and by punishing disobedient residents (and rewarding obedient ones) (p. 56).

Thus, at Belchertown, the physical environment emphasized control: Buildings were set far apart, buildings were locked, windows were covered with bars, sleeping rooms were barren; even toilets needed keys to flush them. Furthermore:

> Forms of punishment included physical force (slapping, hitting), physical restraint (straightjackets, tying to chairs), seclusion rooms, confinement to back wards, forced maintenance of uncomfortable positions for long periods of time, and withholding of privileges. (Hornick, 2012, p. 58)

For some, there was a seclusion room: a bare, unpadded room, with no toilet or bucket. Seclusion rooms were employed in all state institutions we have heard about over the years.

Former residents of Fernald, Belchertown, Letchworth, Willowbrook, or any institution could provide a litany of punishments. Some of the stories, even in the sources cited in this book, are horrifying, almost defying imagination.

Because of their availability and agreement about their utility, at Willowbrook drugs often could serve as a form of punishment as well as control. This was illustrated by a former resident, Eileen, who spoke on the occasion of the 25th anniversary of the Willowbrook Consent Decree, an event at which former New York governors Hugh

Carey and Mario Cuomo also spoke.[26] She told about how she had been punished for being the ringleader of a bunch of the "working girls" who slipped out of the institution at night to try and find guys off Willowbrook grounds to sleep with. They would sneak out on certain nights when they knew night staff would sleep and get back before they would wake. Eventually they got caught, and Eileen was identified as the ringleader (which she readily admits and is proud of today). She was punished with a series of actions: first withdrawal of privilege; next, isolation; after that, drugs. Drugs were the last option because the ones used in this way were very strong, such as Prolixin, which could produce prolonged periods of virtual catatonia and paralysis. Eileen suffered this treatment at first and told her punishers that she would not stop, no matter what they did. But eventually she gave it up because it was just not worth the consequences. When she related this to the audience, she was a proud survivor, happily relating her battle with the institution, even if it eventually won.

The threat of violence, or violent acts themselves, punishments, are a form of social control. There is widespread evidence of punishment at Willowbrook. George, a past resident, described one of the punishments he saw used: standing a child in the corner with his or her hands up. Bronston documented injuries obviously created by attendant keys. A ward key is in the Willowbrook Collection at the College of Staten Island. It is a large key, and the keys at Willowbrook were kept on a key ring. Bronston and workers who were interviewed clearly remember that the keys on the ring were used in defense against aggressive residents and as a weapon against those the staff felt needed to be punished. It is probably not farfetched to think that they may have also been used by aggressive staff to terrorize residents. Irma confirmed that ward attendants used keys to hit the residents:

> I heard Building 23 was awful. I had friends who worked there, and they said it was awful. Many of the girls in Building 23 were disturbed. They would get some pretty severe beatings. In the buildings with more severe behavior problems, the attendants would really lace into the residents. Some of the teachers that I knew did not stay there very long. They said it was disgusting, and they could not handle it.

Ronnie also confirmed the use of keys:

> Yes, you know the big keys? I witnessed this. Willowbrook people learned how to abuse people in a way that left no marks. For instance, in the genital area. It was important to leave no marks because each day,

26. May 1, 2000. Center for Performing Arts, College of Staten Island, Staten Island, New York. An unedited video of is part of the Willowbrook Collection, Library Archives, College of Staten Island.

on your shift, you had to check. You had to strip a client and search for bruises. It was your responsibility. If someone found a bruise later, then you could be blamed for it. I always felt that nobody really did a whole lot about it, if bruises were found.

Irma described another common way used to maintain control:

There were various techniques to keep control of a ward. You would take the most violent clients out and put them in a place where they would not be involved with the rest of the clients on the ward. Rooms were created which were called "Pits." It would be like solitary confinement. You would be placed in "The Pit" and left there. A client would be left there through the entire shift. The client would be left there for five, six, or even eight hours, depending upon how violent he was. Eventually, they padded these rooms, because the clients were so violent and self-abusive. The rages would be so bad that they would split their own skulls open or bite off their own fingers. Some wards could get so terrible, so insane, that there would not be enough padded rooms. You worked in an insane world. It was impossible to beat . . . the clients into submission. Many were so used to beatings that they were immune to pain. After a while you were no longer shocked by these behaviors.

John remembered:

order being kept by banging broom handles on the floor and yelling at them. The brighter ones and the attendants would also . . . herd them into a corner and make like they were going to beat them with the stick and some of them actually did hit them with it. That would get their attention.

Clearly, for John:

It was about control. It was about not losing control. The stories that were told from the attendants to me was it was a dangerous place to work and if you didn't maintain control you could get hurt there. And there was stories of attendants who did get hurt there. Although I never did see any. The only people I saw hurt were the clients themselves and that happened quite often. The only time that any of that was ever reported was when medical care was needed, stitches, or whatever. I can remember times when if it was iffy, they wouldn't call it. They would wait a little while longer to see if the bleeding would stop.

In another interview, a worker was asked about "the Pit" and how order was maintained:

> Well, imagine yourself in a ward with a hundred residents. Many of these people would not or could not keep their clothes on. Many could not control themselves. They would defecate right where they were. The stench was awful. When you went on one of these wards for the first time you would vomit. You had to work there on a daily basis to get used to the stench, if you could. If you were a ward attendant the conditions were impossible.
>
> There was one ward attendant, whose job it was to try and control all of this madness. There was no way anyone could control this. If an attendant tried to keep one resident who was in a rage from hurting another resident, quite probably the attendant would get hurt too.

In sum, from the staff's perspecive, these were the various techniques to keep control of a ward. When faced with a virtually impossible situation, they found methods to achieve a certain degree of control, for all practical purposes and obviously not always successfully.

Worker Solidarity

One of the problems in the institution was that the workers simply did not trust or communicate effectively with each other, and this led to significant problems with worker solidarity. There were hints this might be the case, for it was true elsewhere. In Belchertown State School, for example, Hornick (2012) documented a ward attendant's displeasure: "If you did as I did and brought attention to problems, you were harassed and threatened. The residents had no voice, the staff was silenced, and authority was corrupt. It was institutional corruption" (p. 68).

Tensions between frontline staff and administrators were commonplace. One study of institutional life in the northeastern United States in the early 1970s portrayed ward attendants as routinely suspicious of psychological testing, especially IQ scores (Bogdan et al., 1974). Attendants viewed the largely foreign-born psychiatrists and medical doctors as isolated and lazy and disparaged state officials for giving them inadequate resources. This is similar to the description provided by Bronston about Willowbrook.

There were several examples of this provided by Reiss in her account. For instance, although the psychologists played an important role in assessing the needs of residents, it was widely believed that their intelligence tests were inaccurate and never adequately assessed residents' abilities. Teachers at the school would level punishments at their students, but ward attendants would doubt what happened at school, second-guessing the punishment, and the residents would often not actually receive the prescribed procedure. There seems to have been at Willowbrook, and at Pacific State, distrust on the part of direct care staff of the knowledge and recommendations made by professionals employed at the institution. The direct care personnel, understanding that realistically the professionals knew actually very little about the child compared with their own firsthand knowledge, would simply ignore professionals' reports as much as possible.[27] As the professional staff virtually never came on the ward and interacted with the child only during very short periods of examination and assessment, workers' mistrust was justified under the circumstances. It was one way in which people who worked at places like Willowbrook did not trust one another.

Reiss also addressed the issue of staff theft of clothing and other supplies which created a lot of dissension among the staff, who were in their own right poor and often in serious need for their families. Supplies were usually kept in locked cupboards, but with temporary and full-time employees working three 8-hour shifts, the keys passed through many hands. Reiss believed that sometimes attendants might steal supplies from one ward to give to another:

Sent, usually unwillingly, to cover a ward which she or he did not know, for just one shift, they would inspect the closets carefully. If they contained, for example, garments which were in short supply in her area of the institution she would take them, feeling quite righteously annoyed that one ward could have so much when hers had so little. No thought was given to the hours of planning and careful strategy that had gone into making a reserve of that particular garment.

Sometimes I believe the clothes did indeed go home with the attendant. Certainly the pretty china that we were given at one time, and which disappeared completely during the night as if off the face of the earth, must have been taken off the grounds of Willowbrook. It had been a donation, and since the dinner set was just enough for our ward population we were selected to receive this really very cheering gift. The

27. On the ward for deaf-blind children at Pacific State, Goode was told in so many words not to waste his time reading the formal assessments of children made by professionals at the hospital. "If you want to know what a kid sees or hears, ask me," the ward charge said. She then demonstrated with a particular resident whose file said he was unable to see anything other than overall dark and light. She brought him to a table and put a small bowl of M&Ms on the table. She gave him one, then another, then stopped. He clearly moved his head and looked at the bowl on the table and then reached over to take some more candy. The staff member had a good sense from first hand long term observation about what this child could see. Professionals who did not know the child well at all and virtually never observed them in the normal conditions of ward life, and often few valid intruments to assess children, nevertheless filled out the forms require by law. They were generally not of clinical value; this was the case both at Pacific State and Willowbrook.

boys had one meal off that china, and it was never seen again. The china was kept in an open kitchen which could be entered by several different doors, including one leading directly from the elevator. Even so, it was hard to believe that a dinner set for twenty could be removed so silently in the night that no one was aware of the thievery.

There were ways to file complaints or accuse employees of theft, but as Reiss remembered:

> To bring a charge against a fellow employee was a long and arduous business. It was not only unwise personally because it made you enemies among the other staff members, even those who were in no way involved with the particular incident, it was also difficult because you had to be a witness and prove your case beyond a reasonable doubt.
>
> Most attendants avoided this situation like the plague. They might wail and scream at each other and abuse the suspected culprit, but they didn't if they could help, go to the authorities. 'It wouldn't,' as one attendant said, 'get us no clothes, but it would get us big trouble.'
>
> If an attendant was harsh with the children, or neglectful to the point of abuse, other employees would sometimes get so emotionally involved that they would report the incident, and even press charges. This was courageous of them, and they were often frightened. They suspected that they might suffer reprisals, and sometimes they did. The reprisals again were often ones in which it was difficult to establish origin. Threatening anonymous letters arrived at the attendant's home; mumbled obscenities came over the telephone in the early hours of the morning; car tires were slashed; home windows broken. Such an attendant was often fearful of walking the short distance from her car to her assigned building on a dark night unless someone else came with her.
>
> Without supportive evidence the supervisors were unable to press charges and had little to go upon except gossip. They would then try and get the unsatisfactory attendant moved to another area of the institution, so that they circulated the grounds causing varying amounts of disruption and damage. After six months it is very hard to dismiss a State employee without a very good cause. They have the backing of the State system of employment that was set up long ago to encourage workers to stay in what was once a poorly paid, but secure, position. Now the attendant had also the union, which uses its muscle to protect its members to make sure that they get the benefit of every doubt.
>
> Unfortunately, the children had no union. They were also not allowed to give evidence against employees, or at least that was the situation

when I worked there. Many of the children could not give evidence under any circumstances, and are not aware of anything except their own pain and discomfort.

As described in an interview in the documentary *My Country* (Ward, 1997), this situation also existed at Southbury Training School, where T. J. Monroe lived his childhood. Children there were easy victims because without corroborating testimony of another staff member, nothing they said would be taken seriously. To paraphrase Monroe, if a staff member wanted you to do something, you had to do it. Children who spoke up risked reprisals far worse than sexual harassment, making cooperation the only practical option. Monroe described how when the situation became unbearable at Southbury, some young people would elect to kill themselves rather than continue on. The "Hanging Tree" was a tree used by the older boys to help other residents kill themselves. These boys had become experts at hanging. "They knew how to do the rope . . . and one would hold the feet." Monroe explained that sometimes they did not even use the tree, as they had become expert at strangulation as well. Monroe described how they would use a towel to prevent marks on the body "to spare the parents" and how "guys" would smuggle it back into the ward after. This is an almost unbelievable thing to hear, an appalling consequence of creating such terrible conditions that mercy killing actually became part of the underlife of the children in the institution and that such young people became expert practitioners. No anecdote could more chillingly relate the difference between a regular childhood and one in a total institution. Staff who perpetrated these abuses were also feared by other staff members. Thus as at Willowbrook, staff mistrust and fear were directly linked to the problem of abuse.

Staff distrust and lack of cooperation existed at many levels at Willowbrook. The maintenance department seemed, to Reiss, unwilling to help out with repairs. In one case, she tried to explain why several windows needed repair. Below is her memory of her conversation with the window glazer:

> "Well, you see, it was a fight. They threw shoes. Yes, they were wearing outdoor shoes. No, we don't have slippers. How could we have slippers? We don't even have enough outdoor shoes. That isn't logical? . . . Well, maybe you're right. It isn't logical but that's how it is. Well, yes, they are breaking more windows, but that is because they are much better. I mean they are more alert and active . . . happier, I think. Well, once when they threw shoes they hit each other on the head but now they dodge around like anything and the shoe goes through the window. You don't think that is much of an improvement? Yes, I suppose from your point of view it isn't . . . but it does get awfully cold up here, especially at night, do you think you could please, possibly?"

Plumbers also seemed, to Reiss, to resist taking orders for repair:

> We met the plumbers on much the same level. As toilets and sinks overflowed the grimly enraged plumbers would bring their soaking trophies and lay them at our feet. "Four diapers, one small teddy bear, a wad of paper towels and two toothbrushes. How do you expect a toilet to work if you use it like a garbage disposal? Do you realize that your ward has blocked up the pipes for four floors and that the sewage is dripping into the dental department? You should all be up on charges."

The plumber's warning was serious. The complaint was brought to the administration, and charges of misbehavior were filed against one staff member.

One of the arguments made by Rothman and Rothman (1984/2009) was that the staff of Willowbrook had a vested interest in preventing the various inquiries from uncovering the true nature of the school. Staff engaged in "window dressing" efforts designed to mislead visitors and obstructed investigations in accusations of violence and abuse of residents. And why wouldn't they? Such window dressing was done under the direct orders of the administration. Most were only doing their best under harsh conditions, and without Willowbrook, they would not have jobs. Further, there was considerable and real risk that one took in ratting out another employee. Such an act, as in Reiss's description of the exchange with the plumber, could lead to confrontation, retribution, and violence, even severe violence. This was particularly true of those working at Willowbrook who were engaged in illegal activities, such as drug dealing, stealing, or victimizing residents. This theme comes up in several sections of our book, that self-protection of one form or another was a main reason for not cooperating with investigations.

Families

For those who lived there, it is fitting to address "family" as part of the "living conditions" at Willowbrook. Family was both central to the lives of residents and, paradoxically, often completely absent. Many residents[28] either had no known family members, or they had family who never visited or showed any interest in their relative. Still others, a relatively small minority given the thousands who lived at WSS, had families who were quite involved and came to the school regularly. Both children and adults could be in either of these situations, and this figured, in part, into one's status on the wards. All knew, residents and staff, that those with family

28. Again it is difficult to make a numerical estimation of how many, but it is clear from staff interviews that most children and adults did not have regular visits from families and many had no visitation at all.

were lucky, in a better situation than those who had simply been cast aside because someone didn't care for them. As reported by workers at WSS and observed by Goode at Pacific State, having family gave residents a higher social status than those without. Family thus was part of the texture of life at WSS, by the normality of its perspicuous absence or less commonly its serial presence.

Often finding themselves without any family, children at Willowbrook invented parents. Although Reiss does not report the use of the terms "daddy" and "mommy" on her ward, such language was described by Katie Meskell (1996) in her documentary, *Unforgotten*. Children at Willowbrook did use these terms. It was observed by Davenport on Randall's Island in the 1860s and by Goode at Pacific State in the 1970s. For those abandoned by family, staff were the only people available to them to be their "mommy" or "daddy," and it was easy, if not inappropriate, to allow these forms of address to become an accepted part of ward argot. This form of reference followed residents into the community, and in the 1970s Goode obtained a video of a man with Down syndrome living in a community residence who continued to use these forms of address with people he considered special (Goode, 1983). Goode also noted in this research that these names served an adaptive function for this man, whose choices of "mommies" and "daddies" were not at all arbitrary but involved figures of authority and power. One presumes that these terms may have served similar functions on wards, that is, that there was a logic to who was, or was not, called daddy or mommy on the ward.

Reiss reported that many of her children had been abandoned by their parents: "Nothing had been heard from their relatives since, and the case records were uninformative about their early years." Because many had no viable family connections, they reached out to the ward attendants. Most of the boys on Reiss's ward were envious of children who had relatives or visitors. Interested family members who visited were a primary source of status for children (and adults) at Willowbrook. Although having visiting parents might have been such a status symbol for children, such a symbol glosses the very different relationships that existed, for example, between the children on Reiss's ward and their parents.

On Reiss's ward, some kids made up stories to account for their relatives' absence, though only a few concocted as elaborate an explanation as Nelson, who had been placed at Willowbrook because his parents had either given him up or abandoned him:

> He . . . was generally a cheerful boy, except at Christmas time. He would spend hours on the construction of a Christmas card. His ideas of design were unexpectedly attractive, but many were discarded before he was satisfied. He would then enlist Peter's aid in printing 'To my Mom' on the card, and take it to the attendant saying, 'Mail this. Don't forget the stamp.'

We had no address to which to send the card but Nelson would not accept this as an excuse. At sometime or other he had decided that in the basement of the administration building there was a piece of paper with his mother's name and address on it. If an attendant would just take the trouble to go over to the building and search the basement they would find it. He could not understand our obstinacy, or worse still, our spite, in this important matter.

He waited throughout the Christmas holidays for the arrival of a response from his mother. When no mail came for him he grew progressively more sullen and suspicious. He would announce that he wished to return to his 'real home.' Asked where that was he would say, coldly, 'The Children's Shelter, of course. They were good to me.'

Sometimes residents would make connections with distant family members. Reiss told a story about the visits from José's father:

José's father was greeted with joy. He was not really José's father at all. He was José's mother's second ex-husband. He had no idea where José's mother lived now, and neither had we, but he had heard from a neighbor that the child he had loved was now living in Willowbrook. A sailor, he was away from home for months at a time, and had not seen José for over three years. Whether he had any legal right to come and see the boy we never knew. His moral right was established the moment José saw him standing shy and uncertain in the doorway. Before the attendant could ask him his name José had hurled himself across the ward into the man's arms, shouting, "Dad!"

Mr. P. explained, apologetically, that he had no place to which he could take José. He spent so little time ashore that he didn't have places to live that would be, he thought, suitable for a child. José didn't mind because when his father came to see him it was for the whole day. He either stayed in the dayroom playing cards, telling stories or repairing toys, or, if the weather was good, he would take bat, ball, and all the kids who wanted to go with him out onto the grass. They always ended up at the PX. This was a small building in the center of the grounds. It had retained its name from the time Willowbrook had been an army hospital. Apart from selling a number of small items such as Cigarettes, candy, pencils and some clothes, it provided sandwiches, coffee and ice cream.

José's father treated the boys to as much coke and ice cream as they could hold. He made the occasion festive with his own open delight in their pleasure. During the year postcards came from all over the world and José carried them around until they fell apart.

Some parents were just simply overwhelmed by a child whose needs required more of them than they could offer. Reiss described Sam's parents, who were:

> devoted, gentle people, but they could not cope with him, their eldest son. At 16 years of age he felt that he should be allowed to join in all the activities that his brothers enjoyed. He wanted to go on dates, learn to drive the car and play baseball. The fact that his appearance horrified the girls and his lack of coordination made it difficult, if not impossible, for him to throw a ball, did not deter him. Refused permission, he would lie on the floor and scream. This might have been effective when he was two years old, but it was terrifying in a boy with the height and weight of an adult.
>
> The family doctor prescribed a tranquilizer. This medication stopped his tantrums, but instead he grew morose and quiet, began to wet his bed and occasionally soil himself. Sometimes the parents managed to keep him for a month. This was the longest period. Usually, after two or three weeks they would return him to the ward, dejected and depressed by their failure.

Families who visited WSS developed their own ways of dealing with what they faced. As we shall see, to a large degree relatives were "steel-doored" off the ward and were not permitted to actually see the conditions on the wards. But they could not be sheltered from their effects on their loved ones. They could not help but see their psychological and physical state, their low weight, bruises, broken bones, psychological distress, and so on. As much as Willowbrook employees blamed other residents for the bruises parents saw on their children, parents blamed Willowbrook. In an almost overt attempt to obfuscate the reality of the situation, when families visited, each child was inspected before leaving and upon return, so there was a log of the damage families might have done while the child was off the ward. A mirror image of this same form of examination is described by the Rivera family in the film *Unforgotten* (Meskell, 1996) and was seen performed by parents by Goode at Pacific State Hospital. Upon arriving for visits, these parents inspected their child for harms done by the institution.

Reiss also described Donald and his mother:

> Every month his mother came to see him, traveling from the Bronx by subway, ferry and bus. She would enter the ward, walking heavily on her swollen, bandaged legs, and hug and kiss Donald as if the separation had been longer than she could bear. They both looked forward to the day when he would be done with school and could come home and have a job.

Several times it was suggested that she might apply for permission to take Donald home. Although his IQ remained constant in the low sixties, most people who knew Donald were sure that he could live and thrive outside the institution. The authorities were only too happy to discharge a patient, especially to his own home.

Donald's mother would not hear of it. She was very practical. Donald was happy, as she pointed out, and did 'real good' in school. She thought he might by unhappy in her neighborhood school. He might hang around the streets. There would be trouble. Donald listened thoughtfully and nodded.

Lenny had an unpredictable relationship with his mother, who seemingly had other priorities in life but would be supportive when asked:

He had settled quietly into Willowbrook, communicating with his family through carefully printed messages on postcards or, when desperate, by telephone when he had a dime.

Sometimes his mother came to see him. She was a small, very pretty woman often dressed rather incongruously. With plunging neckline and high heels she would totter through the snow, frequently with only a shawl to protect her from the cold. She agreed to everything. She made appointments to see the social worker, but never kept them. She arranged to take Lenny home for a weekend, but seldom came on the appointed day.

Lenny did not seem to be upset by this. He was very protective towards his mother, who had spent some time in one of the big mental hospitals. Lenny seemed to take the view that as long as she remained well everything would work out. If she did not come to see him for several weeks he would grow progressively more worried, until someone gave him a dime and he could telephone home. His mother was always delighted to hear from him and, reminded of his existence, would turn up the next weekend, smiling, pretty and agreeing to everything.

Peter is featured in one of Reiss's most interesting stories about family:

Peter just said that all his family was dead. He wrote letters to whichever attendant had recently won his favor, ending with, 'From your son who has only dead people.' It was not quite true. He was one of eleven children all living around the State in homes for the retarded or orphanages. One year we received a letter from a social worker. She wrote that three of the Hunter [pseudonym] children lived in the orphanage where she worked. She had heard that Peter was in Willowbrook and proposed bringing the children together for a visit.

Since she did not know Peter and had no information about him except his bare existence, she asked, tactfully, if in our opinion such a visit would be 'meaningful at this time?' We were delighted and wrote back at once to assure her that Peter could well appreciate such a visit. Finally a date was set, and Peter carefully prepared. With all the time and energy spent on clothes the boys still looked shabby. A boy could look acceptable, even smart, in Willowbrook, but the moment he left the grounds, or special visitors were expected, his clothes seemed to droop, to hang baggily upon him, to shout, 'Institution!'

Peter got dressed three times in all. The only mirror in the ward was a small piece of polished metal about twelve inches square, fastened high upon the bathroom wall. He had to rely upon the reaction of the attendant and the other boys. He certainly had their full attention. They watched, fascinated, as the attendant searched through her closets coming out with one shirt or pair of pants after the other. Finally everyone was satisfied, or at least agreed that it was the best that we could do.

The social worker was young, a serious and pretty girl. She brought the three Hunter children to the ward and introduced them to Peter. There was a remarkable physical resemblance between them. We had been told that their mother was a prostitute whose frequent pregnancies had been fathered by many different men. If so, she must have been consistent in the type of man she solicited, or had impressed her image on these four children at least.

Tyrone was three years older than Peter, considerably taller, and more sturdily built. The two girls were younger, shy and quiet. We didn't hear them speak until they were leaving, when they whispered, 'Goodbye,' to Peter.

We were all standing around rather awkwardly in the entrance to the ward when Tyrone initiated the proceedings. Apart from the facial resemblance between the boys there was a similarity in their behavior. Tyrone had, from the moment they arrived, concentrated his attention upon Peter, considering him, inspecting him and sizing him up. Since we had often watched Peter considering people or situations in the ward with that same intent detachment, it was with some inward amusement that we watched Peter, nervous but impassive, undergoing scrutiny for once.

Finally Tyrone walked up to within a few feet of Peter and started an interrogation.

'Do they give you soup?'

Peter, very dignified, replied quietly, 'Often.'

'Do you have a bed?'

'Yes.'

'Is it just your bed?'

'Yes.'

'Where is it?'

Peter led his brother and the two girls on an inspection of the ward. Tyrone continued questioning and checking into everything. We noticed, with interest, that Peter did not show him the playroom or discuss the games he invented. He was a little awed by his brother and perhaps felt it was best to take no chances. Tyrone looked quite capable of taking over completely.

While the children were wandering around the ward we talked to the social worker about them. She described the family as 'socially adept but academically poor.' That seemed to us an excellent description of Peter, and gave us the opportunity that we wanted. Thinking about Peter's future, it seemed that he might have a better chance if he emerged into the working world from an orphanage rather than from a home for the mentally retarded.

We inquired about the possibility of transferring him to the orphanage. The poor girl blanched visibly. The home was, she explained, packed to the ceiling. She had, however, wondered about reuniting the family in Willowbrook. It was our turn to turn pale. We hastily led her down to the Willowbrook Social Workers' department. Such policy decisions were well above our heads.

After that visit Peter wrote to his brother about twice a year. He did not seem to be elated about having a family, and continued to write letters to the attendants ending with, 'From your son, who has no one but dead people.'

These vignettes about how families functioned on Reiss's ward reveal a detailed knowledge of life and compassionate perspective taken toward the children who lived there, in this case, about the importance of family to children who did not see them often, or may not even know them. Of course, children also lived on the custodial wards of the hospital and sometimes had been so neglected and unsocialized that it was difficult to know to what degree they were aware of their own abandonment or its effect on them.

As briefly mentioned, one of the ideas asserted by workers was that there was something inappropriate going on with placements of children at Willowbrook. Several past employees have asserted that parents and the authorities (judges, psychologists or psychiatrists, and the administration) dumped unwanted children at Willowbrook. Irma explained what she saw:

For whatever reason, the child was a bother. This way, they did not have to keep the child at home. So they just dumped them. If you knew someone who would alter the test results for you, you could get your child admitted to Willowbrook. Doctors and judges would alter IQ scores in order to make a child eligible for admittance. If you checked the records of many of the higher-functioning residents you would find that a remarkable number of them had IQs of 69. You wondered how it was that so many of these residents had IQs of 69. Some children were literally dumped at the doors of Willowbrook. There was a story about a boy who was blind. His father drove up to the grounds in a Cadillac and just let him out of the car with a note saying, 'Never want to see the kid again. Do not notify in case of death.'

This kind of story has much repeated by people who worked at Willowbrook and has a symbolic value, expressing how the inhumanity of Willowbrook effected children and adults, disabled or not. Some workers stated in interviews that they knew of well-to-do Staten Island families who got their children into Willowbrook just because they could not deal with the children's behaviors. They implied that these families had taken advantage of the relatively easy procedure to place someone in Willowbrook. That procedure required that the person be examined by a physician, admitted for observation, and, based on the results of observation, placed in the institution or not. Virtually everyone examined got in. Although there may have been people who were not admitted, we are not aware of such a case. Willowbrook became so famous as a place to take unwanted children that, for example, children were found in Grand Central Station with a sign "Take me to Willowbrook." Placing a child at Willowbrook was made about as easy as possible.[29]

Conversely, there were families embroiled in decades of struggle with the school to protect and help their children. Often such families, because they wanted more for their children and advocated on their behalf, were regarded as troublesome, maverick, or uncooperative. They were subject to various forms of social control and manipulation to ensure that they did not "rock the boat" too much.

The Benevolent Society for Retarded Children began as a parent organization, as described by Diane McCourt[30] in 2005:

29. This anecdote was first encountered in an interview done by Fusillo, but has been much repeated throughout the years. It is purported to appear in a newspaper article but we have not located that source.

30. Diane McCourt is a parent of a child who lived at Willowbrook. Her husband, Malachai, a well-known New York radio personality helped bring the Willowbrook case to the public. Diane and Malachai were among the parents who picketed WSS and created public awareness about the School.

In the early days before Bill [Bronston] . . . there was a parent organization. But it was very focused on dealing with emergencies. There were constant emergencies at Willowbrook. Somebody was severely beaten, the heating plant broke, and so everybody was freezing, there were no clothes in building six, so everybody was running around. Also volunteerism, people put a lot of effort into going on trips, bringing candy, things like that. But there was no vision for a different way of doing things. There was only an emphasis on making friends with the administration to try and make a little change. And parents, believe it or not, were really grateful to have a place to put their child, even though it was Willowbrook. Because the culture was such that these were basically throw away people. There was really no possibility of doing anything better. They act that way because that is the way they are. Instead of having an alternative vision that a different environment, a home life environment and community environment would nurture them and people could flower and grow like anyone else. So the parent movement was sort of stuck in a rut, and the reformists were sort [of] stuck in the mode of let's fix the thing like it is. . . . The outside reformers . . . they had a vested interest in keeping things quiet, you know they had made some inroads, and they actually came to one of our meetings and said, you know, keep it quiet, you don't know where your bread is buttered. . . . So that whole thing of making that leap of vision, is very scary to a family because they have gone through this tremendous decision to finally turn their children over to the state, and then to think of having to do it again, facing change, really facing what was going on in the institution. I brought my mother there and all she could do was look at the curtains, and say, the curtains are nice, you know she could not look at what was going on. . . . There is a kind of blocking when you see something horrible going on. (McCourt, 2005)

At the same gathering, Bronston added the following about the parent organization:

The Benevolent Society mightily, mightily tried to ameliorate the situation there. And, did you know, whatever they could. But they operated in a very vassal-like relationship to the director, you know, who essentially was like a Pasha, who had absolute power, absolute authority. The administration, Hammond, had every conceivable excuse for why things were abysmal, making what was abysmal ok, and the best that he could do, which implied the best that could be done. There was an absolute conspiracy of silence, containment, secrecy, and control, and the parents, you know, had to do whatever they could do to get whatever kinds of privileges they possibly could to protect their own sons and daughters which, you know, was futile because there was no protection in there. (Bronston, 2005)

Bronston's characterization of the pathetic treatment of the parents he met at WSS is heart-wrenching. He witnessed their manipulation by the administration, being kept ignorant by being kept off the wards and being threatened (with change of ward, removal of services, having to pay for institutional placement) if they spoke out against what was happening:

> You have the families and that is the tragedy of all tragedies. Their experience there. Incapable of accessing the physical place where the people really are because there are steel doors there. And there are hostile workers there who don't want them to be seen because they know in their heart of hearts they're administrating over crimes against humanity. They may not call it that. They may not say it to themselves. But they are defensive and scared, and ruthlessly rejecting of any caring family. Certainly to bring in the gold and diamonds to put on the altar of taking care of their kids? Well, we'll take care of that. . . . What was going on there is a way of creating an artificial system, a hermetically sealed context for systemic human abuse. The only possible witnesses and voices of love and identification, and recognition by name (said with emphasis) of who's here in the concentration camp, is steel-doored out! The individual is propelled out the door on a weekend visit. There is no support, because there is no money to support those families to help take care of their kids. And the families have had to make an adjustment. They have been told: it's here or nowhere. It's this or nothing. And the result is this incredible heartbreaking transformation of families, who can't even cry anymore. Because nobody will listen and nobody gives them an explanation of what it is that is going on; that this is man-made, that this is corruption, that it is criminal negligence, that this is a violation of the constitution, at every level. That this is a violation of medicine, that this is a violation of fundamental anything! . . .
>
> The real energy and inspiration for all of this comes from families who would come. But one of the things I wanted to do was just to say to them, I want you, you know, to be together with your son or daughter. I mean I will do everything I can to close that gap. I will open that steel door. There is no reason for that steel door to be there in the first place. I can't tell you why the clothes you brought for your kids last week aren't there. Somebody stole them. I can't tell you why your kid looks like he got hit by

a truck. Broken nose, torn ears, scars, hair pulled out, key marks on their backs because of those steel doors, because the administration doesn't care, and because the parents are not raising hell about the fact that their kid doesn't belong here. That the 50 to 80 thousand dollars for your kid here could be going . . . into your community." (Bronston, 2006)

Thus, families' attempts to intervene on behalf of their children were thwarted by keeping them ignorant of actual conditions, threatening them with transfers or even with returning the child to the home, using professional authority to question their efforts, threatening them with bills for services (technically, families were supposed to pay for the services at WSS, but this was virtually never enforced), and by purposefully misleading families about events that occurred. Family members were also met with a wall of silence when they asked about why something bad had happened to their child. Sal Giordano, a member of the Benevolent Association, when asking how his son's leg had been broken, was told that nobody knew. "Nobody knew nothing" (Meskell, 1996).

There was a core of families who were very dedicated to their children at WSS and were active in the Benevolent Society. As mentioned earlier, *Unforgotten* is a documentary about the experiences of several families with children there. In it, the Meskells, Riveras, Giordanos, and Willa Mae Goodman share their memories of WSS. They were very active families in terms of keeping in touch with and visiting their loved one. We will not, in this text, reproduce the stories they told about their experiences there or about the later consequences of the institutionalization on them. This film, an award-winning documentary, should be seen by anyone interested in WSS. It clearly presents the suffering and devotion of these families and their confusion and sadness engendered by the Willowbrook experience. It reveals how loving families were advised to do the best for their children and put them in a place where they could be helped. Such advice was common back in the 1950s and 1960s and would be given by both physicians and clergy. Unforgotten shows how disturbed both the parents and siblings of these families were, and continue to be, about leaving a relative there and about what happened to that relative. It illustrates that the effects of Willowbrook on families were quite general, including many aspects of their lives. It also shows how the siblings of children placed at the institution suffered in certain ways that were different than that of the parents, probably, from what we know today, because the siblings were themselves children and could not comprehend and were fearful of the complexities that were involved or the pain and suffering of their parents and themselves. During the film, the siblings consistently break down while discussing WSS; the parents, less so. One cannot help but be impressed by the siblings' depth of feelings. The overall impression one gets from watching these three families discuss their histories is that they continue to experience deeply upsetting feelings surrounding Willowbrook—which is probably the case for many families who placed loved ones there.

We offer this final note about WSS and its effects on families: Noteworthy are the intergenerational effects of the Willowbrook experience. The effects on the personality of the individual who lived at WSS was so profound that it left its stamp on that person's entire life and on those who were close to him or her.[31] One moving example is provided by Vanessa Debello, the daughter of a woman who lived at Willowbrook for many years, who spoke at one of the Annual Willowbrook Lectures at the College of Staten Island (in 2005). She reflected on the effects that Willowbrook had on her mother, including her mother's then current life, as well as the ways Willowbrook had influenced her own life and even her children's lives. It is not hard to imagine how any parent who had lived at Willowbrook for any appreciable length of time might have difficulties raising children, if not technically then certainly emotionally, if for no other reason than lacking any parental role model.[32] Thus, Debello related aspects of her own childhood that were damaged by the experience of her mother. She used humor to illustrate some of them—people who are involved in the lives of those who lived at Willowbrook have learned to appreciate that there can be humor, however dark, in the situations that the institution created in their lives. (Debello told a telling, funny story about her mother's lack of fashion sense.) But she was also very clear about how hurtful many of the emotional effects of Willowbrook on her mother were to her and her children. Her touching description of having to tell her mother to hug her in front

31. The effects of living at Willowbrook have often been compared, by residents and former workers, to those of living at a concentration camp. The parallel seems reasonable as both were total institutions that involved similar social processes. Without equating one expression of total institutions with another, and without a review of the literature on holocaust survivors and their families, we believe the comparison may be worthwhile examining.

32. We make this distinction because, as noted in the section on institutional peonage, many young woman at WSS worked taking care of children, thereby learning not only the basics about child care but even more technical aspects about caring for a child with a disability. One former resident stated openly that not only did she like this work but also that it specifically prepared her for her own children, two of whom were born with disability. However, this kind of technical knowledge is not at all the same as having a parental role model, that is, experiencing caregiving from a person who loves you in the way parents in our society do (or are supposed to). Thus, although some women were able to learn the practicalities of child care at WSS, none were able to learn (at least there) what it meant to be a mother. While other older residents may have helped them in ways a mother might have, for example as Bertina was reported to have done with scores of woman she lived with at Willowbrook, this experience of group motherhood would have been substantially different than being in a family.

of her children (her mom's grandchildren) is illustrative. Her mother was beaten and raped at WSS and was not the most affectionate person physically. At some point, Debello realized that this was affecting her children, that they needed to see their grandmother giving physical affection, So she simply told her mom, "You need to hug me in front of your grandchildren," and she understood, and began hugging Vanessa and her grandchildren more regularly, perhaps breaking a hurtful cycle begun at WSS.

Death

The objective fact of death does not reduce it to a biological event. The appreciation that people's deaths are socially organized events is no more powerfully portrayed than in the sociologist David Sudnow's (1967) classic book on the topic, *Passing On*. Sudnow, also a student of the ethnomethodologist Harold Garfinkel, studied social life as consisting of mundane everyday practices. From this perspective, all events are socially ordered: walking your dog, having a conversation, praying, shaving, or whatever else. People, both children and adults, learn via socialization how to produce and recognize these everyday events. Sudnow looked at death in this fashion while doing ethnographic research at L.A. County Hospital, and his report was a remarkable "unpacking" of the social events that constitute death at a large public hospital. The variation and complexity of the ways death was organized in different parts of L.A. County is, at least to many readers, completely shocking. Perhaps part of this surprise is because most people, insofar as they know about death at a hospital, do so out of personal experience. Very few have ever actually wandered the floors of a hospital with the specific intent of observing death, so the differences in practices in different parts of the institutions are unknown to most readers. In addition, most people do not think about death in these terms, that is, in terms of its social organization—the mere idea that death could be organized differently socially is not part of our commonsense thinking. We believe that Sudnow's study can serve as a kind of model for thinking about death at Willowbrook.

Sudnow reported a high degree of variation in how death was both organized and given meaning within the institution. His reports were not based on how things were supposed to happen (i.e., written hospital rules and regulations) but what he saw, how things happened, observably (this corresponds to the rhetoric–reality disjuncture explored by Wolfensberger, 1989). Thus, it may not have been according to the rules to allow the perceived moral character of a patient to influence medical decisions about revival procedures or treatment procedures in cases of acute trauma, but this was routinely observed by him (see especially the chapter "Dead on Arrival," where he describes the emergency room discussions around saving a chronic drunk who was being constantly readmitted for bleeding ulcers or about a woman who had shot herself).

Death was neither organized nor given meaning in the same ways in different parts of the hospital. His observations about the organization of child death are poignant. The comportment of staff on pediatric wards reflected their complete defeat, usually of a battle hard fought, and it was always acceptable for any nurse or even doctor to be seen crying after a child died, although there were also limits to such displays. This is in marked contrast to how people working on geriatric wards acted and felt after a death. On such wards, death was so common an occurrence that it was an expected part of daily life. It was death at the end of lived life. Staff generally did not engage in the same kinds of energetic life-saving procedures found on the pediatric ward. Nor did they express intense grief in the way Sudnow saw in the pediatric wards.

It is this conceptualization of the social organization of death at a hospital that can serve as a framework for thinking about it at Willowbrook. Our question is, how was death produced and organized at Willowbrook?

First is the important observation that death was a regular feature of life at Willowbrook. As we have seen, the conditions there created high rates of disease and malnutrition, a lack of health care and basic hygiene, as well as psychological alienation and neglect, which in combination resulted in the regular occurrence of death at a high rate.

Hill and Starogiannis examined the Willowbrook patient data files in the New York State Archives. They examined the "death files," which comprise 197 cubic feet of file boxes. There were about 60 files per box. Hill estimates that there were approximately 12,000 deaths at Willowbrook between 1950 and 1980, approximately 400 per year. This is an awesome figure. Assuming an average of 5,000 residents, it means about 8% of those residing at Willowbrook died each year. The national death rate in the United States in 1972 when Rivera did his exposé was 9.4 deaths per thousand, or 0.94%. Had this been the rate at Willowbrook, there would have been 47 deaths a year there, instead of 400. Willowbrook, and places like it, were regular producers of death. Other institutions similar to Willowbrook suffered from disease and death as well. Fernald State School increasingly served larger numbers of dying residents, as it became the place for "handicapped newborns" to die. In 1954, they had 48 deaths in the year, mostly "sick babies," overwhelming the autopsy lab (D'Antonio, 2004).

These estimates from the patient files at the New York State Archives are even more astonishing because they are incomplete. There was another store of patient case files, a mix of discharged, transferred, and deceased residents. Hill sampled files from every 10th box in the archive of files and found an overall death rate of

6%. A simple tally showed that the most common causes of death were broncho-pneumonia followed by hydrocephalus and, third, status epilepticus.[33]

Conditions at Willowbrook were bound to produce high death rates among residents. Unlike Nazi death camps, there was no explicit plan to do so and no formal monitoring and evaluation of how successful the program was, but it nonetheless became a system to produce death and suffering. This may not have been the perpetrators thought of what they were doing, but stepping back and looking at the situation with the eyes of history, it is hard to conclude otherwise.

Death at Willowbrook was produced in two main ways. First were the physical and social conditions of life, which produced all sorts of diseases, neglect, and psychological trauma. These conditions were coupled with a system of completely inadequate medical care. Bronston testifies to the public health and medical mismanagement nature of the problems most residents faced. Again, although Willowbrook may not have been explicitly set up to create this situation, it was allowed to occur and known to be happening, and for a very long time nothing was done to remedy the situation. Indeed, the politics and profiteering behind Willowbrook is condemning of government to the extreme. Bronston in his forthcoming book describes in detail how he was punished for trying to clean up public health problems and treat diseases on the children wards for which he was responsible. As a reward for his efforts, he was transferred to two large, custodial wards, a clear punishment from the director for his 'extracurricular' efforts. He and his lawyer tried to appeal this treatment but, predictably, failed in the state controlled legal process. Bronston explains how the administration maintained an iron grip on the situation and made sure nothing rocked the boat. Without question, state government, to the highest level, knew about what was going on at Willowbrook but did nothing to stop the abuses, neglect, and death; and suppressed those who tried to do so.

Lack of appropriate medical care was also a main contributor to high death rates at Willowbrook. This occurred in both acute and chronic care. Chronic conditions were not diagnosed correctly, hence not treated correctly, as the following discussion of "mongoloid rash" by Bronston (2007) evidences:

> Thus, physicians at Willowbrook did not diagnose the condition correctly, ascribing it to some vague notion of being related to disability, and not seeing the more obvious environmental cause. This may have represented a general tendency of medical professionals to see people with disabilities as 'having' conditions in the biological sense. The same

33. Table available from Hill documenting the sampling of records and results.

observation could be said about the medical diagnosis and treatment of rampant malnutrition at Willowbrook. Its causes were not identified and appropriate treatment was therefore not given. These kinds of medical mismanagement, indeed in many cases disinterest in really assuming medical responsibility for residents, resulted in many deaths at Willowbrook.

Lack of care extended to routine illnesses and acute incidents, such as accidents or beatings. There was a tendency to overlook sickness and injury generally. Even though there was a central hospital and operating room, it was often very difficult to get residents seen there. There was a definite preference for physicians to take care of things on the ward: sew them up, set the bone, drain the wound, and bring the fever down, whatever. Bronston narrates the case of a young woman who he discovered had a huge hematoma on her skull that had infiltrated into her sinuses and eyes. She was in a very serious condition, but he could not, at first, get the acute hospital unit at WSS to even look at her. When after much threatening on his part they finally did, they returned her to the ward with the comment that they could not do anything. Bronston eventually was able to get this woman admitted to a hospital in Brooklyn (there is a lot to this person's story that we cannot get into here but appears in Bronston's forthcoming book), but the point is the attitude about medical care of residents that existed in the other doctors at Willowbrook.

Another kind of death, one that there is no way to estimate numerically, was when people 'gave up,' decided to die by not eating, or even killed themselves. People reacted to conditions at Willowbrook differently. As discussed, they experienced them divergently because of the real differences in the various parts of the institution but also because of their own sensitivities, weaknesses, and strengths. Giving up, the idea of suicide, has been discussed in accounts of former state institution residents, such as T. J. Munroe at Southbury (Ward, 1997), and it is reasonable to think that these kinds of deaths occurred at Willowbrook, too.

Death related to medical experimentation also occurred at Willowbrook. Some of the workers interviewed mentioned that there were numerous deaths associated with the buildings where medical research took place. Again, there are no statistics about this, but at least two sources related that children infected with diseases in experimental programs did die. Norma Allison, the nurse who worked on a ward where young children were purposefully infected with a virus, experienced enough deaths on her ward that she "became an expert in preparing a child to die," by which she meant that she could administer certain drugs, position the child, and comfort him or her in certain ways. Her story is highly suggestive of the kinds of practices reported by Sudnow (1967). Pediatric death at WSS, in this case caused by medical experimentation, must have been a terrible burden for any nurse (Allison, 1996).

Irma wondered sometimes whether the children were sent to Willowbrook to die:

> I remember one resident who was hydrocephalic. It was unbelievable. His head was three times the size of his body. His mother would not agree to a shunt operation. Some of the parents did not want their children to survive. There would be all sorts of cases like this in the baby building, because most of them would not live to make it into the other buildings.

Indeed, ex-resident Maria had a brother at Willowbrook who died:

> He was like nine months old, but he was Mongolian. But he didn't make it out there because he had died when he was nine months old. He did not live that long, so he died out there in one of the buildings.

She explained:

> But a lot of the kids didn't make it. Because a lot of them they had over-dosed and a lot of them had died there because of the drugs and stuff they gave them. So they had died there, and they would just take them and bury them in Building 2. It was like a morgue.

Arlen explained that the measles research going on at Willowbrook resulted in dead children. He was working in Building 13, where the measles research was conducted, and there were:

> a lot of deaths up there. We had no way of getting them to the morgue [in Building 2] . . . [so] we used to carry the poor little things. So many. I carried dead little babies down into Building 2. You had no way of getting them in, you couldn't leave them all night in there, and we use to carry them.

Death could be violent. There were cases of residents found dead, scalded to death in a shower, beaten to death, hung, or asphyxiated; others simply disappeared. These kinds of death are associated with places such as state hospitals or prisons, where people who matter to no one can meet with an accident or disappear without questions asked.

What happened when a person died at Willowbrook? Where were their bodies taken? Where were they buried? What kind of ceremonies were there?

In most large institutions, the impersonality of treatment in life followed people into the grave. We know that there was no cemetery at Willowbrook. No one was legally buried on the grounds, unlike at other institutions in New York, where one can find cemeteries of unmarked or numbered graves. We know that at Willowbrook bodies were either picked up or taken to a morgue in the main hospital building, in bad weather via tunnels belowground, and then were taken by ambulance to a funeral home. What funeral home, whether it was local or located near the resident's place of origin, whether family was involved, where the person was buried, whether there was a public ceremony—all this would have varied from person to person. One suspects that those who were abandoned in life at Willowbrook continued to be in death. We also know that as a general rule residents did not go to funeral ceremonies, save for those who had very involved families and whose families may have insisted in particular cases that the resident be allowed to attend a funeral of a close relative. Maria, a resident who described the death of her brother, did not know what happened to his body after he died. This was probably the norm. Although residents must have been familiar with death, the lack of experience with grieving created for many residents a specific social incompetence with regard to mourning rituals.

Goode witnessed a group of former residents from Pacific State, many of whom had never been to a funeral before, bury one of their "family." They had lived with this person most of their lives, and they had seen a lot of death in and out of the institution. But they had never been to a funeral. They had no idea what to do or say. Project members had to explain to them how funerals work. Finally, an occupational therapist broke down and started crying, and then the residents seemed to understand (or maybe accept) why they were there and what they were supposed to do. They became almost hysterical, inconsolable. It was as if they grieved all at once for everyone they had not had the opportunity to before. It was an unforgettable thing to have seen and been a part of.

Conclusion

We interviewed workers and residents, analyzed their recollections, and consulted unpublished accounts, public lectures, and media records for clues as to what day-to-day life at Willowbrook was like. Our findings reflect the heterogeneity of WSS, the many Willowbrooks that existed. These many Willowbrooks make answers to the question of what was life like at Willowbrook highly variable.

There was rapidly growing and undermanned Willowbrook of the 1950s and early 1960s, rapidly deteriorating Willowbrook of the late 1960s, discovery and attempted renewal during the early 1970s, and the ultimate closing in 1987. There were the different kinds of buildings and wards and the variation in staff. Experience of WSS was primarily structured by one's status within the institution but one's view of Willowbrook also depended in some measure on one's personal makeup and sensitivities. Reiss's research ward during the period before Willowbrook's downfall faced challenges, to be sure, but it seemed at times a far cry from the Willowbrook seen by Bronston and others later on.

Notwithstanding the peaceful bucolic grounds of Willowbrook and the overall intent to provide for those less fortunate, this is an American gothic tale, a miasma that would perpetuate inhumane living conditions. Willowbrook was overcrowded and severely understaffed, and those who worked under such circumstances were involved in an impossible mission. Basic living conditions were livable for a few at Willowbrook; they were less than that for most. Despite some few concerned families, social events, and a pool, the overwhelming lack of food and clothing, the dearth of treatment and rehabilitation, the lack of schooling at what was called a school, the violence, disease, and death, the unreasonable and unrelenting punishment, and the excessive tranquillization defined life at this institution and disempowered and assaulted its residents. Willowbrook further exploited residents by offering escape from dreariness: the opportunity to work for the institution as rehabilitation. Many doctors, nurses, ward attendants, and teachers were aware of these problems, yet felt powerless to do anything, fearing reprisal or retribution, and so they also fell in line and adapted to an evil institution. Once at Willowbrook, it was too easy to become morally confused and lost, and many people people with good intent and character did so.

Willowbrook, with its excessive social controls, unyielding routinization of life, restrictions on movement, segregation, and isolation, was a total institution. However, in some ways, it did not achieve complete segregation and control. In total institutions such as asylums and prisons, residents are often virtually completely isolated from the outside world, either geographically or physically, with locked doors, police, and judicial orders.[34] This was true, to a degree, at Willowbrook. But there was also evidence of permeability in the border between the institution and outside society. The community came inside to work, as student volunteers, as parents, even establishing a Benevolent Society, and at least some residents experienced the outside world either virtually, through the ever-present ward televisions, or by venturing into the outside world for work, visits to the community, sporting events, band performances, home visits, and even elopement. Willowbrook exhibited many of the features of total institutions described by Goffman (1961). It regulated movement, virtually every aspect of daily life. The interviews illustrate how the institution emphasized the centralization of power over the powerless many and how all involved were assaulted and corrupted by a social form doomed to create victimization and evil.

---

34. By writing this we are not maintaining that prisoners do not find methods of escape, or to smuggle contraband in to prisons. We are simply saying that at Willowbrook the physical and social barriers between inside and outside were less radical than those found with prisons.

The overall physical environment, locked buildings set apart in a wide pastoral campus, gave a sense of isolation, of removal from the surrounding city, of a place where different rules and cultural norms could take root. Willowbrook, like Pacific State Hospital, is often spoken about by those who lived and worked there as if it was another country, or even planet. We do not believe using these terms to characterize WSS is inaccurate or an exaggeration. The words capture the overall feeling of being in such a place, that you are no longer in the regular world; they recall that experience.

5

Being Human

Wolfensberger's (1972) conception of the traditional statuses occupied by people with disability—a collection of deviant, devalued statuses—could be found expressed within the context of a total institution such as Willowbrook. Recall his thesis was that these roles do not disappear entirely but may change in content and become more or less dominant at different periods.

The particular treatment and conditions to which residents at Willowbrook were subject directly reflected the prejudices and antipathies that they faced throughout history. As discussed in the first part of this book, people with disabilities have consistently occupied negative, deviant statuses (roles) in society, which distinguished them from "normal" people. In the development of institutions such as Willowbrook, it is no surprise that several of these roles can be found, including seeing people with disabilities as menaces, as diseased, as essentially innocent and childlike, and as not fully human. Staff used names for these same roles when describing residents at Willowbrook. This is consequential because, as anyone who has ever been described by a devalued label understands, how you are described by others is intimately connected to how you are treated by them and also how you view yourself (cf. the sociologist Cooley's "looking glass self"). To repeat a motif found within these pages, when you are seen as not normal, or as not human like others, this justifies treatment that is not normal or humane by others and promotes disturbed feelings about and perceptions of yourself.

Wolfensberger's *The Principles of Normalization* (1972) argued that all human societies have developed ways of assigning statuses to people who are different, and by and large, these are deviant ones. Deviant statuses are those that are perceived to be qualitatively different from the norm in a negative way (a billionaire is not deviant although he is also qualitatively different from the norm but, in accordance with societal norms, in a positive way). For the reader familiar with disability history, it will be no surprise that people with disabilities have occupied such negative statuses or that these statuses have been used to justify extremely cruel treatment and even death.

Some of these statuses, for example those who are seen as a threat to society because of their low economic status, or those who are considered not fully human, have been applied to other groups besides persons with disabilities. Marginalization and dehumanization are not the exclusive purview of people with disabilities—it is something they have shared with other groups. But, the degree to which these various deviant statuses have been assigned to people with disabilities is remarkable. This theory is parsimonious, organizing the variation of statuses that people with disabilities have occupied in a relatively uncomplicated, comprehensive, and sensible way.[1]

Official accounts of what happened at Willowbrook are concerned primarily with only one of the eight statuses (Wolfensberger calls them "roles," but strictly speaking, according to sociological theory, they are statuses), the deviant individual as a diseased organism. The complete list of the statuses he identifies is: the deviant individual as a subhuman organism, a menace, an unspeakable object of dread, an object of pity, a holy innocent, a diseased organism, an object of ridicule, and an eternal child (Wolfensberger, 1972, p. 12). It is a notable and predictable finding of our work that within the medical context of a state institution, these other statuses were also observed at Willowbrook, illustrating Wolfensberger's contention that these historical ways of thinking about people with disabilities are amazingly persistent, whatever the particular rhetoric of the era.

The argument is that people with disabilities, along with others, have found themselves seen in these ways and that these roles are socially constructed by different societies. They are not exclusive to people with disabilities, and they are not

---

1. Wolfensberger's idea has been criticized by those who felt that its implication was that people with disabilities have had and can only have these devalued and negative statuses. This was not what was intended but rather that he was looking back at the past and noting that this seems to have been the case in many "Western" societies and for a long time. Most of his work (e.g., the service evaluation systems PASS and PASSING) is devoted to precisely creating valued and non-deviant statuses for people with disabilities. However, Wolfensberger believed history has taught us that these social statuses tend not to disappear. They continue to be found today, even though they do not fit into our conscious thinking and values related to disability.

a "natural result" of having disabilities. We will look at these roles briefly before we get into their expression at Willowbrook.

The Subhuman Organism

Many groups have not been seen as fully human by certain societies or social groups. A comprehensive list would be impossible to produce. Close examples to our current focus include African Americans, North and South American Indians, religious groups (e.g., Jews in Nazi Germany), and people with disabilities. Sometimes the idea that such groups are animallike or vegetative is the primary metaphor used in the construction of their status. Seeing these groups in this way justified the most brutal treatment imaginable. For example, early Spanish settlers to South America would hunt and eat native local populations, even setting up butcher shops to sell the meat. The extremely harsh treatment of Africans during the period of slavery, which continued well into the 20th century in the United States in the form of lynching and torture, or the extermination of the Jews are but two of very many modern examples. In the case of people with disability, there is a long history of being associated with non-human status. This includes earlier religious beliefs associating disability with the devil or the evil creation of changelings. In more modern times, we find nonreligious expressions about people with disability that reflect their perception as less than human. Goode remembers the very first resident at Pacific State Hospital he met. It was at the director's office and the person was the director's assistant, a young man with Down syndrome. When he came into the director's office, he was introduced by name. When he left, the director turned and said, "Garden variety Down syndrome." Similar non-human language could be found on the wards, where residents were sometimes referred to as vegetables or animals. Even professionals would characterize their behaviors as atavistic or animalistic (such remarks are found in the interviews). These statements were made openly, without any embarrassment. On one occasion, a researcher at Pacific State asked Goode at a large research conference how his work with a deaf-blind child who had profound retardation and no formal language was any different than working with a chimpanzee.

If you do not perceive a group of people as human, then it is not necessary to treat them in human ways. Being seen in this way has justified extremely brutal treatments—death, genocide, torture, and extreme neglect. Such perceptions have underwritten ideas about using disabled children as organ transplant donors or as candidates for euthanasia, or operating on them without anesthesia. Wolfensberger (1972, p. 18) notes that perceiving someone as less than human is today so contrary to our ideas in general, people who have such perceptions may not be aware of them, may deny or repress them, and may indeed receive social support to do so. For example, at Pacific State Hospital, a very well-intentioned psychologist used a cattle prod to shock residents as part of a behavior modification program. He was unaware of the dehumanization and irrationality of what he was doing and probably felt that he was trying to help his patients. Because he followed research protocol and received a grant to test the procedure, his colleagues supported what he was doing.

The Menace

All societies have statuses or groups that they define as menacing to the whole. Common to all these statuses is the perception of them as "other," that is, not one of "us." Groups are also seen as menaces—for example, criminals, religious or political groups. This certainly has been true of people with disabilities throughout history; they have belonged to groups that were thought in some way to be threatening to society. The primary reason for this was the low socioeconomic status they occupied. Generally speaking, educational and economic opportunity was not extended to people with disability until relatively very recently and even today in many societies they are still the poorest most uneducated minority group. During the Renaissance and earlier, people with disabilities often had no other option other than to become beggars. And some beggars became thieves. Thieves when caught were often punished by amputation (thus creating an association between begging, thievery, and disability). Wolfensberger (1982) cites the example of the growth of pauperism in the 16th century and the brutal response from the privileged classes. In England, begging and vagrancy could be punishable by death; in one instance, 7,000 crucified vagrants and beggars lined a road from one cathedral outside London into central London. People were afraid of those with disabilities for the same kind of reasons they are of gang members today, and beggars of this period were organized as gangs are today. But the point here is that the fear people had of disability was a "real" fear based on the growth of the poor segment in society and the presence of people with disability among them (Wolfensberger, 1982). This idea of disability as a menace to society was later found within the eugenics program, which held that people with disabilities represented a threat to the genetic purity of human beings, coupled with the belief that the absence of such genetic pureness was the cause of almost all social problems.

The Unspeakable Object of Dread

By this, Wolfensberger (1972) meant those statuses that place the individual as unholy, evil, and being punished by God. This kind of way of seeing people with disability can be found, for example, in religious conceptions of people with disabilities as changelings, or witches, or as possessed by the devil. The punishment can be indirect—the outcome of sins committed not by the person but by his or her parents. This belief is also present in the philosophy of degenerationism, and also part of the thinking of phrenologists in the 19th century.

Object of Pity

In this status, people with disability are seen not as culpable for their disability but as "suffering" from their condition. Viewed in this fashion, the individual is therefore worthy of special consideration and support. Wolfensberger writes that the person with disability may be viewed with a "there but for the grace of God go I" attitude (Wolfensberger, 1972, p. 20). There have been various institutional responses to this way of seeing disability. This includes the establishment of the early hospitals within the monastery system; the creation of almshouses, orphanages, foundling homes, and workhouses; the idea that people with disabilities should be taken care of within their communities (e.g., as in colonial America, although as we shall see, its opposite was also practiced); as well as the 18th- and 19th-century charitable institutions of incredible variety and specialization that were designed to provide refuge and care to people with and without disability.[2] In the 20th century, the view of people with disabilities as deserving pity is found perspicuously in the telethon put on by Jerry Lewis or in some of the campaigns of the March of Dimes. It also can be seen in some of the advertising of the parent groups of this era, for example, Eugene Gramm's early 1950s campaign for funds for the Association for the Help of Retarded Children. Gramm used a picture of his own son, that emphasized his disability and innocence (Goode, 1998). People who remember being singled out as representatives of the cause the telethon was targeting—for example Goode's friend Ed Roberts, who was a poster boy for March of Dimes—have emphasized that it was humiliating (and ultimately politically wrong) to portray people as helpless cripples.[3] The disability community has focused a lot of this criticism on Jerry Lewis, but this way of looking at people with disability reached well beyond his telethon. The object of charity is ultimately not a status that we value for people with disability today.

2. A good place to witness this array of charitable institutions in New York City is in the *Manual of the Corporation of the City of New York,* published in 1870 by John Hardy, clerk of the Common Council. Within its 926 pages, one finds 200 pages of descriptions and pictures devoted to hospitals and charitable institutions in New York City.

3. A video of Ed Roberts discussing this and many other observations related to his experience as a person and advocate with disability see: See Effective Strategies for Social Change, May 1, 1987, available at: http://www.mnddc.state.mn.us/parallels2/one/video/ed_roberts-pipm.html

Object of Ridicule

This is a status for people with disability that is very long-standing. Images showing the display of human and animal oddities go back to antiquity and are common by the middle ages. There are many treatments of the phenomenon of the freak show, but two good ones are Leslie Fiedler's (1978) *Freaks* and Rosemary Garland's (1996b) *Freakery* (also her *Extraordinary Bodies;* see Garland, 1996a). Under capitalism, such shows became big business. They were common in the major traveling circuses throughout the 20th century. For some, these shows were a livelihood and a craft. Many cultivated personae and costumes—that is, "an act"—and performers were proud of their show business careers. Another historical thread of the person with disability as object of ridicule is the buffoon or court jester. At least some of these were people with disability, physical and/or intellectual. In the 1960s and 1970s, "midget wrestling" partook of this same kind of spectacle. Today this culture continues to survive in modified forms.[4] Human beings have an interest in seeing unusual other human beings that appears to transcend historical circumstance.

The social status of person with disability as object of ridicule is still with us. Most of the students with disabilities Goode has spoken with at the College of Staten Island have shared that teasing and ridicule were everyday occurrences in their experiences in local high schools and more generally in the community. Sadly, ridicule of people with disabilities is still alive and well.

The Holy Innocent and Eternal Child

We are combining the discussion of these two statuses because they are somewhat different than the deviant ones described above, and they share something in common. To see the person with disability as childlike does not have the same kind of negative connotation as, say, to see him or her as an unspeakable object. Yet this way of seeing and interacting with people with intellectual disabilities is, as

4. Hanspeter Schneider's photo essay *The Last Side Show* (2004) documents the residents of Gibsonton, Florida, in which live many former sideshow performers. Gibsonton has a 1920s Residential Show Business Zone ordinance that allows residents to "put a roller coaster in the front yard and, if you have to, keep an elephant in the back." Consequently, the town has attracted many sideshow and other unusual performers, who continue to reside there to this day. The AMC television show, Freakshow, shows persons performing various side show specialties and includes people who could be described as having a disability, but these current day expressions of 'freak culture' are constructed to avoid the overtly dehumanizing elements that may have been part of the earlier circus side shows. Midget wrestling is still around and may be viewed on YouTube. For a more general treatment of photographic representation of people with disability, including sideshow performers, see Robert Bogden's *Picturing Disability* (2012).

Wolfensberger explains, not a positive thing for the person so viewed. Childlike expectations are extremely limiting and do not present the individual with reasonable "developmental and adaptational demands" (Wolfensberger, 1972, p. 23). It is interesting to note that this status is unusually persistent. It continues to be used in an unreflective manner and even benign intent by workers and even parents. The same can be said of the status of holy innocent, which does not sound like a negative characterization but shares the same problem as the eternal child, that is, expectations that do not jibe with being human. Many cultures (Wolfensberger cites Eskimos, North American Indians, Arabs, Russia, Central Asia, and medieval Europe) have beliefs that people with disabilities are incapable of sin or evil doing, are "purer" than others and in some sense close to God. Wolfensberger explains the different nuances to this perception within the cultures, which are interesting but not directly germane to the current discussion. What is important about the holy innocent status for people with disabilities is that when it is found today, it serves "a reverse form of dehumanization, by elevating the human being almost above the human level" (Wolfensberger, 1972, p. 21). As with the eternal child, the status of the holy innocent places expectations on the individual inconsistent with those held for most people. It is a status that may be used to control people so perceived, who are incapable of guiding themselves. This status was also important to the establishment by religious orders of institutions for people with disabilities. One of the earliest of these was the institution founded in 1410 by Father Juan Gilabert Jofre in Valencia, Spain, for the "innocent ones" (Wolfensberger, 1972, p. 21).

The Diseased Organism

Although Willowbrook was a state school, and although conditions within it were inversely related to preventing or curing disease (see especially remarks by Bronston), it is still fair to say that Willowbrook as an institution was most closely related to the form of the hospital. It was argued that Willowbrook and places like it evolved from earlier institutions that were intended to relieve and cure various kinds of human affliction. There have been such places since antiquity. They are antecedents of more modern attempts that were informed particularly by medical knowledge. Medical knowledge since its inception, and in its various forms, has been used to understand and intervene in a myriad of human conditions, including disability, and since the advent of modern medicine disability was officially and institutionally regarded through a medical model. Certainly, this was still true in the 1970s when several of the authors were working in institutions. Even though they did not cure disease but created it on a massive scale, residents were called "patients." The "medical model," as it is referred to by disability studies scholars, made disability into a constitutional problem of the "afflicted" individual and was used as a rationale to incarcerate people with disabilities into large state-operated institutions. Today, the medical model is rejected by disability studies scholars, especially those with disability, who prefer the social or minority group model.[5]

Having reviewed these statuses historically occupied by people with disability, let us now examine how these statuses expressed themselves in life at Willowbrook.

Dehumanization in Research

In addition to the interview data provided in earlier chapters, the evidence for dehumanization at Willowbrook is overwhelming and well documented through the legal proceedings (sworn testimony and judicial reviews) that resulted in the Consent Decree. In the first legal case, parents' complaints were documented: A 4-year-old girl was left unattended, did not have medical care, was not involved in any programming, fell into a coma, and almost died; others were overtranquillized, and parents discovered new physical injuries and conditions with each visit.[6] The lawyers on behalf of the residents and their parents argued that Willowbrook was a prison and that care of the residents was "in violation of the First Amendment; deprived of rights to privacy and dignity, in violation of the Fourth and Fourteenth; deprived of services given to others, in violation of the Fourteenth; and subjected to cruel and unusual punishment, in violation of the Eighth" (Rothman & Rothman, 1984/2009, p. 64). Already described were the terrible conditions of everyday life that would not be tolerated even for animals. People lost their humanity, their individuality. They ceased to have names, or their names were written on their legs with indelible ink, like branded cattle. At some institutions, like Southbury, where T.J. Monroe lived, residents had numbers.

Perhaps the most egregious violation of human rights, treating people as one might treat an animal, was occurring in the research labs of Willowbrook. We have already described some of this research but in short Willowbrook had been the site of many studies on infectious disease, and it was a natural breeding ground for communicable diseases. Dr. Saul Krugman began a study on hepatitis, feeding live viruses to residents from 1956 to 1971. Between 1953 and 1957, there were 350 residents and 76 staff who were reported to have hepatitis, a rate of approximately 250 per 100,000, ten times the rate in New York State. Residents were enrolled in this study after their parents gave permission, but the letter requesting permission

---

5. For seminal discussions of the social model see Michael Oliver (1990, 1996).

6. As briefly mentioned above, virtually all parents would, upon visiting, would inspect the body of their child as a way to judge their care, whether they had been abused, whether they had gained or lost weight. This ritual is described in Unforgotten and was observed by several of the authors.

contained grossly misleading information and coercive language. Thus, many staff's and residents' human rights and wellness were violated.

Such treatment was not uncommon at other institutions. Sonoma State Home in California, New Jersey State Colony for Feebleminded Men in Woodbine, and Polk State School in Pennsylvania were all involved in early studies isolating polio vaccines. D'Antonio (2004) concluded of Fernald that residents were viewed by the administration and doctors as "a backdrop for their careers, the source of their authority in the outside world, and a handy reservoir of human material for research" (p. 52). He documented the work of psychiatrist Dr. Clemens Benda, who had a collection of over 50,000 samples of brains, thyroids, and pituitary tissues from dead residents. He studied stunted growth in children deprived of adequate nutrition, of whom he had a large sample. He was known to have performed more than 3,500 lobotomies on patients. He would eventually maintain a research staff of 24 people and get large grants with international collaborators.

Dr. Benda used the captive population of residents to conduct experimental psychosurgery, experiments with testosterone, and work on lysergic acid diethylamide (LSD). With Dr. Max Rinkel of Boston Psychopathic Hospital, in 1957 Benda published research showing that LSD administered to a patient would elicit "artificial psychosis." D'Antonio described Benda as a "master mind" who "showed an unseemly callousness for a man who promoted himself as a champion of vulnerable children" (D'Antonio, 2004, p. 251). Biographers point out even more sinister connections: Both Benda and Rinkel had fled Germany prior to World War II, the LSD research was funded by the CIA, and Benda's collection of eugenics literature included a photo of Nazi autopsies at Dachau concentration camp.

At Fernald, there was also an experimental psychology laboratory based on the behaviorist B. F. Skinner's work:

> The behavior modification program involved rewarding children for good behavior—mostly this involved giving them candy—and punishing bad behavior. Punishments included tying children to chairs and confining them to closet-like spaces. One child was subjected to a week-long program that included electric shocks. (D'Antonio, 2004, p. 213).

And in strong echoes of what happened at Willowbrook, Fernald had its own scandal over research. In 1993, the story broke that a privileged group of boys called the "Science Club" has been subjected to undisclosed danger: The oatmeal they were eating in one experiment was laced with radioactive calcium. Parents had been misled in an informational letter informing them of the experiment, and thus none of the participants or parents could have reasonably been said to have given informed consent. Even by 1953, medical research had already accepted the standard of "informed consent" for research, according to which this study would have had to mention radiation. As early as 1950, a memo to the Atomic Energy Commission warned that human experimentation was unacceptable.

These abuses were not rare. Other historians have documented similar conditions at Fernald. D'Antonio (2004) summarized conditions there: "Once locked away, [residents] endured isolation, overcrowding, forced labor, and physical abuse including lobotomy, electroshock, and surgical sterilization" (p. 5). The residents "viewed beatings, torture, and sexual assaults as if they were watching a film. Moments later, it would be almost forgotten" (p. 51). They even had a name for this forgetting: "the ether" (p. 51). D'Antonio wondered whether "They were victims of a way of thinking, or perhaps a dark part of human nature, that allows otherwise reasonable people to decide that a certain few are lesser beings" (p. 252).

As noted earlier, Willowbrook, being the largest institution of its kind, and with a history including the hiring of George Jarvis and building of the Institute for Basic Research, had very many research projects going on at any one time. For these researchers, Willowbrook was a big human laboratory in which to experiment. Residents became research subjects, or even worse, their value was defined in terms of the research. Saul Krugman's work not only dehumanized the human subjects but also victimized their families through deception and social pressure.

Characterizations of Residents

Residents of Willowbrook were described in terms evoking the statuses described by Wolfensberger (1972). Not surprisingly, all of the statuses described by him were found at Willowbrook. People were seen as menaces, as subhuman, as unspeakable objects of dread, as objects of pity and diseased organisms, and as holy innocents and eternal children.

Menace

Clearly, one of the more common constructions of social identity for Willowbrook residents in our sources was "the menace." Because of the endemic violence and lack of control that existed, menacing behaviors took many forms. Descriptions of residents as dangerous reflected actual conditions of life, as well as prejudices about people with disabilities generally.

We have already commented on how many physicians and nurses were afraid of residents, because of aggression and contagious diseases. As a result, as much as possible, doctors and nurses shifted their work to others and tried to have minimal contact with residents—and that only in controlled circumstances.

Comments by past employees sometimes suggest that workers feared certain residents. That some residents were felt to be a "menace" by some workers appears to be true. Irma told this story:

One of the last classes I taught was a group of blind children. There was one student who would attach himself to the teacher. If I were absent, he would have temper tantrums. He would throw tables and behave very badly. I found that if I told him the day before that I would be absent the next day, he would be much better behaved. He was a very bright boy. He was also very powerful. He weighed about fifty pounds, but he could throw those big tables across a room.

Descriptions such as this one are not unusual. Goode was also privy to many stories of children exhibiting incredible strength at Pacific State Hospital, and witnessed several occasions where it took several grown adults to restrain a small child. Their unrestrained, yet highly focused anger was awesome to see. Certain children, even small ones, were known to have this potential, and staff were accordingly careful with them. (see Reiss's description of Robinson below).

At Willowbrook, a less threatening but nonetheless common form of menace was embodied by Tom, whose hobby was tinkering and then ruining beyond repair anything mechanical or electrical. This unruly child was in constant trouble and feared by some. Reiss recalled:

He was a well-developed boy with an unruly mop of fair hair. He talked in bursts, the words tumbling out so rapidly that they were impossible to understand. Asked to slow down and he would make an immense effort, but it often took two or three attempts before he could produce a comprehensible sentence.

Tom could not read or write and was a menace in the schoolroom, but he had a definite mechanical flair. He loved to take things apart. He enjoyed adjusting the sound and picture on the television set, but having absolutely no interest in the program it was hard to get him to change the station.

Reiss explained that staff tried to focus his interests:

At one time it was thought that Tom's mechanical ability could be put to good use, and he was encouraged to try and repair some of the toys by cannibalizing them. Instead he dismembered them all, fascinated to find out how they worked, but he could not be persuaded to put them together again. It bored him.

His acts were a combination of sabotage and unruliness. He was a menace in the sense of being a constant threat to social orderliness:

He went to school impatient and untidy. He was always in trouble. He didn't seem to hear his teacher, had no interest in letters, numbers or coloring. He liked to take his desk apart, play with the window catches or dismantle a pen, watch or toy. He seldom sat still for any length of time. Letters of protest from his infuriated and harassed teachers arrived daily. Tom was spoken to, pleaded with, yelled at and threatened. None of it had any effect. He would listen with a look of genuine distress on his face.

After his conditional release to the community, he returned to Willowbrook because he was a perceived as a direct menace to others:

> One evening horrified neighbors found him by the hedge, in the back yard, carefully undressing a little six year old girl. It was her crying that brought them to investigate and Tom was surprised, but not embarrassed or guilty, when they shouted at him and pulled the little girl away.
>
> No foster home could be responsible for a boy with such frightening tendencies. Tom returned worried, anxious, and confused. We were confused too. In all the years we had known him Tom had not shown the slightest interest in sex. He had neither cuddled up [to] the boys, nor tried to date the girls.

It is likely that many of Willowbrook's released residents were accused of acts they did not commit, often to have them returned to Willowbrook, or in some cases, even if they committed the act, did not have the cognitive capacity to understand its morality or the ability to articulate why, as in Tom's case, they were undressing a young girl. At Pacific State one regular occurrence that plagued residents who left the institution were inappropriate behaviors related to gender and sexuality, the result of institutional gender segregation.

Among the residents who came to Willowbrook through orders of the courts, both juvenile and criminal. There were some children who readily assumed the role of menace. Reiss described them thusly:

> They arrived with records of arson, purse snatching, robbery and malicious mischief. They came on neglect petitions; some were lost and abandoned children who had been taken by the police to a Children's Shelter.
>
> Many came from homes so disrupted that the child's early experiences were never known. Others were from families whose lives had been so destroyed by alcoholism and psychotic episodes that it was astonishing that these children still retained some shreds of sanity.
>
> Many of the children in this last group came to Willowbrook fighting mad. They saw the school as yet another brutal episode in their lives, which had, so far, contained little that was kind, gentle, or even normal. They smashed windows, benches and toys. They fought with attendants twice their size and attacked each other with the same unthinking ferocity.

Some residents, children and adults, were characterologically aggressive and dangerous. Even a very young child, a 7-year-old boy named Robertson, scared many staff members, Reiss remembered:

> I was scared of Robertson too. That boy fought to kill. Very little was known about his early life. He was about seven years old when the police picked him up and they believed he had been living in the streets of Manhattan for, at least, two or three months. He said his name was Robert and that his mother was dead. His case records, from admission on, were a written record of the communal wail that went up from all staff members that came in contact with the child. His deadly aggressiveness could be contained while he was small, though barely muted by counseling, punishment and/or tranquilizers. As he grew physically stronger he grew more dangerous.
>
> When he was nine years old he was found fighting in a quiet part of the schoolyard. He had a smaller boy on the ground, and a rock clasped in his hand. By good fortune a strong male attendant saw what was happening and wrestled the rock away from him before he killed the child.
>
> When he came to our ward he was 12 years old. A quiet, self-contained boy, he immediately assumed a leading position in the group. He received tribute in the form of candy, clothes, and toys as if it were his right. No attendant ever heard him threaten the other boys, or even ask them for gifts. Whenever fights broke out among the children Robertson was standing at one side. No one could prove he was the source of the conflict, but he was always there.
>
> Several times he ran away from the institution but got no further than the Staten Island Ferry Terminal. One morning the night attendant found that both her wallet and Robertson were missing. That time he was picked up by the police but not returned to Willowbrook. In a dark hallway he had used a length of lead pipe on a woman's head and she had not survived.
>
> Willowbrook was not planned nor designed to deal with such patients. Counseling, tranquilizers and threats were used, often to no avail. Detention wards, with barred windows, locked doors and strong attendants were established for the unmanageable children.

Hill confirmed the story of Robertson; in his review of Willowbrook patient case files in the New York State Archives, he found a resident file with similar events documented. Goode recalled a "Robertson" on one of the wards he worked on at Pacific State Hospital, a small young man of whom everyone, staff and resident, was afraid. Aside from a few minor details, their stories are similar. If either of these children fought with you, he was after blood. Robertson's status as "menace" was not prejudiced or ill-founded; it reflected the reality that all groups contain some persons who can exhibit extremely aggressive behaviors.

As noted earlier, all social categories at Willowbrook were heterogeneous and contained many different variations of personhood. Menaces were real in the various ways described. Staff and residents engaged in dangerous and threatening behaviors, although it is important to appreciate that social conditions at the institution contributed substantially to their acting in the way they did. It was easy for staff to be afraid of residents who were largely unsupervised, unsocialized and given literally nothing to do, just as it was sensible for residents to fear staff who could be either nice or horrible to them but in any case controlled their lives to an extreme degree.

Reiss's description of Robertson and his role on the ward, and the complete bankruptcy of Willowbrook to deal with the children who were admitted through the courts, echoes observations made by Bronston and some of the interviewees. In a somewhat parallel process to prisoners who control life at the bottom, residents at Willowbrook developed natural hierarchies of control and dominance. The currency of such social systems was often violence and violent staff and residents like Robertson. Such violence was only reported in the press only when a patient actually died, was seriously hurt or because of some exceptional circumstance, but their less dramatic, ubiquitous power and control were never reported in the press.

Subhuman

Past employees, even well meaning ones, were aware that residents were often viewed as subhuman. For example, many referred to the "freak shows" put on for visiting students from Wagner College. Past employees specifically recall the "bird babies." They were a brother and sister with facial abnormalities that made them look like birds.[7] Another ex worker described seeing children with heads that were horribly huge. John spoke about how the training he received as a ward attendant was to be told that most of the residents were less than human, "the dregs of humanity." We have heard about children in the Baby Building who had very significant body abnormalities. Thus, some people, because of the degree of their disability, were perceived as not really human. On top of this, the physical and social conditions of Willowbrook created people who looked and acted abnormally. Thus, perception of these residents as less than human were also grounded both in stereotypes

---

7. As mentioned earlier, these may be the same residents studied by Hillman, Hammond, Noe and Reiss and described in their research as bid headed dwarfs. As we conjecture in the section on research at WSS, these may have been children with progeria.

about people with severe disability, as well as conditions of life conducive to making people look and act 'less' than human.

Thus it was not just an abnormal appearance that led staff to regard the residents as less than human. Ronnie, in particular, recalled two instances that struck him as incredibly dehumanizing:

> One of my responsibilities was to take my clients to their dental appointments. I can remember being really shocked. The dentist would start to work on a patient without giving them any anesthesia. It was my job to restrain, and I would. I said, "Why don't you give them something?" These were professionals. I remember the dentist telling me that they (the residents) felt no pain, so they did not need any anesthesia. I remember going back there and telling the dentist, "Well you hold him, because I am not going to hold this person." The dentist wanted to do an extraction. After the extraction he would put some gauze in the client's mouth and send him on his way. When I refused to hold the patient down, they called and made a complaint about me.

He also spoke about treating residents like cattle during their showers:

> You would hose them down, like cattle. We would line them up, pour shampoo on top of their head and take a hose to them. If a patient was being difficult, some of the staff would take the hose to the genital area or to their face. We showered the whole ward at the same time. This was done on the day shift, too. Breakfast was at 7:00 AM. After breakfast we would line them up for their showers. That was one of the reasons I liked working with the spastics. The spastics were in what were called cripple carts. You did the job and put them back. They stayed still.

These remarks reflect the "people work" character of staff typifications of residents. It was often that references were job related—here the spastic residents being described as "good" to work with because they were in cripple carts and could not move when being showered. These kinds of descriptions fill our interviews, and were extremely easy to hear at places like WSS or PSH.

Goode heard former residents of Willowbrook, Pacific State, and Wassaic relate stories of their experiences of surgical procedures without anesthesia. There is reason to believe this practice may have been widespread in many institutions of the era.

Unspeakable Object of Dread

For all the residents whom staff found charming or appealing, there were also those children and adults at Willowbrook who were perceived with fear and dread.

Children, some of them newborn infants with incurable and significant brain damage, were often viewed with sympathy mixed with horror, as were the adults who could not care for themselves, sitting nude covered in their own feces, muscles starved for food, rocking their boredom away. Such sights, even with the desensitization that occurred at such places, must have made it difficult to come to work some days. So it is not surprising that for those who worked there, residents could be thought of as most unpleasant looking and acting. Having to work closely with large numbers of persons who were perceived in this way, may account, at least partially, for some workers who drank or used drugs on the job.

At both Willowbrook and Pacific State Hospital there were children who were born with extremely severe defects of the body, sometimes requiring special hospitalization and care (at Pacific State, there was an "acute unit" to house cases requiring such specialized medical treatment). Children with hydrocephalus who were born before the invention of the cerebral shunt often had very large heads and stunted bodies and were paralyzed, sometimes deaf and blind, and profoundly intellectually disabled. Children with profound disturbances of bodily formation, internally and externally, could be seen in institutions. These children were regarded in both institutions with a certain degree of awe and horror. Goode (1985) described a first encounter with such a person and how monstrous he appeared to him.

Some parents, upon discovery that their child was disabled in some respect, upon learning their child was given a diagnosis such as "mongoloid," "moron," or "cerebral palsy," reacted with horror or depression and gave up their children to places like Willowbrook. Fearing the responsibilities that come with having a special needs child, unable to meet the financial and emotional burden of such a child, often fearing for the child's and their own safety, and encouraged by physicians and clergy, they concluded that their child was better cared for by the state.

The term "mongoloid," with its racist overtones, filled parents' hearts with fear and survived well into the 1970s in state institutions and in medical settings. Mongoloids were thought to be something monstrous by people ignorant of disability. Thelma Ragland, a Willowbrook parent who appeared in a training video made by the Association for the Help of Retarded Children, spoke about being told in the delivery room, in the 1970s, that her daughter was "mongoloid." Hearing that term "freaked me out." She thought that she would see a "monster" when she first saw her daughter. (Pictures of her very beautiful baby appear on the tape.) Thelma, like many other parents, was so depressed at the birth of her daughter with Down syndrome that she thought of committing infanticide followed by suicide. Such thoughts are not uncommon, but very few parents act on them, and Thelma instead maintained a committed relationship with her daughter throughout her life (Goode, 1988).

At Willowbrook, some employees perceived residents as monstrous in some ways. An employee, Helen, described a few memories that clearly show how she was horrified by the residents:

I saw them treat a patient who had bitten off her pinkie finger during the night. She felt no pain. The bleeding had somehow stopped and there was no pinkie found in her bed or surroundings. He assumed she ate it! Many of the disturbed patients were "pickers," incessantly picking areas on their arms and legs until the areas bled and became infected. He showed me the arm of one patient who had a large, oozing, picked wound and pointed out a white area in the center. He said that was her arm bone. She had picked all the flesh away. Again, this patient felt no pain.

Even the highly sympathetic Reiss noted the horror on the faces of visitors to Willowbrook: "All the visitor could see was a travesty of humanity. The attendant would become confused and embarrassed at the sight of the visitor's involuntary expression of horror." She acknowledged the links between normalization and happiness for Willowbrook residents:

> A child born with multiple physical and mental disabilities has very little chance of leading what would be regarded by most people as an acceptable existence. This is true even if the child is surrounded by loving relatives, expert attention and even luxury.
>
> However, working on the overcrowded, understaffed wards of Willowbrook anyone who has had close contact with the children is forced to recognize that there are many levels of experience, even of happiness. Some of the levels are distasteful to the point of being horrifying to the average person, but this does not mean that the child is painfully aware of his, or her, deprivation, or is incapable of joy.
>
> An understanding and acceptance of the narrow range of their experience is essential to give them the pleasure that they can appreciate. Who has not seen the parents weeping by the child's bed? The child is seldom crying.

This asymmetry of emotional expression regarding the residents suffering is reported in other interviews. Workers who worked with children with more severe disabilities mentioned that they often had trouble figuring out how aware the child was of his or her own situation.[8]

Again, it bears repeating that conditions at Willowbrook created people who did not look and act normally. Perceptions of this kind are a reflection of these

---

8. At the deaf blind ward at PSH Goode regularly observed people visiting the ward who found the residents too horrible to even look at. On one occasion a visitor vomited when introduced into the day room. It is also true that ward personnel at PSH found it difficult to determine what particular children were and were not aware of. This is similar to what was observed at Willowbrook.

conditions as much as of the individual. It is also true that workers at Willowbrook were members of a larger "disablist culture" and came to Willowbrook with their own prejudices and ignorance.

Object of Pity

In the face of such suffering and misery, against the helplessness and hopelessness, Willowbrook's residents often were spoken about with pity. It was hard perhaps in the end to not think "there but for the grace of God." Perhaps pity was an undeniable recognition of their less fortunate circumstances; perhaps it was driven by guilt. Objects of pity could be deserving of such an attitude because they are victims of a villain, faulty genes, uncaring and incompetent parents, or uncaring state schools. Even the children sent by the courts were in Reiss's eyes pitiable because of their impoverished and chaotic family life. Pity as a reaction to seeing people living in state hospital conditions was common. It occurred among workers, visitors, and families. It was a response to residents' situation that was grounded in an understanding of its details. When first encountering the children on the deaf-blind ward at Pacific State, Goode had a powerful, overwhelming feelings of sorrow and writing at the time asked himself observed, "How could I not?" Many former Willowbrook staff over the years noted this same reaction. But at least some also realized that while acknowledging pity as a part of their response to institutions, they could not let it guide them in how they tried to work with those who lived there.[9]

Diseased Organism

Willowbrook was filled with diseased people. Conditions of life ensured that and most residents were made ill by the place itself. Whatever their disabling condition, whether the result of some disease process or not, they acquired anemia, malnutrition, rickets, scabies, shigella, or hepatitis; their bones and brains became stamped by early neglect and undernourishment, their heads too big for their frail bodies; their minds were damaged by emotional neglect and sexual and physical abuse. Willowbrook case records detail in unemotional "medicalese" the facts of illness, incest, prolonged and agonizing deliveries, chronic neglect and passionate concern,

---

9. This brief treatment of the role of pity at Willowbrook just begins to examine this topic. At PSH when Goode was dealing with this emotion while working on the deaf and blind ward, others shared similar feelings but also, as in the workers at Willowbrook, said that they did not let that emotion prevent them from doing their job and from keeping a certain emotional distance from the children. But it is difficult to make any generalization about the role of pity in working on the wards at WSS or PSH.

children infected with a destructive virus, babies who "never grew," and unwanted babies from women whose lives were as sad and confused as those of their off-spring—stories ending in the final despair of institutionalization.

Some children, the so-called total care residents, had such a precarious hold on life that it could be maintained only by continual medical care. Clearly, some of their problems were related to a biological condition, although the diseases they contracted (i.e., infectious diseases, malnutrition, aspiration pneumonia) often were not directly related to their particular disability.[10]

In addition to these aspects of being a diseased organism, in fact, during the period when WSS was open, "the medical model" dominated how most people thought about disability. People were seen as biologically damaged and in need of fixing. Their disabilities were a result of organic things and were "theirs" in the sense that they were part of the person (the proprietary model of disability). The social processes associated with disability, as understood today via the social model, were not appreciated back then and were more or less ignored in the way residents at Willowbrook were thought of. Thus, the extreme lack of progress in human growth that many residents at Willowbrook displayed was attributed primarily to their disability and not to the deplorable social and physical conditions. This viewpoint permeated most institutions of the era, where behaviors more sensibly explained by social factors were interpreted via a medical model as examples of persons' constitutional limitations or abnormalities. There is no clearer example of this kind of thinking than the way medical personnel interpreted stereotypy—repetitive rocking, hand flapping, and similar behaviors—as resulting from retardation, rather than from boredom.[11]

Thus, the medicalization of disability that occurred in places such as Willowbrook, rather than providing a logic of intervention and rehabilitation that helped or cured people, created one that blamed them for the results of the conditions under which they lived. Because of situations like this the medicalization of disability rightfully became a target of the intellectual wing of the disability rights movement during the 1980s.

10. We are trying to emphasize here the idea that conditions at Willowbrook infected all residents with diseases, whether or not they had other medical conditions. We are not arguing that particular kinds of disability or illnesses that residents may have had when they came to Willowbrook did not effect their susceptibility to certain illnesses while there.

11. There is an interesting parallel here to eugenic researchers who also, in the face of social conditions that were from today's perspective obviously and clearly related to the development of disability, completely ignored them in favor of an explanation that saw disability as a result of genetic factors. See especially Rogers and Merrill (1919). See Chapter 2, Goode, 1994, for a discussion of how stereotypy in institutions is often interpreted as a result of in-born or disease factors, rather than the overwhelming emptiness and boredom of life within the institution.

Holy Innocent

It is not hard to imagine the "holy innocent" at Willowbrook especially when we think about the children. The children, as they are sometimes able, could be just sweet and charming but also sometimes completely unaware of what they had done wrong. Reiss described two "holy innocents"—at least they were at times. Peter returned to the ward with a note from his teacher:

> The notes were always opened apprehensively. "Head Attendant: Please punish Peter. He has been acting up all day and is fresh at the mouth."
> "What did you say Peter?"
> "Nuttin."
> "What did you do Peter?"
> "Nuttin."
> "Don't you give me nuttin! Your teacher wouldn't write you up unless you'd been bad. Now what did you do?"
> "I never done nuttin! He hate me. He pick on me all day!" Eyes round and slowly filling with tears, face angelic, he presented a picture of innocence cruelly misunderstood.

Reiss also described Tom in terms not distant from a "holy innocent." One day on the ward, the attendant noticed that Tom was missing:

> Lenny said casually, "Oh he's on top of the elevator, fixing it." There were two large old elevators in the building, which ran up either side of the central hall. The boys were strictly forbidden to enter them unless accompanied by an attendant. This was no hardship because one flight of stairs brought us to the ground level.
> The attendant, dragging Lenny with her, raced out into the hall to find Tom was indeed on top of the elevator. He had noticed it was not working and that it was stuck between the first and second floor. Prying open the doors on the second floor he climbed down onto the top of the elevator and was happily engrossed in the mechanism.
> When the attendant was frightened she spoke in a special voice, which carried enormous authority. Tom, astonished, looked up to see her peering down at him and unwillingly, but quickly, clambered up out of the shaft to where she was standing. He could not understand her. He was being good. He was mending the elevator. Everyone had been so happy when he repaired the television the other night, why was it wrong to repair the elevator? Yes, he knew he wasn't to touch the elevator, but

he wasn't going to go riding in it. He was just getting it going. There were lots of wires. It was very interesting.

Tom loved the senior attendant. She had been his friend long before he had been acceptable to anyone else. He was genuinely sad to have upset her. He promised he would never touch the elevator again. He would never try to repair anything unless she said that he might do so, and yet it was quite obvious that he did not understand. He had run up against yet another of the complicated rules in an incomprehensible world.

This is the innocent's basic problem: not understanding the complexities of the world. The holy innocents construction is similar to the "eternal child" characterization, as one basic attribute of childhood is relative innocence. In Reiss's narrative, some residents "shuffle, grunt and babble through life diapered like babies and made amenable by tranquilizers" or are like Paul, eternally childlike:

> Paul, undersized for his age and perpetually sniveling, always looked as if he had been beaten and then half drowned. He appeared unattractive and seedy in the very best of the State's clothes. He had a pale little pinched face and anxious expression, and the attendants found themselves continually chiding him, "stand up Paul—blow your nose—pull your pants up—don't stoop like that . . . etc. . . . etc." and yet he was, despite his outward appearance, one of the most lovable children in the ward.
>
> He had few possessions, but was generous with them all. If someone gave him a candy bar an alert attendant would stand over him to make sure he ate it, otherwise he would give a bite to whoever came near him. He had a most repulsive habit of allowing any other child who asked to have a quick chew of his bubble gum, and never complained if it was not returned.

Reiss also observed that many residents remained childlike in their attitude toward work and some were more of a burden than a help to the staff. Again, these characterizations are produced within the institution because of its very conditions. Children who are kept isolated from the outside world are not able to learn the most rudimentary facts of life outside or the most common outside ways of doing things.[12] Depending on when and how they arrive, they may never have received

---

12. An simple example from a staff member at Willowbrook at a conference. He had some chidren on a trip to Manhattan and they discovered a pay phone booth. He related how they just stood and stared at it, with no idea of what it was or how to use it.

even the most rudimentary processes of socialization or development. Whatever the disability and cognitive limitations of the individual might be, such children may act like innocent children because a state of innocence and ignorance, at least about most things, is perpetuated by the institution.

Wolfensberger (1972) and others have described how people with disability in some societies were considered innocent and pure, in some sense closer to God than others. This is different than the innocence described here. Although nothing about holy innocence is mentioned explicitly in the interviews, such a perception was present at Pacific State and probably Willowbrook as well. Goode engaged in many discussions with psychiatric technicians on the deaf-blind ward about God's purpose in creating people who were unable to share in the most basic ways of thinking and of doing things. Several staff believed that God had made them that way, innocent of the larger world, for a reason. Further, at PSH staff at other some of the adult buildings shared similar observations about some of the residents, that they seemed to have a kind of spiritual innocence and development inspite of their disability and circumstance. So holy innocence was not just a matter of childhood and it was a status afforded to some residents by staff.

Eternal Child

The child role for people with intellectual disabilities is a very persistent one, even in current society. Despite its inappropriateness, it continues to be used by family, service providers, and the general public. Its usage may function in different ways for different speakers. For example, a staff member at a group home introducing a visitor to "the boys" in the house (when they are 50-year-old men) may not serve the same social function as a parent saying that his 50-year-old son has the mind of a 10–year-old. Both, however, are examples of using childhood status as a way to characterize an adult with developmental disability.

At state hospitals, residents were often spoken about as having an adult body but the mind of a 5-year-old. This infantilized adults, in the face of the obvious physical fact of their adulthood. Seeing residents as children or as innocents rationalized forms of activity and treatment that today we would call "age-inappropriate." First and most importantly adults were not given choices or allowed to control their own lives, much as children are treated by adults in ordinary society. Additionally, adults were provided swings and slides for recreation. The wards were decorated with childlike murals. No attempts were made to provide individuals with adult forms of recreation or activity, other than work for the working residents. Keeping the residents ignorant, largely uneducated, dependent, and socially isolated maintained their innocence.

Lost Childhoods[13]

> Have you ever wondered what it would be like to raise a kid without giving him any love at all? Don't hold the kid, don't praise him in any way? Have you ever wondered what that would be like? That's exactly how I was raised. I don't even remember being held, except by Madril Caine. And she didn't do that very often because she would always get scolded for playing favorites. (Mickey Finn, as cited by Pratt, 1998, p. 15)

According to the State, Willowbrook was supposed to be an institution for children, more school than hospital. As it turned out, it was never a place for only children, although many did spend their childhoods at WSS, an experience that affected them in profound ways. Whether or not families were involved, young people at Willowbrook found themselves, first and foremost, to be essentially on their own in a difficult, capricious, sometimes cruel situation. Judging by the accounts in this book, children had to become in some way as "hard as steel." They faced assaults at every level: psychological isolation and confusion, insufficient nurturance and food, physical violence and sexual assault, chronic drugging, medical mismanagement and indifference, even death. If by "childhood" we mean that time of innocence when the young are supposed to be nurtured and loved, protected from these horrible aspects of life, encouraged to engage in exploration and discovery, and so on, then it is no exaggeration to say that many young people who were at Willowbrook simply had no childhood. This observation was also made by Goode (1986) on the deaf-blind ward at Pacific State, where he wrote at he could find people with few years and small bodies but no kids or children.

Throughout this book, you have read many statements about things that happened to children at Willowbrook. We know that children, even ones with active families, were abandoned and alone, often wondering why it was they had to be away from their family. We know that some residents, perhaps those who were most abandoned and simply dumped into the institution, would use the terms "momma" and "papa" to refer to staff members, partly because of their need for the human love and

---

13. A short explanatory note about this topic and section. It is not one of the statuses discussed by Wolfensberger. It is a kind of opposite status to the one just discussed, and an extremely common one at Willowbrook and other state schools where young persons were routinely denied the most common experiences of children on the outside. We can see that at least some people were quite aware of this denial of childhood. We include the section here as a contrast to the eternal child, and as a sad addition to Wolfensberger's list. Another deviant status, the not-child. Many children, with and without disabilities, are denied the experience of childhood because of circumstance—extreme poverty, war, and institutionalization being common causes.

acceptance that they had been denied and partly perhaps as ways of influencing their circumstances. We know that children had fantasies about living a normal life, where they were back with parents, their brothers and sisters, in their own home, and going to school. We find incidents where children eloped from the institution to go home to visit. In some cases, we see that children were placed out of Willowbrook, into foster homes, only to return again because of problems adjusting to the outside world.

We find, at Willowbrook and all total institutions, a general lack of "kids' culture"—of the games, fashions, language, popular media, usual gender-related activities, and other cultural practices that are part of childhood in the mainstream of society. Children in such places live lives that are much more dominated by adult practices and adult ideas. They are entirely surrounded by adults and lack any contact with nondisabled children. In addition, because of gender segregation, at Willowbrook and other such places, children did not learn about the other gender, and many became culturally incompetent in these relations. In the face of these facts of life it is remarkable that we come across at WSS and other institutions expressions of children attempting to do kids stuff and in kids ways.[14]

Perhaps the most insidious effect of being a child at a place like Willowbrook was on the person's development of a self-image. In the outside world, many children have parents and families who help them feel good about whom they are, who support them and give them positive feedback about their accomplishments. Most children at a fairly young age begin to develop a self-image that is related to their peer group, other children of the same age and what they do and say. Relations with family and peer group can be difficult for many children. Of course, neither provides only positive feedback about the self. At WSS, children were surrounded by other children who were victimized and lacked appropriate socialization and care and thus were unable to provide peers positive feedback about who they were. The other group in their lives was the relatively few adults who as a rule did not adopt parental roles toward their charges, and some of whom could even be cruel and punitive. Thus, the self-images that developed at Willowbrook were, in comparison to the norm, ungrounded, inaccurate reflections of the self—a self reflected in a most highly distorted mirror who would often become "internalized" and stay with that individual long after he or she left the institution. Those who know former residents of Willowbrook who grew up there can recognize these effects, often sad and difficult to witness because they are so deeply a part of the person and so deeply dysfunctional.

14. We make these observations about institutions only in Willowbrook's era. It is difficult to know today to what degree conventional media and Internet access may have changed for children living in institutions today this relative ignorance of children's culture and children's affairs in the larger society.

A lost childhood is something that cannot be recovered. The emotional scars of neglect and abuse are not easily removed, and it is difficult to assess in any simple way the effects of living in a place like Willowbrook. Babies there learned that crying did no good, and it was not uncommon on entering the Baby Buildings to hear complete quiet (as related to Goode by a former college student who worked over the summer at WSS). How does one evaluate what that did to these children?[15]

The following are two short statements about growing up in Willowbrook. The first was made by Bernard Carabello in conversation with the interviewer Mike Dillon, during the documentary *Recollections of the Institution:*

> BC: I was born with cerebral palsy and they thought I was mentally retarded. Don't forget back in the '50s there were no kind of programs like we have today like school integration, education programs that would have helped me live a productive life in my community. . . . In the end I was put in the institution, and I left the institution in '72.
>
> I went with my mother and my aunt to this strange place and I didn't want to let go . . . [nods his head affirmatively].
>
> Q: *You still remember that day?*
>
> BC: Oh yeah. It's embroidered in my mind.
> I remember being put in the crib. I remember my mother leaving.
>
> Q: *You couldn't walk?*
>
> BC: No. It took me eight or nine years to learn how to walk. The first couple of years was easy for me because I was a cute baby that everybody liked. But as you get older you are no longer this cute little kid. You become this difficult person that they used to knock the hell out of me every day with sticks and key chains and that I never had to walk. I used to roll on the floor. Lay on the floor and roll to get around.
>
> Q: *You never had a wheelchair?*
>
> BC: No. I learned how to crawl . . . and when I wanted a drink of water, I had to drink out of the toilet bowl. Because no one would give me water to drink. . . . It took me three years to get a pair of special shoes.

---

15. We are not implying an obvious answer to the question. In some cultures it is considered beneficial to the development of the child to swaddle him or her and to ignore crying. However, in those cultures there are also expressions of parental love and bonding. At Willowbrook, these were, by and large, lacking. So the ignoring of the babies was part of a more general pattern and would have had different outcomes.

They were orthopedic shoes and I came from a poor family who could not afford for to pay for them and the state had to pay. [They cost $24.]

I remember the time I had a case of appendicitis. And the doctor was scared to examine me and said I needed an enema. Luckily the staff knew better. They knew I had appendicitis. But it almost ruptured.

Q: You're serious when you say the doctor was scared? Like he might catch something

BC: Oh yeah. I can never forget that my family came to see [me] about every five or ten years. I was too scared to tell 'em.

Q: Why were you scared?

BC: Because of the repercussions.

Q: You witnessed that?

BC: Oh yeah. I got it.

Q: Like what?

BC: I got my head kicked through a wall. I got beaten up by staff. . . .

Q: What was the thing that got you to get out?

BC: When I met Mike Wilkins. [Wilkins was the physician who contacted Geraldo Rivera and invited him to film what was going on at Willowbrook.]

Another statement about growing up at Willowbrook comes from Gary Cohen, from the same documentary. Gary arrived at Willowbrook in 1952:

GC: Yes, it was a nightmare. I slept in a dormitory. There were like 60 people in the dormitory and the beds were so close people were breathing in your face.

Q: How do 60 people bathe?

GC: They had one shower stall. Everybody used one shower stall. There were feces in the shower stall. There were feces on the toilet.

Q: How often could you have a shower?

GC: Every night mostly, but the shower. But the shower was so overcrowded you had to wait. At least an hour to an hour and a half. I was beaten at one time because this woman saw me urinating on myself.

And every time she saw this she would beat me with a stick, a sneaker, a belt, slap me in the face. . . . I could have been helped. There are agencies out there that could have helped me.

Most people are fortunate enough not to have experienced such events as a child. As we noted earlier, the children at WSS had paradoxical childhoods. On the one hand, they had nothing to compare what they were experiencing to, and this made the absence of normal childhood perhaps easier to accept. On the other hand, some children did have experiences of the outside world, admittedly often negative in some important way, which is why they ended up at WSS. Or they may have gained knowledge about the outside world through conversations with other children or adults. Many children did have ideas and fantasies about living a more normal existence, even if they had a very limited experience or knowledge of it.

Normalization Fantasies and Strategies

In the last decade of Willowbrook's existence, some reformers' answer to the long-standing prejudice against disabled people was normalization (Wolfensberger, 1972). The only thing, they believed, that could counteract the negative view of disabled people in American society was for them to live lives that were valued by others—a regular life, like nondisabled people. Being normal, as much as possible, was the new language.

Normalization reconstructed people who were "retarded" as like everyone else, "deserving conditions of everyday life that are as close as possible to the mainstream society" (Rothman & Rothman, 1984/2009, p. 48), enjoying things such as living in a family-like setting, going to school, getting adequate medical care, eating food, making friends, enjoying sex—overall, enjoying what Bob Perske called the "dignity of risk" (Wolfensberger, 1972). Because the term "normalization" seemed to implied that the person should live a "normal life," Wolfensberger renamed normalization "social role valorization" to in part combat the tendency to equate the philosophy of normalization with strict conformity to idealized norms.

Although Willowbrook failed to provide anything like a life similar to that of the mainstream, in what ways did ideas about living more normally surface? Did staff use normal life in their thinking about what they did? Did the residents reassert their humanity, resisting dehumanizing forces at Willowbrook? We think the reader will agree that despite widespread evidence of dehumanization, there are several important and meaningful signs of resistance and subversion in the resident accounts.

The philosophy of normalization was an ideal, a guiding set of beliefs for the field, and was known to professionals and workers at many state institutions, including Willowbrook. In field notes while observing at PSH, Goode wrote about what normalization meant to the psychiatric technicians working on the deaf-blind ward. They had been given a 2-day workshop on normalization and how it could be implemented at the hospital. (Goode assumes this could have had nothing to do with Wolfensberger, who would not have supported such efforts). Recall that the philosophy of normalization, borrowed from the Scandinavian countries, held that all persons should be able to live a life as close to the norm as possible and, further, that the methods used to enable persons to achieve this goal should themselves be normal and accepted ones. Goode found that the staff at Pacific State implicitly understood that neither a normal life nor normal ways of helping people to achieve it were possible there. Normalization thus was seen by staff as a kind of dream, fantasy, or, sometimes, a shibboleth, "just another name for what we are already doing . . . you know teach kids not to make in their pants, to dress, use a fork and spoon."

Putting aside the issue of what "normal" is (a concept that had perhaps more meaning in the highly homogeneous Scandinavian societies of the 1950s), the reality for residents at Willowbrook (or PSH) was usually starkly different than what is "normally" found in regular society. How could it be otherwise, given that they lived in the circumstances described by the authors and those interviewed?

These facts of life apparently did not prevent the goal of normalization from serving as an ideal for the service providers, nor did they prevent residents from forming a fantasy of normal life. Of course, the residents' ideas of living a normal life was not the product of a training workshop. It was not a philosophy out of a book. It was a dream, a deep desire, to be able to have the kind of lives that existed outside the institution. Reiss and several interviewees reported that such fantasies were maintained even by children who had no or little direct knowledge of life outside. At Willowbrook and similar institutions, a constant stream of children were admitted, with varying life experiences, so that even those who grew up at the institution could be aware that children on the outside have a mother and father, live in a house, go to school, take vacations, have a boyfriend or girlfriend, have pets, and so forth. While, on the one hand, as Bernard Carabello put it, "we didn't know any better . . . we had nothing to compare it to," on the other hand, children, including Carabello, were in some general sense aware of their relative deprivation. Carabello has been eloquent about this. In *Unforgotten,* he recalls his experiences of visiting days at Willowbrook, when no one would come to see him and bring him cookies, ice cream, and candy, "things like that." Although this reads as somewhat contradictory, some children at Willowbrook were both naive about the details of what they might not have and cognizant of their deprived circumstances.

Reiss presents one fantasy of normalization from the perspective of 14-year-old Peter, whose vivid imagination portrayed both the hope and the reality of these dreams.

A few months earlier an attendant who usually worked in another ward had come to the unit for about a week. During this time she had been amused and touched by Peter, with his vivid imagination and affectionate ways. She had taken him home one Sunday and he had spent a very happy day playing with her children and helping make a barbecue in the garden. For him, it was the fulfillment of his dreams, the ambition of his life. He built upon this one incident a whole world in which the attendant adopted him, took him home, and he grew up as her child.

The attendant had four children of her own, and a small house. Both she and her husband worked, one at night and the other during the day, just to make ends meet. There was no room for another child. Her momentary kindness in taking Peter home for the day had been intended as exactly that—momentary. He could not accept this. For two months he wrote her letters almost daily, mailing them under the door of the ward in which she worked. They were impassioned, pleading, letters scrawled in pencil on scraps of paper, all saying the same thing. "Take me home. I am your son. I will be good forever. I love you. I have only dead people, etc. etc."

The attendant was shaken by the passion her kindness had elicited. As the weeks passed she began to feel harassed and somewhat indignant. Many children in Willowbrook asked to be taken home, but few showed the single-minded determination that Peter was displaying. The attendant worked at night in another ward. Finally she wrote a letter . . . to the senior attendant in his ward. She asked that someone explain to Peter the impossibility of his dreams, "And, please, for heaven's sake stop him writing all those letters. It is getting so that I can't sleep for worrying about it."

At public Willowbrook events at the College of Staten Island, former residents described feelings and ideas similar to those expressed by Peter. Some had memories of the outside, many had fantasies about the outside, and for them the outside represented the possibility of living like everyone else, normally. This fantasy provided hope in what was a hopeless circumstance, and some, after they were released or transferred from Willowbrook, put their dreams into action by pursuing having their own place, family, pet, friends, and so on.

Resistance, Parody, and Sabotage

Resistance and sabotage against those with power were engaged in by both residents and staff at Willowbrook. Goffman's (1961) writing conveys an image of total institutions in which the large mass of controlled persons are usually pushing back against those few who are regimenting and otherwise controlling their lives. It is the hands-on staff, the prison guards, psychiatric technicians, and nurses aides who are sandwiched between those on top, who push for efficiency and standardization, and those below, who want to be free of control and to act according to their own desires and who resist in the various ways available to them. These "low-level" staff are themselves subject to high degrees of social control and, like those they supervise and try to control, sometimes rebel and resist centralized authority. In the case of staff, we might label these acts "worker sabotage," and although there is not a lot about such efforts in our data, they were witnessed firsthand by at least two of the authors and there are other, anecdotal, reports of them in other institutions. Workers apparently regularly acted in ways that they knew would not be sanctioned by those in power and even in ways that were in opposition to their stated purposes.[16] In similar fashion, direct care workers at Willowbrook reacted against centralized control over their lives in as the residents did, to exert control over theirs.[17] In this section, we do not concern ourselves with forms of worker resistance or sabotage. These are mentioned in interviews, and we acknowledge that they were a regular part of life at Willowbrook. Acknowledging the sociological importance of such events in understanding Willowbrook, our focus is on ways in which residents fought back against their subjugation.

As described fully in Chapter 3, Goffman was one of the first social scientists to report methodically on the different patterns of coping that persons living within total institutions display. Some of these patterns, for example, the "intransient line," involve active, consistent resistance to forms of control brought to bear on the individual. These people react to attempts to dominate them with utter defiance. Others give in to them, others try and lay low and avoid them, and still others try and become part of the controlling force. Even at Willowbrook, where

16. The dynamics of resistance to authority is explored in Milgram's (1965) shock experiment, which demonstrated that when authority is exercised indirectly at a distance, it is less effective and can even result in subjects deceiving the experimenter (e.g., lying to the experimenter about what they were doing when the experimenter was out of the room and communicating to the subject via telephone). This kind of dynamic was also operant at Willowbrook for those providing the actual care to residents. They were subject to a high degree of social control, but it was exercised from a high level, not so much on the ward where these staff worked in a relatively high degree of social isolation and invisibility to administration. There were eyes and ears of administration on the wards, but they could not be everywhere.

17. This situation is persistent. In group homes, direct care workers are often treated without respect, not given discretion, and expected to do what they are told. These same persons are told that their job is to treat the residents as individuals, respect their choices and foster their independence.

conditions were such that most choices were taken away via a lack of opportunities and resources, residents developed their own style of coping. Some of the more courageous routinely engaged in resistance, parody, and sabotage. It is difficult to say to what degree these ways of coping are learned or characterological. All forms of resistance involved the risk of getting caught, which was part of the very nature of the act. Although they did the best they could to avoid it, people were caught and punished regularly.

A great example of resistance was briefly described in Chapter 4: Eileen, the ringleader of the group of "working girls" who regularly eloped in the evenings to find sex and drinking partners in the community. Eileen, who Goode has met on several occasions is open about the fact that she doesn't take anything from anybody. She's proud of it. She said she has always been this way, strong-willed. Willowbrook was a place that tried to break her will, and although it won many of their skirmishes, it ultimately couldn't destroy her. For a long while, Eileen was punished for her recreational efforts. She refused to stop. Even when the punishments became severe, she persevered in her role as ringleader of the elopees. Eventually she was forced to abandon her activities, the cost having become unacceptable, the drugs too strong, the isolation too depressing.

Eileen for many years worked as a trusted inmate, helping to take care of the babies in the baby complex. She lived "the best I could" while at Willowbrook, never being entirely cooperative. Eventually when released, she was able to start her own family. Her history at Willowbrook shows what Goffman (1961) described as a "moral career," that is, of the changes in self-worth and value that Eileen underwent as part of her progression through the institution.

Eileen was not at all alone in her defiance. Many residents, amid the horror of their lives, stripped of family, friends, and school, bouncing amid forces colluding to destroy and dehumanize them, resisted through a variety of strategies. At Fernald, for example, open, direct rebellion was a dominant approach: Disorder, fires, and break-ins throughout the institution were "the product of boredom and resentment" (D'Antonio, 2004, p. 120). Similar incidents were reported at Willowbrook, which had its share of rebellion, but there were other less confrontative forms of resistance. Toilets were particularly available targets and were constantly being stopped up by residents with paper, objects, and whatever else they could find. Windows, unscreened and unprotected at Willowbrook, were also easy to break (at Pacific State they were grated so that residents could not break them).

Residents lied and deceived staff in an effort to resist and manipulate them, a practice that must have been massive at Willowbrook given the mix of residents in the various wards and buildings. We find several examples of this in Reiss's writings. Those more capable of understanding and communicating would have had a distinct advantage over those who were not. They would have had available to them the various arts of deception that people have and use in everyday life. Under the kinds of conditions we find at Willowbrook, people living there would do everything and anything they could just to get by, including lying and deception, if they were able.

We know that the activities of parents and professionals that led to the class action lawsuit to close Willowbrook—resistance through public demonstration, political pressure and the courts—was perhaps the strongest act of defiance in any American state school, and it was resistance to dehumanization through certainly the slowest but most spectacular strategy (Pelka, 2012; Rothman & Rothman, 1984/2009). But residents themselves had virtually nothing to do with the suit.

In day-to-day life, their stage was smaller, but the victories were still sweet. Maria described her approach to resisting Willowbrook: "We would stand up to them. We used to run off the grounds. We did what we wanted. They had no control of us." She lived in Building 32, among the "delinquent girls." Her advice was:

> You had to stand up and fight for yourself and you had to show them that you are not going to let them keep you there. No matter how much they lock the door, you will always find a way to get out, so that was my way of showing them that I am going to get out.

And she connected this attitude directly to her freedom to leave Willowbrook:

> So that is why I'm [in] the world out here today: I don't let nobody push me around. I would tell them "Don't push me around because I am a human being. You're no better than me. I am not going to be pushed around." I would talk back to them, but I would not fight. I would just tell them with my mouth that I am not going to be pushed around.

Reiss told one story that shows, in one small way, how a resident resisted the control of his mind and body. Tom resisted the efforts of psychologists to study his behavior:

> Tom had been included in one of the psychological conditioning series. The technician administering the tests pointed out that his responses were different from those of any other patient. Whatever the stimuli, a light or a noise, for example, the length of time it took him to react was always exactly the same. If the technician changed the stimuli in the middle of the series there would be several confused responses, and then he would swing back into his unchanging rhythm again. Intrigued, the psychologist waited until a test was in progress, and then quietly peered over the partition to watch him in action. Tom, absorbed and serious, was timing his responses with a stop-watch. He could not explain how he had learned to use it. He would not explain where he had "found" it.

In her writing about Peter, Reiss mentions a small, unused storeroom between the main ward and the dayroom. It served as a kind of fantasy space where Peter and his ward-mates could act out their critique of ward life, express their wishes for a better life, or work out the horrors of their current situation. On Reiss's ward, Peter unofficially owned this room:

> This was not a conscious decision on the part of the staff; it was just his by right. He was the producer, inventor and organizer of all games. Without him the room was a barren little cupboard, with him it was magically changed into a schoolroom, ship, laboratory or church. He taught school with a blackboard and pieces of chalk. A black sweater pulled over his head and a black raincoat round his waist and he was transformed into a nun, swinging a broken rosary. In a white cotton nightgown and carefully constructed paper cap, he was a nurse.
>
> The room was a source of delight and anguish. On many occasions it had to be closed because the games had gotten so thoroughly out of hand. One such time was when Peter, in his nurse's uniform, tried to get blood out of George. He was using a straightened safety pin strapped to a ball-point pen. George only started screaming when Peter decided to try his abdomen, having inexplicably failed with his arm.
>
> The boys were tested frequently by the psychologists. At one time there was a long series of conditioning tests, which the boys enjoyed. They pushed levers in response to colored lights and were given candy for their trouble. After a while it was noticed that the boys did not eat their candy at once as they had done in the beginning, but rushed back to the ward with it clenched in their hands. There they gave it to Peter who had set up his own psychological test.
>
> A screen across one corner of the room represented the conditioning apparatus. Peter stood at a small table making marks on a piece of paper, while one boy after the other went behind the screen and pressed imaginary levers. When they came out Peter rewarded them with candy and lofty statements such as, "You're doing fine," or, surprisingly, (and surely a direct quote) "This is an interesting series." In between he maintained a serious, preoccupied air, puffing occasionally on a piece of rolled paper and lounging against the door-post.

Peter organized for himself and others a form of resisting the dehumanizing experience by providing a fantasy space, and a space for social commentary, to parody psychological testing, as a form of ridicule, or perhaps a show without meaning. This was a resistance to dehumanization at its most creative. Peter's dramas were also moral plays, as commented on above, and to some degree served the purpose of showing all the children what was "really" right or what "ought" to have happened if things were fair and just.

One form of subversion was sabotage of the physical plant. There are many stories, but one will have to suffice here. Each building was heated by radiators. Many people remember these unreliable sources of heat, but in Reiss's ward, they were a "contested terrain":

> The radiators were enclosed to prevent accidental burns, but the covers could be removed for cleaning and repair. It was difficult to open them without a special key, but our boys found one in the dayroom that they could manage. How long they preserved this secret we never knew. As the winter came on and the heat roared up in the pipes, the ward was filled with a strange smell. It was not an unpleasant smell; more reminiscent of hot wax than anything else. When we finally traced it to its source we found out it was hot wax indeed. The boys . . . had found that they could ease the front of the radiator cover out several inches. It gave them enough space to insert their hands and place crayons on the hot elements. The crayons melted, running down the metal in wild and beautiful colors and patterns. The radiator finally looked like a psychedelic candle. It was difficult to clean and impossible to explain to the plumber. The boys' eyes shone with pleasure when the full atrocity was revealed. They denied any knowledge of it but, by taking one look at their faces, we knew it had been a secret treasure and ward resource possibly for months.

One cannot help but laugh with and root for the boys as the underdog in these stories. Given the overall hopelessness of their situation (no action they could have taken would have changed their basic circumstance), residents found ways to have small victories, almost symbolic expressions, via making trouble for those who made trouble for them. Projects such as the radiator must have provided a needed relief from the boredom of everyday life.

Sabotage and parody, for worker and resident, were social ways to resist the oppression and boredom to which both were subject. For residents, these were ways to claim some degree of control over the situation, to get back at their oppressors, and, given their meager daily existence, to have, perhaps, a heck of a lot of fun. For workers, resistance may have performed different functions, but they were equally a product of their own social circumstances.

Elopement

Prolonged resistance could not be sustained for a long period at Willowbrook, because of the likelihood of being caught eventually and the high costs if one was.

The final outcome of resistance could be problematic; one could fail entirely. And even if one was successful, one could be caught, with the eventual costs outweighing the victory. Escape, a solution to one's problems in one fell swoop, was an option for residents at Willowbrook and places like it. Many staff who we interviewed recalled instances when children and adults went missing, and that most of these incidents were not reported in the newspapers. This occured at other institutions as well. At Fernald, for instance, going AWOL was common. As D'Antonio (2004) put it: "With attendants organizing fights by day and sodomizing them by night, running away became increasingly attractive" (p. 94).

Running away could be a long- or short-term solution. For many, getting out of Willowbrook, through an overnight, weekend, or summer furlough, was a temporary form of relief, but many could not earn this privilege, so eloping was common. Eloping meant running away, being absent without leave. For some residents, escape seemed the most practical or possibly only available option. This accounts for the regularity of their occurrence.

Reiss reported:

> Every week one or two patients would run away. The police were informed, the required forms filled in, and if the child never returned there was a quiet sigh of relief.
>
> The children, however, seldom had anywhere to run to, except homes, which had already proved incapable of looking after them, or streets which could not sustain them. Most of them came back, either quiet and cowed, in the custody of an angry parent, "Why can't you look after this kid?" or quiet and rather happy, in the back of a police car, having been filled up with hot dogs and milk shakes by the station patrolmen.

These children probably knew beforehand that they would be caught. Similarly, we have heard residents say that they would escape the grounds to go back to their old neighborhoods, despite knowing that their parents would take them back to Willowbrook. They eloped knowing that it was a temporary, not permanent, absence, an unofficial vacation. It was fun and an adventure.

Irma observed: "Some of the girls that I taught said they hated it and did threaten to run away. They wanted to go home. Nobody wanted to be there." This was confirmed by Maria:

> I didn't want to stay there so I would just take off and run away for a week and stay with my mother for a week. And they would send the cops after me. And then I would wait for another month and I would take off again. Seven times in seven months. I just kept running and running.

Many ran away and were returned, but some just vanished. There were simply too many opportunities and not enough staff. The newspaper clippings at the College of Staten Island Library Archive report regular elopements and police searches. One can only guess what happened to the people who were never found, whether theirs was a successful escape or a sad event. There were some who eloped and died accidentally. Diane Buglioli, an agency director on Staten Island who worked at Willowbrook in the 1970s, recalls leading a group of horseback riders searching the woods near Willowbrook for a severely retarded child. He had escaped from the ward in the dead of winter. They found him, frozen to death. He had made a bed in the woods nearby, taken off his clothes, folded them and had gone to sleep.

Gender Segregation of Children

Today it is commonly recognized that both gender and sexuality are matters of social convention and experience. Whatever one's biological makeup, one learns from others about the gendered nature of people and society and about sexuality and how it works in everyday life. One of the most dehumanizing aspects of institutional life is gender segregation--virtually a universal feature of total institutions. Separating the genders is usually rationalized as a way to prevent sex and as part of the overall plan to control those living at the institution. Yet, anyone who has worked at a gender-segregated institution knows that separating the males from the females does little to prevent sex (Starogiannis & Hill, 2008). It does, however, severely limit opportunities for social and sexual contact with the other gender, which creates various kinds of problems for residents.

Reiss described the situation this way:

> The boys and girls in Willowbrook were segregated in different buildings. They met at school, dances and movies. Every year one or two of the girls became pregnant, which was a modest number considering the size of the population.

Although gender segregation may aid slightly in the management of residents, it provides an abnormal social environment for people and functions as another force of dehumanization. Perhaps the status of not being human or animal-like is operant here—as if children with mental and physical disabilities need to be separated like animals to avoid reproducing. Whatever the rationale, the social relations of the residents become distorted, abnormal, and inconsistent with those found outside the institution. These distortions then become reflected in the experience and behaviors of those inside, and in their self-images.

Willowbrook at its best tried to provide corecreational activities where boys and girls were explicitly permitted to interact. These occasions were relatively infrequent, and when they did occur it was in large, anonymous, highly supervised gatherings. Most of the boys and girls who came to Willowbrook at a young age and who grew up there had very limited knowledge about how to actually act with a person of the opposite gender because of institutional segregation. This is clearly demonstrated in Reiss's account of a party given for the boys on her ward and some girls from another ward. The party was partly in response to Peter's desire to spend time with one of the girls, whom he called his "girlfriend." Reiss's account is disturbing and compelling:

> From the very beginning it was a problem. We called the boys together and told them of our plan. They were dumb-founded. Girls in their ward? Yes, we explained, we would have food and music and dancing, and it would be fun. Round-eyed they regarded us with amazement. No one, not even Peter, would admit to having a girl friend, or even knowing what a girl was. George finally muttered that girls made him embarrassed. Willie scanned everyone's face anxiously, sure that there was something being discussed which threatened his peace, but unable to understand what it was all about.
>
> The boys' reaction seemed to us to be extreme. The children were not completely segregated into sexes; they met at school, dances and movies. They went on many trips together, and they were only separated as far as living and sleeping accommodations were concerned.
>
> We decided to pursue the plan. We invited Peter's girl friend, whose name had been drummed into our heads, and nine other girls, the names to be selected by the supervisor of that building.

Reiss continued the story:

> The boys were growing excited and cheerful, brief squabbles breaking out over possession of a particularly brightly colored shirt or a comb. Finally they were all dressed and were eyeing the food with anticipation when the girls arrived. As the girls marched into the ward, decorous and shy in the company of their own attendant, there was complete silence, for a moment, and then the boys retreated in a body to the other end of the room.
>
> Willie panicked completely. He had forgotten his foreboding about the party and was quite unprepared for the girls' appearance. After one wild look at them he climbed into the furthest window embrasure and crouched there, too agitated to listen to reassurance.
>
> Matthew and Jimmy eyed the girls with mild dislike and proceeded to ignore them, and everything else, except the food for the rest of the afternoon. George told everyone repeatedly that he was "Embarrassed."

He was, he said, much too embarrassed to eat. Eating would make him feel much worse. He thought he might be sick to his stomach.

It was at that moment of crisis, with the boys poised in flight at one end of the room, and the shy knot of girls looking bewildered in the doorway, when Walter strode forward to the rescue. Walter had lived in the ward for some months without much notice being taken of him. A shy quiet boy, he was always smiling, obedient and somehow neutral. At the party, however, he suddenly blossomed into the most genial of hosts. Striding forward, he welcomed the girls with grave courtesy and led them first to the table where the paper hats were lying and helped them adjust their choice of headgear. To encourage everybody he blew one of the most strident noisemakers as each girl put on her hat. He then led them to the tables where the food was set out, and hovered over them anxiously while they made their selection.

Gradually the boys were persuaded to come and take their food. Once they found that they could take a paper plate and put on it whatever they wanted they became fascinated, unselfconscious and busy.

Reiss explained that the party had been originally planned because Peter was feeling sad, yet:

He did not make any effort to participate, but seemed happy in a dispassionate and aloof way. His girl friend had gravitated to his side soon after entering the ward but we never saw him speak to her. A shy pretty girl, she remained throughout the party attentively about two paces behind his left shoulder. He apparently considered that the correct place for her, and once or twice turned and benevolently gave her a can of soda or a bite of something choice from his plate.

The boys were shocked and unnerved by the idea of having a small party for 10 girls on the boys' ward because they would actually have to interact and speak with a girl. Indeed, what Reiss describes happening at the party, a game of tag, eating, and dumping soda on the girls heads, appears to have nothing to do with the gendered relationships of "outside" children in that age group. Peter, finally able to be with his "girlfriend," does not appear to speak to her, although she by gravitating to his side acknowledges her status. She stayed dutifully two paces behind him and received offerings of food and drink. And, poor Willie.

Reiss's description of this party captures the social damage that had been done to Willowbrook children when compared with noninstitutionalized children of their age. What happened at the party is thus not surprising. What perhaps is surprising is how many children who grew up in this fashion at Willowbrook were able to eventually establish close relationships with others of the opposite sex. Their lack of experience retarded their development in this regard, but it did not prevent them, once liberated from a gender-segregated environment, from learning the necessary skills. How sad, and how many children like those at Willowbrook found themselves in similar circumstances?

Kindness, Love, and Sex

As we have already pointed out, it is remarkable that under conditions such as those found at state institutions, one finds human beings providing one another compassion and kindness. Even short of love, acts of kindness, under such circumstances could leave lasting, profound effects. One of the most poignant examples of this can be found in the following narrative from a former resident, not of WSS, but of Weston State, in West Virginia. Mickey Finn talked about being on the verge of despair and suicide when:

> I met this girl who turned my life inside out. I remember the first time I laid eyes on her I walked into a wall and fell backwards. Well, that got her attention. . . Two weeks later I got up enough nerve to introduce myself to her, and we became friends. For the next three or four months, she paid attention to me as a friend and that was something to live for. Just a little sweet taste of affection, to me that was the sweetest thing I'd ever had. (Mickey Finn, as cited by Pratt, 1998, p. 8)

The importance of simple kindnesses in institutions, a little sweet taste of affection, cannot be overestimated, as so well put by Mickey Finn. Horrible as institutions are, they are also places where human beings show compassion and even love. Because of the severity of situations children and adults faced, even ordinary kindness could have a profound impact on the individuals. Throughout the years, many emotional stories about WSS have been shared at the College of State Island's Willowbrook Annual Lecture.

For Reiss, the impulse for human love and affection was obvious, yet often denied at Willowbrook:

> When they were young the children were often held and kissed, petted and loved. As they grew older the attendant withdrew physical warmth. It was, "Stand up, don't lean on me," "Stop pawing people," or, somewhat illogically, "Be a man."

In a sense, relationships between staff and "favorites" helped assert some humanity into an otherwise depressing situation. Irma called the staff member who had a favorite a "ward mother":

In the baby building, if you had a ward mother, you were very lucky. I will always remember Karen. The first time I saw her. She was dressed like a little princess. She was dressed in a lace outfit, with lace stockings and little patent leather shoes. It was a gorgeous outfit. I said, "Oh my God, these parents must be loaded." I was told, "Her parents don't do it. Her mother on the ward takes care of her." It seems her ward mother's husband had a dry-cleaning business. She would bring the clothes in for Karen and bring them home again and clean them herself. Everybody who worked on the ward had a ward baby. When Karen's ward mother was not there, she was dressed in rags. What a shock I got, when I saw the difference.

Goode heard many Willowbrook staff and residents speak about having special relationships. The idea that an attendant would reach out emotionally and socially to a resident is understandable given the intimacy of their circumstances. But the numbers dictated that only a very few were able to experience such special treatment. At Pacific State, Goode knew many of the "long termers" who had similar relationships with residents. They took on as a special cause one resident with whom they had some particular rapport. It is almost as if, by going beyond the bureaucratically defined "people work" relationship, the attendant does, with at least this one, what he or she knows should be happening with every child. People working at Pacific acknowledged that this was an inherently unfair practice, that is, to the vast majority of others who did not have similar benefits. Yet no one ever questioned the decision of an attendant to take a particular interest in a resident. It was simply understood as part of what happened: You got attached to certain people, kids and adults.

Favorites were essential to order on the ward, according to John:

Most of the other attendants had favorites. Like a favorite client or two who were usually more intelligent. They took over the job of attendant while the attendant would sort of sit down, and just sit there. Those brighter ones who were the favorites would keep order.

He explained:

These clients would get rewards, such as gifts, candy, or soda. Their job was to keep the rest of the residents quiet. If the ward was quiet, then everything was fine. It did not matter what they were doing, as long as they were quiet.

Another worker interviewed by Starogiannis and Hill (2008) noticed this:

There were people who were people's favorites. And so they would say to them, you know, "You look pretty," . . . maybe do their hair a little differently to make them feel more attractive or something like that. Particularly with the little girls, the younger girls.

However, playing favorites with youth who were so vulnerable led to some inappropriate affection, as this same worker observed: "Sometimes the female [resident] would get very attached to the male [attendant], and acting inappropriately . . . with the male staff. So limits had to be set." This worker explained that the female residents would sometimes flirt with the male attendants, saying "You're my boyfriend," "Gimme a kiss." There were rumors that some high-functioning residents were sexually involved with staff members.

Reiss's observations often focused on close bonds between residents and ward attendants. One involved Phillip, Willie, and a treasured ward attendant. Stories like the following take seriously and elevate the lives of Willie and Phillip out of the thousands of anonymous and forgotten people who lived and died at Willowbrook. Willie and Phillip appear as individual children with whom we can identify and understand. They are not "retarded residents," "favorites," or "low grades," or any of the typifications that appear even in the interviews. What happened between these two children and an attendant was something so simple and yet, in its telling, requires the reader to recognize them as real people and to identify with, in some way, what they were feeling.

Humanity was possible to find at Willowbrook, if you knew how to look. Reiss knew how to look and introduces us to Phillip, a new transfer to her ward, who became involved in a love triangle:

> Phillip was enormous, a great lumbering boy-man, five feet tall and weighing 250 lbs. Scientifically he was interesting, and this was the reason he was brought to the ward, but it was obvious that Phillip could not understand his changed circumstances. Unable to talk, understanding only simple sentences, he lurched into the ward like an old bear, expecting to be baited. Head down, hands hanging by his side, he allowed himself to be led to the bed that would be his without glancing [to] either side. The boys in the ward studied him with amazement and some contempt.

Because clothes were a problem, one attendant brought some clothes from home and dressed Phillip up. She began by:

> buttoning a bright shirt around him. She combed his hair, trimmed his nails and patting him on the shoulder told him he was a "fine boy." He fell in love. She was the first person in the ward that he seemed to "see." Up until then he had neither smiled nor shown recognition of anyone, but once his attention was caught his devotion was complete. When the attendant entered the ward he would heave himself up out of his chair

and follow her like a shadow, until exasperation made her order him back to his place. After that he would follow her attentively with his eyes.

This would have been unremarkable since many of the boys became attached to one or other of the attendants if it had not been for the fact that Phillip selected Willie's love, and Willie couldn't bear it. Not only was Phillip following Willie's own special attendant but he was continually in the ward. He was cluttering up the happy time when the boys went to school and Willie and the "bibby" were the attendant's only concern.

Willie objected loudly and often. The attendant hoped she wasn't understanding the words he seemed to be using. It was not long before Willie was on the offensive and, mumbling angrily, would insist on mopping the floor wherever Phillip was sitting, repeatedly bumping his chair, splashing him with water and spraying him with what sounded like a string of obscenities.

Phillip bore all this stoically but the attendant did not and rounded upon Willie with the full force of her majestic wrath. Willie was punished cruelly by having his mop removed. He was not allowed to fold clothes, or follow busily to the telephone. The whole purpose of his life collapsed. His distress was so evident that after a few days the attendant had to gently reinstate him in his activities. Willie was humbled by this experience and carefully avoided Phillip, never going near him and avoiding even looking at him.

Phillip had, we were assured, an extremely limited intelligence. The psychologists explained that only the most primitive orders would be understandable to him, and yet he soon demonstrated an acute appreciation of the situation.[18]

After watching stolidly the downfall, distress and gradual reinstatement of Willie, Phillip quietly started plotting his own revenge. He no longer sat heavily in his chair just watching. He got up and would plod over to the area where Willie was mopping and stand just behind him, gazing apparently fascinated out of the window. Inevitably, Willie stepped back onto Phillip, and then burst into agitated chatter, trying to explain it was not his fault. Silently Phillip would move away, but onto the wet floor that Willie had just mopped. If Willie was folding clothes Phillip would pass slowly by and just happen to stumble so that the clothes flew all over the floor. Twice Phillip "mistook" his bed and fell heavily on Willie's just as the latter had fallen asleep.

18. Here is a good example of the way psychologists at places like Willowbrook and PSH would, from the direct care staff's perspective, systematically underestimate the capacities of the individual residents.

Eventually Phillip was transferred back to his old ward, away from Willie:

> When the transfer took place the attendants made a fuss over Phillip. They gave him the large clothes they had brought for him, packing them neatly in a brown paper package. They gave him candy, patted his shoulder and said "see you soon" but from the moment the familiar attendant from his home building entered the ward Phillip refused to look at anyone. He dropped his head and remained inaccessible and impassive, lumbering off after the attendant without a glance [to] either side. His beloved attendant saw him to the door but he would not acknowledge her presence, and as he left she said, sadly, "Now I know how a traitor feels."
>
> Willie was not jubilant, but cautious. It took several days of peace before he began to feel safe. Even then, whenever one of the secretaries from the laboratory entered the ward carrying a piece of paper, he would rush to her side and scan it from top to bottom. He could not recognize any letters but he knew that changes in the ward population would be listed on a piece of paper. When the attendant said, indulgently, "He's looking for Phillip's name," Willie would give a cry and hurtle himself back to his mop, working furiously for the next few minutes.

WSS was also a place where, despite attempts to prevent it, people had sexual relationships. The distinction between love and sex is part of our commonsense knowledge, and the observation that sex can serve different purposes is not something at all unique to total institutions, but it is very much part of life in them. Commonly sex in total institutions can involve pleasure, love, aggression, revenge, and/ or protection. The photographic essay *Concrete Mama* is a collection of photos and stories of prisoners at Walla Walla prison describing what sex in prison means to them, how sexuality works for them in prison (Hoffman & McCoy, 1986). Under conditions of strictly enforced gender segregation, for the men incarcerated there, there were really no opportunities for heterosexuality. Sex meant intercourse with men, whether one was gay or not. Sex also could mean a way to form an alliance, to appease an aggressor, to get back at a former boyfriend, or to dominate and humiliate. Without firsthand knowledge of these kinds of events within the world of the residents at Willowbrook, we can say at least this—that under the enforced conditions of gender segregation there, institutional homosexuality was created as a basic condition of everyday life. Again, without having asked specifically about the details of events of these types, we suspect that sex at Willowbrook was not simply a matter of love and that it served perhaps the same kinds of functions as described by the Walla Wall inmates.

In this book, we cannot explore the topic of institutional homosexuality in any detail. It was a fact of life at Willowbrook but one that people avoid speaking about, perhaps understandably. This reticence, and the effects of this experience on a non-homosexual, was talked about by Howard Cobb, a resident at Weston School, West Virginia:

> Another thing happened to me while at Weston that I would like to bring up. Even though I am not too comfortable talking about it, I think it needs to be said. In these institutions men and women are separated. Much of the time there would be sexual acts done by men to each other. The aides would try to keep that down because they felt that it wasn't right. . . . When you're so young, and when you're a man, your testosterone levels are so high that the desire is pretty hard to handle. When you throw the medicine in, that creates a double whammy, and it's hard to control your sexual urges. . . . I was told on by one of the patients. That resulted in me getting caught in the act of a sexual act. The doctors pretty much made up their minds that I was homosexual. It was written into my records, and it made my social life a disaster because there were other patients who did not or would not understand. After getting out of Weston, it took me some time for me to even figure out who I was. I was so messed up, it even reflected in sexual actions after I got out of Weston. (as cited by Pratt, 1998, p. 42).

One assumes that Cobb's experience was not unique.

Sex can be a sharing of love and warmth; it can be a form of subjugation and domination; it can be intimate or public. At WSS, all these expressions of sexuality existed. The quest for loving close relationships or simply the pleasures of sex are two of the most basic human needs. One strategy for resisting dehumanization is to seek the pleasures and comfort of another. Despite serious efforts to repress this, there is broad and substantial evidence of sex, and even love, at Willowbrook (Starogiannis & Hill, 2008) and Fernald State Schools (D'Antonio, 2004). Although most of what was written about was newsworthy reports of rape, pregnancy, and sexually transmitted disease at Willowbrook, there were other stories that spoke to a quest for love and sex (Starogiannis & Hill, 2008).

We have some telling anecdotes about sex in Reiss's writing and some interviews. Because the implications of various forms of sex were understood by staff and residents, it could be invoked as a topic of conversations, for various reasons. Reiss relayed one story involving Anthony and a teacher where Anthony used talking about staff sex, in this case a complete fabrication, as a way to seek attention and entertain his friends:

> He was delighted to tell his story. Sitting down comfortably in the attendant's office he said that his teacher zipped down his pants. He took his thing out. He zipped down Anthony's pants. He took Anthony's thing

out. "The girls all watch. He do it every day." Anthony smiled shyly, obviously pleased by the rapt attention his story received.

In Willowbrook no staff member can be accused of misconduct on the basis of a patient's word alone. Another employee had to be a witness, and prepared to testify. Uncertain how to proceed, the attendant in charge of the ward was determined not to report this story until it could be validated. A woman of wide experience with small boys both at home and in the institution, she had an uneasy feeling that something was not right. She decided that the best thing to do would be to go to the school, ostensibly on a social visit. She had often been invited by various teachers, but seldom gone. There were always one or two boys in the ward who could not be left alone. This, however, was a crisis and she reacted decisively. Dressing Willie and Jimmy in their best clothes she set off for the school building.

The school, in common with almost every department in Willowbrook at that time, suffered from a paranoid feeling that they were unloved and unappreciated. The unexpected appearance of the attendant, flanked by her small boys, was greeted with caution, inquiry, and finally pleasure. Someone, it seemed, was interested at last. They took her on a tour of the school, showed her different classes and even demonstrated the talking typewriter.

Finally they took her to Anthony's class. His teacher was there and welcoming. A small black lady she said she had been teaching Anthony for two years now, and believed she was, at last, getting through to him. Somewhat taken aback the attendant asked if substitute teachers were employed at times, or if Anthony attended any other classes. The answer was no. The teacher was proud of the fact that he had been in her total care for so long, and equally proud of her own attendance record. She held up his recent drawings, and hunted through her desk for examples of his letters and sums. Later that day the attendant took Anthony aside and asked him "Why?" He was not worried or upset. He agreed readily he had made up the stories. Asked again, "Why?" he answered, after a long pause, "They like it."

In this instance, knowledge of sex, its being forbidden with staff, was used as a way to entertain. Anthony understood that what he was saying was both a fabrication, something "bad" or nasty," and, more important, that his peers enjoyed it when he told these sex stories. Sex was used as a way to make life more interesting for his mates, who undoubtedly enjoyed hearing him tell these tales and seeing the staff react to them.

Sex was going on among the residents, children and adults. Reiss describes how this quest for pleasure and warmth was not always welcomed by the staff:

> Most of the boys had no relatives or visitors. They craved warmth and love, and found it in each other's beds. The more uninhibited didn't wait for a bed and, periodically, all over Willowbrook there could be heard attendants wailing "Oh, you nasty things! Stop that right now."
>
> The official view was that the problem was inevitable and unmentionable. Standards became oddly twisted. A visitor once exclaimed in horror, "Those kids are screwing around behind the drapes!" and the supervisor of the building answered, indignantly, "Before I came to the building they never thought of going behind the drapes!"

Many residents sought out relationships with each other. A recreation worker noticed that residents: "would hug each other. . . . Some people would kiss. Some people would refer to people as their boyfriend or their girlfriend. They would see each other . . . in some of the bigger recreational events." A mental health counselor described seeing romances develop at the dances and noted that sometimes residents would claim each other as boyfriend or girlfriends and fight among each other over these relationships.

At Fernald, the situation was pretty much the same. For the boys at Boys Home, picking girlfriends was done at a distance, given that the genders rarely had opportunity to interact. On weekend nights, older boys might sneak out and peek in the girls' shower room, while yet others would sneak through utility corridors in tunnels between the buildings. "They would meet a girl at a designated spot, usually in the basement, exchange a few kisses, attempt to grope her breasts, and then flee" (D'Antonio, 2004, p. 107). Yet the reality of Fernald was that residents' earliest sexual experiences would likely be with same-sex residents late at night or at the hands of adult staff.

Because romantic relationships existed, of course, so did unplanned pregnancies. Arlen remembered one resident who would get picked up by guys at night and take her around Staten Island. She eventually got pregnant. And young women got pregnant sometimes when they went on home leaves. They would come back and have the baby. The babies were then kept in Building 13, tested for medical or cognitive problems, and then handed off to the Foundling Hospital. Indeed, Maria became pregnant at Willowbrook when she was 19. There was a rumor that physicians began prescribing birth control pills to all the female residents. Two ex-employees recalled a staff member who impregnated a resident who was quadriplegic and spastic.

Things happened routinely at Willowbrook and other institutions that would have been considered inappropriate because of their sexual dimensions. Today it is not considered appropriate to kiss or hug children in educational settings. In the 1970s at Pacific State, Goode described routinely kissing and cuddling with children. To do otherwise, it was reasoned, would have been horribly cruel under the circumstances. The children desperately and naturally sought such affections, and staff would not have been happy with the kind of prohibitive regulations that exist today. Hugs and kisses were simply a natural outgrowth of the nurturing capacities of caregivers, male and female, and given the terrible emotional neediness of the children could not be withheld, on the part of the staff member, without crossing a certain human boundary. On the deaf-blind ward, every attempt was made to show affection, to hug and kiss children and even adolescents. Some residents had become "tactically defensive" and would not accept affection, but even some of these children could be "convinced" of the value of human warmth and contact. Similarly, at Willowbrook, many of the workers mentioned hugging and kissing the younger children for the same reasons.

Just as with work, sexuality at Willowbrook involved children as well as adults. Children were regularly objects for sexual abuse by staff. Many former workers mentioned knowing of these kinds of abuses. But it is difficult to know exactly how widespread this practice was or to what degree these practices may have been heterosexual or homosexual.

Sex was also a reality of life at Willowbrook for children. Children are known to be capable of sexual behavior, but their behaviors are shaped and molded by social norms. Under conditions of minimal socialization and supervision such as at Willowbrook, it is no surprise that we find reports of open expression of child sexuality. Reiss documented an event involving Peter that illustrated just how effective gender segregation was at preventing sex and the consequences of giving in to the comfort of other bodies. In her nonjudgmental narrative Peter and his friends appear as just being human when they got into trouble:

> There was a small door at the end of the playroom which led onto a covered terrace. Protected by a roof and surrounding wall it was an ideal place for the boys to play during wet weather or on the warm days of winter. Every evening the door was locked, as much to keep intruders out as the children in. One night the attendant forgot to lock it.
>
> As she sat dozing in her chair, Peter and three small companions crept quietly out onto the terrace. They took with them pillows and a blanket. It was a warm night with a full moon. They were discovered next morning, fast asleep, wrapped around each other like a nest of puppies.
>
> Peter never lied. He seldom volunteered information, but if asked a direct question he always spoke the truth. "We was corn-holing each other on the terrace and we fell asleep."

The night attendant reported the scandalous affair to the day attendant when she came on duty. "You punish them real good," she warned, feeling very guilty about the unlocked door.

In fact, Peter was transferred to another ward as punishment, and a teacher, who had noticed his sadness and despondency after the transfer, pleaded to have the punishment lifted. Reiss recorded her reaction:

> We, however, were sure that Peter would sin again and again. He was of no particular interest to the laboratory, which had long since transferred its total attention to metabolic disorders, but we did have a vacant bed. Somehow, good or bad, he seemed to be our child. The transfer was made.

In this incident, we see clearly how the meaning of social acts was transformed within the total institution. Sex, violence, and kindness took particular forms and significances because of the different nature of society there. One became desensitized to violence because it was ever present, and the same was true with nakedness. Apparently, as this nonjudgmental account, written about the time of the event, clearly demonstrates, this was also true about child sexuality. Staff were aware but in some sense could not really condemn the children for their "nastiness," a recurrent, ubiquitous feature of ward life. Staff and residents understood this. And it was not that either group was unaware of the larger significance of sex, that staff should not do it with residents, that residents should not force other residents to have sex, that having sex was punishable, and so forth. Such knowledge constituted a backdrop to sexual activities, the secrecy that was observed about them, and in their organization as practical matters. Such awareness existed but within a climate that did not guarantee bodily security and provided ample opportunities to engage in certain forms of sex.

Finally, sex had a diurnal rhythm and was especially prevalent in the evenings. Because of the dullness of life in places like Willowbrook, with days being empty of activities but more full with staff, many residents slept. The activities one did not want others to know about thus naturally occurred at night. In practice, at night residents were sometimes completely free of supervision (which was at best minimal in larger wards), and the ward became a growth medium for unacceptable behaviors that would never be tolerated if seen by staff. This has been reported by a number of former residents. It was also observed by Goode on the ward for deaf and blind children at Pacific State Hospital. There the children would sleep a good portion of the day. At night they were wide awake, engaging in a variety of activities, including sexual. One evening Goode witnessed a young resident climb on top of a young girl and begin to "hump" her. The evening ward charge told him that she had found these children in this same position but had seen nothing more. She had interrupted children engaged in even more overtly sexual acts. Where and how these behaviors were learned can only be speculated about.

Careers of Residents: Gena

When Goffman (1961) wrote about the "moral careers" of mental patients in his book *Asylums,* he observed that every person who lived in a total institution, such as Willowbrook, had a unique story that can, in retrospect, be characterized as having had certain stages and outcomes. Residents at Willowbrook followed certain paths and stages before, during and (presumably) after leaving the institution. What determined one's career, its ultimate outcome, and its character while in the institution was a reflection of many factors, programmatic, personal, and chance. It could probably also be argued that people who worked and visited relatives at Willowbrook had a kind of career, a path with stages along the way.

Bronston, in his forthcoming book, provides a detailed narrative of a young woman resident he calls Lillian. It is a pathetic tale, ending terribly, and can only be summarized by the phrase "descent to death." It is a story of the institution slowly killing a person, psychologically and physically. It is a common story about what happened to many people. That narrative is recommended to the reader as an illustration of what happened to a person who never made it out.

The idea that people had different careers in their tenure at Willowbrook is consistent with one of the basic tenets of this book, which is that the experience of Willowbrook had a lot to do with when one was there, the particular situations one faced, and the individual's particular way of seeing and making sense of things. What resulted was a person's story about what happened to them at WSS. Goode has heard many such narratives over the years, each unique but also with features in common. It is fitting, we feel, to end the section of our book about what happened at Willowbrook with a short narrative about one of its residents, who came to Willowbrook in 1956, spent her entire childhood there, experienced terrible abuse, and not only made it out of Willowbrook but eventually was able to take control of her own life and live independently.

Goode met Gena (a pseudonym) over 10 years ago when he heard her speak about her life at one of the annual Willowbrook lectures held at the College of Staten Island since moving to Willowbrook campus in 1993. Since then, he has heard Gena speak about her experiences at many public forums and also during personal conversations. Recollections of these events and personal conversations are used to reconstruct Gena's story.

Gena and Goode are about the same age and comfortable in one another's company. As a custodial worker and professor, they do not occupy similar positions in society. Gena works in a janitorial capacity for an agency providing services to people with developmental disabilities, in fact, on the same campus she grew up on, Willowbrook. Through their shared mutual interest, Willowbrook, though arrived at via very different paths, they have become friends over the years.

Gena came to Willowbrook in 1956 as a young child. She is of African American heritage, as many children at Willowbrook were, and was born in Brooklyn, also as many Willowbrook residents were. She came to Willowbrook when she was 4 years old and spent the next 22 years of her life there.

When Gena was an infant, she developed a growth on the right side of her head near her ear. She remembers that she was put into a hospital that treated her for a cancer by irradiation. That treatment had terrible iatrogenic effects. Gena's right ear, and area surrounding, was essentially "burnt off." This is the story that Gena remembers, and if you saw her today, her physical appearance would substantiate her almost Mengelian story. She is such a beautiful person in many ways that one easily and quickly becomes desensitized to her physical deformities.

Gena's mother apparently had problems of her own, and when it came time for the hospital to release Gena, her mother would not, or was judged unable to, take care of her at home. With medical advice, her mother was convinced to place her into Willowbrook.

In one interview, Gena was asked the question, "what was Willowbrook like when you got there?" Her answer went something like this: "Most people were nice to me at first. There were not so many kids, like later. There were nurses in uniform." People think that when Willowbrook was opened, it was not bad in the way it was in 1972, the year of the Geraldo exposé. But that is wrong. According to Gena, Willowbrook was never a good place. Even though when she first arrived and things were relatively uncrowded and people were nice to her, Gena commented that "People teased me and called me names, 'monkey,' 'one eared gorilla,' 'one half side.'"

Gena was very young and in her mind there was only one question: "Why am I here? Why can't I go home to be with my mother?" In addition to the abuse at Willowbrook, she suffered intensely simply because, as she has said, she could not understand why she had to be in a place like Willowbrook and not with her family. It is a question that we do not know the answer to. In the various conversations and narratives, Gena did not disclose exactly what was wrong with her mom, other than to say that she could not take care of Gena.

When Gena observed that Willowbrook was never a good place, she meant that there was never a time there when abuse of children did not occur. Her narrative included descriptions of terrible psychological and physical abuse that were part of her life. Her fate, like that of many other children in any given ward, was largely up to those who worked there. The first workers at Willowbrook largely were transfers from other state institutions. They knew the ways of those places. It is not surprising that Gena related the following kind of abuse:

> One of the staff would always tease me about how I looked and how I was stupid and ugly. She would tell me that I would never amount to anything and that if I were lucky I would die at Willowbrook. At one point she began to hit me. Then one day when she found dirty underwear under my mattress—I told her I did not put them there—she turned on me. She beat me with a mop handle across my face. She hit me, three or four times, but it was done.

When Gena's mother, whatever her problem and however functional, came to visit her next weekend, she found Gena covered with makeup in a thinly disguised attempt to cover her injuries. Gena recalled her mother's visit and discovery of her injuries. Her mother immediately complained and eventually was able to get the responsible staff member fired. Gena thinks this occurred about 1958, but there is no record of this event in the newspapers at the time, which is not to question Gena's memory. Her narrative provides her recall of the incident, and there is nothing unusual about it not reaching the *Staten Island Advance*.

Many people at Willowbrook teased Gena about her appearance. She suffered abuses of all kinds: beaten with a broom, made to kneel on the floor for hours, injected with Thorazine and Mellaril to keep her knocked out, whipped with a belt, and forced to stand naked in a dark room in the winter with the window left open. This kind of list could be made by virtually any former resident. But Gena, because she was a person who stood up for what was right and openly criticized how residents were treated, got more than her share of punishment. As Carabello put it, those who spoke up at Willowbrook knew the consequences.

Yet when asked about Willowbrook in these early years, Gena also remembers that there were some good things. There was not the overcrowding that existed in the 1960s, and there were good summers, the carousel, friends, and swimming. Gena made a life; there was nothing else she could do. She could not, and did not, do so alone.

Gena talked about friends she had made at Willowbrook, some of whom she retained well after its closure. Among these there is an attendant whom she recalls in great detail and with tremendous affection. This woman staff member, after the incident of abuse recounted above, took a special interest in Gena, an easy decision to relate to as Gena is a person who is easy to like and take an interest in.

On the basis of several narrations of this event, we know the following: After the beating, Gena was befriended by this staff person, who began speaking with Gena about her disability. Having listened to Gena's protests, this woman had connected with Gena in a maternal way:

After I was beaten I was barely able to see. An attendant began to take an interest in me. A lot of the children and even the staff would tease me about being ugly. She talked to me and made me do certain things. One thing I remember was that she would make me look in the mirror and say out loud, "I am beautiful." She did that to me a lot. She said I needed to do this. She would bring clothes for me and dress me up. Eventually I began to understand that I was not just ugly. She was kind to me and made a big difference in who I became.

When Gena talks about this experience she is understandably emotional.

You would think that a story like this is an exception to the rule, but it is not. As discussed above, over the years, Goode has heard many staff and residents from Willowbrook speak about having these kinds of special relationships. The idea that an attendant would reach out emotionally and socially to a resident is understandable given the intimacy of their circumstances, and Gena was one of the lucky minority to experience such special treatment.

Gena lived all her childhood at Willowbrook. During this time, she worked on the wards, developing the custodial skills that she continues to use to this day. She attended school but just enough to learn some basic reading and math. She wanted to go to school once she left Willowbrook, but that did not occur. Still, she has been able to make a full life for herself, rebelling against the idea of living in congregate facilities, using deception and cunning to escape a group home, and eventually acquiring her own place and living the life she wants. At one point, she eloped from the home, saved money, rented an apartment, and moved in without "permission." Today, she is part of the protected class under the Willowbrook Permanent Injunction.[19] She receives benefits because of her disability, which limits her pay today and reminds her that she was not paid for her work at Willowbrook. It is remarkable the way these things follow you through life.

Today if you speak to Gena, she will tell you openly that Willowbrook prevented her from living a normal childhood, which she probably could have had. She says she would have gone to college, bettered herself, and sought a professional job. She has worked hard to have a "normal life," with a job, boyfriend, and her own apartment. She recently moved into an apartment that she really likes. It is very close to the Willowbrook campus.

19. On March 11, 1993, the Willowbrook Permanent Injunction replaced the Willowbrook Consent Decree, the previous legal agreement that had been in place for eighteen years between the Plaintiffs and Office for People With Developmental Disabilities. The Permanent Injunction guarantees Willowbrook Class members certain enumerated rights, sets standards for residential, treatment, and case management services, and sustains an advocacy structure through the Community Advisory Board (CAB).

Gena would like to raise money to pay for plastic surgery on her face. She has considered writing a book about her life. Like many other former residents Goode has met over the years, Gena has been able to get on with her life, despite its less than promising beginnings.

There was a newspaper article written about Gena (under yet another name). It concludes with a story about Gena and her mother:

> When I was younger, and I would go home sometimes on the weekend, when we would walk down the street, she would either walk way behind me, or to one side of the other. When I got older, a year before she died, I told her, "We need to talk about this." I told her, "Don't be ashamed of me; I am your child." I told her, "You did the best you could." When I said that, something lifted inside of her.

This is a wonderful story about forgiveness and moving forward. Life after Willowbrook, a topic perhaps for another book, would be as interesting and complicated to explain as life in it.

Conclusion

The essential aspect to a total institution such as Willowbrook is its capacity to change and control those who reside there. The change is usually described as being for the better, to help rehabilitate someone or to teach residents to be better (e.g., monks, soldiers, human beings). Because of the nature of total institutions, the actual changes produced by them can alternatively be quite negative, and in places like Willowbrook, humanity and even life itself was uncaringly removed from its residents. Dehumanization, being made to be seen as inhuman or less than human, is a key aspect of some forms of total institution, and the living conditions at Willowbrook certainly stripped many of their humanity. Daily life at Willowbrook and state schools like it created conditions that were degrading in the extreme, causing residents to look and act abnormally, which in turn underwrote widespread characterizations of residents as lacking in human character. In the midst of these processes of dehumanization at Willowbrook and PSH, staff discourse about Willowbrook residents included characterizations of residents that Wolfensberger (1972) called "deviant statuses"—menace, subhuman, unspeakable object of dread, an object of pity, the holy innocent and eternal child, diseased organism—and these statuses were used to justify on various levels the neglect and cruel treatment that existed there. This description fits with assertions that the legacy of disability in America is based on a history of widespread prejudice and antipathy toward disabled people and that these beliefs and practices continue to exist in institutions and other places where people with disabilities are by policy congregated.

Despite being characterized with such negative language, despite overwhelmingly dehumanizing physical and psychological conditions, there were reports about Willowbrook residents at least partially fending off the crushing assault against their humanity. Residents engaged in fantasy, resisted mischaracterizations, escaped, sought out normalizing experiences, including friendship, love, and sex, and parodied and sabotaged the efforts of staff, giving them small but precious victories, often achieved in cooperation with others. The residents resisted the desexualization and degendering of the total institution, remaking their identities through escape, play, fantasy, and explorations of the kind of boy or girl, or man or woman, they could become. They shared intimacies with fellow residents.

6

Epilogue and Conclusions

Close the doors/Close the doors/Close the doors/
Behind us forever/Cus we deserve better.

Till you throw away the key/I won't have my dignity/
I won't be really free to live/While my brother's locked
away/While my sister's in that place/I can't see the
light of day myself.

Till the day you announce/That you've torn the last
one down/You will hear me calling aloud and clear.

—Williams and Self-Advocates Becoming Empowered
(1998)

The Sociology of Total Institutions

Large institutions such as Willowbrook were known and written
about by social scientists in the 19th century. Their study became
increasingly a part of sociological and psychological research in
the 1930s. Through largely observational studies, we began to
understand how these places worked and the logic of the behaviors
of the people in them. Because the purpose of many total institutions is to allow a relatively small number of persons to either
shape (socialize) or reshape (resocialize) a large number of people, conditions are created such that the agent of (re)socialization
controls, to a very large degree, the lives of the inmates, residents,

patients, initiates, inductees, or prisoners. The massive nature of the work required to "cure," "habilitate," "change," or "rehabilitate" people is the basic rationalization for this division and organization of power.

Erving Goffman's (1961) book, *Asylums,* presents many of the common features of total institutions. Total institutions are "place(s) of residence and work where a large number of like situated individuals, cut off from the larger society for an appreciable period of time, together lead an enclosed, formally administered round of life" (Goffman, 1961, p. xiii). All such places exist on the basis of some social rationale, although that rationale may differ considerably, from punitive (a prison) to self-realizing (a monastery). What Goffman so convincingly argues and demonstrates with examples are the forces of social organization that become operant within a total institutional context and how these powerfully influence behavior of all groups involved.

Goffman notes that institutions exist on the basis of a certain social rationale justifying the exercise of power of those in charge over those who are there. Because of the strong social status divisions in total institutions, different groups have different expectations for same- and other- status individuals. The groups see the situation differently and behave in notably different ways. For example, and as illustrated in the narratives and interviews, administrators and physicians had a certain role and kind of involvement at Willowbrook that was substantially different from that of professional staff, direct care personnel, or residents. Each of these social groups was subject to, or produced within specifically understood restricted circumstances, a workday that allowed the institution to function. Administrators did what administrators often do: plan, rationalize, deny, minimize, and control. Those working on the wards had their own daily round of life that involved trying to meet the human needs of those of whom they were in charge, but without sufficient personnel or resources. And the residents, or "patients" at Willowbrook, did what they could do to construct a meaningful life under highly inadequate, dangerous, abnormal and even bizarre circumstances. As the weakest status in the institution, with minimal power to effect their own circumstance, the social expectations established at Willowbrook were powerful influences on the behavior and experiences of the residents there, in processes analogous to those reported by Zimbardo (1973) in his mock prison experiments. But unlike the temporary status that students occupied in the Zimbardo experiement, the individuals who lived at Willowbrook were in a real confinement without end. They "internalized" these expectations, which influenced how they saw themselves and other groups, and how they behaved.

In Goffman's model of total institutions, part of the official job of such places is to mortify or kill the old identity of the individual in order to construct a new and more acceptable social self. This occurs to some degree in all total institutions, even monasteries or bootcamp, for example, but at places such as Willowbrook this aspect of total institutional life was particularly brutal and torturous, and was without an analogous process of rebuilding the self, as would be done in monasteries or bootcamp. People with recalcitrant behavior problems were subject to extreme treatment, including the use of long-term restraining devices, isolation, and powerful medications. By and large, the attempts to break the spirits of many residents were "successful" (i.e., produced compliance) although as we have read by no means completely. Hence we find Reiss's descriptions of children's attempts to live meaningful lives under highly restrictive circumstances, Eileen's nighttime excursions, Peter's "magic theater," or Gena's constant objections to her terrible treatment. There is no way to estimate how much resistance and parody occurred, but we do know it was a feature of life at Willowbrook.

Administrators, professional staff, direct care staff, and residents to some degree occupied separate worlds within total institutions. Physicians and nurses did not interact with residents except under highly structured conditions such as physical examinations or being given medicine or medical care. While some of the long-standing nurses at the institution became familiar with the residents in their care, many of the more transient professional staff did not, generally speaking know the residents as individuals very well. The residents and direct care personnel shared a common world. Their daily work on the ward was where, as the expression goes, the rubber met the road. Direct care staff was subject to pressures from superiors above to do their jobs effectively and efficiently, from below to do it fairly and humanely. Thus, the concerns of direct care staff often reflected the nature of the "people work" they were required to do and the responsibilities they were assigned as a result. Administrators interacted primarily with other administrators, medical and nursing staff. While they may have shown up on a ward from time to time, their presence on and knowledge of the wards was minimal.

Street-level bureaucracy, on all levels at Willowbrook, was used to control and minimize official reports of negative or inappropriate things. In general, each level of the social hierarchy managed information both within and out of their group. Administrators manipulated information, and often revealed little about the rationale for decisions. They used misinformation to manage difficult circumstances when they developed. Many staff recalled cover-ups and lying in order to keep those higher up from finding out about an incident of violence or severely inappropriate behavior. Generally, the staff attempted to deal with problems at their own level and did not report the truth or bring in those higher-ups, unless it was unavoidable. Finally, among those lowest on the social ladder on the wards a structure of self-policing existed that was often put into place by direct care personnel, using 'favorites' as ward monitors to keep the piece. In addition, the residents had their own methods of dealing with things without calling in the attendants. They managed information in the ways they could and under circumstances that they knew could have, to use Bernard Carabello's term, "repercussions."

Within a framework of control of information and bureaucracy and lack of resources, residents at Willowbrook made attempts to build and live meaningful existences, even if these, for those at the bottom of the social hierarchy, often ended tragically. The capacity of people, in this case many with intellectual, physical and psychological disabilities, to find ways to exert some control over their lives even within a total institution is a sociologically important finding when we examine Willowbrook.

The residents, patients, or inmates in total institutions are subject to the rules and demands of those above but, through a process Goffman calls "fraternalization," also construct their own rules and underworld, managed largely by themselves. In prisons, for example, an ethnically based gang-oriented society can be a more powerful influence on day-to-day inmate behavior than any rule or administrator. For many reasons, there was no similar kind of organized underworld at Willowbrook, but there was fraternalization and a system of street-level bureaucracy on the wards. As most clearly portrayed in Reiss's work, in at least a few wards, including hers, the children were able to develop personal relationships with staff and each other and even a culture of a sort (e.g., Peter's theater). This same kind of thing seemed to be going on in Eileen's ward, where the girls organized themselves and engaged in actions that involved serious breaches of institutional rules. Reiss's account of sexuality among the boys on the ward is one aspect of fraternalization that developed under strict conditions of gender segregation and severe overcrowding, sometimes referred to as institutional homosexuality.

Other studies about the social psychology of institutions clearly bear on how we are to understand what happened at Willowbrook. Zimbardo's (1973) work demonstrated the power of social roles and their associated social expectations to affect behavior, independent of the particular psychologies of those involved. Thus, average people can be put into situations where the social forces around them will largely override their better judgment or self-concept. This is what occurred at WSS. The power of social expectations when coupled with authority was also explored by Milgram (1965), who clearly demonstrated most persons' compliance with what they perceive to be legitimate authority, even when it means seriously hurting another individual. This kind of dynamic undoubtedly also operated at Willowbrook and accounts for the overwhelmingly accepting response from almost everyone who worked at Willowbrook at every level. At the same time, Milgram showed that the more distant the authority, the less it was obeyed. Under conditions of an authority that is absent from the setting (i.e., communicated with only over the telephone), subjects in Milgram's experiments were deceptive and lied about what they were doing. This same general social dynamic also existed at WSS.

Finally, research about abnormal behaviors in total institutions found that these actions may not be a reflection of the "condition" of the individual as much as a reflection of the social organization of the institution. This same logic can be applied to Willowbrook, where extreme neglect and abusive treatment led to a variety of behaviors that were often interpreted as evidences of disability but, as stated clearly by Bronston, were really reflections of conditions at Willowbrook. Circumstances made people look and act in ways that appeared less than human. Making residents look and act these ways made it easier to treat them as less than human, and a self-fulfilling circularity was built into how things worked at Willowbrook and places like it.

Bronston has often commented about how difficult it was to actually "see" what was going on at Willowbrook. It was hard at the time, although in retrospect this can be puzzling to those who were involved, to understand that the bizarre behaviors and appearances of residents were a product not of their disability but of the environment of the institution. The medical model, "constitutionalizing" the behaviors of individuals, so dominated professional and worker perspectives that it prevented them from seeing what was so obviously, in retrospect, in front of their faces: that the residents were people just like them. So this is one clear lesson about what happens to people in total institutions, whether they work or live there. Not seeing what was happening at Willowbrook is also puzzling to those who see it from the vantage point of history, for example, the students at the College of Staten Island. Many of them, and understandbly, ask how people could not have recognized that they were involved in evil and why they did nothing about it. Hopefully, having read this book, they will have gotten some insights into that question.

The Sociology of Willowbrook

There seems to have been a general way that things worked at Willowbrook that is reflected in many of the narratives about life on the wards. Subject to the authority of the administration, the director and his assistant directors, we learned that medical doctors, usually white men and sometimes with foreign medical degrees, were in charge of wards and a staff of nurses, also often white, and direct care attendants, who were more likely to be women and men of color. Many of the doctors conformed to the very low, professionally compromised standards of care that had become characteristic of the chronically overcrowded, underfunded institution. As stated above, many physicians did not go onto the ward but had patients requiring care brought to them in the nurse's station. The routine care and treatment of the residents was done almost entirely by the direct care staff, who were often helped by the more capable residents. Staff relied heavily on the residents themselves to keep control on the ward, employing "favorites" to whom they assigned this task and rewarding them with various material and psychological benefits for doing so. This form of social control was also evident in the 1867 account of the orphanage on Randall's Island and appears to have been a regular feature of institutions for a very long time.

Even though the conditions at Willowbrook were, almost from the outset, close-quartered and difficult, in the early years the nature of the labor on the wards was not alienated. If a worker on the ward wanted something done, he or she did, perhaps with the help of other workers and residents, whatever was involved. People knew each other, looked after each other, and there was more of a climate of cooperation and trust. With the exposé of Willowbrook, and the hiring of additional workers to alleviate conditions, the number of workers went up, but the quality of work life went down. Work on the wards became alienated, as reflected in some of the workers' narratives. Strangers worked with one another, trust was lacking, and fear began to dominate staff relationships. To actually get anything done, once the work on the ward became segmented and hierarchically organized, became almost impossible. It required a kind of teamwork that did not exist at Willowbrook, especially after the exposé. To some degree, this accounts for why after the Willowbrook exposé, some aspects of life actually grew worse in the late 1970s instead of better, when unqualified workers were brought in to fill court-mandated staff hiring.

Many interviews contain remarks about unpaid and paid resident labor. This arrangement has generally been part of institutions for the poor and disabled, as we saw in earlier European examples and in Davenport's (1867) account of Randall's Island Nursery. When looked on from the outsider's perspective, institutional peonage appears to be almost a form of slavery, especially when it was entirely unpaid labor. When looked at from an insider's perspective, as, for example, in Reiss's narrative about Willie, giving residents a task such as mopping the floor could be a way to break their boredom and encourage a sense of pride and even emotional devotion. From the outside, such work could seem unfair, demeaning, and detrimental to the resident's welfare. But as Maria said in her narrative, it was because she learned to take care of babies at Willowbrook that she was able to take care of her children with disabilities after Willowbrook. We need to appreciate that in a place where real work was not possible for residents and boredom was the normal condition, for those incarcerated, unpaid work was better than no work; it was a form of exploitation that also had positive social and psychological functions. It would be a mistake sociologically, at least from the accounts, to think of the unpaid labor as simply slave, unwanted, or forced labor. Such labor is defined by this contradiction.

It is interesting to contrast the different ways of looking at Willowbrook even within institutional statuses. When reviewing our primary data, especially the interviews and speeches, we are struck with the contrasts in accounts. These contrasts and even contradictions are "positive" sociological phenomena. They represent different people's perceptions of particular places and circumstances, not accounts whose differences need to be reconciled. The differences are instructional, not nuisances to a simplistic and facile account of Willowbrook. As stated in the Introduction, there were many Willowbrooks, literally and subjectively.

To illustrate the theme of many Willowbrooks, the contrast between Reiss's and Bronston's accounts is helpful. The conditions on the particular ward Reiss wrote about were not representative of the vast majority of wards. The ward she served on was one funded by a research grant, and children housed on it were subject to different standards and received different supports than those housed on "custodial" wards such as those described by Bronston.

Anyone with whom we shared Reiss's complete unpublished text agreed it is a powerful and honest piece of writing about life on a state hospital ward for children with disabilities. There are really no comparable examples, nothing quite like it, as Reiss is not a trained social scientist and did not write for the purpose of advancing an academic career. She wrote to give herself some distance from what was occurring every day, as a way to survive the difficult circumstances of her job. This makes her writing so worthwhile to anyone interested in Willowbrook or, more generally, in life in total institutions. Because she stayed at Willowbrook for many years, her writings are unique, compassionate glimpses into what occurred on a ward day to day.

She wrote as a way to honor the lives of the children she knew and loved. After reading her work, one cannot think about Willowbrook without being reminded of Peter or Willie, or Reiss's deep empathy for these children. Although she never comments about her feelings, it is simply evident in the writing, in her beautiful preoccupation with this very strong personality and person. Her writing about Peter, Willie, Donald, or Lenny, make real for us the terrible and yet completely human circumstances within which they lived. We can identify with them as persons. Her words are a tribute to the human spirit of children, in this case with disabilities, who found themselves in extraordinary, brutal, unimaginable life circumstances.

In contrast to Reiss's almost diary-like reflections on life in her Willowbrook, Bill Bronston's remarks about Willowbrook in general were taken from public statements and from interviews and lectures. Because Bronston was both a physician and political radical who openly confronted the administration's complicity in creating inhumane conditions at Willowbrook, his views about medicine and politics are particularly telling. Medically, Willowbrook was a disaster, and Bronston even today will not allow people who speak about it to call it a hospital. The conditions on the ward promoted both disease and death, including widespread malnutrition. Extremely high rates of all kinds of infectious diseases were the norm. Unclean and wrongly cleaned wards created skin conditions that promoted an epidemic and chronic infection known as cellulitis. On the larger wards, such as those Bronston was in charge of, there were often extremely inadequate medical reviews of children, and in Bronston's view, problems were often and detected only when they became acute. The administration and physicians (Bronston and Wilkins being exceptions) accepted the lowest denominator of medical care possible.

Families who remained involved with their relative were also systematically disenfranchised, and conditions of life at Willowbrook were hidden from them. Children were taken out of the wards on visits, and parents and relatives were not let in. They were "steel-doored" out, a literal description of what occurred. When families did protest or pressure the administration for better treatment, they could be threatened with return of the child to the home, or by asking the family to pay for services for which they were technically fiscally responsible. In essence, the same kind of uncaring attitude that was taken to the residents of Willowbrook was also extended to their families.

Given the medical neglect and lack of sanitary and, generally speaking, "healthy" conditions, Bronston noted a certain path or trajectory that some residents at Willowbrook would follow. This involved on the one hand becoming, or being made to become, good residents (i.e., "institutionalized" and no trouble to the staff). Children without families to advocate for them (and even those with such families) were often transferred from building to building, experiencing serious illness or abuse, and could begin a downward spiral, resulting in psychological and physical deterioration and sometimes death.

Bronston, because of his previous training in care of children with developmental disabilities at Children's Hospital in Los Angles, knew that the assumption that the children were ill and could not get better was a wrong one. He also knew that the lack of sanitary conditions and adequate medical treatment, even given the budget cuts and lack of resources at Willowbrook, was not something that had to be but was a result of administrative passivity and physician neglect. He tried, on the wards he was in charge of, to do something about these matters. It was when he tried to address these problems that he began to get into trouble. His alliance with the families at Willowbrook was also part of the reason he got clashed with the administration, but it was Bronston's insistence on good medical practice on his wards that began his long term fight to close Willowbrook. His commitment to medical standards went against how things were done and challenged the basic authority and legitimacy of the administration. His familiarity with the potential of children with developmental disabilities made their behaviors at Willowbrook interpretable to him in ways unavailable to other professionals there; that is, that what they were doing was a reflection of conditions at Willowbrook, and not their disability.

Bronston's description of the grievance process shows, among other things, how it was virtually impossible to influence things at Willowbrook if one stuck to formal bureaucratic structures. Despite the fact that he conformed strictly to their legal process and consistently showed what appeared to be reasonable arguments about how the administration had singled him out for punitive treatment, and that he provided (via his lawyer Gene Eisner's brief) very strong evidence that he was being unjustly punished for trying to improve things at Willowbrook, Bronston was not surprised when the commissioner of the Department of Mental Hygiene ruled against him.

Bronston openly confronted the administration and called them into account, via their own procedures, and lost the initial battle with them, although, with the eventual transfer of Director Hammond, winning the war. In Bronston's forthcoming book on Willowbrook, you will find a narrative of him developing various strategies in addition to these bureaucratic ones, to confront and defeat the administration, which he repeatedly and appropriately holds accountable for conditions at Willowbrook. These other strategies included worker organization and also working with families and concerned parties to help organize them to protest what was being done to the children and adults. These matters are covered in *The Willowbrook Wars* and Bronston's book.

Bronston's writings and interviews about Willowbrook represent instances of a person stepping outside the official framework of interpretation that surrounds him and recording things in a way that reflects, as best one can, the non-official viewpoints of those being observed. His remarks are emblematic of an epiphany that occurs to some of those working at a total institution: When you look at things on a state hospital ward, if you want to understand what you are seeing, you have to forget about your practical interests. Instead, you need to take off institutional blinders while thoroughly focusing on how things are made to appear as they are by those in power.

A Total Institution

One contribution of this study is some reflection on Goffman's (1961) explanation of total institutions as it applies to the Willowbrook case. Beyond being an isolated place, a total institution is about social control, the regulation of life and identity through institutional policies. In the case of Willowbrook, it was also about the formation of resident identities, as *disabled, incapable, without hope, care, sex, or friendship,* and the regulation and reproduction of these identities. Total institutions control over time and personal space, through the rigid time-tabling and scheduling, mostly at the convenience of staff and administration. This was descriptive of Willowbrook. There was also strong evidence of another common feature of total institutions, an underground or underlife, at Willowbrook, both for the staff and the residents though in very different ways.

Although some of the basic structures and qualities were present for Willowbrook to be a total institution, any particular institution will contain individual, even idiosyncratic, features. For instance, when considering the isolation of Willowbrook, it turns out that it had a PX, a unique reflection of its Halloran Hospital history. The boundaries between it and the Staten Island community were relatively permeable. Police, court orders, locked doors, and other forms of control were never absolute, as residents found their way into the outside world, and the community found their way onto the Willowbrook campus. This is a more generally shared feature of institutions like Willowbrook. So each place was a mixture of the particular and and general.

Like Goffman, this research found that autonomy was not entirely lost at Willowbrook State School. Agency of inmates in Goffman's total institution was to a large degree overlooked, and it is a mistake to construct the total institution as totally repressive (see also Scott, 2010). On the one hand, Goffman portrayed actors often as passively shaped, lacking autonomy, and deindividuated by the institution. On the other hand, at Willowbrook, there was evidence of agency. For example, there were some residents who "knew the ropes" and how to "play the game," suggesting they had some control over their lives. As has been discussed, individuals to some degree chose their own styles of dealing with conditions they faced. Also, Goffman (1961) referred to small but significant victories, the "make dos" (p. 187) or, as Scott (2010) called it, a "micropolitics of resistance in everyday life" (p. 217). Goffman explored other strategies, such as withdrawal, intransigence, and colonization (playing at being compliant). Scott proposed that the total institution is simultaneously repressive and enabling (i.e., evoking defiant acts of resistance). Our study of Willowbrook supports this understanding; life at Willowbrook provided opportunities for resistance and defiance even if these may have had certain 'consequences.'

Politics, Economics, and Power

If you want to understand life at Willowbrook, then the politics, economics, and power that were involved are essential. It was a place controlled by a few very powerful people, and its inhabitants were kept deeply oppressed and mostly powerless. It is clear from Bronston's testimony to the state, his book, and the excerpt we included from a public event at the CUNY Graduate Center (Bronston, 2005) that he found the administration at Willowbrook deceitful, controlling, and evil in their willful and cognizant mismanagement of the situation at WSS. Throughout the years he has repeatedly referred to them as arrogant and accused them of unfairly using power to suppress any dissent. He portrays them as Machiavellian and not hesitant to use untruths, punishment, and threat as management techniques. In trying to repress dissent at Willowbrook, "radical organizing tactics" were used, including Red-baiting and, in the case of Bernard Carabello, threats about revoking privileges if he did not cooperate with the administration's efforts to discredit Bronston and Wilkins. Moreover, Bronston noted that the administration had a view of the people they were taking care of that was completely inaccurate (that they were unable to learn or progress in any significant fashion), which was what lay at the heart of the neglect and lack of care at Willowbrook. They brought in experts to justify their understanding and management of the situation. Bronston describes the administration as incorrigible in this belief and in the conviction that for persons with such irremediable conditions they as professionals organized things the best possible way.

It goes without saying that if it were possible to have Jack Hammond's comments about these matters, they would likely be very different. It is important both to note that we do not have that opportunity but also that Bronston's viewpoint about Willowbrook did ultimately prevail over Hammond's. The state, in the face of uncontestable evidence, was legally held responsible for the conditions at Willowbrook. Hammond, in a socially transparent fashion, was transferred upstate and those seeking to end the inhumanity at Willowbrook celebrated.

Bronston and Castellani (2005) raise serious questions about the political economy of Willowbrook and the system of institutions in New York State. Bronston directly attacks Governor Rockefeller, and certainly one can find reason in what Bronston says and writes for holding government ultimately responsible for what happened at Willowbrook. By "ultimately," we mean that both authors advance a somewhat conspiratorial point of view. The Rockefeller government, while spending millions of dollars on construction of the Capital Mall, issued government bonds that were sold at 2% to financial institutions associated with the Rockefeller family. Then New York State government benefited tremendously, as described by Castellani in his writings, by keeping beds in places like Willowbrook filled and receiving federal Title XIX dollars at extremely high rates. Castellani described how, under Rockefeller in the 1960s, New York State became the most effective in the country in figuring out how to maximize the flow of Title XIX dollars into the state. A ridiculously complex and expensive rate setting structure, hugely benefiting New York State and developed during the Rockefeller governorship, has been recently challenged and will no longer going to be the basis for funding the state system of services for people with developmental and intellectual disabilities. As of this writing, New York State is currently redesigning its rate setting structure based on a new waiver system that will not allow for the high rates of the past. Many are worried about what this new system will mean for quality of life for people with developmental disabilities and their families.

Workers and their unions were another aspect of the political economy of Willowbrook that Bronston comments on. The overall climate at Willowbrook was not conducive to critical union actions, although unions did exist. He is very sympathetic to workers, although he saw them as largely impotent to affect the situation, to think critically, and to avoid being used by the administration in helping to crush dissent. However, workers had little job security. If they stepped out of line or said something seriously critical of the status quo, or if they "raised a stink," they were out (Bronston & Castellani, 2005). On the union side there was an active Black union, but its agenda was respondent to national rather than Willowbrook-specific concerns. Other unions represented at Willowbrook seemed to take a conciliatory position with regard to the conditions there. Even during the years when the exposé and trial were going on, unions, and for that matter most local Staten Island government officials, said little about Willowbrook. Neither politician nor unions, or for the most part individual workers, ever became part of the group that advocated for, and eventually achieved, the closure of Willowbrook.

The topic of culpability for what went on at Willowbrook is naturally related to the discussion of political economy. In some ways, Bronston's view is a bit different from that of Wolfensberger, who in writing about the Nazi extermination of handicapped people found all levels of participation to bear responsibility for the situation, including even those who had no role in it at all but knew and did nothing. Bronston sees the residents, workers, and families as victims of an institutional logic and system within which they had little or no power, which was designed and operated by those with significant authority. The logic he has used on several occasions when he has spoken about Willowbrook at various venues is that you cannot hold workers, residents, or family members responsible for what they did under the highly abnormal conditions that had been set up for them.

Responsibilities involved for various groups are not equal or qualitatively the same. Those who set up the system, operated, and oversaw it bear primary responsibility for its existence even if history was their accomplice. But we also understand Wolfensberger's thinking, that everyone involved took on some of the blame, whether they were the designers of the system, those who administered it, those who rationalized it intellectually, the medical personnel who worked in it, psychiatric technicians, bus drivers, designers and servicers of equipment, grave diggers, parents who did not protest, or clergy who said nothing. These are different levels, or even types, of culpability, and it is important to acknowledge that they are also part of the moral landscape. With the current media saturation of society, it is possible to think of it becoming a commonplace situation where people would be generally aware of a situation like Willowbrok that involves great injustice and inhumanity, and yet fail to act. The question Wolfensberger asks is, does this make them in some way responsible?

Contemporary thinking is sympathetic to explcitly sociological views of human behavior, as we provide in this book. If you want to understand what happened at Willowbrook and who bears the responsibility for it, you look to the institutional arrangements that were put into place and that powerfully structured experience and behaviors of those within them. Thus, practically speaking, using

Destruction of Ward Building

Destruction of Main Building

what we know about human behavior in institutional settings, in a sociological sense staff and residents at Willowbrook could not have done anything other than occupy their institutional statuses—statuses that came with powerful social expectations that we know profoundly influence their and others' behavior. As the literature has demonstrated, centralized authority of a few staff over many inmates produces behavior that only makes sense within this pathological social situation. Further, at Willowbrook, staff and residents occupied these social statuses under conditions of social isolation, extreme overcrowding and lack of resources. Given what we know about the sociology of total institutions, and consistent with Bronston's description of workers, professionals, and residents at Willowbrook, it does make sociological sense to understand them primarily as having been victimized by the existence of such an institution.

Can one explain away responsibility in a situation because of an understanding of its social structures and dynamics? Does the existence of statuses, powerful social expectations set up by these, and sanctions imposed when expectations are violated "explain away" individual culpability? Or are we all responsible in different ways for the Willowbrooks of this world? We submit that both approaches contain an element of the truth. We have heard that people at Willowbrook made moral choices, even under the most extreme of circumstances. An appreciation of this may lay at the heart of what bothers people who worked at such places, people like Norma Allison who, while proud of the efforts she made as a nurse at Willowbrook, is still haunted by the things she did. People involved who did not lead a revolt at Pacific State Hospital, the way Bronston did, may well feel some level of guilt at not having protested about what they saw there and about what they participated in while working there, as well intended as they were and as understandable their actions under the circumstances.

Being able to embrace both these ways of looking at responsibility is one of the important lessons of Willowbrook. On the one hand, political and economic forces can produce institutions (in both senses of the term) that mislead and take advantage of the poor, powerless, disadvantaged, and disenfranchised in society. The powerful institutions and individuals involved in this level of responsibility need to be differentiated from those who end up staffing the arrangements. Good people do and ignore bad things, but the sociology of why and how does not absolve them of responsibility for their actions or lack thereof.

Willowbrook State School Today

Ambiguity continues to surround Willowbrook State School today. In the late 1980s work began to convert the abandoned Willowbrook campus into the College of Staten Island, which moved there in 1993. Some of the buildings were demolished, but many were refurbished and converted into college classes and offices. Today,

Mounted Plaque near Building 1P,
College of Staten Island

the campus is the largest in the CUNY system and the center of higher public education on Staten Island.

On the one hand, Willowbrook is far from forgotten at the College of State Island. There are yearly Willowbrook Memorial Lectures held, and the 20th annual event, was held in April 2012 and cosponsored by the student Social Work and Green Thumbs Garden Clubs, along with the Friends of CSI, was organized around the theme "Inclusion: Far Reaching Benefits for Social Growth." We celebrated how far we have come since the days of Willowbrook. Plans for a walking path about human rights, with historical points of interest identified throughout the college campus, are being finalized as the book goes to press. This path is being developed cooperatively with the Staten Island Developmental Disabilities Council. Students at the college now have a history of Willowbrook available to them through professors who teach about it in their classes, events at the college, and, of course, through a few recent movies representing aspects of life at Willowbrook (e.g., *Cropsey:* Mortensen, Brancaccio, & Zeman, 2009; *Willowbrook:* Cohen, Iosotaluno, & Cohen, 2012). Willowbrook continues to occupy the hearts and minds of Staten Islanders, and captures the interests of the younger generation there.

On the other hand, and here is where the ambiguity enters, there is very little physical representation of Willowbrook on campus, and what there is, two small plaques, are unmarked, and one not accessible to people with disabilities, so most people do not even know they are there. The disability community on Staten Island has remarked that more should be done on campus to mark its important history. Some sort of Willowbrook Memorial has been suggested but no political will appears to exist at this time to actually make this idea into reality. There has been some discussions about establishing a Willowbrook Museum on campus, but again nothing concrete has resulted from them.

There is interest in Willowbrook that goes beyond Staten Island. Both *Cropsey* and *Willowbrook* were shown at the Tribeca Film Festival to a warm critical reception. In the fall of 2012, the Office for People with Developmental Disabilities (OPWDD) organized the traveling exhibition "Remembering Willowbrook" to memorialize the 25th anniversary of Willowbrook's closure. It was shown in the Port Authority Bus Terminal in Manhattan throughout September 2012. Throughout New York, there are former employees of the Willowbrook State School; some are retired, but others are still service providers for disabled New Yorkers; some now, in the apex of their careers, are leaders in their community. We have met past employees, along with former residents, at Willowbrook-related events through the years, a tradition that we hope continues. Willowbrook remains alive in the minds and hearts of anyone who worked or lived there, wherever they are today.

The "Willowbrook Class," the residents at Willowbrook at the time of the Consent Decree (today the Permanent Injunction), are under considerable state scrutiny (OPWDD, 2012). OPWDD has a comprehensive Web page set up to facilitate provision of services to the Willowbrook Class. The class members are represented with an OPWDD "Administrative Liaison to the Willowbrook Parties," special counsel and attorneys, and a network of district Developmental Disability Reigonal Office Willowbrook liaisons, a Consumer Advisory Board (board of parents, siblings, and advocates), the OPWDD Commissioner's Task Force on Willowbrook, and an "independent evaluator." The Web page details the expectations for service standards to Willowbrook consumers, guidelines on service provision, incident reporting guidelines, consent and rights, and really any details one would need to know about providing services to Willowbrook Class members. With all this oversight, the former Willowbrook residents should be experiencing a richer life than at Willowbrook.

Having said this, despite these provisions for former residents of Willowbrook, there are indications that life at state-run homes continue to be risky places to live. There have been regular incidents and problems involving the members of the Willowbrook class. The *New York Times* conducted an investigation and reviewed hundreds of cases of neglect and abuse, yet employees were rarely fired, even after repeat offenses (Hakim, 2011). This report found that fewer than 5% of 13,000 allegations in 2009 were referred to law enforcement. Only 25% of cases involving physical, sexual, or psychological abuse were referred to police. State employees alleged to be abusive were often simply transferred to other homes. The state tried to fire 129 employees, yet succeeded in just 30 cases because of opposition from the

Civil Service Employees Association, their union. Even a whistle-blower, a developmental aide, who refused to falsify fire drill records, was subjected to repeated questioning and pressure. After hearing of these findings, Governor Andrew Cuomo accepted the resignations of the head of OPWDD and the chief operating officer of the state's Commission on Quality of Care and Advocacy for Persons with Disabilities.[1] Then he ordered a review conducted by Charles Sundram, the lawyer who helped establish the Commission on Quality of Care.

Sundram's (2011) report observed that dangers remain in the New York residential care system: People who live in residential care facilities in New York State are still vulnerable to abuse and neglect. This report found that as of December 31, 2010, there were 274,000 children and adults with disabilities in residential facilities in New York. An investigation into abuse and neglect with primary consumers, family, providers, direct support staff, advocates, state agency staff, and over 1,700 e-mails and letters revealed wide variations in reporting and responses to these incidents such that "These gaps and inconsistencies expose vulnerable people to needless risk of harm" (Sundram, 2011, p. 5). This report documented, for the 2010 year, 5,209 abuse or neglect allegations in OPWDD facilities; 1,713 allegations at residential facilities run by the Office of Child and Family Services; 758 allegations at Department of Health, Residential Health Care facilities; and another 1,202 allegations from assorted Office of Mental Health residential facilities and state and private psychiatric hospitals. This was an overall rate of 119.68 allegations per 100 beds. Sundram's (2011) report recommends a series of practical steps to solve the problems, so practical that it is astonishing none have been adopted as of yet: a common set of policies and reporting and investigation standards across the state; a 24-hour hotline for reporting of abuse or neglect; a statewide register; background checks and training for staff; clear standards of expected conduct; and the implementation of preventive, corrective, and disciplinary actions. Some critics of Sundram's solution emphasize the danger of centralization of these processes and especially its remaining a form of self-policing, rather than creating a truly independent authority with this overview function.

The Current and Future Relevance of Willowbrook

Hegel (1832/1956) proposed that people, individually and collectively, do not learn the lessons of history and, in a vein later popularized by George Santayana, will repeat its errors. At this point in the book if readers feel that the history of Willowbrook does not contain lessons of current import, then we certainly have most failed in our writing in at least one important way.

---

1. The New York State Commission on Quality of Care is part of the national system of protection and advocacy originally set up in 1975 under the Developmental Disabilities Act.

To conclude that the history and accounts provided in this text are irrelevant to current circumstances could be argued in this way, that somehow the social, psychological, political and economic forces that produced Willowbrook and the many other places like it across our nation to exist were somehow unique, a result of historical and social abnormalities that will not recur. This argument would make of WSS an oddity of the 20th century, an historical blip, a kind of perfect storm, that made the terrible circumstances for Willowbrook residents and workers. It is a possible argument but a weak one given the overwhelming historical evidence to the contrary, as we have tried to indicate. We proceed on the opposite assumption, which is that the history of disability is cyclical and that the reports of the experiences of those who were involved at institutions such as Willowbrook are indicators of what is likely to come to pass again, if in a reworked and altered form. The past reveals a societal predisposition to differentiate and devalue people with disabilities and separate them from mainstream society. Differentiation more often than not resulted in the devaluation and segregation of people with disabilities. This is not to say that there are not examples of social forces and forms more sympathetic and inclusive of people with disability or that one day we might not have a society composed mostly of inclusive institutions. But to ignore the regularities of the past, their production in the present, and their possible reproduction in the future, would be indefensibly naive.

In considering the implications of this history and sociology, it is important to emphasize that the dynamics of exclusion and punishment for all groups, not just persons with disabilities, are culturally and historically relative. If we view the eugenics movement as an example of this general dynamic, we can appreciate how its basic belief about socially desirable and undesirable groups became culturally adapted: in the United States, to target people with disabilities, Blacks, and immigrants; in England, to bring the poor under control; in Sweden to perfect the human race; and in Germany, to eliminate not only people with disabilities but even more primarily those with 'undesirable' religious, political and ethnic characteristics. It is important to realize that there is no particular inherent quality of a person that makes him or her socially valuable or not. Criteria involved in such judgments are historically and culturally relative, even if their overall pattern is virtually universal (Wolfensberger, 1972). Examples of this social dynamic are found all over the world and it very likely will continue.

In the United States today, despite the Americans with Disability Act and progress in our thinking about disability, people with disabilities continue to be subject to exclusionary and devaluing dynamics. They continue to experience extremely high rates of un- and under-employment. There are supports and services available to them, but these are of highly variable quality and funding is eroding; the very real possibility of people with disability ending up in total institutions when they cannot take care of themselves, even just temporarily, is increasing (McBryde-Johnson,

2003). The warning by Staten Island state representative Elizabeth Connelly that Willowbrook is "one cut away" should give us reason to reflect. Current political and economic realities create concern in the disability community about the reappearance of places like Willowbrook and Willowbrook-like conditions in community residences. If the money goes away, will conditions turn back to what they were like in the 1950s and 1960s? If the money goes away, can government be trusted to oversee conditions for those who are unable to care for themselves? Does what happened at Willowbrook have any relevance to our present thinking about these problems?

The question of who lives in total institutions today is a complicated one. Its occurence is widespread, even more than indicated in McBryde-Johnson's (2003) article. How we think about this question and more generally about the relevance of total institutions today depends to some degree on how one defines the term (today many people in the disabilities field leave off the word "total" and just talk about institution). If we refer strictly to places of great size that are physically cut off from the outside world, such as suggested by Goffman (1961) and as embodied by Willowbrook, then there are fewer Americans with disabilities living in such medical institutions today than there were when Willowbrook first opened. But if we take a broader definition, one not linked so much to size but to the idea that "institution" refers to places where people live under one authority, relatively cut off from society, or, put alternately, not integrated into it, then it could be argued that we continue to see many, many people with intellectual disability living in this way. In 2000, Goode and Braddock prepared a paper for a Willowbrook-related event that examined the number of people with intellectual disability who lived in institutions and used Braddock's state-of-the-state report and reanalyzed the data according to a broader definition of institution than just very large size and census. They found that nationally a significant number of people with intellectual disabilities continued to reside on the grounds of old state institutions, at that time some 56,000.[2] But far greater were the numbers of those who lived in nursing care facilities, prisons, mental hospitals, and large congregate care homes. Including nursing home, prison, and mental hospital population estimates meant that hundreds of thousands of people with intellectual disability were living in total institutions.[3] They had not been deinstitutionalized but *laterally transferred* to other kinds of institutions. Recognition of this situation is what prompted one of the first national

2. Larson et al. (2012) at the Research and Training Center at the University of Minnesota found this figure to be almost 43,000 in 2010.

3. The incidence of disability in prison is estimated by the US Census bureau to be 20%. These estimates vary according to disability and even within disability categories (for example, with mental retardation, studies vary from 3 to 9.5%). Given that the US has the largest prison system in the western world, and the highest rate of incarceration of any developed nation, deinstitutionalization may well have resulted in a kind of lateral transfer for people with disabilities, from medical to penal institutions. This is argument is empirically and theoretically explored by Stewart (2001).

self-advocacy groups, Self-Advocates Becoming Empowered, to formulate their "Close the Doors" initiative. The leadership of this organization, some themselves ex-residents of institutions, wanted to remind all of us that many of their "brothers and sisters" remained locked away in places that are hidden from our view. The group has a Web site describing their position concerning such large institutions.[4]

If we expand the definition of total institution to include places of any size where people live an administered round of life that is mostly segregated from the society at large, we could conceivably include many group homes and even small apartments (ILAS or independent living arrangements). Although these places are intended to enhance the social integration of residents, at least sometimes their actual day-to-day operation does not effectively allow them to assimilate into their communities. Goffman (1961) used the term "total institution" to refer to places with walls and barriers that physically separate life inside from the outside; we might profitably expand the usage to include more generally any place that segregates one from society and does not provide opportunities for choice and control over one's life. We refer to such places as *relatively total institutions*. Depending on a variety of factors, ending up in a relatively total institution is realistically what can happen to many people today, including people with intellectual and other disabilities. People with disabilities may live their lives in places that are physically part of the community but may not provide them with opportunities and appropriate supports to control their own lives and that, in effect if not intention, segregate them from mainstream society. This can be due to poor agency management, lack of resources, and/or lack of community awareness.

Some years back, Goode was speaking with a friend who worked at a large New York City agency serving people with intellectual disabilities and their families. The topic was a group home located in an apartment building in Manhattan where Goode had visited and interviewed the residents, some of whom had lived at Willowbrook. They were an incredible bunch of characters, and his friend could see that Goode had enjoyed meeting them and asking questions about their lives. She shared that she had been visiting this group home for many years and had many friends there. She spent free time with friends there and went to dinner and movies with them. She visited to relax and hang out, she and they enjoyed being with each other. But, she noted, she was one of the only people from outside the agency who visited them. The residents of this group home, although in an apartment building in Midtown Manhattan, were physically *located in* but not socially *integrated into* their community, if one means by integration, engaged in meaningful, social relations with their neighbors and other community members. People who live in group homes on Staten Island have also complained about

4. SABE's website is at www.sabeusa.org.

the relative lack of opportunities to meet and hang out with people who are not involved with their agency. They and Goode's friend agree with Ed Roberts, the disability rights leader and poster boy for the March of Dimes, that the primary problem that people with disabilities face continues to be the prejudiced attitudes and ignorance of others.

It is impossible to determine how many people with intellectual disabilities today live in circumstances that could be described as 'in' but not 'a part of' their community. Unfortunately, when reading the various listings on the disability List-servs to which the authors belong, it appears that many persons with cognitive and other disabilities continue to feel as if they are not accepted by others. Thus, one of the important lessons from Willowbrook is to look for relatively total institutions—institutions in changed forms, cloaked in different clothes, in a variety of sizes. It is important to be sensitive to new social conditions and places that may not be physically like total institutions but that accomplish similar purposes.

Another obvious relevance of Willowbrook today is institutions for people with disabilities that continue to thrive in poor countries, countries lacking both knowledge about people with disabilities and resources to address their needs. Willowbrooks today exist all around the world, as was described in the *New York Times Magazine* January 16, 2000, article, "The Global Willowbrook" (Winerip, 2000). There are many international organizations—in New York City, Disability Rights International is an important example—that provide technical assistance to governments that operate such places. Disability Rights International has reported abuses and conditions in institutions that have included extreme overcrowding, inadequate heating, lack of toilet facilities, use of cage bed (beds with cages around them), people living in cages or chained to beds, massive overmedication, and so on.[5] The existence of Willowbrooks around the world has become a motivating factor for a global movement to help these countries close such places and recognize the rights of people with intellectual disabilities.[6]

The observations about Willowbrook's history and sociology are also relevant to people who are not thought of as disabled. As stated, the particular categories and statuses singled out for devaluation and segregation are culturally and historically relative. In the recent past, people with intellectual disability or mental illness, who

5. Disability Rights International has a website: www.disabilityrightsintl.org that contains information about the background of the organization and examples of some of the work in which it is engaged.

6. One reader, Jim Conroy, commented in an email that this book is relevant to the challenges faced by many countries around the world "now struggling with the United Nations Rights Convention on the Rights of Persons with Disabilities. Article 19 states that no person should grow up in, or live a life in, an institution. The story of Willowbrook . . . explains why this is now worldwide fundamental knowledge." (personal communication, June 29, 2013)

were poor and committed crimes or who were old and had chronic and incurable conditions, were increasingly at risk for life in a total institution. This will continue to be the case, and as the baby boomers become old and infirm, we are likely to see the expansion of relatively total institutions for their care. As Bronston (2005) observed, the decision to provide funds for the institutional, rather than family, care of the elderly, ill, or infirm was made many years ago, in the mid-twentieth century, but continues to be the rule today.

Without changes in legislation allowing for reimbursed care performed by family members, baby boomers likely will end up in "facilities," large and small, that segregate them and largely set out for them the routines and rules of daily life. This is not to say that every nursing facility must be a mini-Willowbrook. Some readers have older relatives living in places that may be wonderful and avoid the pitfalls of relatively total institutions. Such asylums exist, one suspects for those with financial resources, but it is difficult to estimate in what proportion.

Another of the lessons of Willowbrook has to do with the confluence of factors that allowed WSS to be. It was a place that largely housed poor people; the number of baby boomers will be immense but not poor. Some of the factors that led to WSS were political and economic. There is no saying that in the future a similar confluence of factors comes to be that will allow for new Willowbrooks again, perhaps this time funded via the accumulated wealth of the baby boomers. Wolfensberger believed something like this could happen (personal communication, by telephone, 2009). What we have presented in this book seems to justify this suspicion. Many of us may come to better understand and appreciate the continuing relevance of Willowbrook. As we have emphasized, older people, those who are ill, and those who live in very poor and disadvantaged circumstances are all at great risk for ending up segregated into institutions of one kind or another.

Currently, there is a rhetoric of individual care for people with intellectual disability, but it is not clear that institutional arrangements correspond to this ideology. There appears to be a national trend toward a managed care model in order to minimize cost. The actual options facing people in these times of fiscal austerity and insecurity are unclear, and the fears that people with disabilities and their families face today are real. On Staten Island, this is causing agencies to cut back on supports and services. Agencies are uniformly worried about both quality and continuity of care. While there is political movement toward 'non-institutional' supports and services for people with intellectual disabilities, for example via the Olmstead legislation passed in 1999, the enforcement of that legislation has been difficult to achieve. There does not appear to be any general awareness in our society that history and science have shown us that we need to turn away from institutions as a way to deal with various standing social problems. In the current debate about health care reform, there is no arguing that this could be a good occasion to avoid Hegel's (1832/1956) observation and to change the structure of *how* we care for those most in need, not just how we fund care. By and large we are not having this discussion, and many lay persons and social scientists probably do not appreciate the number of groups and individuals in our society who are and will become institutionalized and live in total institutions.

A long-term debate in sociology is to whether society should be thought of as a stable set of social relations and institutions that exist in a relative equilibrium with one another (called the functionalist or equilibrium model) or whether is it constantly in change, conflict, and disequilibrium (called the conflict or Marxist model). When one examines the history of total institutions such as Willowbrook, one cannot escape the tensions created by both these views. On the one hand, there can be no question about the changes that have occured since Willowbrook's closing. Willowbrook itself became part of a movement to close institutions in America and it contributed directly and indirectly to the ultimate betterment of conditions of life for many Americans with intellectual disability. On the other hand, one is highly impressed by the stability of institutions, recalling the dual sociological uses of that term. Their persistence, resilience to mortality, ability to mutate, and, again depending on definition, their widespread presence in society, is remarkable.

One might argue that the closing of state hospitals and developmental centers around the country signifies the final chapter to total institutions for people with intellectual disabilities. Of course these are good things to have happened, but they do not foreshadow the end to institutions by any means, either for people with intellectual disabilities or for others. Given a cyclical, or at least non-progressive, view of history, what we have is more likely a case of "The institution is dead; long live the institution."

Problems of Method

If one understands methodology to refer to a logic of inquiry, then there are several methodologies used in this text. First is that of historical method, in which various artifacts were analyzed and utilized as part of a story about how things worked in the past. Much of this work was achieved via this method, which requires that some limits be placed on the overall conclusions. We have used clinical case files, newspaper accounts, speeches and reflections, oral history interviews, and narratives written by authors who worked at Willowbrook and by those who worked or resided at other institutions for people with intellectual disability.

As we stated in our Introduction, if one begins with the assumption that there is one truth about Willowbrook, that there is one narrative, story, experience, or piece of writing that could tell "the Truth" about Willowbrook, in any comprehensive or objective way, then we have a significant epistemological problem as the data do not bear this assumption out. But this is not the case, and there are different sources of data that need to be looked at and assessed.

As pointed out earlier, the clinical records we examined told to a degree what was required by law, avoided reporting incidents that could be dealt with without official involvement, and generally did not convey anything like 'what really was happening' with the individual in question. They are notoriously inaccurate, and were not valued as resources by those actually working with the residents. The staff attempted to deal with problems at their own level and did not report the truth or bring in the higher-ups, unless it was unavoidable. Similarly, on the wards, apparently the residents, those capable, had their own system of self-policing and dealing with things without calling in the attendants. In an analogous process, the administration also used procedures to control the leaking or spread of incriminating information. So the formal information available to us through files is inherently selective and political.

The narratives and accounts of Willowbrook evidence the variety of institutional roles that existed there as well as the real differences people have in making sense of their lives. In introducing the narratives about Willowbrook, we remarked that this "fact" of life about the institution seems to shock people when it is pointed out. It is as if some sort of homogneous image about life there has been constructed, and one is surprised by the fact that Willowbrook, in fact, did not work that way. Even if we take the interviews and narratives at face value and assume that people are telling what their best memory permits, we need to acknowledge their reconstructed nature. Even given this limitation, that they are recall data, what is most convincing is the pattern of responses, where many people remember things more or less the same way. Despite the Rashomon nature of memory it is reasonable to conclude that such patterns reveal what we today may take as 'truths,' even given their recalled nature and nuances.[7]

We acknowledge that the estimation of quantitative measures at Willowbrook—how many children went to school, the degree to which sexual abuse existed, or how many children may have eloped, how many had visitors and so on—were based on the impressions of the authors and individuals interviewed. Again, in speaking about such matters, we relied on the pattern of responses reported in interviews and the content of the narratives as the basis for general

7. Mannheim in his book 1936 *Ideology and Utopia* discussed a conception of truth with a small t. He called his concept "relationalism" and by it meant to point to the truth value that certain descriptions or ideas have relative to the social situation in which they take form. Not all descriptions of things are equally true or of equal value, when judged according to their socio-historical circumstance. Some turn out, with the benefit of hindsight, to be simply misleading and incorrect. We believe that the patterns located in our interviews reveal 'relationally' true statements about Willowbrook,

conclusions. The procedure is wanting, but the alternative would involve inspection of such a mass quantity of records that the undertaking would be immense and beyond the capacity of most individual researchers. Even if this were to be done, the way actual events get placed into institutional files would create questions about validity of their own.

In sum, we feel that while acknowledging the limitations of the types of data used in our analysis, both a picture and critical understanding of everyday life at Willowbrook has been presented, which was, as stated in the Introduction, our purpose. We hope that the reader will have been able to find in these narratives and interviews at least a sense of what life was like there and why it was that way.

Further Research

Many areas related to Willowbrook deserve separate and thorough treatment. A serious monograph or book about the experimentation that occurred at Willowbrook has yet to be written. A book such as Bronston's about the power structure at Willowbrook, its *modus operandi*, how it was defeated, and the significance of this for current society will be a great contribution. An analyis of the political economy of Willowbrook, although brought up in various sources, would make a case study of great interest. An examination of the 10-year existence of Halloran Hospital, the world's largest and most advanced military hospital of its time, also needs to be written.

Many of our discussions lead to further questions about Willowbrook. Because the data were actually collected before this writing, the authors were unable to ask more pointed and systematic follow-up questions about many matters in order to produce more complete views of them. We have tried to indicate some of these topics within the text, such as the hierarchies that existed among staff and among patients; the underground economy at Willowbrook; the difficulty of finding information out about certain topics at Willowbrook, such as violence, death, and sexuality; the role of gender and race at Willowbrook; and so on.

Perhaps of most needed is something that would allow us to document the promise made to those who were incarcerated there; research about what happened to the members of the Willowbrook Class members after leaving the institution. Such a work would be eye-opening, and despite being belated, we believe is something that can and should be undertaken in the near future. There has been no academic study of what happened to people who lived and worked at Willowbrook after it closed. This is an important piece of research because it would provide answers to what many scholars in the field would want to know: What happened after deinstitutionalization? To what degree and in what ways was deinstitutionalization successful or not? Were the promises made to those at Willowbrook and their families kept? What is the legacy of Willowbrook for those who lived and worked there?

The reader is not to come away from this book with the idea that Willowbrook has "been done"—that there is no reason to write anything more about it. One of the authors, Bronston, will be publishing another treatment of Willowbrook, with an emphasis on policy and the implications of what happened at Willowbrook for our current circumstances. His book will also make use of the very rich visual images that he photographed while at Willowbrook. From this, we will learn even more about what constituted life there.

In addition, the reader should not conclude that other institutions need not be researched again because we already know what we are going to find. We are already aware of a volume about Pennhurst State Hospital that is in preparation, and we hope there will be others. Each story can add to our corpus of knowledge about this period of history and these kinds of institutions. Each may contain possibly relevant lessons from the past, whether we choose to act upon them or not.

History shows that books, especially academic ones, possess limited potential to produce social change. When they do, it is because they come along at the right time, and then their circumstances propel them to influence. Accordingly, we have realistic expectations about whether this work will lead to a political movement against congregate care for those who are infirm or disabled, as much as we might want that to happen. Yet we wrote this work with conviction that, to paraphrase Williams and Self-Advocates Becoming Empowered, as long as our brothers and sisters are made to live in total institutions, we cannot ourselves see the light of day. Our book was created with the hope that readers will be made aware of and better understand the history and dynamics of total institutions such as Willowbrook State School. This understanding and awareness should guide us to, in whatever ways available, resist the production and reproduction of large and small Willowbrooks in society. While we are not likely to succeed in their elimination, knowledge and resolve can minimize the presence and influence of total institutions in our lives.

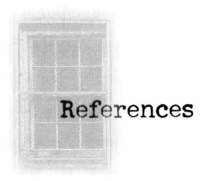

References

Allison, N. (1996, September). *Address at the dedication of Building 4S at the College of Staten Island*. Video on file at the Willowbrook Collection, Archives of the Library, College of Staten Island.

Asch, S. E. (1955). Opinions and social pressure. *Scientific American, 193*, 31–35. doi:10.1038/scientificamerican1155-31

Bartlett, F. L. (1964). Institutional peonage: Our exploitation of mental patients. *Atlantic, 214*, 116–119.

Bateman-House, A. (n.d.). *A history of Willowbrook State School, Staten Island, New York*. College of Staten Island Library Archives, Staten Island, New York.

Berman, H. H., Albert-Gasorek, K. E., & Reiss, M. (1959). Gonadal immaturity as an etiological factor in some forms of mental deficiency, and its therapy. *Diseases of the Nervous System, 20*, 106–110.

Berman, H. H., & Jacobs, M. (1956). Electro cerebral stimulation in mentally defective patients. *Diseases of the Nervous System, 17*, 264–265.

Berman, H. H., Lazar, M., Noé, O., & Schiller, H. (1957). Pentylenetetrazol (Metrazol) in mental deficiency. *Journal of Diseases of Children, 94*, 231–233.

Berman, H. H., & Noé, O. (1958). An evaluation of the nutritive supplement Dietall. *American Journal of Mental Deficiency, 62*, 657–662.

Bettelheim, B., & Sylvester, E. (1948). A therapeutic milieu. *American Journal of Orthopsychiatry, 17*, 191–206.

Black, E. (2003). *War against the weak: Eugenics and America's campaign to create a master race*. New York, NY: Basic Books.

Bodgan, R. with Elks, M. & Knoll, J.A. (2012). *Picturing disability: Beggar, freak, citizen, and other photographic rhetoric*. Syracuse, NY: Syracuse University Press.

Bogdan, R., Taylor, S., DeGrandpre, B., & Haynes, S. (1974). Let them eat programs: Attendants' perspectives and programming on wards in state schools. *Journal of Health and Social Behavior, 15*, 142–151.

Braddock, D. L., & Parrish, S. L. (2001). An institutional history of disability. In G. Albrecht, K. Seel-man, & M. Bury (Eds.), *The handbook of disability studies* (pp. 11-68). London, England: Sage.

Braginsky, B. M., Braginsky, D. D., & Ring, K. (1969). *Methods of madness: The mental hospital as a last resort*. New York, NY: Holt, Rinehart, and Winston.

Braginsky, D. D. & Braginsky, B. M. (1971). *Hansels and Gretels: Studies of children in institutions for the mentally retarded*. New York, NY: Holt, Rinehart, and Winston.

Bronston, W. (1972, February 17). *Testimony to the New York State Joint Legislative Committee for the Mentally and Physically Handicapped*.

Bronston, W. (2002). Interviews by Kathy Cowan.

Bronston, W. (2005, March 19). Presentation to CUNY Graduate Center, Program in Sociology 6th Floor. Video available at the Willowbrook Collection, Archives of the Library of the College of Staten Island.

Bronston, W. (2006, April). Willowbrook Annual Lecture, College of Staten Island, April.

Bronston, W. (2007, August 19). Interview by the Civil Service Employees Association, New York. City, New York

Bronston, W. (forthcoming). *Public hostage, public ransom*. Washington, DC: American Association on Intellectual and Developmental Disabilities.

Castellani, P. (2005). *From snake pits to cash cows: Politics and public institutions in New York*. Albany: State University of New York Press.

Caudill, W. (1958). *The psychiatric hospital as a small society*. Cambridge, MA: Harvard University Press.

Caudill, W., Redlich, F. C., Gilmore, H. R., & Brody, E. B. (1952). Social structure and interaction processes on a psychiatric ward. *American Journal of Orthopsychiatry, 22*, 314–334.

Cohen, J. M., Iosotaluno, M., Cohen, R. (Producers), & Cohen, R. (Director). (2012). *Willowbrook* [Motion picture]. Los Angeles, California: Independent.

Crookshank, F. G. (1924). *A mongol in our midst: A study of man and his three faces*. New York, NY: Dutton.

D'Antonio, M. (2004). *The state boys rebellion*. New York, NY: Simon & Schuster.

Davenport, W. H. (1866, November). Blackwell's Island Lunatic Asylum. *Harper's New Monthly Magazine, 32*, 276–294.

Davenport, W. H. (1867, December). The nurseries on Randall's Island. *Harper's New Monthly Magazine, 36*, 6–24.

Debello, V. (2005). The Annual Willowbrook Memorial Lecture. College of Staten Island. Video available at the Willowbrook Collection, Archives of the Library, College of Staten Island.

Deutsch, A. (1948). *Shame of the states*. New York, NY: Harcourt Brace Jovanovich.

Devereux , G. (1944) The social structure of a schizophrenic ward and its therapeutic fitness. *Journal of Clinical Psychopathology, 6*, 231–265.

Dillon, M. (Producer) (2004). Recollections of the Institution. Program Development Associates, Cicero, New York. Available at: www.disabilitytraining.com

Ferguson, P. (1994). *Abandoned to their fate: Social policy and practice toward severely retarded people in America, 1820-1920*. Philadelphia, PA: Temple University Press.

Fiedler, L. (1978). *Freaks: Myths and images of the secret self*. New York, NY: Simon & Schuster.

Fisher, D. (Producer) (1996). *Unforgotten: Twenty-five years after Willowbrook* [Motion picture]. USA: City Lights Production.

Fowler, O. (Editor) (1844). The American phrenological journal. Vol. VI. New York: O.S. Fowler

Freeberg, S. (2001). *The education of Laura Bridgman: First deaf and blind person to learn language*. Cambridge, MA: Harvard University Press.

Freud, A., & Burlingham, D. (1943). *War and children*. New York, NY: International Universities Press.

Fusillo, M. (1994). The Willowbrook State School: An oral history, Staten Island, New York: unpublished Master's Thesis in Special Education, 202 pp.: Willowbrook Collection, Library Archives, College of Staten Island.

Garfinkel, H. (1967). *Studies in ethnomethodology*. Englewood Cliffs, NJ: Prentice-Hall

Garland, R. (1996a). *Extraordinary bodies*. New York, NY: Columbia University Press.

Garland, R. (1996b). *Freakery: Cultural spectacles of the extraordinary body*. New York: New York University Press.

Goddard, H. (1914). *School training of defective children*. New York, NY: World Book.

Goffman, E. (1961). *Asylums: Essays on the social situation mental patients and other inmates*. New York, NY: Anchor.

Goode, D. (1983). Who is Bobby? In G. Kielhofner (Ed.), *Health through occupation* (pp. 237–254). Philadelphia, PA: F. A. Davis.

Goode, D. (1985). Socially produced identities, intimacy and the problem of competence among the retarded. In S. Tomlinson & L. Barton (eds.), *Special Education and Social Values*, (pp. 228–248). London: Croom Helm.

Goode, D. Kids, Culture and Innocents.(1986) *The Journal of Human Studies*, pp. 83-l05. Also appears in Studying the Social Worlds of Children, Frances Waksler (ed), London: Falmer Press, 1992, pp. 145–160.

Goode, D. (1998, December). *"And now let's build a better world": The history of the Association for the Help of Retarded Children, 1948–1998*. Retrieved from http://www.nysarc.org/files/9913/0703/8158/AHRC_History.pdf.

Goode, D. (1994). *A world without words*. Philadelphia, PA: Temple University Press.

Goode, D. & Braddock, D. (2000) . The history and status of state institutions for persons labeled 'mentally retarded.' Unpublished paper written for the occasion of the celebration of the 25th anniversary of the Willowbrook Consent Decree. Available from the author.

Gould, S. J. (1981) *The mismeasure of man*. New York, NY: Norton.

Hakim, D. (2011, March 12). At state-run homes, abuse and impunity. *New York Times*. Available at http://www.nytimes.com/2011/03/13/nyregion/13homes.html

Hammond, J., Sternlicht, M., & Deutsch, M. R. (1969). Parental interest in institutionalized children: A survey. *Hospital and Community Psychiatry, 20,* 338–339.

Hardy, J. (1870). *Manual of the Corporation of the City of New York*. New York, NY: Clerk of the Common Council.

Hegel, G. W. F. (1956). *The philosophy of history*. New York, NY: Dover. (Original work published 1832)

Hillman, J. C., Hammond, J., Noé, O., & Reiss, M. (1968). Endocrine investigations in De Lange's and Seckel's syndromes. *American Journal of Mental Deficiency, 73,* 30–33.

Hillman, J., Hammond, J., Sokola, J., & Reiss, M. (1968). Changes in plasma growth hormone levels in retarded children. *Journal of Mental Deficiency Research, 12,* 294–306.

Hoffman, E., & McCoy, J. (1986). *Concrete mama: Prison profiles from Walla Walla*. Columbia: University of Missouri Press.

Hornick, R. (2012). *The girls and boys of Belchertown: A social history of the Belchertown State School for the Feeble-Minded*. Boston: University of Massachusetts Press.

Knight, G. H. (1891). Colony care for idiot adults. *Proceedings of the National Conference on Social Work, 19,* 107–108.

Krugman, S., Giles, J. P., & Hammond, J. (1967). Viral hepatitis: Overview and historical perspectives. *Annals of Internal Medicine, 66,* 924–931.

Kuhlmann, F. (1940). One hundred years of special care and training. *American Journal on Mental Deficiency, 45,* 18–24.

Larson, S. A., Ryan, A., Salmi, P., Smith, D., & A. Wuorio (2012). *Residential services for persons with developmental disabilities: Statues and trends through 2010*. Minneapolis: University of Minnesota, Research and Training Center on Community Living, Institute on Community Integration.

Lerner, H. J. (1972). *State Association for Retarded Children and New York State Government, 1948–1968*. Printed in Israel: Yessod Publishing.

Levine, M. M., Rice, P., Gangarosa, E. J., Morris, G. K., Synder, M. J., Formal,. B., . . . Hammond, J. (1974). An outbreak of Sonne Shigellosis in a population receiving oral attenuated shigella vaccines. *American Journal of Epidemiology, 99*, 30–36.

Mannheim, K. (1936). *Ideology and utopia*. London: Routledge.

McBryde-Johnson, H. M. (2003, November 23). The disability gulag. *New York Times*. at: http://www.nytimes.com/2003/11/23/magazine/the-disability-gulag.html?pagewanted=all&src=pm

McCourt, D. (2005, March 19). Presentation to the CUNY Graduate Center. Program in Sociology. Video available at the Willowbrook Collection, Archives of the Library of the College of Staten Island.

McMurtry, L. (1999). *Crazy Horse*. London, England: Weidendfeld & Nicolson.

Meskell, K. (Producer) (1996). *Unforgotten: Twenty-five years after Willowbrook* [Motion picture]. USA: City Lights Production.

Milgram, S. (1965). Some conditions of obedience and disobedience to authority. *Human Relations, 18*, 57–76.

Mortensen, Z. (Producer), Brancaccio, B., & Zeman, J. (Directors). (2009). *Cropsey* [Motion picture]. USA: Ghost Robot.

Murphy, T. F. (2004). *Case studies in biomedical research ethics*. Cambridge, MA: MIT Press.

Noé, O. (1964). Amsterdam dwarfs: Four cases of typus degenerativus amstelodamensis. *Clinical Pediatrics, 3*, 541–549.

Noé, O., & Hammond, J. (1967). De Lange's Amsterdam dwarfism: Case report and etiological considerations. *American Journal of Mental Deficiency, 71*, 994–1003.

Oliver, M. (1990). *Disablement in society: A socio-political approach*. London: Thames Polytechnic.

Oliver, M. (1996). *Understanding disability: From theory to practice*. London: Macmillan.

Office for People with Developmental Disabilities. (2012, October). *Beyond Willowbrook*. Available at http://www.opwdd.ny.gov/opwdd_resources/willowbrook_class

Pelka, F. (2012). *What we have done: An oral history of the disability rights movement*. Boston: University of Massachusetts Press.

Penny, D., & Stastny, P. (2008). *The lives they left behind: Suitcases from a state hospital attic*. New York, NY: Bellevue Literary Press.

Pernick, M. (1996). *The black stork: Eugenics and the death of "defective" babies in American medicine and motion pictures since 1915*. Oxford, England: Oxford University Press.

Pratt, J. (Ed.). (1998). *On the outside: Extraordinary people in search of ordinary lives*. Charleston: West Virginia Developmental Disabilities Planning Council.

Pustel, G., Sternlicht, M., & DeRespinis, M. (1971). Tree drawings of institutionalized retardates: Seasonal and color effects. *Journal of Genetic Psychology, 118*, 217–222.

Pustel, G., Sternlicht, M., & DeRespinis, M. (1972). Institutionalized retardates' animal drawings: Their meanings and significance. *Journal of Genetic Psychology, 120*, 103–109.

Pustel, G., Sternlicht, M., & Siegel, L. (1969). Pleasant vs. unpleasant early childhood recollections of institutionalized adolescent and adult retardates. *Journal of Clinical Psychology, 25*, 110–111.

Ragonese, P., & Stainback, B. (1991). *The soul of a cop*. New York, NY: St. Martin's Press.

Reiss, J. (n.d.). *They learned to do without: Untold stories from Willowbrook, Staten Island*. Unpublished manuscript, available at the Willowbrook Collection, Archives of the Library of the College of Staten Island.

Reiss, M. (1960). Castration [Review of "Asexualization: A follow-up study of 244 cases"]. *British Medical Journal, 2,* 652.

Reiss, M., Berman, H. H., Pearse, J. J. Albert-Gasorek, K., & Hillman, J. C. (1961). Investigations into the interrelation of physical and mental retardation. *Journal of Neuropsychiatry, 2,* 109–137.

Reiss, M., Wakoh, T., Hillman, J. C., Pearse, J. J., Reiss, J. M., & Daley, N. (1966). Action of anabolic steroids on the metabolism of mentally retarded boys. *American Journal of Mental Deficiency, 70,* 520–528.

Rivera, G. (1972). *Willowbrook: A report on how it is and why it doesn't have to be that way.* New York, NY: Random House.

Roberts, E. (1989). Effective Strategies for Social Change, May 1, 1987, available at: http://www.mnddc.state.mn.us/parallels2/one/video/ed_roberts-pipm.html

Rogers, A. C., & Merrill, M. A. (1919). *The history of a feeble-minded community: Dwellers in the Vale of Siddem.* Boston, MA: Gorham Press.

Rothman, D. J. (1990). *The discovery of the asylum: Social order and disorder in the New Republic* (rev. ed.). Boston, MA: Little, Brown.

Rothman, D. J., & Rothman, S. M. (2009). *The Willowbrook wars: Bringing the mentally disabled into the community.* New Brunswick, NJ: Aldine Transaction. (Original work published 1984)

Rowland, H. (1938). Interaction processes in the state mental hospital. *Psychiatry, I,* 323-337.

Rowland, H. (1939). Friendship patterns in the state mental hospital. *Psychiatry, II,* 363-373.

Schneider, H. (2004). *The last side show.* London, England: Daze Books.

Scott, S. (2010). Revisiting the total institution: Performative regulation in the reinventive institution. *Sociology, 44,* 213–231.

Ségun, E. 1870. New facts and remarks concerning idiocy, being a lecture before the New York Medical Association. October 15, 1869. New York, NY: William Ward.

Siegel, L., Sternlicht, M., Pustel, G., DeRespinis, M., & Brandwein, H. (1972). Differential reactions to frustrations of adolescent and adult institutionalized retardates. *Journal of Psychology, 80,* 193–196.

Stanton, A. H., & Schwartz, M. S. (1954). *The mental hospital: A study of institutional participation in psychiatric illness and treatment.* New York, NY: Basic Books.

Starogiannis, H., & Hill, D. B. (2008). Sex and gender in an American state school (1951–1987): The Willowbrook class. *Sexuality & Disability, 26,* 83–103.

State of New York. (1852). No. 30 in Senate, First annual report of the Trustees for the New York State Asylum for Idiots. located at the Samuel Gridley Howe Library, Fernald Developmental Center, Waltham, Massachussets.

State of New York. (1854). No. 54 in Senate, Third annual report of the Trustees for the New York State Asylum for Idiots. available at the Samuel Gridley Howe Library, Fernald School, Waltham, Massachussets.

Stern, E. (1948, August). Take them off the human scrap heap. *Women's Home Companion, 75,* 62–64.

Sternlicht, M. (1964). Establishing an initial relationship in group psychotherapy with delinquent retarded male adolescents. *American Journal of Mental Deficiency, 69,* 39–41.

Sternlicht, M. (1966). Treatment approaches to delinquent retardates. *International Journal of Group Psychotherapy, 16,* 91–93.

Sternlicht, M. (1969). Parent counseling in an experimental rehabilitation center. *Journal of Rehabilitation, 35,* 15–16.

Sternlicht, M., Bialer, I., & Deutsch, M. R. (1970). Influence of external incentives on motor performance of institutionalized retardates. *Journal of Mental Deficiency Research, 14,* 149–154.

Sternlicht, M., & Cavallo, M. (1965). Screening techniques in the selection of practical nursing candidates. *Nursing Research, 14,* 170–172.

Sternlicht, M., & Deutsch, M. (1971). The value of temporary institutionalization in habilitating the mentally retarded. *Mental Retardation, 9,* 37–38.

Sternlicht, M., Hammond, J., & Siegel, L. (1972). Mental retardates prepare for community living. *Hospital & Community Psychiatry, 23,* 15.

Sternlicht, M., & Schaffer, S. (1973). Employing mentally retarded ex-residents in the institution. *Hospital & Community Psychiatry, 24,* 698–699.

Sternlicht, M., & Siegel, L. (1968a). Institutional residence and intellectual functioning. *Journal of Intellectual Disability Research, 12,* 119–127.

Sternlicht, M., & Siegel, L. (1968b). Time orientation and friendship patterns of institutionalized retardates. *Journal of Clinical Psychology, 24,* 26–27.

Sternlicht, M., Siegel, L., & Deutsch, M. R. (1971). Evaluation of a remotivation program with institutionalized mentally retarded youngsters. *Training School Bulletin, 68,* 82–86.

Sternlicht, M., & Wanderer, Z. W. (1962). Nature of institutionalized adult mongoloid intelligence. *American Journal of Mental Deficiency, 67,* 301–302.

Stewart. J. (2001). Disablement, prison and historical segregation. *Monthly Review* (July 1). Available at http://monthlyreview.org/2001/07/01/disablement-prison-and-historical-segregation

Sudnow, D. (1967). *Passing on: The social organization of dying.* Englewood Cliffs, NJ: Prentice-Hall.

Sullivan, H. S. (1931). Socio-psychiatric research: Its implication for the schizophrenia problem and for mental hygiene. *American Journal of Psychiatry, 10,* 977–991.

Sundram, C. J. (2011). *The measure of a society: Protection of vulnerable persons in residential facilities against abuse and neglect.* Albany, NY: Author.

Szurek, S. A. (1947). Dynamics of staff interaction in hospital psychiatric treatment of children. *American Journal of Orthopsychiatry, 17,* 652–664.

Tolstoy, L. (1904). *War and peace* (C. Garnett, Trans.). New York: McClure, Philips and Co.

Trent, J. W. (1994). *Inventing the feeble mind: A history of mental retardation in the United States.* Los Angeles: University of California Press.

Wagner, P., & Sternlicht, M. (1975). Retarded persons as "teachers": Retarded adolescents tutoring retarded children. *American Journal of Mental Deficiency, 79,* 674–679.

Wanderer, Z. W., & Sternlicht, M. (1964). Psychologists discover the value of volunteers: 2. Psychology students work with retardates. *Mental Hospitals, 15,* 271–272.

Ward, P. (Producer). (1997). *My country* [Television documentary]. New York, NY: Public Broadcasting Service. Available at: http://www.ada.gov/mycountryvideo/hi_speed_rp/mycountrydslgallery.htm

Williams, K., & Self-Advocates Becoming Empowered. (1998). *Close the door* [Audio recording]. USA: CD Baby. Available at www.amazon.com/dp/B001I475JG

Winerip, M. (2000, January 16). The global Willowbrook. *New York Times.* Available at http://www.nytimes.com/2000/01/16/magazine/the-global-willowbrook.html

Wiseman, F. (director) (1967) *Titticut Follies.* Available Zipporah Films, Inc. (1992)

Wolfensberger, W. (1972). *The principle of normalization in human services.* Toronto, Canada: National Institute on Mental Retardation.

Wolfensberger, W. (1982). *The history of human service institutions.* Notes by Goode on a lecture given at the Training Institute for Human Services and Change Agentry, September. Unpublished manuscript.

Wolfensberger, W. (1989). Human service policies: The rhetoric versus the reality. In L. Barton (Ed.), *Disability and dependency* (pp. 23–41). London, England: Falmer Press.

Zimbardo, P. (1973, April 8). A Pirandelian prison. *New York Times Magazine.* Available at http://www.prisonexp.org/pdf/pirandellian.pdf

Zimbardo, P. (2007). *The Lucifer effect: Understanding how good people turn evil.* New York, NY: Random House.